The Business of Venture Capital

Founded in 1807, John Wiley & Sons is the oldest independent publishing company in the United States. With offices in North America, Europe, Australia and Asia, Wiley is globally committed to developing and marketing print and electronic products and services for our customers' professional and personal knowledge and understanding.

The Wiley Finance series contains books written specifically for finance and investment professionals as well as sophisticated individual investors and their financial advisors. Book topics range from portfolio management to e-commerce, risk management, financial engineering, valuation and financial instrument analysis, as well as much more.

For a list of available titles, visit our Web site at www.WileyFinance.com.

The Business of Venture Capital

*Insights from Leading Practitioners
on the Art of Raising a Fund,
Deal Structuring, Value Creation,
and Exit Strategies*

MAHENDRA RAMSINGHANI

John Wiley & Sons, Inc.

Published by John Wiley & Sons, Inc., Hoboken, New Jersey.
Published simultaneously in Canada.

For general information on our other products and services or for technical support, please contact our Customer Care Department within the United States at (800) 762-2974, outside the United States at (317) 572-3993 or fax (317) 572-4002.

Wiley also publishes its books in a variety of electronic formats. Some content that appears in print may not be available in electronic books. For more information about Wiley products, visit our web site at www.wiley.com.

Library of Congress Cataloging-in-Publication Data:

Ramsinghani, Mahendra.
 The business of venture capital : insights from leading practitioners on the art of raising a fund, deal structuring, value creation, and exit strategies / Mahendra Ramsinghani.
   p. cm. – (Wiley finance series ; 612)
 Includes index.
 ISBN 978-0-470-87444-8; ISBN 978-1-118-13038-4 (ebk);
 ISBN 978-1-118-13039-1 (ebk); ISBN 978-1-118-13040-7 (ebk)
 1. Venture capital.   I. Title.
 HG4751.R36 2011
 332'.04154068–dc23

                                                                        2011017545

Printed in the United States of America.

10 9 8 7 6 5 4 3 2 1

In the memory of my parents

and

to Deepa and Aria,
the light, the song, and the dance

Contents

Foreword   xiii

Preface   xvii

Acknowledgments   xxix

PART ONE
Raising the Venture Fund   1

CHAPTER 1
The Universe of Limited Partners   5
An Overview of Alternative Assets   6
Sources of Capital   10
Comparison of Limited Partnerships   29
Summary   29

CHAPTER 2
Fund Due Diligence   33
Sourcing and First Screens   34
Fund Due Diligence: How LPs Evaluate Venture Firms   36
Evaluating the Fund Managers   39
Emerging Managers: A Promise of the Future   53
The Quest for the Elusive Top Quartile Managers   61
Fund Investment Strategy   67
Market Timing   77
Fund Size and Portfolio Construction vis-à-vis Fund Strategy 80
Fit within the LP's Current Portfolio   85
Why LPs Terminate Existing Relationships   87
Summary   87

CHAPTER 3

Terms of Investment: The Limited Partnership Agreement   89

Sample Terms in a Fund's PPM   90
Other LP-GP Terms   105
What Matters Most   110
Summary   110

CHAPTER 4

Fund Structure, Governance, and Operations   113

Key Constituents of the GP Team   114
Finding Suitable Partners   125
Fund Governance and Economics   126
Governance of Management Services GP LLC   127
Summary   134

CHAPTER 5

Getting to the First Close   135

Build Your Target List of Investors   137
Fund Marketing Materials   141
Presentation Slides   142
Making the Presentation Pitch: Drink Your Own Kool-Aid   144
Attracting the Lead Investor: Your "Nut"   144
Communicate, Create, and Maintain Momentum   146
Offering Sweeteners to Attract LPs: A Double-Edged Sword   147
The Role of Placement Agents in Fund-Raising   147
Caveat Emptor   151
Summary   152

PART TWO

The Investment Process   153

CHAPTER 6

The Art of Sourcing Investment Opportunities   155

The Best Source: The Network   157
The Fountainheads of Academia and Research   160
Corporate Research   161
Venture Events and Trade Conferences   163
Venture Farming   165
Angels and Pledge Funds   167
Business Plan Competitions   171
Cold Calling   172

You Win Some, You Miss Some 172
Summary 174

CHAPTER 7
The Art of Conducting Due Diligence 177
What Is Important: Jockey, Horse, or Markets? 178
Attributes of the Jockey 179
Serial Entrepreneurs versus First-Time Entrepreneurs 183
What about Charisma? 184
Management Team Due Diligence: How to Assess the Jockey 185
The Importance of Conducting Background Investigations 192
Assessing the Market 194
Evaluating the Idea or Product 199
Reviewing the Business Model 201
Considering the Financial Projections 202
Weighing the Importance of Business Plans 203
The Due Diligence Checklist 203
Summary 206

CHAPTER 8
The Basics of Corporations, Ownership, and Control 209
Authorized Shares and Issued Shares 211
Shareholder Rights 217
Role of the Board 217
Summary 218

CHAPTER 9
Valuation Methods and Other Voodoo Arts 219
The Drivers of Valuation 220
The Simplified Form of the VC Method of Valuation 221
Comparable Valuations of Similar Investments (Comps) 224
Discounted Cash Flow Method 226
Summary 228

CHAPTER 10
Structuring Investment Transactions 229
The Spirit of the Term Sheet 229
Negotiation Stress Points 230
Milestone-Based Financing: Risk Mitigation or Distraction 238
Structuring Terms to Generate Target Returns 239
Governance and Control: Protecting Your Securities 246
Exit-Related Provisions 247

Other Terms   248
Toward a Simpler Term Sheet for Smaller Investments   250
Syndicating Investments   251
The Closing Process: After the Term Sheet   252
Summary   253

CHAPTER 11
Behind Every Successful CEO Stand a Few Good Board VCs   **255**
The Need for Director Education   256
Roles and Responsibilities of a Board Member   257
Board Composition and Orientation   261
Board Practices   263
Get That Gavel: Overview of Robert's Rules of Order   265
Value Creation: How to Support Your Portfolio
    Company's CEO   268
The CEO's Perspective on Venture Capitalist Value Add   269
Setting the Tone through Board Culture   275
Improving the Board Game   284
Summary   289

CHAPTER 12
Exit Strategies   **291**
Preconditions for an Exit   292
Acquisitions: The Primary Path to an Exit   297
The Sell Process   302
When an Acquirer Comes Knocking   307
The Buy-Side Acquisition Process   307
Deal Killers   310
Acquisition Case Study: Mint.com Generates 5x Cash-on-Cash
    Return in Two Years   310
Initial Public Offering   313
Private Exchanges: Necessity Drives Liquidity Solutions   324
Summary   327

CHAPTER 13
Summing Up   **329**
Aptitudes and Attitudes of Successful Practitioners   330
Drawbacks   338
What about Luck?   339
Key Takeaways for Practitioners   340
As You Go Forward   344

About the Companion Web Site   **345**

Notes   **347**

Suggested Reading   **375**

About the Author   **379**

Index   **381**

Foreword

I f the business of venture capital is driven by the entrepreneurial forces that cause creative destruction, venture capital is the primary fuel that drives these forces. Armed with this ammunition, entrepreneurs leapfrog toward the new frontiers at a rapid pace. Closely teamed up with these entrepreneurs are venture capital professionals, who bring insights and direction and, at times, act as guardrails for the entrepreneurial energy and enthusiasm. This book, *The Business of Venture Capital,* whose primary audience is an entry-level venture practitioner, addresses the critical elements of the venture capital investment process: raising the fund, sourcing and structuring investments, creating value as a board member, and, finally, leading investments to exits.

The quest for new frontiers has led to the significant growth of venture capital over the past two decades. I was recruited to lead the National Venture Capital Association (NVCA) in 1991. Since then, the venture capital industry has grown significantly and venture capital is now recognized as an asset class with distinctive merits. In the early nineties, annual venture investments in U.S. companies was $7 billion. Fifteen years later, this has grown threefold to $20+ billion. (Of course, we will ignore the 1999–2000 era when investments grew to $100 billion.) Tied to this growth is the flow of capital—assets under management, the number of funds, and the number of professionals in the venture business, all of which have grown at an equal pace. Institutional investors are driven by financial returns. Corporate and government entities invest in venture funds to spur technological development and social change.

Christopher Columbus said, "Following the light of the sun, we left the old world." After all, it's primal for man to seek new frontiers. While those in earlier times sought to discover unknown lands and bring home spices and gold, modern-day entrepreneurs and adventurers seek to break down the frontiers of technology and business. As we know, venture investments started in the late sixties but the nineties experienced rapid growth and formal structures were established into a norm. The first wave of venture investments grew with the advent of the semiconductor industry, closely followed by the growth computing industry. The mainframe and desktop, software, networking, and the Internet led to the peak of the frenzy in the year 2000 with venture investments reaching \$80–\$100 billion. This frenzy also generated triple-digit returns for venture funds for a brief period, leading to more capital flows into this asset class. However, recent years have created a new set of demands on venture professionals. As the technology wave shifts to mobile computing and social networks, energy and clean-tech sectors have attracted much attention. While these sectors have different return dynamics as compared to the technology era, a steady flow of capital and opportunities is drawing the battle lines for the next wave of creative destruction. Life sciences and health care, sectors that have largely remained steady, have seen a spurt of recent activity. The underlying drivers of cost and insurance premiums combined with aging demographics will sustain the pace of investments. However, in recent years, political drive to reform health care has spurred adoption of technology in areas such as medical records, where venture investments may see growth. Drug discovery—the other end of the life sciences investment spectrum—also continues to see considerable opportunities due to consolidation within the industry and the growing cost of drug development combined with pressures of generics.

On the geographic front, the United States continues to lead the venture activity due to underlying structural advantages of a judicial, taxation, and regulatory environment peppered with innovation and entrepreneurial mind-set. Despite several challenges, the European Union, China, India, Israel, and other countries in the Middle East have experienced growth in venture capital, private equity, and infrastructure investments. Venture professionals know the importance of a supportive government in paving the way for growth—be it through research grants or tax incentives. Several countries are closely following the proven recipe of success that the United States has experienced. The entrepreneurial drive combined with the set of market conditions gives the United States the edge that is not easy to replicate across cultural nuances. For example, the rate of formation of anchor companies (companies that started from scratch and are listed in the 1,000 biggest companies by market capitalization over the past 20 years) in the United States is four times as many as are found in the European Union. In the European Union, entrepreneurs are perceived as "exploiters" of resources at twice the rate that they are so perceived in the United States. Despite which, successful companies like Skype have generated wealth for venture professionals. Singapore leads governmental reform and investments in technology research parks. Five percent of companies in Singapore are venture backed. Israel leads in entrepreneurial drive and innovation, especially in security and defense, turning the political issues into opportunities. Creating a stable political environment combined with a strong legal infrastructure that speedily addresses corporate, shareholder, taxation, and intellectual property concerns is the foundation on which venture investments can be established. The harder challenge is not government mandates, but social acceptance and change. A government cannot create, but only support, entrepreneurial drive as it's largely a complex interplay of emotional and social dynamics. For instance, while Japan leads the world in filings of intellectual property, the linkages with venture capital and start-up formation have not been visible. The Global Entrepreneurship Monitor (GEM) global report gives Japan the lowest score for entrepreneurship of any large country, largely due to its risk-averse orientation. Bankruptcy in Japan equates largely to being ostracized and in the extreme, leads to suicide. Eventually, some regions will march, some will drift, and some will be dragged into the entrepreneurial domain. And no matter what your zip code is, the basics of the business remain the same—the ability to raise capital, invest it prudently, add value as a board member, and generate exits. *The Business of Venture Capital* seeks to offer valuable insights to a rookie venture practitioner or a business school student aspiring to pursue a career in venture capital. While parts of the subject have received attention from publishers in the past, this book promises to be the first comprehensive attempt to focus on the four critical elements of the venture capital business. Raising a venture fund calls for a deeper understanding of what investors (Limited Partners) seek in venture funds. The art of sourcing investments is dependent on the team's operating expertise, the fund's past successes, and brand identity. While structuring term investments may appear fairly straightforward, Mahendra Ramsinghani touches on the underlying logic that is embedded in term sheets. And most professionals learn how to be good board members by watching the senior partners at work. This book helps the reader to understand the basics of boardroom behavior and the ways value can be added in the arc of a portfolio company's growth. And while exits occur as acquisitions of public offerings, this book helps with understanding the underlying aspects that lead to the final step in return creation. Mahendra's career progression as a venture practitioner, former limited partner, and entrepreneur encompasses the 360 degrees of venture capital. He has sought insights of leading venture capitalists and compiled their views in this book, which can be a good starting point for any practitioner. These insights combined with experience allow him to structure the contents of this book in a relevant manner. This book not only informs and educates on the process of venture investments, but also balances the glory with the reality—this is a business where only returns matter and time is not your friend! Venture capital is a lifelong apprenticeship. The business of investing requires equal parts logic and intuition; the yin and the yang; the alpha and the omega. As in life, much can be taught by books but most is learned on the battlefield, where a few earn the honors, most become martyrs, and the rest carry the scars for a lifetime.

MARK HEESEN
President—National Venture Capital Association
August, 2011

Preface

Life is continually a creation—a formation of new higher forms.
When this formation comes to stop in our view, or goes
backward—when existing forms are destroyed, this only means
that a new form is taking shape, invisible to us. A caterpillar sees
itself shrivel up but does not see the butterfly which flies out of it.
  —Leo Tolstoy in *Tolstoy Diaries*, Kochety, October 27, 1900

A leading U.S. pension fund manager was flummoxed when recently some venture capitalists called for a meeting. Those seasoned venture capitalists (or General Partners, GPs) did not walk in with a presentation slide deck or a fund memorandum. "I walked in fully prepared for a fund-raise pitch," he recalls. "But here was a group of proven VCs with over 25 years of venture investment expertise telling me that the venture model is broken." What they brought instead was a candid assessment: that they did not see a future in this business. Lack of exits and poor performance, regulatory challenges, and shrinking capital pools had led to structural challenges; hence, significant investor disillusionment.

The pension fund manager walked away from the meeting scratching his head and asking himself, "Did that meeting just happen?"

It seemed to the pension fund manager that the venture model must be broken, but within walking distance of the office where this happened, a different picture (or as Tolstoy puts it, a new form) emerges. Andreessen-Horowitz, an up-and-coming venture firm had raised over $1.6 billion in 22 months across three funds. As LPs beat a path to this door, neither Marc Andreessen nor Ben Horowitz asked themselves if the venture model is broken. Instead, they were busy investing in Facebook, Twitter, and Zynga. As this book was being written, one of their portfolio companies, Skype was acquired by Microsoft for over $8.56 billion.[1]

But the underlying challenges of the business of venture capital are significant. Investors (Limited Partners, or LPs) seeking venture funds have been disillusioned by the aggregate performance over the past decade—an industry that has not produced meaningful "risk-adjusted" returns. Peter Dolan, Director of Private Equity for Harvard Management Company, once said, "When I ask a VC to explain a fund's poor performance, he just says: 'Be patient—the cycle will turn.' Society, venture capitalists, and entrepreneurs would all be better off if VCs quit their jobs and started doing something different."[2]

So which is it, a broken model or a booming asset class? As with most things, the answer depends on where you stand. Any practitioner keen to dip their toes in this business of venture capital may stand on a stronger foundation if the following characteristics are considered.

VENTURE CAPITAL IS A SMALL ASSET CLASS WITH A LOT OF PIZZAZZ

Despite its powerful impact on innovation and economic impact, venture capital is a very small portion of any institutional fund's assets. Any institution typically sets aside no more than five to six percent of its entire asset class for private equity (PE). Within this PE universe, VC is an even smaller subset; other private equity players like buy-out, mezzanine, and distressed investing eat up a significant chunk of this PE allocation, leaving a tiny bit for the VCs. Why do LPs even care? "LPs come to venture capital for sex and blood—it's that dark alley—everyone is intrigued and wants in—the curiosity and interest level is very high, but very few LPs know what truly goes on," says Chris Douvos, an LP with investments in some of the leading venture funds in the country.

Take an example of a $50 billion pension fund, which typically sets aside 10 percent, or $5 billion, for alternative investments. Of this pool, about 15 percent, or $750 million, would fall into the PE asset class. This PE pool is subdivided in multiple funds, sliced by sectors and geographies—you could end up with 20 to 50 different funds. A typical investment amount in a venture fund would be, say, $25 million. Should this venture fund yield a 5x return in 10 years, the impact of this outcome on a $50 billion fund on an annualized basis may be good, but not enough to move the needle (or as one LP wryly puts it, just about enough to get a flower basket from the chief investment officer). The asset class is deemed risky, thanks to the fact that at last three out of every 10 investments are total losses and another third of the investments generate a modest outcome. This, combined with illiquidity risks and the fact that only a few funds have generated such strong returns, consistently across economic cycles, keeps the VC pool small. In contrast, hedge funds have grown to as much as 10 percent of any alternative assets portfolio, swelling from $39 billion in 1990 to $1.9 trillion in 2007.[3]

ONLY A SMALL SUBSET ARE CONSISTENT PERFORMERS; THE REST IS NOISE

According to the National VC Association 2010 yearbook, there are at least 800 firms with 1,188 funds in existence managing about $179.4 billion. Of these, funds actively investing may be far lower—as much as half. In any given year, VC funds raise about $25 billion from limited partners. Consider 2009, which was a challenging year for VC by any standards. LPs deployed about $15 billion in all venture funds but the amount raised by the top seven VC firms was a staggering $7.08 billion, or as much as 46 percent of the total. At least 127 venture funds were in the market at this time, fighting for the other 54 percent of the pie. If seven funds can attract as much capital, there were as many as 15x of "not-so-fortunate" funds trying to kick down LP doors without much success.

LPs seek top performers that demonstrate consistently superior returns across economic cycles. The universe of top performers is small and can absorb as much as 50 percent of the total LP capital. The rest of the capital is being sprinkled in subpar funds, which yield subpar returns, which creates more noise for the top performers.

ACCESS TO THE BEST-IN-CLASS IS LIMITED

LPs have limited access to the top quartile managers. In a 2010 J.P. Morgan survey of 325 institutional investors, as much as 42 percent of the respondents described top-manager access as an advantage of this asset class.[4] We saw earlier that a $50 million investment does not do much for a larger institutional investor. But once LPs gain access to a top-performing fund, not only do they heave a sigh of relief, but they gradually try to up their position and seek a larger investment size. This creates an interesting problem—those on the inside seek bigger bites, and yet, those on the outside are eager to get in. The top quartile funds start to expand in size to accommodate this growing demand, but few funds can maintain performance. Success begets bloated funds, and thus lower performance. Research shows that a 50 percent increase in fund size leads to 1.5 percent decline in IRR. Performance peaks with $200 million fund and declines once funds cross $500 million.[5]

"It's a swell offer, Brad, and you're a great guy, but I've just got out of a bad limited partnership, and I'm not ready for that kind of commitment yet."

Size is not the only problem. Strategies shift (think cleantech). Stage-related dynamics (early-stage investors become later-stage or multistage investors) cause LPs to walk away from funds. With stronger performance come GP-friendly investment terms (high carry structures, fatter fees per partner, little reporting, or minimal LP control provisions). As LPs shift away, the dance starts all over again.

CAPITAL SUPPLY AND DEMAND

Every good VC investment a la Facebook, Twitter, and Google leads to a mad scramble for LPs to invest more capital. This leads to emergence of subpar LPs who do not fully comprehend the dynamics of this asset class and end up investing in GPs who do not deserve to be in this business.

Chris Douvos, who blogs as SuperLP, draws an interesting analogy:

> *If the public markets are like an ocean with trillions of dollars at play, the private equity as an asset class is like a bathtub (LPs invest ~$300 billion each year in PE in United States). Venture is like a tiny sink or a bucket—at $20 billion each year—and when you pour a lot of capital in a small bucket, you end up making a big mess.*

Douvos is alluding to the $100 billion that eager LPs invested in VC during the 1999–2000 bubble era. Such excesses will need another few years for cleanup.

But with every triple-digit IRR a Facebook, Zynga, Groupon, and Twitter generates, the hoi polloi jumps back in the asset class and throws a lot of fresh water in the sink. The level rises but, unfortunately, there is no ringing of alarm bells to alert LPs that the overall bucket is about to overflow—that the capital supply-demand curve is shifting. Several LPs bemoaned the fact that over supply of capital causes a mess and it takes upward of a decade to mop things up. On the other hand, eager GPs argue that more capital is better, and the market can expand with technological trends. After all, LPs invested about $2 billion each year in the early 1980s in VC—a number that has now grown to $20 billion a year.

Embedded within this debate is the inherent cyclical nature of all investment trends—with more money, valuations go up, returns go down, and LPs scream that the venture model is broken, take their toys away, and go home. And the ones who know how to play the game grin silently—stay consistent and generate strong returns in the down markets and the cycle starts all over again.

THE CHALLENGES OF FUND PERFORMANCE MEASUREMENT

Often it feels like every GP who walks in the door is in the top quartile. FLAG Capital, a fund-of-funds, calls it the Lake Wobegon effect: where all VCs are above average. The first problem is fundamental; past performance does not guarantee future results. The second is that public benchmarks are of little help because the "private" in PE translates to lack of meaningful datasets. While this has improved significantly over the years, the sample size and returns reporting (largely sourced via Freedom of Information Act requests of public pension funds) can create challenges for any LP. Compare data from two highly respected sources:

Vintage Year	Top Quartile IRR (Data source #1)	Top Quartile IRR (Data source #2)
2002	3.8%	6.2%
2004	8.9%	4.8%
2007	0.3%	(13.0)%

To position themselves in the best light, GPs choose one data source over another.

Additionally, the best performers do not have any incentive to report their data and the worst of the GPs quietly leave through the back door. Thus, sample size for most datasets is small, making this debate spirited, to say the least.

The other challenge is the propensity of the media to create "news" using premature data. For any vintage year, all IRR data in the first three to five years will be negative (it's called the J-Curve), but try explaining that to a green journalist who is bent on getting a byline on the front page. This hurts the entire VC asset class. And for VC associations across the board, this is an opportunity—ensuring data quality is relevant and the media thoughtfully presents it would mean less noise and more opportunities. Quarterly reporting on a 10-year fund is like trying to gauge the performance of a marathon runner at each mile; the data is great but not as relevant till the race is complete.

COMPETITION FROM WITHIN IS HIGH

Venture is an asset class that competes for LP mind-share. The line at the door includes other private equity players (Buy-outs, Mezzanine, Distressed Debt), hedge funds, real estate, oil and gas, and more. And risk-return profiles of other asset classes can be compelling, if not better. While some LPs dedicate a portion of their assets to venture capital, even within venture, LPs have ample choices.

According to the NVCA, there are approximately 800 active venture firms in the United States. In 2010, there were over 120 funds in the market seeking over five times the capital that is typically invested in this asset class. Only an average of 10 percent would successfully raise their funds. Of these, a smaller portion will actually deliver some meaningful performance.

No database captures trends of those who tried and lost in this game. And there are no barriers to entry in this business—every entrepreneur who sells their company successfully wants to raise a venture fund, but there is only one Marc Andreessen. Performance remains concentrated within the few pockets of expertise.

A BUSINESS OF HOME RUNS

Each year, VCs invest as much as $20 billion in some 2,500 companies (and that is not even counting Yuri Milner's investments, a Russian investor who exploded in the VC arena with investments in leading social media companies such as Facebook and Twitter). Competition for good opportunities can be intense. VCs do not seek also-rans—companies that could end up with modest revenues. Each year about 600,000 start-ups are launched. Less than 0.5 percent attract VC. Of *Inc.* magazine's annual list of the 500 fastest growing companies in the United States assessed over a decade (1997–2007), less than 20 percent of companies were venture backed.[6] Obviously, VCs seek the ones that have proprietary technologies, can scale up quickly, and can become big winners, the kings of new categories—not "also-ran" companies.

Despite all the due diligence, the loss-ratios are significant. According to Professor William Sahlman of Harvard Business School, 62.4 percent of VC investments were completely lost while 3.1 percent of the investments accounted for 53 percent of the profits for roughly 600 investments.[7] According to the National VC Association data, as many as 35 percent of the venture-backed companies may have quietly failed. But a few big hits make up for all the losses—as Gordon Hargraves of Rho Capital, a fund-of-funds, puts it, "We should count ourselves as very lucky a 'Facebook' comes along once every five years. VC is a home run business, and our experience, the roughly 20 percent capital-weighted success rate of winners makes up for the 80 percent of losers. In 2010, less than $12 billion was raised in the U.S. for VC, yet the valuation of Facebook was $50 billion while Groupon, Zynga, and Twitter were all around the $5 billion mark and, given that, it was surprising more money wasn't going to VC."[8]

Exits, from a quick three-year flip in 1999, have stretched to an eight-year arduous journey in 2008. But at the same token, it took only three years for Zynga to reach a $3+ billion valuation. Squeezed in between these investment-exit dynamics are some seven thousand venture professionals, some hugely successful and some in between. Promod Haque of Norwest Venture Partners, one of the leading venture practitioners, once summarized a presentation with this New Testament James 4:13 quote, which I hope you find true to the daily struggle with immense failures or flamboyant successes:

> Now listen, ye who say,
> Today or tomorrow we will go to this or that city,
> Spend a year there,
> Carry on business and make money.
> Why, you do not even know
> What will happen tomorrow.
> What is your life?
> It is a mist that appears for a little while
> And then vanishes.

DON'T BOTHER PRETENDING THAT THE BUSINESS IS SCALABLE

Successful venture firms grow in size, or expand geographically—China, India, Europe, Israel—franchises open at a rapid pace but at some point these groups break off and the splinters take on a life of their own. While the DFJ and Village Ventures franchise models are intriguing, several funds have tried expansion without much success. It irritates LPs and does no good. But any GP with triple-digit IRR can quickly get afflicted with the desire to dominate the world—success seduces one and all. While this business is driven by several interwoven factors of opportunities, talent, technology, and capital—it's not easy to whip up a recipe for making astute investments. At the outset, buy low, sell high is an easy mantra to chant but difficult to implement.

Another axis of scalability within a firm is succession—firms with senior GPs should attract the next layer of talent and build the bench. But the majority of GPs really have no good way to solve this problem—and Warren Buffett at the age of eighty is still trying to figure out succession. Brad Feld of The Foundry Group was candid when we discussed succession: "We don't intend to hire associates and train them; we are just going to shut shop and go home. Done!"

FRONTIER CHALLENGES OF EMERGING MARKETS

Private equity has grown significantly in emerging markets—for example, Asia is now on par with developed countries with respect to private equity deal value as a percentage of GDP.[9] About $20 billion is invested in PE transactions in Asia—which is about one-tenth of the global PE investments. Driven by GDP growth, infrastructural challenges, consolidation, and financial engineering opportunities, PE has entered emerging markets easily. However, VC demands a different fabric for growth.

While the 6 percent to 8 percent GDP growth in India or China is appealing, consider the fact that, in the United States, the emerging market of one time grew at the rate of 1.3 percent for the period of 1820–1870[10]—that's one generation of single-digit growth, not just a year or two. Such growth drives public market returns and to a certain extent PE investments but venture capital trends in Asia have a long way to go before it can come close to mirroring the levels of the United States. Eager GPs have expanded or relocated in the new markets. While the growth may seem obvious and infrastructure-level investments may seem intriguing, it is truly a venture market that remains to be seen. The ecosystem is evolving—regulatory frameworks, judiciary, and intellectual property foundation, financial markets, service providers, syndicates, and exit opportunities are nascent and unpredictable, compounding the risk for LPs. And with respect to entrepreneurial talent, the jury is still out. In general, the society still has to believe in the promise of start-ups! Getting a job in Microsoft's Hyderabad offices is considered cool. An eligible bachelor can command some decent dowry and social standing, but stock options are neither sought nor granted. One institutional LP was candid: "At the grass-root entrepreneurial level, I just don't see the hunger in India—the burning desire to start companies that could change the world." And what about the ecosystem—an entrepreneur who relocated to India from the United States and raised his Series A bemoaned, "I had to fire my entire senior management team because the productivity and pace was eons away from that of United States."

The situation in Europe may be slightly better but the frequency of exits and returns for venture are lower in comparison to the United States. Paul Morris heads Dow Chemical Company's investments in venture funds in Europe. He points out that the challenges in EU markets are of a different kind. "The barriers of language are obvious," he says. "But each country has a different financial and regulatory framework which impairs the ability to generate rapid exits, which is the lifeblood of this business."

While the underpinnings of a bright future are evident in emerging economies, will these markets become as efficient as United States VC markets? The United States can export the VC model to the world. But this business is driven by factors such as entrepreneurial, socioeconomic, and regulatory and innovation—it does not operate on flows of capital alone.

WHAT THIS BOOK COVERS, AND WHAT IT DRAWS ON

This book aims to address the entire spectrum of investing and is focused toward seed and early-stage venture investments. Those who are eager to get in the business, MBAs or, say, an analyst-level person, may benefit from this book. Raising a fund, sourcing and investing, being a good board member, and exits are interlinked aspects of the business—it all starts and ends with the quality of people and the investment strategy. The front end of the investment cycle, due diligence and entrepreneurial debates, is fun—the other half, value add and exits, is hard work and tests the mettle of one and all.

Part One of this book focuses on raising the venture fund—we look at the sources of capital and LP investment criteria. Raising a fund is not for the fainthearted but that is only half of the equation. Generating a return is what matters. Part Two of the book focuses on the sourcing, structuring, and value add of portfolio companies. The web site has some tools such as due diligence checklist, LP GP Due Diligence criteria, and links to essential white papers.

While venture capital is a subset of the private equity (PE) asset class, this book does not delve into the PE universe. PE is more heavily oriented toward existing, higher-revenue companies, is agnostic to technology, and the value-creation drivers are primarily financial and operational engineering. VC on the other hand is more about building companies, can be technology intensive, leans heavily on management teams and intellectual property, and does not rely as much on financial jugglery of reducing costs, consolidation, or improving gross margins. The common threads in PE and VC are generic from an investment standpoint—the sources of capital are similar, and the investee companies are "private" and require strong management teams, rapid results, and some clarity on exit timing.

This book builds upon the earlier works of professors Josh Lerner, Andrew Metrick and authors Justin Camp, Randall Stross, Udayan Gupta, and Jeffrey Bussgang—all of whom have made significant contributions. I strongly suggest indulging in their works—it is much expansive and will make a better practitioner out of you. This book is a slight variance in which I have attempted to cover the entire investment cycle. Roughly, about a third of the content is derived from peer-reviewed journals and publications, a third from interviews and insights from some of the world's leading practitioners, and the rest from my own experiences. In some situations, interview sources have requested anonymity to allow for candor. While I could have eliminated these comments easily, I chose to include them to help readers understand the mind of any LP.

Certain subjects such as valuation and exits are treated in a rudimentary manner, a bit sparsely because these have been addressed in other books earlier. When it comes to exits, reading any instruction book and trying to negotiate an exit would be akin to learning to fly an airplane while reading a user manual. Get a pilot!

Tax matters, regulatory aspects, accounting matters, and the role of government in stimulating venture capital are beyond the scope of this book. Usage of data trends is minimized to allow for longevity—data gets irrelevant and stale quickly. Also, leading practitioners are moving away from industry jargon like "deal" and "projects," which is not the most respectful way to address an entrepreneur's lifeblood, sweat, and tears. I have tried to minimize usage of these terms without losing the essence of the subject.

Amidst all the hype and hoopla around this business, I wanted to emphasize the challenge—it is seductive but the failure rate is very high. And those who fail have no good place to go. Jack Ahrens of T-Gap Ventures has successfully navigated the venture capital waters for 30 years. I once asked Jack, "Where do failed VCs go?" and he said, "There is no good place, really—VCs think they could be good at running companies but that is a stretch. A consultant maybe? You become bad at everything." Jack's dry wit shows. "Maybe I could make it easier for them and offer my 9 millimeter?" My goal in sharing such comments is not to deter a reader from this business but rather to offer reality checks—in conducting interviews with various successful practitioners like Jack, it was evident that there is no straight path into or out of the top quartile.

After reading the insights of various practitioners, aspirants may be able to appreciate the intricacies of the VC business and have a stronger understanding of basics. I sincerely hope this book benefits all those who seek to get better at the art and science of VC investments.

Acknowledgments

T his book is a collage of the investment experiences of some of the world's leading venture practitioners—I merely wielded the brush. These experts offered their ideas in an attempt to make the uphill incline of venture capital (VC) a bit easier for the future practitioners. Without their participation, support, encouragement, threats, and sometimes the much-needed kick in the rear, this would have remained just another idea. A mere acknowledgment seems inappropriate, considering the time and effort invested by several people in making this book a reality. Deep gratitude would be more like it.

First and foremost, Harry Cendrowski, author, mentor, and mensch, helped me get started on this project. If Harry had not offered his generous advice and support, a few trees would have been saved. Denise Shekerjian, author of *Uncommon Genius*—a seminal book on creativity—chose to guide me, then a random stranger, and offered valuable pearls of wisdom along this path. Denise and Harry prove that this world still has people who are selfless, generous of their time, and a force for the good in this universe. Thank you, Harry and Denise. May your tribe increase!

In its original form, this book was headed in a different direction. The worldwide financial debacle of 2008, combined with so-called denominator challenges in the venture industry, called for a reboot. It would have been a shame to let this (hopefully) once-in-a-lifetime recession go to waste. Amid all this, John DeRemegis at John Wiley & Sons was very patient as I plodded through re-creating this canvas. John teamed me up with Emilie Herman, senior editorial manager at Wiley. Emilie, who speaks softly and knows how to get these crazy writers to meet deadlines, assures me that sanity is overrated. She well knows that writers procrastinate and can conjure up very compelling excuses—"hitting the wall" was my favorite. In her ever-so-gentle style, she would find ways to help me climb over such walls and keep me on track. Next time, I promise not to ask Emilie for so many extensions. To avoid these, just a serene waterfront stone cottage in the Bahamas or Aruba would suffice—thanks in advance for that, Emilie!

Mark Heesen, president of the National Venture Capital Association (NVCA), generously agreed to contribute the Foreword for this book. Mark, a one-of-a-kind social entrepreneur who has led the NVCA for over two decades, was an active supporter throughout the process, for which I remain grateful. In developing the framework for this book, Lisa Edgar, managing director at Top Tier Capital Partners, offered critical and insightful guidelines. I had to discard about a hundred pages of the manuscript after our brief 15-minute conversation. And heck, I was even grateful as I hit "delete"; *gracias*, Lisa—perfect timing! Dr. David Brophy, director of the Center of Venture Capital and Private Equity at the University of Michigan, was kind and patient enough to indulge my ideas and advise me on how to make the book more valuable. Thank you, Dr. Brophy!

As I conducted interviews, gained insights, and gathered information, many leading practitioners and friends offered their time, advice, and direction.

My deep gratitude to:

- Institutional investors Robert Clone (director of private equity, Indiana retirement plans); Catherine Crockett (Grove Street Advisors); Chris "SuperLP" Douvos (TIFF); G. Thomas Doyal; Gordon Hargraves (Rho Capital); Erik Lundberg (University of Michigan Endowment); Paul Morris (Dow Venture Capital, Europe); Georganne Perkins (Fisher-Lynch Capital); James Plonka (formerly of Dow Venture Capital, USA); Christopher Rizik (Renaissance Venture Capital Fund); Igor Rozenblit; Kenneth Van Heel (Dow Venture Capital, USA); and Kelly Williams (Credit Suisse).
- Howard Beber (Proskauer Rose) for his valuable guidance on the chapter addressing LP–GP terms. My deep gratitude to Pascal Levensohn (Levensohn Venture Partners and The Presidio Group) for his insights and guidance on corporate governance. Pascal is the author of a series of white papers on the role of VC in the boardroom, which address a critical challenge in the industry.
- Brad Feld and Seth Levine of the Foundry Group, Boulder, Colorado, who went out of their way to offer their expertise, contacts, and ideas—thank you for making this journey easier!
- Various GPs and venture practitioners who agreed to share their experiences:
  Brent Ahrens (Canaan Partners)
  Jack Ahrens (T-Gap Ventures)
  Lindsay Aspegren (North Coast Technology Investors)
  Rajeev Batra (Mayfield Fund)
  Tom Bredt (formerly with Menlo Ventures)
  Frank Caufield (Kleiner Perkins Caufield & Byers)
  Punit Chiniwalla (Panorama Capital)
  David Cowan (Bessemer Venture Partners)

Todd Dagres (Spark Capital)
Liam Donohue (.406 Ventures)
Tim Draper (Draper Fisher Jurvetson)
Bill Elkus (Clearstone Venture Partners)
Jan Garfinkle (Arboretum Ventures)
Matt Garratt (Battery Ventures)
Promod Haque (Norwest Venture Partners)
Rob Hayes (First Round Capital)
Rick Heitzmann (Firstmark Capital)
John Hummer (Hummer-Winblad)
John Jarve (Menlo Ventures)
Chris Jones (Dow Venture Capital)
Deepak Kamra (Canaan Partners)
Mitch Lasky (Benchmark Capital)
Marty Lehr (Osage Venture Partners)
Mary Lemmer (RPM Ventures)
Rich Levandov (Avalon Ventures)
Terry McGuire (Polaris Ventures)
Steve Mercil (Rainsource Capital)
Ravi Mohan (Shasta Ventures)
Hany Nada (GGV Capital)
John Neis and Jim Adox (Venture Investors)
Bob Nelsen (ARCH Venture Partners)
Mark Olesnavage (Hopen Life Sciences Fund)
Tim Petersen (Arboretum Ventures)
James Plonka (Dow Venture Capital)
Andy Rappaport (August Capital)
Bryan Roberts (Venrock)
Bryce Roberts (O'Reilly Alphatec Ventures)
Seth Rudnick (Canaan Partners)
Lip-Bu Tan (Walden International)

- Kelly DePonte (Probitas Partners) and Gus Long (Stanwich Advisors) for their industry insights. To Tim Mayleben and Roger Newton (of Esperion fame) for all their support and guidance. To uber-angel Terry Cross and Matthew Neagle for their timely support. To Amanda Ross at Stunning Creative for key introductions with industry leaders. To Tim Friedman (Preqin) for offering valuable industry data and always being responsive and helpful—thank you, Tim! To Kim Gagliardi at Dow Jones VentureSource for generously assisting with IPOs and M&A trends. To Brant Moxley (Pinnacle Group) for sharing hiring (and firing) trends in the venture capital/private equity (VC/PE) industry. To Ian Bund and Mark Horne at Plymouth Venture Partners.

- Edward "Chip" Miller, David Blaskiewicz, Karen Harris, Karl Bell, Jamie Grimaldi, Mary King, Steve Rose, and Andrea Washington—my wonderful family at Invest Detroit—thank you. It is a joy to work with *all of y'all!*
- John Kerschen and Dale Grogan, VC kings in the making, who know how to enjoy full-belly laughs.
- Michael Finney, CEO of the Michigan Economic Development Corporation (MEDC), for having given me the opportunity to dip my toe in venture capital, and to Cindy Douglas, formerly of MEDC, for having made the legislative ride easier.
- Dr. Sankara Bhagavadpada, astrophysicist, mentor, and guide extraordinaire for his invaluable support.

And finally, to my parents—wish they were here—and my dear family members, Deepa, Aria, Amar, Geeta, and Sunita; my in-laws, Appa and Amma; and my "out-laws," Ratan, Nitin, Chirayu, Prajakta, Uncle Sree, and Sanjay (Turbo-dada)—thank you all for being patient (or more correctly, supremely tolerant) of my idiosyncrasies.

My karmic debt to all of the above weighs heavy. If you, dear reader, should cross paths with any one of these industry leaders, please join me in extending not just your acknowledgments, but your deep gratitude. The venture world is a better place thanks to them. And, of course, while all the good ideas and insights are theirs, at least one bad idea and the mistakes are mine.

Ann Arbor, Michigan
May, 2011

The Business
of Venture
Capital

Raising the Venture Fund

When Jan Garfinkle decided to be a venture capitalist, she polished her resume and approached several early-stage venture funds and was turned down. Jan had spent 20 years in various operational capacities and had cut her teeth primarily at two venture-backed cardiovascular device companies. A large publicly traded company acquired both these companies, leaving Jan a bit richer, wiser, and hungrier. She joined these start-ups after the initial idea had been vetted and the strategic direction of the company was being crystallized.

Early in her career, Jan joined Advanced Cardiovascular Systems (ACS) as an associate product manager, the company was seen as the forerunner in over-the-wire angioplasty—a technique that reopens narrowed or blocked arteries in the heart (coronary arteries) without major surgery. The founder of the company, John Simpson, once remarked, "When we started the company, there was no interventional cardiology device sector."[1] C. Richard ("Dick") Kramlich, founder of New Enterprise Associates (NEA), one of the world's leading venture capital (VC) firms with over $10 billion under management today, had then invested in Advanced Cardiovascular Systems. Dick once said of ACS, "The procedure was entirely non-invasive ... the body didn't have to go through the trauma it once had to endure."[2] At Advanced Cardiovascular Systems, Jan spent six years in marketing and sales of angioplasty systems. When Eli Lilly came knocking and acquired the company, the foundation stone for Guidant Corporation was laid. "We were the largest single shareholder in [Advanced Cardiovascular Systems]. ... The company did extremely well,"[3] Kramlich would say. That was over 25 years ago, when Jan was at the threshold of her career. To be in an NEA-backed start-up was certainly fortuitous for Jan's career path.[4]

Like all good serial entrepreneurs, Jan moved on to John Simpson's next company, Devices for Vascular Intervention. The same founder who had built Advanced Cardiovascular Systems was now leading the charge in the next wave of the cardiovascular sector. Devices for Vascular Intervention laid its bets on atherectomy—a procedure to remove plaque from arteries. Here, Jan wrote the first business plan, and over the next six years, as director of marketing and clinical research, she dove deep into the universe of regulatory trials and approvals. Again, Eli Lilly had been watching closely and came knocking at the door. These two companies acquired by Eli Lilly became the foundation for Guidant Corporation, which was eventually spun off by Eli Lilly as a separate company and listed as GDT on the New York Stock Exchange (NYSE). Boston Scientific acquired Guidant in 2006 for $27.2 billion. At that time, the vascular intervention business was valued at $4.1 billion.[5]

When venture firms turned her down time and again, Jan decided to do what any entrepreneur does—never take no for an answer! She decided to raise her own fund and launched Arboretum Ventures, a fund focused on early-stage health care and medical device companies. Having lived close to Nichols Arboretum in Ann Arbor, and with her own DNA of a nurturing type, she found the name to be the appropriate encapsulation of her philosophies and style.

Like Jan, John Hummer, cofounder of Hummer-Winblad, interviewed at five venture firms. "All five turned me down—on the same day," reminisces John with a smug smile. "I climbed in from the window, as most do to get in this business of venture capital," comments the towering John, who once was a professional basketball player.

Most venture professionals agree that there is no straight path into the business of VC. You have to climb in from the window, if that's what it takes!

A venture firm's functions can be broken down into four key parts:

1. Raise a venture fund.
2. Build a portfolio of investment opportunities.
3. Monitor and add value to this portfolio.
4. Generate a superior financial return via timely exits.

Part One of the book addresses the various aspects of raising a venture fund. It starts with the universe of investors, or limited partners (LPs). We consider their investment criteria, LP-GP terms of investment, and fund structures.

Investment professionals, or general partners (GPs), develop an investment strategy and raise a fund, a process that may take anywhere from a few months to a few years. The investment period commences after the "close" when the money has been raised. This period typically lasts for four to five years, when the GPs, or practitioners, search for opportunities and make the initial portfolio company investments. The initial capital is deployed in four to five years with follow-on rounds being funded in years 5 to 10. Ideally, all the invested capital would be harvested and returned to the investors, the LPs, in 10 years. The fund would then be fully liquidated.

Successful firms do not necessarily wait until liquidation of the previous fund; they raise their next fund as soon as the majority of the capital of the current fund is invested or designated as reserved for existing portfolio companies. Leading venture firms raise a fund every three to five years. Typically, funds are labeled with Roman numerals, such as ABC Ventures Fund II, III, IV, and so on. Roman numerals are a soft indicator of a venture fund's ability to survive and to generate returns across the various economic cycles. A firm's true measure of success is its ability to generate consistent returns over multiple economic cycles. The VC business is subject to pressures from multiple ends: the supply of capital, the availability of investment opportunities, liquidity time frames, and regulatory dynamics.

Successful venture fund-raising is 90 percent preparation. Investors or limited partners seek a blend of strong investment expertise, a compelling investment strategy, and supportive market conditions. For proven top quartile fund managers, fund-raising is a breeze. Good fund managers, like good brands, have customers knocking at their doors at all times. At the other end of the spectrum are the unproven: the first-time fund managers, for whom the fund-raising process can best be described as crawling uphill . . . on broken glass.

A thorough analysis of the LP universe can help a GP target the right LPs and beget unusual results. This section starts with identifying the universe of LPs. LPs follow predetermined investment processes and criteria. We look at how LPs assess GPs in making 10-year blind pool commitments. Finally, LP-GP investment terms are covered, along with details of terms that matter.

In considering investments in private equity and venture capital, LPs adhere to certain norms and practices. The objective of this section is to help a fund manager to understand these clearly. The fund-raising process, that uphill incline, may become a tad bit easier.

CHAPTER 1

The Universe of Limited Partners

Before beginning a Hunt, it is wise to ask someone what you are looking for before you begin looking for it.

—Winnie the Pooh

Potential investors in venture funds, or limited partners (LPs), do not hang a largish dollar sign at their doors, but they do have what all venture capitalists (VCs) seek—capital! These LPs include a mix of institutional investors (e.g., pension funds, foundations, and endowments) and family offices, including high-net-worth individuals (HNWIs). As seen in Figure 1.1, typically, the bulk of capital for venture funds comes from pension funds. Each LP follows a unique set of characteristics:

- *Asset allocation strategy.* A set of investment principles and portfolio construction guidelines designed to generate an overall target rate of return. Venture capital is treated as a subasset class of private equity that falls under "Alternative Assets."
- *Investment criteria.* The factors that help choose target investments within each of the asset classes.
- *Investment process.* Time lines and steps to make an investment within each asset class

This chapter describes the various types of LPs such as pension funds, finance companies, endowments, and foundations. All LPs aim to manage risk and returns and construct portfolios that aim for a target return. Targeting the right mix of LPs is a bit like matchmaking; understanding the array of potential investors and their decision-making process is the first step to raising the fund in an efficient manner. For example, a first-time

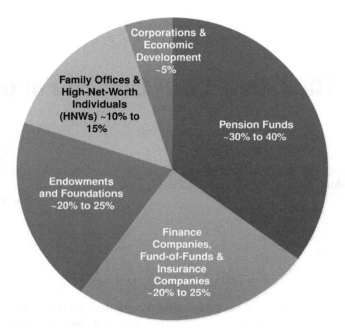

FIGURE 1.1   The Limited Partner Universe: Typical Sources
of Capital for Venture Funds

fund launched by first-time managers is likely to raise capital from individuals and family offices but will seldom get the attention of institutional
investors. In this chapter, we look at allocation strategies of various LPs and
develop a framework for targeting suitable LPs. For any venture fund, it
is prudent to know that competition does not come necessarily from other
venture funds, but from asset classes that offer a better risk-adjusted return
to the LPs.

AN OVERVIEW OF ALTERNATIVE ASSETS

The four major asset classes are stocks (public equities), bonds (sources
of fixed income), alternative assets (private equity, VC, hedge funds, real
estate), and cash. Investors establish asset allocation strategies to adopt
optimum allocation percentages in each of these asset classes. Asset allocation, a prudent method to manage risk and returns, is driven by each investor's appetite for risk, rewards, and liquidity. Consider Figure 1.2. VC is a
subasset class of private equity and falls under the alternative investment asset class, and for most LPs, it is a small fraction of the overall portfolio.

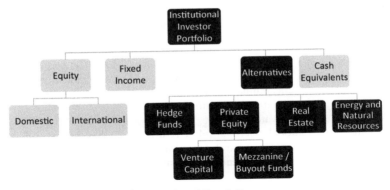

FIGURE 1.2   A Typical Institutional Portfolio

ASSET ALLOCATION 101

Put your eggs in different baskets and watch *all* baskets. The risk/rewards of various assets are evident from this simple example: If an investor had allocated 60 percent in stocks, 30 percent in bonds, and 10 percent in cash, an average annual return would be 9.2 percent. If allocation is increased to 100 percent in stocks, the return would increase to 11.0 percent. If the entire portfolio is shifted to bonds, the return falls to 6.1 percent.

Risk is measured by standard deviation, an indicator of uncertainty, which increases about three times between the stocks and bonds portfolio. Investors expect higher returns when the risk is high.

Impact of Asset Allocation on Returns

Portfolio and Returns*	100% Bonds	60% Stock/30% Bonds/10% Cash	100% Stocks
Average annual return	6.1%	9.2%	11.0%
Standard deviation	6.4	10.8	18.0

*Calculated over the 60-year period from December 31, 1949, to December 31, 2009.
Source: T. Rowe Price Associates.

TABLE 1.1 The Alternative Investments Universe

Class	Subasset Class	Investment Goals
Private equity	VC, Leveraged buyout funds (LBOs), distressed debt, mezzanine funds, special situations, and international private equity	Higher returns and diversification
Hedge funds	Global macro, absolute return, market neutral, long/short, 130/30, event driven, and derivatives	Higher returns and diversification with better liquidity as compared to private equity
Real estate, infrastructure	Real estate investment trusts (REITs), private real estate funds	Diversification
Commodities	Energy, oil, gas, timber, agriculture, and managed futures	Returns/cash income streams from other assets

Alternative assets are alternatives to equity and include a growing array of options, listed in Table 1.1.

Certain types of alternative assets are illiquid and do not provide the same advantages that equities provide—that is, investor capital remains locked in for longer periods, which can be as long as 10 years in private equity and venture capital—and interim resale is not efficient. The concept of liquidity affects allocation outlays. Liquidity allows an investor to get out of investments without much friction, a concept that has continued to be debated through the years. In 1964, noted economist John Maynard Keynes stated that there is an "anti-social ... fetish of liquidity" that drives investment institutions to concentrate their holdings in liquid assets. He added that "there is no such thing as liquidity of an investment for the community as a whole."[1]

More recently, David Swensen, chief investment officer of Yale University, shares Keynes' view. In 2000, he wrote, "Investors prize liquidity because it allows trading in and out of securities. Unfortunately, liquidity tends to evaporate when most needed," offering examples of the stock market crash in 1987.[2] In the 2008 subprime crisis, his predictions rang true when liquidity evaporated and public markets crashed.

Keynes also wrote, "The spectacle of modern investment markets has sometimes moved me towards the conclusion that to make the purchase of an investment permanent and indissoluble, like marriage, except by reason of death or other grave cause, might be a useful remedy for our contemporary evils. For this would force the investor to direct his mind to the long-term prospects and to those only."[3] Unfortunately, neither marriage nor investments are treated as permanent in current times. Despite the emphasis on liquidity, alternatives as an asset class continue to grow steadily.

Market surveys affirm that alternative assets are an attractive asset class. Institutional investors plan to increase their allocations to alternative assets over the next few years. In 2010, Russell Investments surveyed 119 large institutional investors that manage $1.3 trillion in assets around the globe. These investors sought to increase their allocation to alternatives to 19 percent (from 14 percent in 2009) of the total portfolio. In addition, private equity (which includes VC) is projected to rise to 6.8 percent of the total portfolio (up from 2 percent in 2009) by 2012.[4] See Figures 1.3 and 1.4.

To address the liquidity risk, these alternative asset classes offer a higher return than do public equity or other lower risk asset classes. Fees and expenses, valuation and regulatory challenges, and limited control over investment decisions are major drawbacks to alternative assets. A measure of risk, volatility, is estimated to be twice that of equity. Despite these drawbacks,

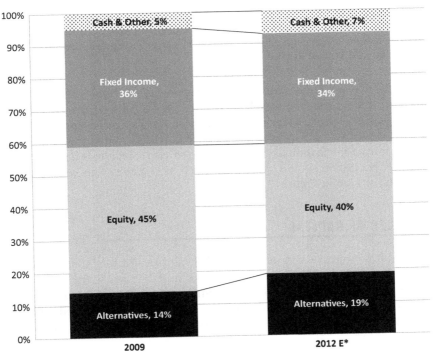

FIGURE 1.3 Growth in Alternatives Assets
Source: Russell Investments, 2010 survey of 119 large institutional investors managing $1.3 trillion in assets.

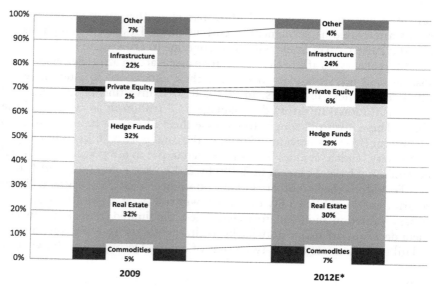

FIGURE 1.4   PE Is Projected to Rise 3X from 2 Percent to 6.8 Percent by 2012
Source: Russell Investments, 2010 survey of 119 large institutional investors managing $1.3 trillion in assets.

these alternatives remain attractive to investors for several reasons, including enhanced returns, improved diversification of their investment portfolios, and a hedge against inflation risk. Investors see alternative investments as a way of lowering the overall risk of their portfolios without giving up the opportunity for substantial returns. In recent years, investors have expected that PE portfolios should deliver as much as 4 percent above the public markets, as seen in Figures 1.5 and 1.6.

SOURCES OF CAPITAL

Capital flows into venture capital funds from pension funds, university endowments, foundations, finance companies, and high-net-worth individuals. While pension funds are the largest contributor, these are also conservative with respect to PE and VC allocations. Endowments and foundations are comparatively more aggressive and allocate larger portions to private equity (PE) and VC asset classes. Finance companies function as specialized intermediaries and follow the guidelines established by their sponsors. A fund-of-funds (FoF) is established as an intermediary to allow larger institutional investors to research, access, and manage PE and VC investments.

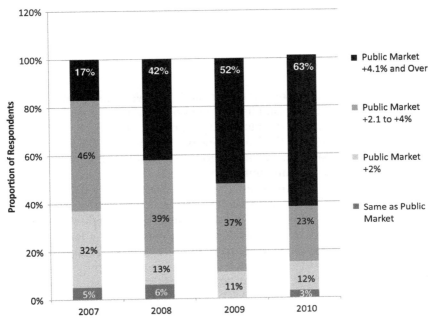

FIGURE 1.5 Growing Expectations: 63% of Institutional Investors Expect +4.1 Percent Above Public Market from Private Equity Asset Class
Source: Preqin.

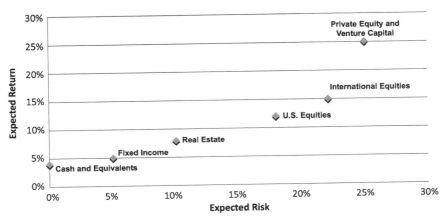

FIGURE 1.6 Expected Risk and Returns for a Portfolio

High-net-worth individuals and family offices generally lean toward conservative investments. Within all these players, some have a stronger penchant for PE and VC and will often deviate from the aggregate.

Pension Funds

By far, the largest source of capital for the VC universe are pension funds. A public or private entity establishes a pension fund to manage employees' investments. Employees contribute a portion of every paycheck to a pension plan (such as a 401(k) in the United States). The pension fund is typically established as a separate entity and is governed by a board of trustees. Employees set aside a certain amount at a fixed interval of time, with the goal of enjoying their years of retirement. Employers, with an objective of attracting employees and incentivizing savings, match the employee contribution into the pension plan. Thus, the primary sources of cash inflows are a sum of contributions made by individuals and employers. With a larger pool of employees, the steady trickle of contributions grows to a significant amount over time. The primary goal of such a pension fund is to provide financial security to the employees and their beneficiaries.

The top pension funds in the world by assets under management are listed in Table 1.2, and the leading investors in venture capital are listed in Table 1.3.

The typical asset allocation strategy for this pool of capital depends on the cash needs of the pension plan. Pension fund cash outflows are a factor of the benefits paid to retirees. Consider California Pension Retirement System (CalPERS), the largest public pension fund in the United States, which had over $200 billion in assets in management as of September 30, 2010.[5]

TABLE 1.2 Top 10 Pension Funds

Rank	Fund	Country	Assets ($M)
1	Government Pension Investment	Japan	$1,315,071
2	Government Pension Fund-Global	Norway	$475,859
3	ABP	Netherlands	$299,873
4	National Pension	Korea	$234,946
5	Federal Retirement Thrift	United States	$234,404
6	California Public Employees Retirement Systems	United States	$198,765
7	Local Government Officials	Japan	$164,510
8	California State Teachers Retirement Systems	United States	$130,461
9	New York State Common Fund	United States	$125,692
10	PFZW	Netherlands	$123,390

Source: *Pensions & Investments*, as of June 2010.

TABLE 1.3 Top Pension Funds Investing in Venture Capital

Pension Fund	Investments in VC ($M)
California Public Employees Retirement Systems	$2,689
New York State Common Retirement Fund	$2,424
University of California Retirement Systems	$1,438
Pennsylvania Employees Retirement Systems	$1,432
Verizon	$1,294
California State Teachers Retirement Systems	$1,138
Colorado Public Employees Retirement Systems	$998
State of Michigan Retirement Systems	$956
New York State Teachers Retirement Systems	$889
Massachusetts Pension Reserves Investment Trust	$866

Source: *Pensions & Investments*, as of June 2010.

CalPERS has over 1.6 million beneficiaries who receive pension and health care benefits every month. A pension fund's investment team has to juggle these cash inflows and outflows. Since a pension fund needs to pay retirees a set amount each month, the demands on its cash position are high, and thus the fund allocates a higher proportion of its assets to public equities, where liquidity is higher. A typical pension fund will allocate around 10 percent to 15 percent of its assets to alternative assets, which include hedge funds, natural resources (such as oil and gas partnerships), private equity, and VC. Table 1.4 shows the typical asset class allocations of public pension funds in the United States and the expected rate of return for these asset classes.

Pension plans are divided into defined benefit (DB) and defined contribution (DC) plans. DB plan sponsors promise a specific cash benefit to an

TABLE 1.4 Asset Allocation of Public Pension Funds in the United States

Asset Class	Typical Allocation	CalPERS	Expected Return
Equity—domestic and international	52%	54.6%	7.5–9.5%
Fixed income	28%	23.1%	4.5–7.5%
Real estate	5%	7.1%	8.0%
Alternative assets	14%	13.9%	6.0–8.5%
Cash/cash equivalents	1%	1.3%	3.5%
Weighted Average Expected Return			7.0%

Source: Karl C. Mergenthaler and Helen Zhang, "Public Pension Funds: Allocation Strategies," J.P. Morgan, accessed January 23, 2011, www.jpmorgan.com/tss/General/Public Pension Funds Asset Allocation Strategies/1289431691010.

employee upon retirement, with the benefit depending on years of service and salary grades. State pension funds typically offer DB pension plans. Under DC plans, also called 401(k) plans in the United States, the plan sponsor agrees to make contributions only to the employee's pension fund.[6]

The distinction between DB and DC plans has important consequences for asset allocation. For DB plans, the combination of the sponsor's contribution policy and asset allocation strategy must be designed to fund the sponsor benefits as they become due. This translates to long-term liabilities. In recent years, the number of DB plans in the United States has steadily declined as more and more employers see pension contributions as a large expense that can be avoided by disbanding the DB plan and instead offering a DC plan.

For DC plans, however, there is no similar issue of asset-liability matching. The sponsor has no obligations beyond the prespecified contributions. Instead, the theoretically optimal investment policy for DC plans depends on the participant's preferences with respect to risk and return and the composition of assets held in other accounts.[7]

Besides cash flow demands for retirees, other constraints that affect pension funds include growing health care costs, legislation, and political dynamics. As of 2010, 19 states have taken measures to manage the growing costs of health care and manage long-term liabilities. Since the pension funds manage public money, state legislation attempts to ensure that assets are preserved and a steady income stream is generated to pay for the retiree benefits. In many cases, the government mandates investment activities and prescribes language requiring that pension funds "maximize returns without undue risk of loss."[8] Pension funds are also subject to political pressures, and political interference can severely affect a pension fund's viability.

Endowments

A university's cash inflows are a sum of student fees, grants, and contributions. On average, student fees and grants constitute 48 percent of a university's revenues; as these sources are uncertain, universities seek to insulate their position by creating endowments.[9] For example, in 2009, 23 percent of revenues at Yale University resulted from grants and contracts; 16 percent from medical services; 9 percent from net tuition, room, and board; and 6 percent from gifts and other income. The rest of the university's operating income—a whopping 46 percent—came from its $16 billion endowment.[10]

The largest endowments, ranked by size, are listed in Table 1.5.

An endowment generates investment income and provides a cushion against any potential uncertainties. With it, a university can focus on its

TABLE 1.5 Top 10 Endowments

Rank	Institution	Assets ($B)
1	Harvard University	27.60
2	Yale University	16.70
3	Stanford University	13.80
4	Princeton University	14.40
5	University of Texas System	13.68
6	Massachusetts Institute of Technology	8.30
7	University of Michigan	6.75
8	Columbia University	6.50
9	Northwestern University	6.12
10	University of Pennsylvania	5.70

Source: *Pensions & Investments*, as of June 30, 2010.

primary goals of providing education and conducting research (or building a football stadium, depending on priorities)—activities that further social causes and knowledge. The grants and contributions are fickle and insufficient—neither of these tantamount to predictable revenue streams. Research grants largely depend on government and political priorities.

Donations received by universities or other nonprofit entities such as cultural and religious institutions are set aside in endowments to accomplish certain investment objectives. Donors frequently specify a particular purpose for gifts, creating endowments to fund professorships, teaching, and lectureships; scholarships, fellowships, and prizes; maintenance; books; and other miscellaneous purposes.

Institutions without permanent financial resources support day-to-day operations with funds from transient sources, limiting an organization's ability to shape its future, David Swensen, chief investment officer of Yale University, wrote in his book, *Pioneering Portfolio Management*. In 1755, the Colony of Connecticut refused to give Yale an annual grant, which resulted from the political backlash due to the college's religious character. Swensen pointed out that the Colony refused the grant under the guise of rising wartime expenditures.

Asset allocation for endowments is shown in Table 1.6 and Table 1.9. The Yale endowment's asset allocation is heavily aligned toward alternative assets: absolute return, real assets, and private equity. Swensen has made bold moves by shifting assets away from U.S. equities into illiquid securities and racked up strong returns. Table 1.7 demonstrates how Yale's assets have shifted toward alternatives over time. Swensen's portfolio management and

TABLE 1.6 Asset Allocation Target for Yale Endowment

Asset Class	Yale Endowment (%)
Absolute return	19
Domestic equity	7
Fixed income	–
Foreign equity	9
Private equity	33
Real assets§	28
Cash	4

Source: *Yale Endowment*, http://opac.yale.edu/news/article.aspx?id=7789. Yale endowment grows by 8.9%, a gain of $1.4 billion. Published: September 24, 2010. Asset Allocation Data as of june 30, 2010.

asset allocation strategy have been studied and duplicated by experts across the investment industry.

More than 90 percent of endowments typically spend around five percent of their assets each year. They use these cash outflows for university operations or capital expenditures. Due to limited demands on their cash

TABLE 1.7 Yale Endowment's Asset Allocation: Private Equity Slice Grows Steadily

Asset Class	1985	1995	2009	2010
Absolute return	0%	20%*	24.3%	19%
Domestic equity	65%	30%	7.5%	7%
Fixed income	15%	20%†	4.0%	X‡
Foreign equity	10%	10%	9.8%	9%
Private equity	0%	10%	24.3%	33%
Real assets§	10%	10%	32.0%	28%
Cash	0%	0%	1.9%	4%‡

Source: Yale Endowment Annual Reports and *Yale Daily Bulletin*. Endowment was valued at $16.7 billion as of June 30, 2010.

*In 1995, Yale defined absolute return asset class as hedge funds.
†In 1995, the fixed income asset class was categorized as U.S. bonds.
‡In 2010, bonds and cash are lumped into one category at 4 percent. No allocation was defined in fixed income.
§Real assets include holdings of real estate, oil and gas, and timber.
Data has been clubbed within the asset class for clarity and consistency of presentation.

outlays, endowments are better suited for investments in alternative strategies. In comparison with pension funds, *endowments have invested as much as four times the percentage of their assets in alternative assets*. In a perfect world, endowment funds can potentially last forever, while pension funds can run out of money due to existing liabilities.

Foundations

Like endowments, foundations are a significant force in the world of private equity. Foundations exist to support charitable and nonprofit causes. Governed by federal laws and regulated by the Internal Revenue Service (IRS), foundations are managed by their trustees and they aid programs such as childcare, arts and education, health care, climate and environment, and religious and social causes. Foundations support programs that are likely not supported by federal or state grants. The emphasis placed on health care by the Bill and Melinda Gates Foundation is one such example. Foundations offer grants to various nonprofit organizations to conduct these programs.

As of 2008, over 75,000 foundations in the United States manage over $583 billion in assets.[11] Foundation assets have grown 20 times as large over the past three decades, as shown in Figure 1.7.

The majority of these are independent or private foundations. The 10 largest foundations are listed in Table 1.8.[12] Private foundations are established and endowed by corporations (e.g., Ford Foundation, W. K. Kellogg

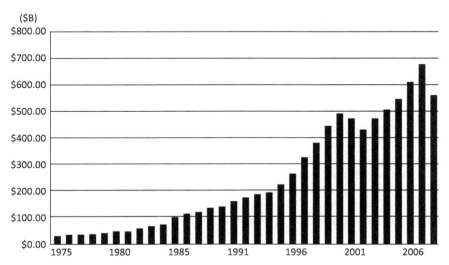

FIGURE 1.7 Growth in Foundation Assets
Source: The Foundation Center, Foundation Yearbook, 2010.

TABLE 1.8 Top 10 Foundations by Asset Size

Rank	Foundation	Assets ($B)
1	Bill & Melinda Gates Foundation (WA)	33.9
2	Ford Foundation (NY)	10.7
3	J. Paul Getty Trust (CA)	9.3
4	The Robert Wood Johnson Foundation (NJ)	8.4
5	W. K. Kellogg Foundation (MI)	7.2
6	The William and Flora Hewlett Foundation (CA)	6.8
7	The David and Lucile Packard Foundation (CA)	5.6
8	The John D. and Catherine T. MacArthur Foundation (IL)	5.2
9	Gordon and Betty Moore Foundation (CA)	5.2
10	Lilly Endowment Inc. (IN)	5.1

Source: The Foundation Center, as of December 2009.

Foundation) or families or individuals (e.g., Bill & Melinda Gates Foundation) and fund programs that are important to the donors. To meet IRS eligibility, private foundations have to give away as grants, as much as 5 percent of their assets each year. The balance, 95 percent, is invested using asset allocation strategies. Foundations have to report their assets and grants information publicly, as IRS guidelines mandate this disclosure.

Besides private foundations, other types of foundations include community foundations, which attract a large number of individual donors from a geographic region, and corporate foundations. Corporate foundations exist to further the cause established by the donor corporation and are funded from the corporation's profits. Over 2,000 corporate foundations in the United States hold approximately $11 billion in assets.[13] Other forms of foundations include operating foundations, which conduct research or provide services, as opposed to grant-making activities.

To understand a foundation's asset allocation strategy, let's consider an average allocation plan (as of 2010) of 850 foundations and endowments (see Table 1.9).

Compared to an endowment, the short-term cash needs of a foundation are not as significant. Hence the allocations toward long-term assets, such as alternative assets (which includes VC), tend to be higher in comparison to those of a pension fund or an insurance company.

Finance Companies

Within the LP universe, finance and insurance companies provide as much as 25 percent of capital for venture capital and private equity. Finance

TABLE 1.9 Average Asset Allocation Plan of 850 Foundations: VC Attracts a Small Portion of Overall Assets

Asset Class	Allocation (%)	Alternative Strategies	Allocation (%)
Domestic equity	15	Private Equity	24
Fixed income	12	Marketable Alternatives (Hedge Funds)	41
International equity	16	Venture Capital	6
Alternative Strategies	52	Real Estate	10
Short Term Cash	5	Energy	14
		Distressed Debt	5

Source: 2010 NACUBO Commonfund Study of Endowments

companies are treated as a catch-all category to ensure clarity of presentation in this book. These include banks, nonbank financial companies, fund-of-funds, and other entities like TIAA-CREF funds, investment trusts in which assets are pooled for investment purposes. Operating methods, combined with internal criteria (e.g., cash, target returns, time horizon), define each finance company's asset allocation plan.

For example, Citibank has invested $321 million in private equity.[14] Or consider GE Capital, Equity—the financial arm of General Electric that positions itself as an entity that "maximizes the return on GE's investment capital by combining deep equity investing experience with GE's industry expertise, operating experience and global reach." GE Capital, Equity has invested in over 500 LP funds and currently has over $5 billion of assets under management.[15] Other examples within this category include One Equity Partners—the private equity arm of J.P. Morgan Capital Partners, Banc of America Capital, and Société Générale (France). A fund-of-funds is considered as a subclass within the finance company universe.

Funds-of-Funds In the 1980s, the fund-of-funds model (FoF) emerged to meet the asset allocation and diversification demands of larger financial institutions. Three decades later, a diverse set of FoFs has developed—from large, diversified global funds offered by Adams Street Partners, Credit Suisse, and Pantheon, to sector-focused investment vehicles from HarbourVest and Horsley Bridge, to smaller funds such as LGT's FoF that targets middle market buyouts in Europe, and emerging manager FoFs, such as Parish Capital.[16] FoFs typically attract about 10 percent to 12 percent of all capital within the PE alternative asset class, which is about $25 billion in any given year.

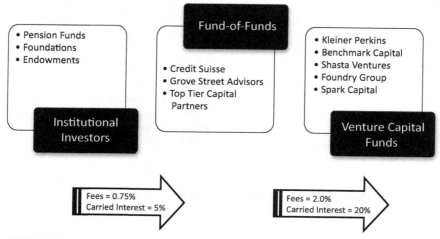

FIGURE 1.8 The Fund-of-Funds Model

The concept underlying FoFs is essentially a variant of the type of collective investment approach that undergirds mutual funds. Individual investors seek to invest in mutual funds using an indirect investment approach, as opposed to researching and investing in various company stocks directly. A private equity FoF can be construed as a mutual fund that invests in a variety of private equity and venture funds: in other words, a superfund whose portfolio is made up of other funds. The FoF model is depicted in Figure 1.8.

FoFs are categorized by region (e.g., United States, Europe, Asia) and subasset classes (e.g., venture, buyout, distressed, secondary markets). Some of the largest FoFs are listed in Table 1.10.

All these FoFs raise capital from various institutions previously mentioned and invest across all the regions and subasset classes previously men-

TABLE 1.10 Top Fund-of-Funds by Assets under Management

Position	Name	Total AUM ($M)
1	Goldman Sachs Asset Management, USA	33,952.00
2	HarbourVest Partners, LLC, USA	31,294.60
3	Credit Suisse Asset Management, LLC, USA	30,791.02
4	Pantheon Ventures, Ltd, UK	22,004.80
5	Adams Street Partners, LLC, USA	18,434.20

Source: Towers Watson; Global Alternatives Survey 2010, June 2010.

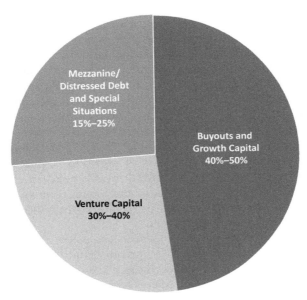

FIGURE 1.9   Typical Fund-of-Funds Asset Allocation

tioned. Consider Figure 1.9, which shows typical asset allocation strategy for a leading fund-of-funds. [17]

Despite the tumult of the past several years, experienced institutional investors continued to invest in private equity and are making new commitments to FoFs. To investors, FoFs offer the following features:

- *An efficient mechanism to access various asset classes/venture funds.* Institutional investors have optimum resources to research or manage certain asset classes. In context, a $50 billion pension fund may have less than 10 percent of its assets in private equity. This could be further sliced into mezzanine, buyouts, and VC. Apply another set of layers of risk diversification—sectors, geography, size, and vintage year—and what you have is a fairly complex matrix of relatively small investments. FoFs allow for larger institutions to efficiently participate in the PE/VC asset class without substantially increasing their overhead. Thus, a smaller venture firm has a lower probability of attracting capital from a large institution such as a state pension fund, but has a higher probability with targeted FoFs.
- *Access to high performing managers.* FoFs offer access to elite funds and knowledge of emerging funds that have the highest potential growth performance in the market. Leading FoFs offer to transfer the relationship to the institutions as the GPs raise future funds. Thus,

an institution may use a FoF to gain access to a tier-one fund and then directly invest in the future funds. This is beneficial for the institution in the long run provided it can manage the relationship effectively.

- *Diversification.* The universe of the private equity and VC managers evolves with the ebb and flow of economic trends and opportunities: venture, distressed, real estate, sector-focused funds; turnaround funds; and foreign funds. FoFs are attractive investment strategies because they enable investors to diversify and spread out risk over a range of different assets (e.g., a typical FoF will invest in 10 to 20 underlying funds, which in turn are investing in hundreds of portfolio companies). In effect, FoFs provide increased access with decreased risk. For example, many private equity funds have a minimum commitment of $5 million to $25 million—amounts that can be inefficient for a larger institutional investor that manages $50 billion.

- *Research and proactive relationship development.* While institutional investors may be experienced in private equity, they often lack the abilities or resources to conduct research and proactively build relationships. FoFs also offer specialized expertise to track and monitor industry trends, identify leading funds, build relationships with key managers, and stay abreast of GP-LP investment terms.

- *Cost structure.* FoFs are cost-effective solutions for institutional investors because the due diligence, negotiations, and post-investment portfolio management is outsourced to the FoF managers. A typical FoF fee structure is 5 percent carried interest combined with approximately 0.75 percent annual management fee. Institutional investors pay two layers of fees in such a structure: one at the FoF level and another at the PE/VC fund level.

CURRENT FUND-OF-FUNDS TRENDS

FoFs raised approximately $30 billion in 2009, as fund managers managed to attract capital from both institutional investors and wealthy individuals. The first FoF, a firm that would eventually become Adams Street Partners, raised a mere $60 million in 1976. Today, Adams Street Partners manages $20 billion and raises about $2 billion each year to be deployed in 15 to 30 new partnership commitments. Its target allocation typically includes 30 to 40 percent in venture capital, with the largest slice allocated to buyout and growth at 40 to 50 percent and the rest of 15 to 25 percent being set aside for mezzanine and distressed debt funds.*

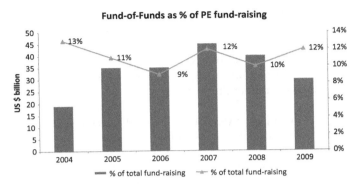

Fund-of-Funds Growth Trends
Source: Preqin, 2010.

The capital is fairly concentrated in the hands of top firms. In 2002, the top five FoFs accounted for more than 50 percent of the total capital raised by managers. As of 2010, the top 10 FoFs have cornered 63 percent of the total pie.[†] The top 50 FoFs control $186 billion and the top 10 control as much as 65% of these assets.

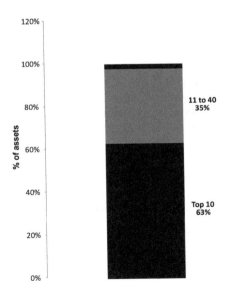

Concentration of Assets in Top 10 FoFs
Source: Towers Watson © "Global Alternatives Survey," June 2010. Reprinted with permission.

Emerging markets are the new darlings of FoF managers, particularly in light of the robust Asian recovery from the crisis and sluggish growth in developed economic markets. Since 2007, the trend among firms such as Asia Alternatives Management, Axiom Asia Private Capital Pte Ltd., and Squadron Capital is to raise FoFs exclusively built on Asian and other emerging markets.[‡]

*Adams Street Partners, "About Us," accessed December 29, 2010, www .adamsstreetpartners.com/about-us.html.
[†]Dow Jones Private Equity Analysis, "Credit Crisis: Prime Time for Some Funds of Funds, but Curtains for Others," http://fis.dowjones.com/products/ fundsoffunds.html.
[‡]Ibid.

Insurance Companies

Like pension funds, insurance companies manage a large amount of cash inflows and outflows. Any insurance company is in the business of managing risk. An insured party pays a premium at a fixed time interval—say, monthly, quarterly, or annually. Insurance companies invest the premiums, but the underlying driver is to meet a potential obligation that may occur in the future. If an accident occurs, the insured receives compensation. The business model of any insurance company can be reduced to inflows via premium payments and investment income. Underwriting expenses and incurred losses are primary outflows. The scope of the insurer's business and required guarantees drives the target rate of return. These factors determine an asset allocation strategy for any insurance company. A sample is presented in Table 1.11.

TABLE 1.11 Asset Allocation for the Insurance Industry

Asset Class	Life and Health Insurance (%)	Property and Casualty Insurance (%)
Bonds	63.4	64.8
Equity	26.0	16.1
Cash	4.7	8.0
Other	5.8	11.1

Source: 2010 Institutional Investment Report, The Conference Board (2009 data).

Insurance companies have a unique advantage as a business model: The customer pays up front and eventually, at some point in the future, may receive benefits. In some cases, all a customer may ever get is the proverbial peace of mind. The primary mechanism to generate investment income for insurance companies is management of "float"—the amount of money that "floats" with the insurance company as premiums arrive and sit around, waiting to be used in the event of any claims.[18]

Insurance companies need to maintain certain levels of capital; if they fail, regulators can swoop in. Solvency requirements are an important factor; hence the need to maintain a certain level of cash is important. Thus, insurance companies have to model their cash needs based on an actuarial assessment of risk and liabilities. In any insurance company, the accounting and actuarial teams develop the overall plan that determines cash inflows and outflows. Inflows are predictable, but outflows are not entirely predictable.

Actuaries invest an enormous amount of time in modeling demographic patterns of fire, floods, accidents, and other acts of God to derive a correlationship between premiums and claims—or risks and rewards. Hence, insurance companies attempt to manage their cash positions and liquidity effectively, as unanticipated events could occur and affect their solvency. Thus, asset allocation for insurance companies is heavily weighted in low-risk investments such as bonds. Venture capital investments are lower on the totem pole and fall in the "Other" category for most insurance companies.

Family Offices and High-Net-Worth Individuals

As much as 10 percent of PE and VC assets come from family offices and HNWIs. A family office is a private company owned and run by a single wealthy family. The family office manages the investments and trusts of the family. A single-family office (SFO) or a multifamily office (MFO), as their names suggest, are professionally managed investment services companies that serve wealthy families. One of the primary functions of a traditional family office is to consolidate financial management with a view to preserving wealth, generating returns, and minimizing the tax impact for any family's fortune. Small teams of confidants, including professional investment managers, are responsible for managing the family's assets and the family office. Among the other major tasks handled by the family office are the management of taxes, property management, accounting, payroll processing, and other concierge-type services such as travel arrangements.

Family offices are classified as Class A, B, or C depending on their administrative structure. Class A family offices are operated by an independent company with direct supervision from a family trustee or an appointed administrator. Class B family offices are operated by an accounting firm, bank, or a law firm, and Class C family offices are directly operated by the family with a small support staff.

MFOs consolidate activities for several wealthy families with the objective of minimizing operational costs. The Family Wealth Alliance estimates there are approximately 3,000 U.S.-based SFOs and 150 MFOs. SFOs manage assets ranging from $42 million to $1.5 billion. Total assets under advisement by MFOs are upward of $357 billion, with an average client relationship size of $49 million. Median asset size at any MFO is close to $1 billion.[19]

According to a study conducted at the Wharton School, the most important objective for the SFO is transgenerational wealth management.[20] The second is to consolidate accounting, tax, and estate planning services. Having an SFO also allows the family members to pursue their own careers, while enjoying the benefits of cost-effective money management. As the wealth comes from family business, 58 percent choose to focus on their strengths and remain involved in operating the businesses, and 77 percent are majority stakeholders in their holding companies.[21] This has implications from an investment decision-making perspective. In Table 1.12, Cap Gemini World Wealth Report reports typical asset allocation for HNWIs and family offices. In comparison to endowment and foundation allocations, this LP category is conservatively slanted, with only 8 percent in alternatives. However, some family offices have a strong propensity to invest heavily in venture capital asset class. The Hillman family office of Pittsburg, PA, played a significant role in the launch of Kleiner Perkins Caufield Byers KPCB Fund I in the early seventies by investing as much as half of the entire fund. KPCB Fund I invested $8 million in seventeen companies (including Applied Materials,

TABLE 1.12　Typical Asset Allocation for HNWIs and Family Offices

Asset Class	Allocation (%)
Equity	35
Fixed income	30
Real estate	14
Cash	13
Alternatives	8

Genetech, Tandem Computers and one called "Snow-Job") and returned $345 million to its investors, making the Hillmans very happy, thank you very much.

SFOs have partnered with banks for better access to information technology and tools. On average, the study found that European SFOs are inclined to outsource fewer activities related to wealth management, especially investment-related activities. In Europe, 63 percent of SFOs perform asset allocation in-house versus 47 percent of SFOs in the Americas. Thus, investment decisions and process may differ if professionals manage the office. Due to the size of assets, and the conservative undertones, the decision-making cycle for investment in PE and VC is comparatively longer.

Family offices and HNWIs are a significant source of capital for venture funds. According to a Cap Gemini Merrill Lynch World Wealth Report, worldwide, wealthy families and individuals control about $42.2 trillion.

More than 100,000 individuals in the United States are estimated to have assets in excess of $10 million. HNWIs have assets worth at least $1 million, while ultra-HNWIs have at least $30 million in investable assets. A typical asset allocation strategy for HNWIs.

North America remains the single largest home to HNWIs, with its 3.1 million HNWIs accounting for 31 percent of the global HNWI population. In terms of the total global HNWI population, it remains highly concentrated, with the United States, Japan, and Germany accounting for 53.5 percent of the world's HNWI population. The fastest growth of HNWIs is in Asia or "Ch-India."[22]

Corporate Operating Funds

Corporate operating funds make up a bare whisper of 2 percent of all capital flowing into venture funds. A number of corporations invest as LPs in externally managed venture funds. Others establish internally managed "corporate VC funds," such as Intel Capital. The source of capital is primarily operating funds (as opposed to corporate pension funds).

At the PE/VC fund level, corporations actively invest significant amounts of capital. In a brief survey, between 2004 and 2006, approximately half of the companies surveyed had invested $5 million or more in VC funds (see Figure 1.10).

Investments via corporate venture capital (CVC) in start-ups and VC-backed companies are as much as 6 percent to 8 percent of all venture capital investments in the United States, or approximately $1 billion each year (see Figure 1.11). Corporate VCs invested as much as 20 percent of all capital in the biotech sector, the largest sector by far, followed by software at 13 percent.[23]

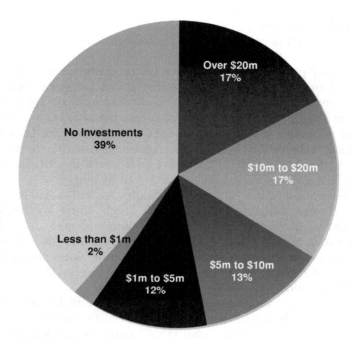

FIGURE 1.10 Limited Partner Commitments Made
by Corporations
Source: Corporate Venture Capital Study, National Institute
of Standards and Technology (NIST), June 2008. Survey
included 48 corporations; total investments made between
2004 and 2006.

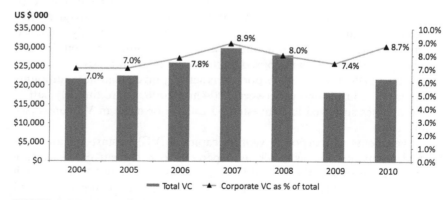

FIGURE 1.11 Corporate Venture Capital Investments
Source: PricewaterhouseCoopers, NVCA, Thomson Reuters.

COMPARISON OF LIMITED PARTNERSHIPS

In comparing the various LPs in Table 1.13, the allocation to alternatives varies, as does their primary driver for investments. Any venture practitioner seeking to raise capital needs to consider the size of an LP's alternative asset pool, decision-making criteria, time lines, and the investment process of each LP.

SUMMARY

For any venture practitioner, it is imperative to know and understand the universe of investors. These LPs come in a variety of shapes and sizes, and each has its own set of constraints. The largest percentage commitment of capital to VC comes from endowments and foundations due to their relatively lower short-term cash needs. The smallest percentage commitment comes from insurance companies.

As discussed earlier, Chris Douvos, co-head of private equity investing at The Investment Fund for Foundations (TIFF), draws an interesting and humbling analogy. "If public markets are like an ocean—multi-trillions of dollars at work—and private equity is a bath tub . . . say \$300 billion a year . . . venture capital is like a small sink."[24] Dick Kramlich, founder of NEA, once said, "As an industry we are only raising 20–30 billion dollars, while private equity as an industry is raising 300 billion dollars. And there's two trillion dollars worth of hedge funds. All of these resources are within the same purview . . . and there's a whole different definition of how rates of return are obtained and who you compete with."[25]

While VC has gained interest and allocation has increased over the years, the asset class faces fierce competition from other classes within the alternatives universe. As Timothy Recker, chairman of Institutional Limited Partners Association, says, "The investment options for institutional investors are growing. Venture practitioners tend to be an insular group and negotiate their place within the private equity/VC category. I think they could easily price themselves out of the alternative class if they put the blinders on and do not aim to compete with other alternatives."[26] Any competitive class that offers better liquidity, a lower fee structure, and equal or higher returns can easily displace VC. Chris Douvos extends the competition beyond alternatives in different geographies. "As an asset allocator—in the eighties and nineties, venture capital asset class was like 'emerging growth' asset class, wrapped in an easy to understand legal and regulatory structure.

TABLE 1.13 Comparing the LP Universe

Investor Type	Typical Percentage of Assets in Alternatives	Decision Maker(s)	Drivers	Constraints
Pension funds	14%	Portfolio manager, CIO, investment committee; state treasurer may be the final signatory	Financial returns	Liquidity and risk management, size of investment staff, regulatory, political perspectives
Insurance companies	6%	Chief investment officer (CIO)	Capital conservation	Liability, liquidity, solvency, regulatory
Endowments and foundations	51%	Chief investment officer (CIO)	Financial returns	Size of investment staff; social and political views
HNWIs/family offices	8%	Managing director; family member may be the final signatory	Returns and relationships	Limited bandwidth; strategy and allocations are highly fluid
Corporations' operating funds	Opportunistic	Corporate development, CFO, or CEO	Insights into developing technologies and new revenue streams	Limited percentage allocation, board approvals; long-term participation is unlikely

And there was no choice but venture. Today, I could commit to emerging markets and generate good returns—the monopoly of venture has gone."[27]

For most institutional LPs, venture capital is a subasset class, a small percentage of their entire portfolio. Now that we know where the biggest pools of capital lie, let us understand an institutional LP's investment criterion. It starts with the people!

CHAPTER 2

Fund Due Diligence

If it takes $10 million to make a good VC, that $10 million better come from the LP next door.

—Anonymous LP

Now that we've explored the universe of LPs and what the sources of capital for VC funds are, we need to identify the criteria for evaluating potential investments. Known as "fund due diligence," this begins and ends with the team—the general partners (GPs). If the GP investment team has a strong performance track record and relevant expertise, and is pursuing a compelling strategy, capital follows. The due diligence process at the LP-GP level is similar to that of a venture practitioner seeking to invest in companies: source a few thousand opportunities, invest in a handful, and get returns from a few. It starts with sourcing, followed by due diligence, negotiating LP-GP terms, postinvestment monitoring, and generating returns. LP-GP terms are presented in Chapter 3. Postinvestment monitoring of venture funds is beyond the scope of this book.[1]

LPs proactively seek, or source, as the jargon goes, prudent and experienced GPs who can be good stewards of their capital and generate strong returns. But no LP hangs a sign at the door—rather, the communication channels are informal. Most LPs look for seasoned professionals, those top-quartile managers with demonstrated track records over multiple fund cycles. Yet some LPs focus on the other end of the spectrum: emerging managers, as these bring a fresher approach, energy, and malleability to the mix. And all fund-raising is at the mercy of markets—with Mr. Market on its side, even a mediocre group may have an oversubscribed fund. But the primary takeaway of this chapter is to understand an LP investment process and how an LP evaluates a GP.

A typical investment process for any LP seeking to invest in venture funds follows the following steps:

- *Sourcing and screening.* The art of finding the right fund managers.
- *Fund due diligence.* The ability to assess the various risk-return measures for investing in such a fund.
- *Negotiations and closing.* Knowledge of various investment terms, the middle-of-the-road positions, and the ability to successfully close in on investments. These are presented in detail in Chapter 3.
- *Postinvestment monitoring.* The ability to build an effective relationship with the fund managers, leading to open, honest, and timely communications.

This chapter looks at the various interconnected elements of fund due diligence, which includes performance, people (GP expertise, stability, and skills), and strategy (sector, market timing, and portfolio construction).

A combination of these criteria helps any LP to make a multimillion-dollar commitment to a venture fund.

SOURCING AND FIRST SCREENS

While some LPs seek to invest in emerging managers, others seek the proven top-quartile established funds. Yet others start the search with sectors—say, technology or cleantech—and whittle down the universe of fund managers based on additional criteria. Certain LPs, especially those with a socioeconomic mandate, will attempt to invest in funds based in certain geographic regions. For LPs, the primary filter—performance—remains high on the list.

Lisa Edgar, managing director of Top Tier Capital Partners, prefers to start her process with performance. "In an environment defined by change, it is important to assess the GP's ability to produce superior returns across various technological and economic cycles," she says.[2] Over the past two decades, Edgar, with her investment experience of 17 years, has seen it all. Top Tier Capital Partners, a fund-of-fund, manages over $7 billion across three platforms and has established relationships with some of the leading funds. A GP's ability to produce superior returns across various cycles is evident only after the venture firm has raised and invested a few funds. Georganne Perkins, managing director at Fisher Lynch Capital, a fund-of-funds with $2 billion under management, seeks proven GPs as well. "A roman numeral V or higher is a good start," she points out.[3] The "V" indicates the firm has invested capital over four previous fund cycles. Such a firm would have established a track record and a brand in the investment arena. Perkins, who formerly managed the PE investment portfolio at Stanford University, receives over 200 fund documents, or private placement memorandums (PPMs), each year.

Most institutional LPs see anywhere from 200 to 600 fund documents on a yearly basis. With such a high volume, the best way to stand above the ambient noise level is to begin a relationship via an introduction. Without a connection, fund documents that come in the door head for the trash can. But who makes the introduction is equally important. A trusted relationship, ideally another peer-level limited partner, an existing GP, or a respected attorney can make this path much easier. An inappropriate starting point could blow up this process very quickly. "For state pension fund managers, getting calls from politicians is typical, including calls from the governor's office. GPs who use such pressure tactics, despite stellar performance, are starting with a deficit," says Robert "Bob" Clone, director of private equity for the $14 billion Indiana retirement plans: Public Employees Retirement Fund (PERF) and the Teachers Retirement Fund (TRF). Bob formerly was a portfolio manager of a $50 billion state pension fund.

Institutional LPs warm up to a new fund manager over time and observe the fund's evolution and performance. G. Thomas Doyal, managing director of global PE investments for a family office, says, "We watch managers over several years and multiple investment cycles before we are ready to engage." Doyal, who sees about 50 PPMs each year, reviews fund documents only after a strong relationship has been established with the investment team. "It is very unusual for us to look at a cold PPM," he says.

For newer managers, the ability to engage via an introduction and proactively build these potential institutional relationships is key: Providing meaningful updates on investments and performance can make the path easier. And GPs can take solace in the fact that they are not the only ones on the hunt. "Like any entrepreneur looking for the next best opportunity, LPs are always seeking the most promising managers—the Kleiner Perkins of the future,"[4] advises Kenneth Van Heel, director—Alternative Investments, at the corporate pension fund for Dow Chemical Company. Van Heel manages an asset pool of approximately $10 billion.

Should You Hire a Placement Agent?

Across the board, institutional LPs prefer to interact with placement agents. A few reputed agents are able to build a matrix of LP relationships and reduce the friction in the process for LPs as well as GPs. Igor Rozenblit, who led fund investments on behalf of a $2.5 billion European financial services company, says, "Many venture fund managers would not bother to do a primary assessment of our investment criteria and send us completely irrelevant PPMs. These would land in the dustbin quickly." Other institutional LPs agreed. Edgar adds, "We get PPMs from all over the world—China, India, Brazil—and a lot of these are not even relevant, nor fit within our strategy."

Several institutional LPs highlighted the role of a placement agent as critical in the sourcing process. A placement agent brings expertise and a set of relationships, along with know-how of market trends. These minimize the friction a GP may face while raising a fund.

Good placement agents are inundated with solicitations and are highly selective of engagements. For the right fund, placement agents will risk their reputation and invest significant time with the expectation of getting paid after the fund is closed. Kelly DePonte, partner with Probitas Partners, a leading placement agency, says, "I review 600+ placement memorandums in any given year, and barely a handful will make the cut." DePonte's perspective comes from his interactions with leading LPs across the world who make multibillion-dollar decisions and who are jaded by the hubris of VC excesses over the past decade.

Augustine "Gus" Long, Partner at Stanwich Advisors, who has recently helped close a $1.6 billion private equity fund, points out that a good placement agent functions as a proxy LP. "If we cannot gather enough confidence and comfort in the GP, we do not engage," remarks Long, who managed a $1 billion fund-of-funds prior to joining Stanwich Advisors. Rozenblit concurs that a good agent can make a significant impact for the right VC firm: "The top venture firms do not need agents, and on the other end of the spectrum, there are firms that are so bad that even a placement agent will refuse to touch them. There can be a few good venture firms in the middle who can benefit from placement agents." Thus, emerging managers with some demonstrated track record, and a compelling strategy, ought to consider whether a Kelly or a Gus can make the uphill task easier. The role of placement agents is described in greater detail in Chapter 4.

FUND DUE DILIGENCE: HOW LPs EVALUATE VENTURE FIRMS

LPs evaluate venture firms on the two primary criteria: the fund managers' expertise and their investment strategy. Secondary criteria include terms and market conditions, as presented in Figure 2.1.

- *Fund managers' expertise.* The foremost and primary criteria—LPs seek to understand investment expertise and entrepreneurial/domain expertise. Performance is one of the foremost criteria.

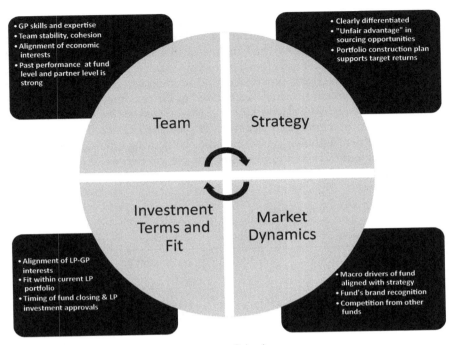

FIGURE 2.1 Limited Partner Investment Criteria

- *Investment strategy.* What is a fund's investment strategy, and how does it stand apart from the rest of venture funds? What unique factors/differentiators or "unfair advantage" does this combination of people and strategy bring to the VC arena?

While all the listed criteria are important, the diligence process seeks to find an answer to a fundamental question asked by Lisa Edgar: "Are we going to make money in this fund?"[5] Kelly DePonte of Probitas Partners, a leading placement firm, concurs: "The first question any LP asks of venture practitioners is quite simple: How can they make money for me?" In "What Drives Venture Capital Fund Raising?" authors Paul A. Gompers and Josh Lerner concluded that fund performance and reputation were the key determinants of fund-raising, in addition to macroeconomic and regulatory factors.[6] Beyond performance, the top due diligence criteria included team stability and a consistent investment strategy.[7]

This theme, "performance is primary," recurs in various strands of academic literature. In a survey of LP investment criteria, over 200 U.S.-based LPs confirm the importance of performance.[8] In order of priority, the LPs started with internal rate of return (minimum floor of 12 percent and ideally closer to 30 percent) to be considered for investment. The returns are also typically tied to a benchmark index for comparing performance (say 400 basis points above the benchmark index, such as Russell 3000 or S&P 500). Other criteria included a consistent track record, diversification of the LP universe, team experience, and fund strategy. In another survey of 75 LPs, 50 percent of which were based in Europe, the conclusions were similar—LPs sought GPs who had access to transactions, a historic track record, and local market experience. In *Beyond the J Curve*, Thomas Meyer and Pierre-Yves Mathonet propose qualitative scoring criteria, which ranks the management team and fund strategy as the top two weighted factors, as shown in Table 2.1.

TABLE 2.1   GP Selection Criteria

No.	Dimension	Weightage	Remarks
1	Management team skills	30%	Investment and operational experience, sector expertise, regional connections, size of team, and complementary skills
2	Management team stability	10%	Clear roles, responsibilities, decision making, historical relationships and stability, economic alignment of incentives, financial stability of fund, and succession planning
3	Management team motivation	10%	GP commitment percentage, incentive structure, reputation, team independence, outside activities and conflicts of interest
4	Fund strategy	15%	Sourcing, stage/sector, fund size, exit strategy, and overall strategy fit
5	Fund structure	10%	Costs/fees, governance and compliance
6	External validation	10%	Track record of previous funds, performance of comparable funds, quality of co-investors and recurrence of investors
7	Overall fit	15%	Considers the overall picture. For example, the fit between the team, fund size, and the strategy.

Source: Thomas Meyer and Pierre-Yves Mathonet, *Beyond the J Curve—Managing a Portfolio of Venture Capital and Private Equity Funds* (Chichester, UK: John Wiley & Sons, 2005), 221.

EVALUATING THE FUND MANAGERS

From any LP's perspective, a VC partnership is a 10-year blind pool—a long relationship in which the investors have limited ability to exit and no clarity of outcomes. Thus, investors seek proven fund managers. Figure 2.2 depicts the stacking order of professionals. A proven fund manager is one who has generated consistent returns across multiple economic cycles. Having demonstrated the ability to source opportunities, invest capital over multiple rounds, add tangible value as a board member, and generate exits, the proven manager is a much sought after star in the VC minefield. Proven managers do not have to struggle with background, expertise, or scientific domain knowledge. LPs don't really care how they got there as long as they rack up the returns. But the rookies eager to enter the business have to establish their credentials.

If a newcomer has entrepreneurial experience—started a company, raised multiple venture rounds, and led the company to an exit—the fundraising path becomes a bit easier. Having generated strong returns for investors as an entrepreneur is a good start. A demonstrated nose for choosing good investments is even better. And if these investments have, at the minimum, stepped up in value, the appreciation builds up. The indicators of an investor in the making are few, but nothing compares to returns.

"If you belong in the 'first-time manager/first-time fund' box, you are in trouble. I mean, what are the investors going to base their decisions on?" asks Kelly DePonte. Some investors are blunt and discourage rookie fund managers. "After all, why should you train to become a venture capitalist on my nickel?" Others are quick to point out that it takes about $10 million of investor capital to train a GP. "I'd let the other LPs pay for this education," they say. "Experienced managers who have attained returns over multiple funds are attractive to any LP," says DePonte.

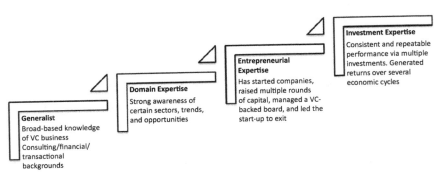

FIGURE 2.2 GP Expertise: Show Me the Money!

Take the example of Shasta Ventures. DePonte helped Shasta to raise its first fund of $230 million and highlights the salient attributes that made fundraising efficient: "Here is a strong team. Each of the three founders had an average of 8 to 12 years of partner-level investment experience in an existing venture firm. Their track records are attributable with multiple investments and exits. The team cohesion is evident—they have invested as syndicate and are former Kauffman Fellows." One fund-of-funds LP who invested in Shasta remarked, "It was a 'quick-yes' investment for us. . . . Such an opportunity does not linger around for too long."

Some key criteria for evaluating fund managers and the investment team include:

- *Performance:* What investing qualifications, if any, does the individual have? Does the individual have an investing track record? Are the managers proven top-quartile performers? Emerging? Or somewhere in between?
- *Team Skills:*
  - What are the operating qualifications and background? Has the individual played relevant roles in industry?
  - What is the individual's domain expertise: Is he or she a generalist or a specialist?
  - Does the individual have any experience as board member? If yes, how many boards, and what is or was the person's specific value/role?
  - What are the role and investment focus of each individual? In larger multisector/multistage firms, this criteria has higher importance.
- *Generalists:* Do the team members have a broad-based business background with little or no discernable differentiated skill set?

Performance, the Primary Metric

LPs assess performance primarily at the fund level and compare any fund's performance against a set of benchmarks. Let us look at the various aspects of performance assessment and the challenges therein. But before we dive into fund level performance, let us start with individual-level performance.

Individual Performance and Attribution

At the heart of it, the business of venture capital is akin to skydiving—small teams form pretty patterns, but each diver has to hold his or her own. Splinter groups are formed frequently. While some glide along, navigating the strong winds, others often crash. The rest of the divers can do little to prevent a crashing partner, so they move on and form a different pattern. Inherently competitive at an individual level,

TABLE 2.2 Sample Format: Individual Performance of a Practitioner

Name of Portfolio Company (Date of investment)	Investment Amount and Syndicate Investors	Investment Thesis	Current Status
SpiderCloud Wireless Inc., Santa Clara, CA. (Feb. 2010) Information technology	$55 million Charles River Ventures, Matrix Partners, Opus Capital, Shasta Ventures	Indoor mobile-broadband networking gear for wireless operators. Helps solve network overload problems caused by handheld devices. Carriers like AT&T can meet the growing demand for mobile broadband on corporate campuses.	Closed a recent Series B round of $25 million. Company was recognized in *Wall Street Journal* as a Top 50 VC-backed company. Likely exit via a trade sale to Cisco or Juniper Networks.
ExactTarget, Indianapolis, IN (May 2009) Information technology	$70 million Battery Ventures, Scale Venture Partners, TCV	Technology tools for e-mail and social media marketing	Company has raised $155 million and is IPO ready, although market challenges prevail. On a rapid growth path, completed three acquisitions in past 12 months.

this business is of hero worship and also-rans, where personal brands often tend to rise above the brand of a firm.

When it comes to individual attribution, practitioners often add a string of successes to their bios. For presentation to LPs, individual performance of practitioners is typically presented with one-page case studies of each portfolio company. Table 2.2 depicts another sample format, a summary table that constitutes the list of portfolio companies managed by each professional.

Individual performance is measured as follows:

- Number and types of opportunities sourced
- Amount of capital invested from fund
- Amount of capital syndicated from other investors, including description of the firms
- Number of boards
- Exits and returns

When it comes to individual attribution, GPs should not only resist the urge to cherry-pick the best opportunities but be prepared to share details of all the investments. "Cherry picking can hurt your credibility: we live in a world where we are a few degrees away from ascertaining the facts," says Christopher Rizik, fund manager at Renaissance Venture Capital Fund, a fund-of-funds. For LPs, it is not just a listing of opportunities that matters but the GP's role in value creation. "Attribution is critical. The underlying factors of value creation are more critical. Was it margin expansion, multiples expansion: what did the GP exactly contribute? If it is just multiple expansion, it could well be a case of a rising tide which benefits all and sundry," says Kelly Williams, Head of Customized Fund Investment Group, Credit Suisse, a fund-of-funds.

Attribution challenges can also cause internal competition within a firm and destroy its chemistry. In a business where hero worship trounces teamwork, it is easy to see why a partner would want to be on the board of a fast-rising portfolio company. But such tactics can create their own set of challenges. In one firm, a newer partner, seeking instant attribution nirvana, assigned himself to the board of a rapidly growing portfolio company, edging the younger partner out. This business calls for a sharp mind, not sharp elbows—the younger partner eventually left the firm and took his skills elsewhere. The opportunity that was once rising soon cratered. LPs are all too familiar with such clever maneuvers. "Attribution ambiguity can be sorted out quickly; in most cases, the person who sourced the opportunity and nurtured it would be the first board member. We also talk to all the CEOs of portfolio companies to double-check the claims. In these discussions, CEOs also help us understand who was a true value creator versus who showed up for the Christmas parties," says Van Heel.

LPs are watchful of poor performance as well. If a partner's performance is uninspiring, LPs candidly share their concerns with the stronger partners and even establish preconditions for investments. This leads to elimination of weaker partners much in advance of the LP commitments. In one example, a new fund was set up by a number of practitioners who had worked at other brand-name firms. But when potential LPs really dug in and got off-the-record evaluation, the luster faded. In fact, these individuals had been pushed out of their firms. "These GPs were not the stars they made themselves out to be," remarked Clint Harris of Grove Street Advisors, a fund-of-funds, in an interview with AltAssets.[9] Despite this, a number of LPs had quickly lined up at the new fund's doors, eager to throw money at these underperformers, according to Harris.

Fund-Level Performance   LPs assess investment track records rigorously at the fund level as well as the contribution of each investment professional. Fund performance is measured via two primary metrics: internal rate of return (IRR) and cash on cash (CoC) multiples. While Table 2.3 shows fund-level performance in a stand-alone format, LPs typically assess stand-alone and benchmarked comparisons, but it is the LP who prefers to choose the benchmark. (See Table 2.4, in which all are early-stage funds with a U.S. regional focus.)

Analyzing the Data   LPs slice performance data in a number of ways, but it all begins with the returns. "GPs give us the aggregate performance numbers—it would be a lot easier if they gave us the cash flows for each portfolio company," says Bob Clone, who has managed over 75 GP relationships. LPs often grumble about the fact that data is not shared to the level of their satisfaction. Thirteen leading pension funds, in conjunction with Pension Consulting Alliance, developed a reporting format for PE/VC funds.[10] This format has two additional schedules that institutional LPs prefer.

Any LP assesses general performance metrics as well as specific data points. These data points are sliced in a number of different ways to understand the risk and GP's ability to adhere to the stated strategy.

- *Sourcing*: Did the opportunity originate via your proactive efforts? Or via a proprietary set of relationships? How well did the opportunity fit within the core investment criteria of the fund?
- *Investment analysis:*
  - Investments by year
  - Investments by industry subsectors
  - Investments by stage—seed, early, or later
  - Investments by dollar amount
  - Investments by series/round
  - Investments led/co-led or syndicated
  - Roles of GPs on boards/observers

For established funds, LPs look into returns and analyze these by fund, year, industry subsectors, size stage of investment, and board representation. "At times, a fund's track record may be due to a 'one-off' event—we seek

TABLE 2.3 Sample Fund Performance: Stand-Alone Format

Company	Date of Investment	Date of Realization	Total Capital Invested ($M)	Total Realized Proceeds (A) ($M)	Unrealized Value (B) ($M)	Total Value = A + B ($M)	Multiple of Invested Capital	Gross IRR
				Realized Investments				
Saver	Dec 08	Nov 09	$18.6	$60.0	–	$60	3.2X	38.1%
Distracter	Jan 09	Jun 10	$8.20	$1.0	$3.1	$4.1	0.5X	NM
Total			$26.8	$61.0	$3.1	$64.1	2.39X	24.2%
				Unrealized Investments				
Potential	Mar 09	N/A	$5.0		$9.0	$9.0	1.8X	9.2%
Middle Path	Jun 09	N/A	$8.20		$4.1	$4.1	0.5X	NM
Total			$13.2		$13.1	$13.1	0.99X	NM
Total Fund Investments			$40.0	$60.0	$17.1	$77.1	1.92X	24.2%

TABLE 2.4 Sample Fund Performance: Benchmarked Format

Fund	Vintage	Fund Size ($M)	Type	Regional Focus	Called (%)	Distributed (%) DPI	Residual Value (%) RVPI	Multiple (X)	Net IRR (%)	Benchmark IRR (%)	Quartile	Date Reported
Avalon Ventures V	1991	9	Early stage	U.S.	100.0	748.0	0.0	7.48	47.7	25.3	1	31-Mar-10
Avalon Ventures VII	2004	75	Early stage	U.S.	94.6	1.2	95.6	0.97	-1.2	-4.6	2	31-Dec-09
Avalon Ventures VIII	2007	150	Early stage	U.S.	36.5	0.0	378.5	3.78	182.0	-10.9	1	31-Dec-09

Source: Adapted from Preqin for illustrative purposes only.

consistent performance over economic cycles," says Van Heel. A one-off event, also called a one-hit home run, occurs when one portfolio company generates the majority of the returns for the entire portfolio. "This business is about home runs indeed, but we aim to dissect the overall approach and strategy of the fund. At times, we remove the outliers from the venture fund portfolio and stress test it to see how the rest of the portfolio stacks up. And during the frothy times, we even take it one step further—we set aside the top two and bottom two outliers to see how resilient the returns are." Chopping off each end of the spectrum allows a rigorous investor to review the portfolio in a more balanced light. Several LPs agreed that this approach is used to stress test the returns. Others do not necessarily subscribe to this approach. "You are investing in VC for their best performing companies: the returns come from the top decile, whether it is in a fund, firm, or the industry. There is no consistency of return," says Perkins of Fisher Lynch Capital. Some LPs also seek to assess the loss ratio: the amount lost vis-à-vis the size of the fund. This ratio is a factor of sector and stage: For example, an early-stage technology fund would have a loss ratio of as much as 50 percent. A later-stage health care fund would be looking at a lower loss ratio. "Anything above 20 percent would make me nervous," says Rozenblit, who invested in a venture fund that had a loss ratio of 3 percent.

The LP seeks all these data points to predict a GP's ability to deliver consistent returns. "We use a number of data points—we start with our own internal notes, look at fund quarterly reports, web research, conferences, and portfolio company meetings—it is multidimensional. This assessment improves our ability to predict a firm's potential to earn the desired return," says Lisa Edgar. Predicting future performance is a harder challenge for any investor, but GPs need to be prepared to address what will make them successful in the current times. "If you don't have credible answers on how you plan to consistently generate returns, don't even bother knocking on any doors," says Gus Long of Stanwich Advisors.

Comparison Benchmarks   LPs compare fund performance with the aggregate returns generated by an entire VC asset class. For example, if a fund is of vintage year 2008 and has generated 24.2 percent IRR, an LP would stack these up against the appropriate benchmark, as seen in Table 2.4.

While selecting benchmarks, a number of "self-selection" caveats crop up here:

- *Vintage year*: A GP may be tempted to assign a vintage year when she started raising the fund as compared to when the final close occurred.

- *Universe of benchmarks*: The data source matters, as does the selection of benchmarks. Several data providers, including Cambridge Associates, Preqin, and Venture Economics, gather returns data. The universe of benchmarks can get equally large. Consider the various benchmarks that can be effectively deployed by a clever GP to posit themselves as shining stars:
  - All private equity funds
  - All venture funds
  - All early-stage venture funds
  - All early-stage technology venture funds
  - All North America early-stage technology venture funds of vintage year 2009
- *Realized versus unrealized value*: The data can become muddier as you try to compare apples and oranges.
- *Veracity of data/self-reporting*: As this industry calls for self-reporting, the skeptical LPs pointed out that the bad managers never report their data—only the good do. Thus, this creates another layer of complexity in trying to assess true performance of the vintage year. Rizik suggests intellectual honesty: "Make it simple: show me every investment you have made. If we smell any issues, it becomes a non-starter. GPs should be forthcoming on the history." Rozenblit says, "We never used any public database due to the veracity issues. We had built our own internal assessment tools, which would give us some very powerful insights. I believe most LPs have similar internal tools." Recall that Rozenblit's firm received at least 200 PPMs each year. His analysts would key in data from all investments within these PPMs, building a substantial database which can be sliced and analyzed in a number of different ways.

The GP Team Dynamics: Stability, Skill Set, and Alignment

LPs assess the team stability, alignment, and dynamics using a number of techniques. Team stability—the ability of the partners to work together through thick and thin—is considered a substantial risk with unproven managers or newer funds. Alignment of interests shifts when senior managers choose to retain most of the profits, leading to potential break-ups of younger partners. Finally, how the members of teams align with each other with respect to roles and responsibilities is a key question LPs often ask.

Here, we describe stability, alignment, and skill sets (soft skills, specialists, and social networks) to help develop deeper insights into a fund manager's due diligence.

Stability and Alignment: Will the Family Stay Together?   Newly minted partnerships are seen as risky: Team cohesion or stability risk is paramount in such firms. If partners cannot get along and there are resignations for any reason, it can be a death knell for the fund. LPs frequently assess each individual's background and expertise, and more importantly, how these cohesively tie together to form an operatic symphony. Redundant skill sets or incompatible personalities are red flags. But while functional attributes can be easily ascertained, no LP can predict whether a marriage can last. Thus, the first-time funds have to demonstrate track records as well as intangible elements like cohesion and stability.

"When we formed Shasta Ventures, the three co-founders knew each other very well, but had never worked under the same roof. We undertook intense efforts to understand how we would function as a team. We discussed, agreed upon, and wrote an operating manual which includes everything from carry distributions down to managing travel decisions and dinner tabs. These aspects were finely calibrated—we were deliberate about this, and the LPs could appreciate it. Seeing this level of preparation, the LPs were comfortable that we could keep the fund together," says Ravi Mohan, co-founder and managing director, Shasta Ventures, a Silicon Valley based early-stage technology venture firm.

To assess team cohesion, LPs look at:

- *Compensation structure* for each team member.
- *Duration of relationship*: How long they have worked together, and under what circumstances these relationships have become stronger.
- *Alignment with LP's financial goals*: Their own capital at play or "skin in the game"; the amount of GP investment as a portion of the GPs' net worth.
- *Distractions*: Sources of other income.

As Clint Harris, managing partner at Grove Street Advisors, puts it, "[One of our team members has] an insight into things like whether the junior members in a fund are talking to headhunters. If they are responding to calls, then you know there is something wrong. . . . [The team member] can make five phone calls and he will get an honest answer very quickly. . . ."[11]

Stability and alignment of interest are closely tied—should a senior partner be unwilling to share meaningful portions of carry, the junior team members will often vote with their feet and head for the door. Table 2.5, a format developed by Pension Consulting Alliance (PCA), demonstrates alignment of interest of various principals in an early-stage fund. Red flags that LPs look for include (1) no significant capital contribution, (2) disproportionate carry allocation, especially to senior partners, and (3) excessive compensation from other sources.

TABLE 2.5 Sample Format: Assessing Alignment of Interest

Principal Name	Expected Capital Contribution	Carry Points (20%)	Total Annual Expected Compensation from This Fund	Total Annual Expected Compensation from Other Sources	Carried Interest Compensation if Fund Meets Objectives
Managing Director 1	$450,000	10%	$400,000	None	$10,000,000
Managing Director 2	$450,000	8%	$300,000	None	$8,000,000
Principal	$100,000	2%	$200,000	None	$2,000,000

Identifying Complementary Skill Sets VC investments call for a varied skill set in a team: raising capital, sourcing investment opportunities, adding value as board members, and leading exits. These skills are prefaced by entrepreneurial expertise, technological strengths, and the ability to perceive future market trends and maintain an even keel in somewhat ambiguous and rough times. LPs also closely look at the duration and the intensity of GP interactions—as investment professionals, not golf buddies.

Table 2.6 shows a complementary skill set of a team at an early-stage health care fund. Note the ability of the managing directors to attract junior as well as senior partners across two separate fund cycles.

The Importance of Soft Skills In a survey of over 145 leading venture capitalists, leading practitioners agreed that listening skills were considered more important for success in VC than quantitative skills.

The skills that were rated most important were:

- Listening skills
- Ability to recruit talented management
- Qualitative analysis skills
- Coaching/counseling/advising skills

"You've got to be a good listener. I find if the venture capitalist does all the talking, he doesn't learn very much about the people he's thinking about investing in. Very important to listen ... and judge who looks and feels like they have the makings of making a real company. Eventually it becomes instinct if you do it often enough," Paul "Pete" Bancroft, former CEO of Bessemer Securities and former chairman of National Venture Capital Association, once remarked.[12]

Financial and technical skills were rated least important by practitioners, while possessing a "CEO perspective" was considered a valuable asset.[13]

TABLE 2.6 Complementary Skills in a Venture Firm

Title (Years with Firm)	Fund-Raising	Early Stage Investments	Operating Qualifications	Board Positions	Exits
Managing Director 1 (Founder—8 years)	Successfully led raise of two prior funds totaling $100 million	Completed 20 investments over 8 years	Over 20 years, launched 20+ products in medical device companies; marketing, clinical research, and sales expertise	Seven board positions	One exit; as operator, two start-ups were acquired by publicly traded company
Managing Director 2 (8 years)	Co-developed investment strategy; supportive role	Completed 20 investments over 8 years	Nine years in consulting services; investment banking expertise	Five board positions	Two exits: one IPO and one acquisition
Principal (4 years)	N/A	Completed 3 investments over 4 years	Eight years in large automotive company; product development, manufacturing, and strategy	Three board positions	N/A
Venture Partner-1 (1 year)	N/A	N/A	Former CEO of publicly traded company	Three positions	Two exits as CEO of venture-backed companies
Venture Partner-2 (1 year)	N/A	N/A	Thirteen years as cardiac surgeon; development of medical devices and FDA regulatory trends	Observer	N/A
Associate (2 years)	N/A	Completed due diligence for two investments	Investment banking with a bulge bank	Observer	N/A

While conducting reference checks with portfolio company CEOs, LPs are able to identify GP strengths in these areas.

LPs also are able to grasp a deeper sense of the culture of the firm. "Naturally, GPs project that all is great within the firm, but while talking to associates, I get a different picture. I have learned how to get to the bottom of that quickly," explains Rizik. Bob Clone, who has made investments in funds across the country, would set aside time to speak with the front-office staff, including the phone operator and the receptionist. "These people may seem irrelevant but are on site every day. They see the entire family at work—the senior partners, and the junior partners and how they interact with entrepreneurs. And they are candid in sharing the true picture."

Other soft aspects LPs consider in GP assessment include the proportion of specialists in a fund team and the quality of the GPs investment networks.

Generalists versus Specialists In a study, the authors demonstrate a strong positive relationship between the degree of specialization by individuals at a firm and the firm's success. A specialist investment professional in a specialist firm will outperform a generalist. The poorer performance by generalists appeared to be due to both an inefficient allocation of funding across industries and poor selection of investments within industries, concluded the authors. In other words, the generalists made bad choices across the board. But if you put a specialist individual in a generalist firm, the performance was weak.[14] Thus, the LP emphasis on domain expertise is intuitively high. Another interesting study of 482 venture practitioners in 222 first-time venture funds asserts the same proposition: *The specialists outperform the generalists.* The specialists were superior, especially when it came to early-stage investments. The study also concludes that the two strongest predictors of fund performance were entrepreneurial experience and domain expertise.

Interestingly, the funds with more MBAs on board performed poorly as compared to others: *We have found at least one place where having an MBA can be a disadvantage*, conclude the authors.[15] But the predominance of MBAs in the business of venture capital is evident. In 80 larger VC firms, of the 615 general partners, 58 percent had MBAs. Of these, 64 percent came from Harvard, Stanford, and Wharton.[16] Guess an MBA from the right school can help you to at least get in the business! Or build a great network to start with!

Social Capital: Who You Know Matters Social capital in the VC arena can help a practitioner access opportunities, conduct due diligence, syndicate investments, accelerate exits, and mitigate risks. Do strong networks among venture capitalists improve their bargaining power over that of entrepreneurs? According to a study, yes, indeed![17] LPs watch for syndication networks and ascribe an intangible value to a venture capitalist's networks. For any LP, VC networks are an indicator of sector expertise and financial strength. Needless to say, the stronger networks were able to extract value from a pricing perspective: Lower valuations were evident in more densely networked markets. Empirical evidence that better networked VCs enjoy better performance has already been established,[18] but lower valuation at the point of entry may also bring a smile to many an LP's face. "My success, frankly, was mostly due to two things: One, as a CFO ... I was a corporate finance expert at a time when biotech and medical devices were becoming very capital-intensive models.... I had an expertise that the industry needed; and I had these great relationships with [venture funds]. Everybody needs an angle, so that was my angle; I knew people,"[19] Alan Frazier, founder, Frazier Healthcare Ventures, once remarked.

Steve Bird of Focus Ventures writes on the importance of networks in the business of venture capital:

"Quality of management" really means the quality of the relationships that GPs build over years in the business. Management means forging relationships with other top VCs that allow both parties to repeatedly form syndicates on the best deals. It means building a network among the entrepreneurial community so that the GP hears about a revolutionary technology when it's still in the lab, not after the company has landed its first round of financing. It means knowing important customers, suppliers, and scientists that can help a fledgling company reach its first quarter of profitability. And it means building trust with the broader financial community so that when the time comes for a portfolio company to get a loan, raise more capital, or go public, company management doesn't have to re-create the wheel.[20]

MY GP IS A ROCK STAR

As a rock star, Bono, the U2 front man, continues to perform at sold-out concerts worldwide. His band has been inducted into the Rock and Roll Hall of Fame, has won 22 Grammy Awards, and has sold over 150 million records in its 35-year career. As an activist, he's no lightweight, either: He has been a Nobel Peace Prize nominee, was the 2005 *Time* Person of the Year, received the Amnesty International Ambassador of Conscience award, and is a passionate advocate for debt and HIV/AIDS relief—these are just a few among his many causes and citations.

He certainly looks and acts like a rebel, although his brand of rebellion defies our expectations of how a rocker should behave. He is still married to his high school sweetheart. They have four children. His band showed capable management and business savvy, unlike many artists, by retaining control of most of its catalog.

Bono continues to defy convention by indulging in his latest un-rock star-like behavior as managing director and co-founder of Elevation Partners, a VC/PE firm that boasts investments in Facebook and Yelp. For a rebel-rocker-activist, such straitlaced, numbers-crunching, right-wing capitalist principles run counter to the free-wheeling, make-love-not-war themes that have been a winning formula of his success as an artist. But the question that begs attention is, what would a Monday morning meeting at Elevation Partners look like? Does Bono attend, complete with shades, annual meetings and sign autographs? Does he meet with LPs to discuss attribution? Some questions that will remain unanswered. . . .

In the following section, we review two types of fund managers— emerging and top quartile. Emerging managers are those with limited track record but strong potential. The top quartile managers are the crème de la crème. LPs gravitate to these bookends of the spectrum. For some LPs, the emerging managers are a definite no-no—perceived as too risky, yet others seek them aggressively for their latent potential. Most LPs seek the top quartile managers, the ones who have consistent performance over multiple fund cycles but few can get access to their hallowed halls.

EMERGING MANAGERS: A PROMISE OF THE FUTURE

Sergey Sheshuryak of Adams Street Partners, a fund-of-funds, asserts, "Our best investment ever was in a first-time fund."[21] Before you rush to call Sergey with your first-time fund documents, read on.

Emerging managers are those practitioners who have yet to demonstrate superior returns in a consistent fashion. Take the example of Steven Lazarus, founder of ARCH Venture Partners. When Lazarus started to raise ARCH Venture Partners Fund I, investors would say, "Your track record is all ahead of you."[22] Those investors threw Lazarus in the emerging manager box and dismissed him. ARCH Fund I celebrated four IPOs as well as four acquisitions and generated 22 percent IRR[23]—a dream scenario for any GP.

The general misperception of emerging managers is that they lack the experience and track record. Perceived as ill-equipped, untested, and unseasoned neophytes, they are considered outside the established. Within the institutional LP community, the perceived risks in investing in emerging managers are high. Rumson Capital Advisors, based in Princeton, New Jersey, observed that less than 7 percent of new firms generate returns in the top quartiles.[24] In essence, they were dismissed as minor league players in the world dominated by juggernauts.

The changing industry offers new opportunities for investors to access investments outside the mainstream PE universe. For investors, striking a balance between established fund managers and tilting slightly in favor of emerging managers is increasingly becoming the norm. In building more mixed portfolios with funds managed by premier names as well as funds managed by emerging managers, investors can build dynamic and diversified portfolios and ensure risk-adjusted returns over the long run.

Several criteria are often used in identifying emerging managers.[25] According to Kelly DePonte, at one end of the spectrum, they may be "first-time fund, first-time investors"—a group of professionals who lack significant PE experience. They may also be a group of individuals who have experience, but no track record working as a cohesive team. There could also be spinoffs of existing, more established funds. Partners who have raised money on a deal-by-deal basis and built their track records would be appropriate candidates for raising funds.

But LPs prefer experienced investors who have played the game well. As Gus Long of Stanwich Advisors points out, "First-time fund is acceptable, but not a first-time investor." Finally, women or minorities who have been traditionally underrepresented in the PE markets are often dubbed as emerging.

Why LPs Seek Emerging Managers

Emerging managers compensate for their perceived shortcomings in many ways, offering a unique edge for investors. Often hungrier, they have a passion for investing in new platforms or areas, such as green technologies or in emerging markets such as Brazil and China. Kelvin Liu of Invesco, a fund-of-funds, writes that "since they do not have historic challenges of poor performance, they are able to pursue unique investment strategies."[26] As mavericks in the capital markets, they often have stronger motivations. As a result, they are more fiercely driven toward achieving high performance and results right out of the starting gate and evolve to be nimble in their decision making. As the underdogs looking to prove themselves, they are often more flexible in working with investors, resulting in a greater alignment with investor interest. Some emerging manager funds allow investors to take bigger percentage shares in their funds—larger than the typical 10 percent cap. Empowered, investors can then wield influence on decisions, terms, and fees.[27]

And some integrate a different cultural mind-set: Much more open, they share their views in blogs and live a transparent life. Their way of doing business makes their more established counterparts look downright prosaic and even backward. Emerging managers tend to be sought out by high-net-worth individuals and family offices, private companies, and government funds, rather than by some institutional investors.[28] Credit Suisse, Grove Street Advisors, and Invesco have started to look closely at this sub-asset class.

Anecdotal evidence and research have shown that emerging managers offer higher returns than more established funds. With entrepreneurial sensibilities, they often seize the market opportunities that their more established colleagues would balk at. In many ways, they run faster and have less to lose and more to gain from investing smarter than the bigger players. In fact, in some cases, it is not lack of experience per se that defines them, but rather the fact that the assets they manage have not reached critical mass. Subsequently, emerging managers are ideal for investors seeking exposure to the "middle market—one that is more fragmented and more susceptible to tactics that can increase earnings at the company level."[29] In effect, these seedling managers fill in the gap when experienced managers outgrow the sector.

All these qualities—smaller fund size, a taste for nontraditional investment strategy, drive and innovation, keeping investor interest closer to heart—are turning heads among investors looking for a different path toward success.[30]

How Are Emerging Managers Born?

As venture firms grow and succeed, partners run into incentive sharing and succession issues.[31] From the old comes the new. These issues may cause the stronger partners to split and form new firms where they are in better control of their destiny, the brand, and the economics. "The investment strategy at Battery Ventures was shifting towards more of a multistage fund, and I had always enjoyed early-stage investments," says Ravi Mohan, who left Battery after eight years and co-founded Shasta Ventures. Catherine Crockett of Grove Street has developed a simple yet effective technique to build an

Life Cycles of Private Equity Fund Managers

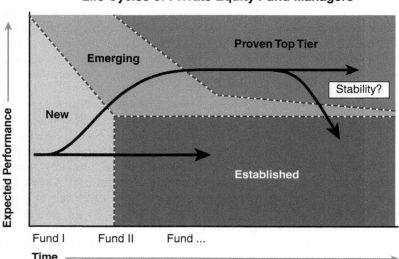

FIGURE 2.3   Fund-of-Funds Allocation for an Emerging Manager Portfolio
Source: © Grove Street Advisors. Reproduced with permission.

emerging manager portfolio. (See Figures 2.3 and 2.4.) Make small bets and build up the position as the performance improves. Crockett explains, "We were fortunate to have backed Granite Global Ventures (GGV). Tony Sun at Venrock decided to recruit a team to lead a fund in China. Grove Street was an early investor in GGV-Fund I (Vintage 2001), which backed leading companies in China, like Alibaba. The timing could not have been better for both GGV and Grove Street."

FIGURE 2.4   Concentrating Capital with Top Performers
Source: © Grove Street Advisors. Reproduced with permission.

Hany Nada, co-founder of GGV, has certainly arrived and is no longer emerging: Ten years later, GGV is on to its Fund III and manages $1 billion across multiple stages. "When we started GGV-I, it was the aftermath of the dot-com crash in 2001—one of the toughest periods to launch a new fund. Our compelling investment strategy was an important factor, but the only reason we made it during the tough economic times of 2001 was because we were 'all-in'—a 110 percent commitment in making this fund successful. We had burnt all boats and there was no plan B. The LPs could sense this commitment," he says. And needless to say, that commitment has led to superior results and a strong global brand.

Crockett and Kelly Williams of Credit Suisse have also invested in Spark Capital, a $300 million technology-focused fund formed by Todd Dagres, Santo Politi, and Bijan Sabet. At Battery Ventures, Dagres had invested $220 million and returned over $1.6 billion to the LPs. What emerging? Here is a proven manager! And lately, the team at Spark Capital has proven that they can spot good opportunities: Bijan Sabet has led one of the early investment rounds in Twitter.

Consider how market conditions drive the birth of emerging managers in the case of Hopen Life Sciences Fund. Fifteen years ago, the Van Andel Research Institute (VARI) was established in Grand Rapids, Michigan, to further research activities focusing on genetic, cellular, and molecular origins of cancer, as well as Parkinson's and other neurological diseases. VARI has blossomed to 250 of the world's leading scientists and a total staff of 800. Eager to leverage and translate an endowed trust of over $1 billion for basic research at VARI, a small group of former life science executives launched Hopen Life Sciences Fund I. Four years and seven investments later, Hopen is on to its Fund II. The GPs, who have operational experience in building a billion-dollar company, have a strong collaborative relationship with VARI. The fund sponsors and VARI also have relationships with Translational Genomics Research Institute (T-Gen), a nonprofit biomedical research organization with 40+ lead investigators and 300 staff engaged in research of diabetes, cancer, and neurological disorders. While these relationships are not exclusive, the GPs have an unprecedented level of access to this network. Such relationships are often considered an unfair advantage—a newer set of GPs may find it challenging to try and build inroads into such a tight-knit network.

Hopen Fund I was an early investor in Intervention Insights, a company that spun out of these research efforts. Intervention Insights assists community oncologists in developing personalized treatments for their patients. By analyzing cancerous tissue, the company can generate a complete genomic picture of over 20,000 genes and corresponding molecular pathways that uniquely define a person's cancer. The improved outcomes benefit patients and payors as treatment costs are generally impacted favorably. Hopen Fund I's seven portfolio companies have gone on to raise additional capital from leading investors in the region. Hopen Fund I led an investment in Metabolic Solutions, a drug discovery company focused on diabetes cure, which has now raised over $46 million. Its two other portfolio companies have syndicated over $10 million. The Midwest United States region is fertile with executive level talent from pharmaceutical and medical device companies such as Upjohn, Pfizer, Stryker, and Perrigo, so piecing together a highly seasoned scientific development team has been relatively easy. But Hopen Fund I has yet to have exits and while the portfolio is healthy, the risk of raising follow-on rounds exists. Despite these challenges of emerging managers, Hopen Fund II has raised 50 percent of the target fund. And speaking of alignment of interest, the GPs have kicked in 30 percent of Fund II. Compare that with typical 1 percent commitment made by most GPs!

Institutional Allocations for Emerging Managers

Major institutional investors, such as California Public Employees' Retirement System (CalPERS) and California State Teachers' Retirement System (CalSTRS), and the pension funds of General Motors Corp. and Motorola, Inc., actively invest in emerging funds. In 2007, CalPERS and CalSTRS—the nation's largest public pension funds, with collective assets of more than $240 billion—set their sights on building a new investment strategy that created opportunities for emerging managers. With the help of Altura Capital of New York, CalPERS and CalSTRS developed a directory that exposed its pension funds to a new world of emerging and undercapitalized managers, funds, partnerships, and broker dealers in a range of asset classes and allocated 2 percent of its total portfolio toward underserved capital markets. The effort kick-started investment returns by "building investment portfolios that tap into the changing demographics and talent emerging in California and the nation."[32] For investment authorities at CalPERS and CalSTRS, the decision enabled beneficiaries to access an untapped and dynamic market. Russell Read, CalPERS chief investment officer, noted that "it's easy to miss emerging firms that are still struggling to raise capital. . . . Most large firms started at the small end of the market and we want to find them on the small end of their asset class. Then we won't have to stand in line for their services on the big end later."[33]

In a Preqin 2010 survey, 42 percent of the world's top 100 LPs were open to considering first-time funds (see Figure 2.5). Note that this is different from spin-off funds. In partnering with emerging managers, both programs have touted many benefits—early access to industry leaders, gains from better returns, higher rates of proprietary deal flow, and a management

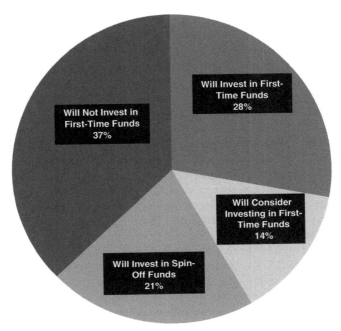

FIGURE 2.5   LPs Preference for Investing in First-Time
Funds
Source: Preqin, 2010 survey.

focus on maximizing profits rather than on increasing assets under management.[34]

Pension programs have demonstrated staunch support for minority representation among their emerging funds. Thus, the definition of emerging has expanded to include demographic factors as well as performance. CalPERS' alternative investment management (AIM) program explicitly states that its goal is to invest in women-owned or minority-owned funds. In particular, CalPERS and CalSTRS partnered with Leading Edge Investment Advisors LLC, a fund-of-funds run by an emerging manager who is working with seven other emerging manager-run funds and has allocated $150 million from its CalPERS investment to those funds—of which "one is African American-owned, one Asian American-owned, and one is woman-owned."[35]

The partnership between CalSTRS investment authorities and Palo Alto-based Invesco Private Capital drew a lot of attention when Invesco agreed to invest $300 million over a five-year period on behalf of the state teachers' pension fund. Kristine Brandt, director and CEO of Invesco, extols the company's strategies to bring diversity to VC and PE investing, which have had superlative returns. She asserts, "The economy is more and more global these days, so you have to have that global mind-set. . . . If there isn't diversity within the [general partner], then where is that diverse thought coming from? In order to build better companies, in order to come up with the next best widget, I really think that diversity is required."[36]

Since 2002, CalPERS has seen a 26 percent annual growth rate in these funds. By 2008, it had committed over $3.4 billion to PE firms that are majority-owned by disadvantaged groups and at least $11.7 billion to PE firms that have at least one woman or minority owner in the partnership.[37]

GPs have found the emerging category to be advantageous, but rarely does an LP make an investment decision solely on the fact that a GP is emerging—it may get a GP's foot in the door, but that's about it. A pecking order, as seen in Figure 2.6, exists and LPs prefer the performers as opposed to the rest. After being hounded by one firm for too long, an LP acerbically commented: "You have been emerging for too long—just call me back when you have *emerged*!" The primary risk that any LP faces with emerging managers is career risk—after all, why would LPs risk the embarrassment of losing their capital (and their job) with an unproven manager? And just look at the return variance in the following section—now put yourself in the shoes of any LP and you can see why every LP eagerly covets a top quartile GP.

FIGURE 2.6 Emerging Managers—Pecking Order

THE QUEST FOR THE ELUSIVE TOP QUARTILE MANAGERS

For all venture funds, being in the top 25 percent of their class is a coveted position. LPs and GPs alike view this golden spot most favorably. Studies show that top quartile PE funds sustain their performance and produce returns of 50 percent greater than public benchmarks.[38] In one study, top quartile PE funds generated annual returns of 39 percent over a 25-year period—more than triple the returns for the S&P 500 (12.1 percent) and the NASDAQ (12.3 percent) in the same period.[39] Table 2.7 and Figure 2.7 further demonstrate the variance between the top and the bottom ends of the spectrum. Despite the fact that the data in Figure 2.7 is dated, the point being illustrated here is the IRR variance due to manager selection in comparison with other factors that may impact IRR. And what's more, as evidenced in Figure 2.8, the top quartile continues to shrink. The good get better and the bad get worse, indeed. With such a wide variation, it is evident why LPs seek the best in class.

With stellar returns, it is no wonder that PE/VC is an extremely attractive investment—and that investors are looking for the crème de la crème of the universe to maximize returns. David Swensen of Yale University writes, "Selecting top quartile managers in private markets leads to much greater

TABLE 2.7 The Best versus the Worst: Performance Variance in Venture Funds

Vintage	IRR Maximum	IRR Minimum
2003	21.1	−4.6
2002	43.2	−27.7
2001	29.0	−100.0
2000	29.0	−25.4
1999	18.0	−40.6
1998	1025.1	−46.1
1997	213.0	−35.0
1996	133.3	−33.3
1995	447.4	−19.9
1994	73.2	−23.2
1993	87.4	−14.8
1992	110.4	−20.1
1991	346.4	1.2

Source: Preqin Median Benchmarks, all regions, Venture, as of September 2009, calculated for 648 funds. Returns net of management fees, expenses, and carried interests.

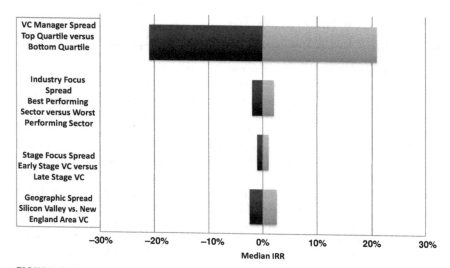

FIGURE 2.7 Manager Selection and Return Variance Manager Selection Trounces Everything Else
Source: General Motors Investment Management Company (2001 Data).

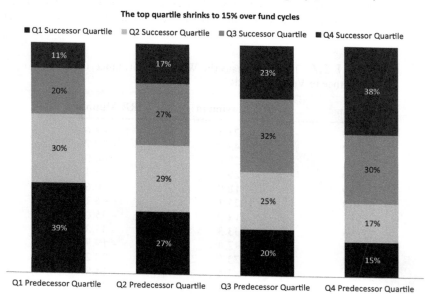

FIGURE 2.8 Top Quartile Pool of Funds Shrinks from 39 Percent to 15 Percent over Four Fund Cycles While the Lowest Quartile Grows from 11 Percent to 38 Percent
Source: Preqin Benchmarks as of September 30, 2009.

reward.... The first quartile venture capitalist surpasses the median by 30.1 percent per annum, providing a much greater contribution to portfolio results."[40]

According to DePonte, the priority among investors is access to high-performing funds.[41] But the top funds are plain inaccessible for the vast majority of investors. A handful of funds have generated superior returns in a consistent fashion. The biggest beneficiaries of this performance have been larger institutions—the public and private pension funds, endowments, and foundations, which have seen their PE investments beating public market indexes. They account for more than 70 percent of the funds invested in the top 100 PE firms since 2005.[42]

An LP based in France came to the U.S. West Coast eagerly seeking relationships with top quartile relationships. And bear in mind that this was a multibillion-dollar financial powerhouse. Here is what the LP had to say: "After a number of calls, one top quartile GP agreed to meet with us. We were told in no uncertain terms that all they would share is a statement of net returns. No details of portfolio companies or the amount invested, nor gross returns. Nor would we get any additional materials for due diligence beyond standard information. This fund was obviously trying to be efficient on the due diligence process as well as hiding the fee income. Their shrug-the-shoulders, take-it-or-leave-it attitude was indicative of the demand-supply situation." This LP eventually passed on the opportunity to invest in this top quartile fund.

MEASURES OF PERFORMANCE: IRR, COC, TVPI, OR DPI?

An informal survey conducted by McKinsey found that only 20 percent of executives understand the critical deficiencies of IRR.* IRR has its allure, offering what seems to be a straightforward comparison of, say, 30 percent returns with 8 percent. IRRs appear favorable but do not consider reinvestment risks and the redeployment of capital in other investment opportunities in the calculation for investors.

Because IRR is expressed as a percentage, a small investment can show a triple-digit IRR. While this looks attractive at the first glance, a larger investment with a lower IRR can be more attractive on a net present value (NPV) basis. To interpret IRR as an annual equivalent return on a given investment is easy and intuitive, but this is only true if there are no interim cash flows. This may be the case with most venture investments, but in any biotech or a pharma exit, where earn-outs are negotiated, the IRR may become misleading quickly.

FLAG Capital Management, a fund-of-funds, points out that LPs often "gauge fund performance by analyzing some nebulous combination of IRRs (dollar-weighted returns, which are influenced by the timing and magnitude of cash flows) and cash-on-cash investment multiples, either total-value-to-paid-in-capital (TVPI) or distributions-to-paid-in-capital (DPI). Each can tell a different story and is important in its own right. But none is sufficient by itself to tell the whole story.[†]

---

*John C. Kelleher and Justin J. MacCormack, "Internal Rate of Return: A Cautionary Tale," *McKinsey Quarterly,* August 2004, accessed February 20, 2011, http://www.mckinseyquarterly.com/Internal_rate_of_return_A_cautionary_tale_1481.

[†]FLAG Capital Management, "Behind the Benchmarks: The Art of Private Capital Performance Assessment," November 2009, accessed February 20, 2011, www.flagcapital.com/pdf/Insights%202009%20November%20-%20Behind%20the%20Benchmarks.pdf.

All the Managers Are Above Average

According to FLAG Capital Management, being in the top quartile is akin to the Lake Wobegon effect, where all the managers are above average. "Like most LPs, I am still waiting for the 'other 75 percent' to show up—none of us know where to find them," quips Chris Rizik, fund manager, Renaissance Venture Capital Fund, a fund-of-funds. To position themselves in the top quartile, 77 percent of PE firms were found to change key data inputs such as the selection of the reference benchmark and the definition of the fund's vintage year.[43] In this vein, one LP sardonically pointed out, "Sure—any fund can be in the top quartile when you self-select the benchmark and compare with funds that have all exits that occurred on a Monday in the month of October when the full moon was shining at its brightest."

The criteria for establishing performance benchmarks are riddled with inconsistencies and ambiguity, with measurements to identify top quartile private capital funds varying widely. While public equity fund managers can look to indexes such as the S&P 500, private fund managers do not have the luxury of straightforward benchmarks. FLAG Capital Management further points out in its newsletter that "Top quartile can mean a net IRR of 25 percent for its latest fund in its class" or a fund whose "CoC multiple" is in the top quartile of its fund class. But the dimensions can get tricky when

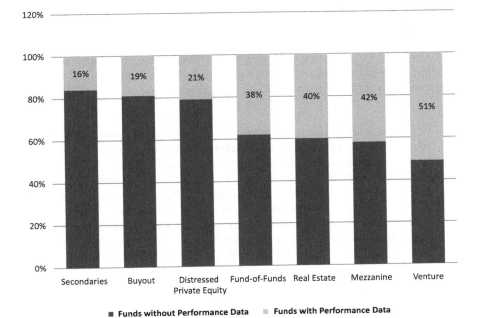

FIGURE 2.9 Private Equity Indeed: 51 Percent of Venture Funds Do Not Share Performance Data
Source: Preqin database, 1990–2009.

you consider more subtle criteria. For example, funds with very a attractive rate of return may have inferior CoC multiples if they have been flipped quickly. Funds may also have impressive projections on performance but no cash distributions. A venture firm may have a range of strong performing funds and one poor fund that, if excluded, can boost the other funds and bring it into the coveted top quartile position. In fact, omission of certain investments from the historical track record to boost performance indicators is a common tactic practiced among funds.[44]

Consider Figure 2.9, where Preqin gathered performance data over two decades. At least half of the performance data in VC remains unreported.

With the imperfect state of performance benchmarking in the PE industry, investors cannot always make accurate investment decisions. Oliver Gottschalg, co-founder of the consulting firm Peracs, has put it this way: "Being in the 'top quartile' somewhere, somehow is not a meaningful criterion to assess the quality of a GP."[45] It is nearly as much an art as it is a science. With these challenges, it is imperative for the LPs to demand better measurements. But as FLAG Capital correctly points out in the following section, the top performers have no motivation to offer their performance data. And those at the bottom of the pile hide the data to avoid any further embarrassment. So what we have left is data from a pile of middle-market players. Any LP struggles with this conundrum—you could end up with "tallest amongst the dwarves." You can sense the challenges in the following excerpt from *Insights,* a FLAG Capital newsletter:

A serious problem in establishing benchmarks is the sourcing and aggregation of financial data because of the lack of transparency and publicly disclosed information from private companies. Often, this data is embedded in quarterly reports typically only sent to a select batch of people. Another source of information is through voluntary disclosure from the fund managers themselves or through performance reporting by clients or advisory services. The existing benchmarks professional investment advisors often compile are also flawed, as a large share of their funds tend to be from higher quality managers that the firm goes on to recommend to clients. Another inherent problem is that data from large institutional investors, such as pension funds, are often compiled from a sample of disproportionately large funds.

Whatever the source, significant biases adversely affect frank attempts to benchmark the data. Sources dependent on accessibility and selective contributions lead to non-representative sampling of the universe of PE funds. Finally, incentives to report are also misleading.

Consider the choices top-performing managers have. There is no incentive to contribute fund data to the index, which only serves to raise the benchmark and makes the performance of the fund look less stellar compared to its peers. On the other hand, poorly performing fund managers also have no incentive to disclose data to a third party because they are highly unlikely to raise another fund. As one LP remarked, "Two poorly performing funds, and you are out of the game."

Existing barometers for investors are therefore the best of what's available, but they should be approached with a grain of salt. Performance evaluation is still important; the key is to be cautious on selection of benchmarks, especially if self-selected by GPs. LPs dig deeper into manager track records, identify quantitative and qualitative indicators of performance on an absolute and relative level, and monitor the fund diligently beyond static indicators, such as the seemingly inviolable top-quartile benchmark.[46]

First Access the Top Quartile, Then Give It All Away

Legacy Ventures, a fund-of-funds, has access to the very best of top quartile VCs. Other LPs would kill to get their dollars in the hands of Legacy's fund portfolio, which includes storied firms like Kleiner Perkins, August Capital, Foundation Capital, or Greylock Partners. In what seems like an interesting karmic circle, former successful GPs provide the capital to Legacy Ventures. After Legacy puts this money to work, and generates obscene returns, the distributions are donated. The goal for Legacy and its investors—not IRR, not filthy lucre, but to give it all away. More than $700 million has been committed across at least five Legacy funds of funds. The spoils have benefitted effective philanthropic, economic development, environmental, and human rights groups.

FUND INVESTMENT STRATEGY

An investment strategy—the very raison d'être of any venture firm—combines GP skills and expertise with a given market opportunity to target superior financial returns. Most venture capitalists use "emergent strategies," where the firm adopts a sandbox but also is flexible enough to deal with exceptions. Boundaries are adjusted periodically, and when exceptions occur, partners decide to invest based on the potential for return. Firms conduct off-site meetings as often as once every quarter to develop or tune such strategies.[47]

Strategy is important but LPs are tired of, and somewhat irritated with, the me-too strategies that abound across the board. After all, which GP does not want to invest in a Facebook or a Groupon? Chris Douvos, co-head of private equity investing at The Investment Fund for Foundations (TIFF), notes, "In the venture business, we have a lot of smart people but not necessarily differentiated: *being smart is necessary, but not a sufficient condition.* And can you demonstrate resonance between the partners' backgrounds and the investment strategy?"[48] TIFF and its related entities manage $9.4 billion for over 750 charities.[49] Adams Street Partners, one of the world's largest funds of funds, seeks to find "the quality of the group's deal flow, with respect to intrinsic quality and competition for opportunities."[50] Chris Rizik, fund manager at Renaissance Venture Capital Fund, a fund-of-funds, takes the long view: "It all boils down to two things: the people and their investment strategy."[51]

A well-established strategy blends macro data with the GPs' insights and analysis. Synthesizing this information, a GP points to the future, where opportunities may grow and generate significant returns.

Any investment strategy would include:

- *Market opportunity, drivers of growth:* What are the key macro trends that identify unsolved challenges? Is the universe large enough to source opportunities? See the example of a health care fund's strategy in the following section.
- *Competitive advantage in this market opportunity:* Does the fund have a significant unfair advantage in the domain? Consider the competitive advantage of Osage University Partners, a fund that has rights of first refusal to invest in leading university spin-offs. Or consider Foundry Group's presence in Colorado.
- *Fund managers' background and relevant expertise:* Does the investment team have relevant background, or sector expertise? As one LP joked, "I was suddenly inundated with cleantech experts who had failed at the dot-com investing."
- *Capital efficiency, investment cycle, and target financial returns:* Is the strategy suitable for generating venturelike returns, that is, 25 percent IRR in five to seven years?
- *Competition from other venture funds:* Certain geographic areas are hypercompetitive, while certain regions are underserved. Each of these conditions impacts a fund's ability to generate returns.
- *Risks and plan for mitigating these risks:* An investment strategy that is based on health care investing faces regulatory risk. Funds playing in underserved geographies face risk from other newer entrants. These need to be addressed effectively.

Many GPs fail to develop a compelling strategy that effectively combines all the above. Such GPs often fall into the me-too category of investing, which irks LPs across the board. "Having seen over 500 funds, I meet GPs who try to convince me that they have invented this asset class. These are savvy, smart people, but ... if they only knew that I have seen the same pitch 300 times before. There are days when, as an LP, you feel like you are a pretty woman in a bar. Everyone is giving you his pick-up line, and it is tiring. You have great deal flow and great team dynamics ... well, how very nice ... now, are you going to tell me my eyes are pretty, too?" asks Chris Douvos. Chris Rizik concurs: "GPs use words like proprietary and unique extensively—in the past 30 days, I have seen 10 funds that have no differentiators." David Cowan of Bessemer Venture Partners warns against a purely market-driven approach. "When you comb through mature sectors that are ripe with proven winners, 'comps' with high multiples, and dozens of well-funded companies, you're not excelling at the craft of early-stage venture capital—you're momentum investing. Momentum is critical for day traders, but it is not how you spot the next Cisco."[52]

Sector-Based Strategy

Certain sectors show promise at certain times, while others run out of favor. Consider the waves within the technology sector. As the bulky mainframe computer transitioned to the ubiquitous desktop, the ecosystem of hardware and software opportunities emerged. In the early 1980s, eager investors backed over a hundred hardware start-ups that focused on disc drives, desktop computers, and allied products. As the desktop wave descended to its nadir, the networking wave emerged, which led to the formation of Cisco, Juniper Networks, Bay Networks, 3 Com, and others.

Venture firms were evolving in the seventies and eighties, and with capital flowing rapidly in this asset class, a sector-based strategy was not as important as it is today. James Swartz, founder, Accel Partners, once remarked, "Biotech was just incredibly difficult. And services—I don't know, we just somehow gravitated to communications and software. I'd like to say we're brilliant and knew that was the way to go, but that wasn't it. We just felt more comfortable in our own skins doing those kinds of investments."[53] In the current times, no GP worth his IRR would appear so casual about their sector-based strategy.

As social media, games, and cloud computing are currently at their peak, leading investors have found opportunities within these sectors with the potential to generate strong returns. On the other hand, cleantech investments have had mixed reviews, thanks to the larger capital needs and lack of liquidity. "In recent years, the venture industry as a whole has lost its 'sectorial' touchstone," says Kelly DePonte of Probitas Partners. "If the 1980s were the decade of PCs and the 1990s spawned the Web, there is no sector in this 2010 decade that has the potential to provide returns," he points out. "And the jury is still out on cleantech returns." The number of pure-play cleantech funds actually closing continues to drop and cleantech, which once was positioned as a primary focus sector, is now included as "one of many" sectors.

An example of a fund's health care investment strategy is highlighted, where the sector's macro trends are amplified to help potential LPs understand the primary drivers for innovation, market challenges, and exits.

Example of a Sector-Based Strategy: Early-Stage Health Care Fund   The primary investing targets for ABC Fund are early-stage health care companies located primarily in Middle America. Key target health care subsectors include:

- Medical imaging
- Bioinformatics

- Health care services and information technology
- Drug delivery, diagnostics, and devices

Medical Imaging   Scientific and technological developments have made the field of diagnostic medical imaging a high-growth industry. In 2010, the U.S. market for diagnostic medical imaging technologies was valued at more than $7 billion, and it is expected to exceed $8 billion by 2013. The top three companies in the diagnostic imaging market—GE Healthcare, Siemens Healthcare Solutions, and Philips Medical Systems—represent 55 percent of the sales of equipment and a 12 to 15 percent CAGR in revenue growth through 2011, according to industry research reports.

3D imaging has become an essential tool for radiologists and plays an increasingly important role in the daily clinical practice of cardiologists and surgeons. Accordingly, customer expectations for advanced visualization are growing rapidly, as they demand more workflow efficiency and enterprise-wide access to these systems. However, workflow-related concerns remain a crucial market restraint because of the need to integrate the new systems into existing practice with minimal disruption to the clinical workflow. Picture archive communication system (PACS) workflow, often requiring that radiologists physically move from one workstation to another several times, reduces efficiency in the interpretation process and service. Cardiovascular imaging is developing rapidly. Image acquisition technologies, particularly the recent leaps forward offered by 64-slice CT and multimodality image fusion, have opened the way to robust cardiovascular imaging capabilities. Cardiovascular imaging is attractive because it constitutes a less invasive alternative to the current standard procedures, often eliminating the need for an invasive procedure to exclude coronary artery disease. Cardiac CT angiography (CCTA), use of which has skyrocketed with the advent of the 64-slice CT, has been driving the adoption of advanced visualization technology since 2004. Accordingly, the vessel analysis package has been the single best-selling set of clinical applications for all advanced visualization vendors. Such applications have the potential to change clinical guidelines and be adopted as standard screening procedures, which will further increase their utilization. Cardiovascular MR is also a contender to CT that displays significant growth potential.

Bioinformatics   Bioinformatics is a key enabling technology in diagnostics and drug development. Bioinformatic tools gather, analyze, and represent information across the many levels of life—genes, proteins, and metabolons—to help scientists understand life's processes in healthy and disease states. These tools enable new or better drugs and pinpoint the makers for diagnostics. As the regulatory scrutiny of new drug candidates increases and failure in late-stage trials becomes untenably expensive, bioinformatics enables early warnings for drugs likely to have interaction with related biochemical pathways, and provides screening for patients who will not benefit from the drug or may experience an adverse reaction. Spending on bioinformatics will increase significantly through 2011. Revenue for bioinformatics software and database content was estimated at $725 million in 2010 and growing at a CAGR of 15.7 percent to an estimated $1.5 billion in 2014.

Healthcare Services and Information Technology Digitalization, health care consumerism, and the drive for cost containment are reshaping the importance of health care IT to the efficient practice of medicine. The spending on electronic medical records, health care information systems, and telemedicine and monitoring are growing faster than the growth rate for health care overall. Outpatient and home care spending are growing rapidly and are beginning to overtake hospital spending on healthcare IT.

According to analysts, the U.S. health care IT market size was $18.5 billion in 2006 and it is forecasted to grow to $34.7 billion in 2014, a 13.4 percent CAGR. The hospital segment accounts for the larger portion of the market with 52.2 percent of sales in 2005, 51.4 percent in 2006, and 48.2 percent in 2014.

The physician/home care/nursing/hospices sector will overtake hospitals by the end of the forecast period and will be worth 51.3 percent of the U.S. market by 2011. The highest growth appears in physicians, home care, nursing homes, and hospices. The market for this sector of the industry was worth more than $7.7 billion in 2010. By the end of 2010, it will grow to almost $8.9 billion and, at a CAGR of 15.0 percent, reach more than $17.8 billion by 2014.

Diagnostics The diagnostics market in the United States is approximately $8 billion (close to $22 billion worldwide), with a 10 percent annual growth rate. This growth will be fueled by the aging U.S. population; the flow of information from the mapping of the human genome, which leads to an increase in molecular diagnostics; and the convergence of semiconductors, nanotechnology, engineering, materials science, and medicine. Advances in these technologies have created investment opportunities in companies developing products for molecular diagnostics to detect and manage diseases as well as new methods for targeting and delivering therapeutics compounds.

Summing It Up: Fund Investment Strategy

Other factors that impact investment strategy include geography (underserved regions yield opportunities due to pricing advantages) and the stage of investments (earlier stage companies need less capital but are deemed to be riskier). Ultimately, an investment strategy is a combination of the GP's expertise, the market opportunity within the sector, geographic advantages, stage of investments, and the size of the fund. No single element stands out as much as the GP expertise. A few examples of fund strategies are laid out in Table 2.8.

Once a strategy is established, leading practitioners not only seek existing opportunities but lead the formation of companies based on the white spaces, road maps, or the open avenues in the market.

White-Space Investing: The Venture Practitioner as a Founder   Leading researcher John Seely Brown of Xerox fame defined white-space research as "radical ... lashing one's self to a problem and taking it wherever it goes. The only guide to where to go is the problem itself; if it takes you out of your discipline, you go with it.... Such research seldom happens at universities because peer review and tenure mechanisms tend to favor research that stays well within established disciplines."[54]

Several leading venture professionals have used this white-space research strategy to proactively form start-ups. Ralph Waldo Emerson's credo resonates well with these mercurial minds: "Do not go where the path may lead, go instead where there is no path and leave a trail." John Jarve, general partner at Menlo Ventures, asserts, "More than half of the companies we finance come out of the research we do—Menlo is a very research-intensive firm." Jarve earned his master's of science in electrical engineering from the Massachusetts Institute of Technology. "This is not something we hire somebody to do: we are pretty strong technically and analytically. Combined with our investment and market awareness, we often identify a new, emerging market, and choose to master it,"' Jarve remarks. Menlo Ventures started investing in 1976 with less than $20 million. Thirty years later, the firm manages $4 billion and has closed its eleventh fund of $400 million.

At Bessemer Venture Partners, David Cowan leads the concept of developing investment road maps. While these road maps have their utility, it's a deeper understanding of technologies and the market challenges that help develop such a road map. Tom Perkins of KPCB writes that "the technical aspect didn't daunt me too much. I figured that I could learn it." While looking at Genentech, Perkins did not get into the scientific details, which he professes would have been over his head. Rather, he focused his questions along the lines of equipment needs and steps to prove the technology. Perkins was playing the role of a classic project manager: setting goals, establishing time lines, and providing key resources—people and money.[55] Like most agile practitioners, he had mastered various technologies as they evolved: lasers, computers, and genetic engineering.

TABLE 2.8 Variations on a Theme: How Strategy Differs in Venture Firms

Fund	Market Opportunity and Drivers of Growth	Source of Investment Opportunities	Fund's Competitive Advantage	Sourcing Advantage	Capital Efficiency and Target Returns	Example	Level of Competition from Other Funds
Arboretum Ventures, Ann Arbor, MI	Health care is a large, growing market fraught with inefficiencies and FDA regulatory challenges.	Universities in Midwest, research hospitals, corporations, and entrepreneurs	Track record, team's expertise, and relationships with VCs across the country.	Underserved/ geographic	Early-stage health care opportunities need at least $20 million and generate exits in the range of $150 million. Average span for exits is seven years.	Accuir Cytometers yielded a 5X return in six years.	Medium
Osage University Partners, Bala Cynwyd, PA	University research and development budgets are growing. TTOs are primary source of opportunities.	Top 10 universities with significant research budgets	Sourcing tie-in with university technology transfer offices	Contractual	Variable. Ability to cherry-pick opportunities with lower capital needs and shorter investment cycle	Avid Pharmaceuticals acquired by Eli Lilly for $500 million.	Low
Foundry Group, Boulder, CO	Technology disruptions in social media, Web, man-machine interactions	Rapidly evolving market space	Relationships and network/ entrepreneurial contacts	Brand recognition of GPs. Launched techstars in various leading cities (New York, Boston).	Lower capital needs to reach break-even. Target returns can be significant in short time frame.	Zynga valued at $3 billion in three years	High
Norwest Venture Partners, Menlo Park, CA	Global shifts in GDP growth, infrastructure, technology usage, and regulation	Large—multistaged investments in multiple sectors and geographic arenas	Brand and track record. Relationships	Firm's network of relationships. Geographic spread	Varied. Energy sectors demand higher capital with uncertain outcomes.	Playdom acquired by Disney for over $700 million.	High

ROAD MAP INVESTING: A PEEK INSIDE DAVID COWAN'S CRYSTAL BALL

"We at Bessemer try to take [the road map investing approach] more seriously than most," writes David Cowan of Bessemer Venture Partners.*

"Fresh out of business school, I joined Bessemer [in 1992] and proceeded to fall in love with every crappy pitch I heard. Fortunately, before I did any damage, my bosses intervened, suggesting that perhaps I should take a few months to Think Before I Fund. I developed a comprehensive list of 38 potential investment sectors of high technology, and I spent the next three months whittling it down to 5. I crossed off sectors, which required deep domain knowledge—sectors that were too early, too crowded, or too unproven. . . . I solicited advice from the smartest experts I could find. I went to conferences, surveying buyers," writes Cowan.

This resulted in sharpening the saw, which allowed him to focus, narrowing down his investment horizon to the data and communications subsectors. Over the next three years, Cowan would find very specific opportunities and invest in them. In the early 1990s, when the World Wide Web did not exist, Cowan's road map included technology subsectors such as network management, telecommunications technology, and enterprise e-mail. Then these investments may have appeared to be "exotic" or science experiments, at best. Cowan went on to co-found Verisign, an Internet security and infrastructure company, and served as its chairman. Within three years, the company's stock was publicly traded.

"Each Bessemer investor's road map begins with an analysis of disruptive catalysts that have the potential to cause major displacements in our economy. Those disruptive catalysts might be technical (e.g., network vulnerabilities), demographic (e.g., aging U.S. population), regulatory (e.g., spectrum auctions or Sarbanes Oxley), psychographic (e.g., consumer concerns about security), or geopolitical (e.g., China's reception to foreign investment)," he writes.

Cowan's road map lays out specific strategies, or "initiatives," to exploit the disruption. "For each of these initiatives [Bessemer] made one investment in the best team we could find attacking the problem—some were follow-on rounds . . . and some were new teams that we incubated in our offices."

Note that by creating a road map, it allows a practitioner to not only spot the growth opportunities and the cracks in the technology landscape but also to gain awareness of the leading start-ups in the landscape. Thus, while Cowan co-founded Verisign, he also followed some existing opportunities.

In 2009, Cowan was working on social networking road maps: companies with a revenue model that does not depend solely on impression-based advertisement revenues. Social gaming (Cowan has invested in Playdom[†]), social music (Smule), crowd-sourced solutions for enterprises (Crowdflower). "Separately, I believe there are opportunities in the online security arena (Lifelock and Reputation Defender)—these emerged from my security road map. Finally, in 2010, the application of technology to solve government problems has rapidly evolved—satellite imagery, health insurance, and health exchanges are some of my recent road map-based investments. Government has been slower to adopt technologies but has strong purchasing power. I am looking to take the ingenuity of Silicon Valley to bring efficiencies to the government," remarks Cowan.

---

[*]David Cowan, "Road Map Investing," Who Has Time for This? (blog), August 12, 2005, http://whohastimeforthis.blogspot.com/2005/08/road-map -investing.html.
[†]Playdom, an online gaming company, was formed in 2008. Bessemer invested in a $76 million Series A round at $260 million premoney valuation. In July 2010, Disney acquired Playdom for $763 million.

For any venture practitioner, it is an important cranial exercise to assess the technological ecosystem and predict the harmonious interplay of the components. "While our competitors seemed happy to wait for fully fleshed-out business plans, and full teams, to walk through their doors, we were incubating our own new ventures, then building the teams to suit the needs. We had found a way to harness our impatience. I have never been good at just waiting," writes Perkins in his memoir *Valley Boy*.[56]

When Investment Strategy Shifts and Drifts   Mae West, the Hollywood star of yesteryear, once said, "I used to be Snow White but I drifted." Any LP dreads strategy drift—those opportune moments when fund managers start to invest in everything else but their core areas of expertise. But a strategic shift, conducted between funds with a well laid out plan, can be beneficial.

"Even with a great road map, it's always necessary to maintain an open mind to great opportunistic investments," writes Cowan, who rues Bessemer's inability to exit telecom investments in the late 1990s.[57] Vinod Khosla exited the technology sector and burned any technology investing road map to start afresh at Khosla Ventures, primarily to focus on investments in energy. Khosla quickly reinvented himself as a thought leader at the forefront of a new sector, challenging assumptions and engaging in strong debates with Princeton scientists on the future of biofuels.[58]

Shifting strategies and developing new road maps are appropriate when the GPs raise new funds. But within an existing fund framework, if a GP attempts to shift the strategy substantially, the LPs see it as a big negative. After all, the investors had bought an original thesis of investment, and unless the LPs approve the shift, the GPs should resist the urge to tinker at such a grandiose scale.

"Strategy drift is an ongoing concern within the LP community. Opportunistic GPs get clever in their definition of how a certain company fits their strategy. This becomes a debate of definitions, and you will be surprised what I have seen pass under the definition of cleantech. I am always intrigued at a fund's success outside of the core fund strategy," says Kenneth Van Heel of Dow Pension Fund. Every fund has a clause that allows the GPs to invest up to 10 percent of the capital in companies that are outside the core investment criteria. "In my world, GPs do not get credit for the success of these opportunistic outliers. Worse, if we see a pattern of successes only in the outliers, then the GPs have a bigger problem."

Brad Feld, co-founder of the Foundry Group, a Boulder, Colorado-based venture firm, writes, "Lots of VCs talk about their 'process,' 'investment thesis,' 'company building model,' 'value add model,' or other such cliche-ish phrase. Some of the great VCs really do have a mental model that they can articulate; the balance of the great VCs don't have one that they can (or choose) to articulate. However, most of the not-so-great VCs will have 'something else' that they use to frame their investing."[59]

Some leading professionals conclude that strategy in venture firms is ever evolving and opportunistic, at times developed to appease investors. "If you had no strategy and great returns, the investors would not care; and why should they? Just do good deals."[60] Rozenblit, who managed investments for a European financial services firm, too, concluded that strategy did not matter to their firm. "Of the four criteria we used: strategy, track record, business sustainability, and alignment of interest—strategy was the least important. I believe many strategies are the same, and if a GP has truly ground-breaking strategy, he or she should go to Goldman Sachs, who is sophisticated enough to understand it and would gladly fund the whole thing. Our risk profile was to be on the lower side of the experimentation," he chuckles. Gus Long says, "If a GP proposes something really novel and unique but the returns are mediocre, no LP will be interested. The novelty needs to be matched with performance." Naturally, when a strategy is unproven, LPs are the ones who bear the risk. Thus, while strategy is important, a word of caution to GPs: Avoid anything too exotic or untimely. If your investment strategy is aligned with market, LPs will listen.

Advice to GPs: If at all your strategy drifts, try not to be like Mae West. Make sure that the performance speaks for the rationale of drift.

MARKET TIMING

Any investment strategy is based on a premise that the market conditions are ripe, ready to be exploited by entrepreneurs. But the LPs need to be ready as well. Too early and LPs will neither understand nor engage—too late and you fall in the me-too category. Market timing is critical when it comes to fund-raising. Let us consider the inherent drivers of market opportunity. If we understand these well, the timing of the fund raise can be planned effectively.

Do structural shifts in the market create new investment opportunities? Management guru Peter Drucker would say yes. Drucker defines systematic innovation as the "purposeful and organized search for changes, and ... systematic analysis of the opportunities such changes might offer."[61] He outlines seven sources of innovative opportunity and agrees that the lines between these sources are blurred and overlap considerably. (See Table 2.9.) Opportunity is embedded in four sources (the unexpected, incongruity, process needs, and structural changes), and three external factors (demographics, changes in perception, and new knowledge) are drivers of opportunity.[62] How does this approach compare with Cowan's road map? Can this be a foundation for creating future road maps?

It is not so much as identifying the market opportunity but tying the opportunity in a cohesive manner with the GPs' expertise and their ability to execute such an investment strategy. After all, LPs expect a bit more from GPs than just identifying the opportunity. As Bob Dylan once sang in "Subterranean Homesick Blues," "You don't need a weatherman to know which way the wind blows."

While market timing is critical for making investments, raising the fund in a strong market is equally important. If the management team and investment strategy are aligned, chances are you could raise a fund, correct? Wrong! A critical element of the strategy relates to the timing of the fund raise. Investors are quick to point out that in any fund document, *"Why you?" is not a sufficient condition. The question "Why now?"—why is your strategy relevant in the present market conditions?—is equally important.* "The one variable that we cannot control—the black swan in the room—is the state of the market," explains De Ponte. "Ten years ago, LPs were in

TABLE 2.9 Drucker's Seven Sources for Innovative Opportunity: Can These Create Investment Opportunities for GPs?

Sources	Definition	Examples
Unexpected	Unexpected events, successes, or failures lead to opportunity	General Motors bankruptcy, Tesla Motors IPO, A123 Systems IPO
Incongruities	Discrepancy or dissonance between "what is" and "what ought to be"; composed of four areas: (1) economic realities of an industry (marketplace), (2) other realities of an industry (optimization of local, nonessential areas rather than system optimization), (3) customer expectations versus the industry perception of customer expectations, (4) internal incongruity with a process	Oil prices, organic foods, and buy-local consumer demand
Process Needs	Missing links or unmet needs in a process that could make the process cheaper, easier, or technologically or economically possible	Biofuels, streaming video on demand, voice-over-IP
Industry and market structures	Changes in industry or market such as new competitors, new customers, more differentiated products, new manufacturing or marketing processes, new substitute, or complementary products or services	E-commerce/Web-based technologies in retail, distribution, auctions, and information arbitrage; outsourcing to low-cost regions creates new competitors
Changes in demographics	Changes in population structure, age structure, cultural composition, employment, education, and income	China and India consumer/economic growth, health care investments in United States due to aging population
Changes in perception	Perceptional shift: "the glass is half full" versus "the glass is half empty"	Energy becomes a hot sector and then cools off
New knowledge	Discovery of new knowledge such as a new technology or materials	Facebook as a gaming platform, touchscreens, solar cells, voice-over-IP

Source: Adapted from Peter F. Drucker, *Innovation and Entrepreneurship* (Oxford: Butterworth-Heinemann, 1985).

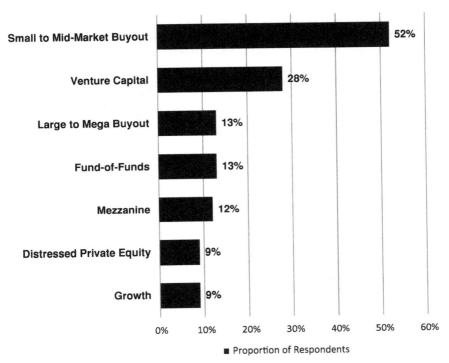

FIGURE 2.10 What the LPs Seek in 2011
Source: Preqin, 2011. Survey of 100 global leading institutional investors.

a stampede to put their money in venture capital. On other days, investors' interests shift: nothing looks better than distressed debt or secondaries." "From time to time we have a market-driven and opportunistic approach within our generally structured portfolio architecture. For example, we have invested in a smaller fund that targets distressed U.S. financial institutions, something we would not have done three years ago,"[63] remarks Christophe Nicolas, executive director, Morgan Stanley Alternative Investment Partners, a fund-of-funds that manages over $6.5 billion. Figure 2.10 shows how various subasset classes within private equity compete for LPs' capital.

Certain market conditions can accelerate the LP decision-making process. Thus, market timing is an important element that often defines outcomes for a fund. Time and again, in unfavorable markets, proven funds have struggled to raise capital. Menlo Ventures raised Fund XI at $400 million in 2010 in tougher market conditions. Its Fund X was at least $1.2 billion.

In favorable market conditions, if the investors seek to rebalance their portfolios or reduce their commitments, it is likely that a GP may not have much traction in fund-raise discussions. "We have exited our relationships on several occasions when we are overweighted in certain categories. At times, we find that the number of relationships cannot be monitored effectively," says Van Heel. On other occasions, GPs tend to be highly opportunistic in timing the raise of a new fund. "I get a chuckle when I receive a PPM right after a big exit has occurred. I mean, the IRR looks fantastic, but most LPs look past the short-term good news," quips one LP.

Thus, for any GP getting ready to raise their next fund, market timing of sectorial shifts are important. But the amplitude of these shifts needs to be closely timed with LP sentiment. While the cleantech opportunity resurfaced, fewer LPs were as enthusiastic as they once were. After all, what good is any market with plenty of fund opportunities but no LPs?

FUND SIZE AND PORTFOLIO CONSTRUCTION VIS-À-VIS FUND STRATEGY

Several technology-focused funds are shifting gears toward raising smaller funds. Whether this is a possible function of a tougher fund-raising environment or an awakening of sorts, the industry seems to be leaning toward the belief that smaller is better. Josh Kopelman, managing partner of First Round Capital, in an interview with TIFF,[64] explains why a smaller fund size is more relevant for VC investments: "Take a typical $400 million fund today. To get a 20 percent return over six years, you have to triple your capital, turning $400 million into $1.2 billion. Now, it's going to take longer than six years, and you have to add fees and carry, so that $400 million fund roughly has to return $1.5 billion to the investors to get a 20 percent return. On exit, that fund will own at most 20 percent of a company—the founder owns some, and there are multiple VCs, but on average it's about 20 percent. That means that a $400 million VC fund has to create $7.5 billion of market value to return $1.5 billion to its LPs in order to deliver a 20 percent return." Fund sizes are not necessarily determined by GPs in a vacuum, but by market conditions and LP appetite.

Portfolio construction design factors in the size and timing of investments with the view to balancing cash flows and minimizing risk. Portfolio construction design involves:

- Total number of companies, typically a range, say 8 to 12. For technology funds this range tends to be higher at 20 to 30 companies.
- Average total investment amount per company, typically around 10 percent of the fund.

■ Average investment amount at the point of entry. Typically, this would be one-third of the average total investment per company.

■ Stage of investment: Seed, early, or growth stages demand differing amounts of capital and offer differing risk-return profiles.

■ Staging of investments: Seasoned firms choose the riskier companies earlier in the investment life cycle, while as the fund matures, they shift toward more mature companies.

Consider a portfolio construction strategy of a Midwest-based early-stage life sciences company. At Arboretum Ventures I, a fund of $20 million was established to focus on the health care sector. This fund size would allow investments of up to $2 million in 8 to 10 early-stage companies. A technology fund is expected to invest in as many as 25 to 30 companies, as the sector is capital efficient in comparison. On the other end of the spectrum is a large fund such as Norwest Venture Partners (NVP). NVP's current fund is $1.2 billion in size, and it targets multi-stage (venture and growth stage) companies. The risk-return profile for each of these stages is different. The size of the fund vis-à-vis the investment strategy is an important consideration for LPs. Funds that have stellar teams but cannot raise a suitable size fund have fallen by the wayside, especially in the biotech and pharma sector. Smaller funds are perceived to be riskier, as they may not be able to protect their positions in follow-on investments.

A rule of thumb is to reserve approximately 10 percent of the fund for each portfolio company while target building a portfolio of 10 to 12 companies. While the life of the fund is legally established for 10 years, the capital is deployed during the investment period, typically the first five years. GPs actively seek to invest and build the portfolio during this period. A fund portfolio that minimizes risk and generates returns within a reasonable time frame is desirable. GPs aspire to generate returns rapidly, say, within four to six years from the time of investment. However, certain sectors and market cycles follow established patterns of capital needs and exit timing.

From this set of parameters, the partners need to ensure the following portfolio construction aspects:

■ *Source efficiently*: The quality of an existing portfolio determines the probability and timing of the raise of the next fund. Venture investors normally invest in about 1 percent of the companies they review. This means that the practitioners will need to review an average of 1,000 companies, if not more, to achieve the desired portfolio size of, say, 10 companies. That is an average of one company a day! Thus, the territory ought to be fertile with opportunities.

TABLE 2.10 Sample Investment Outlay for a $100 Million Fund

Total fund size (million):	$100.0
Total investable capital net of fees (million):*	$83.5
Target portfolio size (# of companies):	10
Average investment amount per company (million):	$8.35

	Y1	Y2	Y3	Y4	Y5
Number of new investments	4	3	2	1	
Amount per investment (millions)	$2.5	$2.5	$2.5	$2.5	
Subtotal—Capital Invested (A)	$10	$7.5	$5.0	$2.5	
Number of follow-on investments		2	2	2	1
Amount per follow-on investment (millions)		$6.0	$9.0	$9.25	$10.0
Subtotal—Capital Invested (B)		$12.0	$18.0	$18.5	$10.0
Total Invested (A+B) (millions)	$10	$19.5	$23	$21	$10
Amount invested as percent of investable capital	11.98	23.35	27.54	25.15	11.98
Cumulative amount invested (percent)	11.98	35.33	62.87	88.02	100

*Fees are calculated as 2.5 percent for years 1 through 5, followed by 2.25 percent in year 6 and 1.75 percent in year 7.

- *Build a quality portfolio*: In about four to five years from closing, a fund's portfolio is fully constructed. Table 2.10 demonstrates an outlay plan for investments. Ideally, toward later years, GPs seek opportunities where an exit is likely to occur within a shorter time frame. For emerging managers, the ability to find a company that yields a strong exit in a three- to five-year window is critical. Else you run the risk of staying stunted.
- *Prepare for losses:* A good portfolio manager knows which companies to keep and which ones to let go. Many a GP has struggled with portfolio companies that cannot meet their value-creation milestones, or raise additional follow-on rounds of capital, or generate target returns in a time span of, say, five to seven years. The faster you recognize those losses, the better it is.

  In constructing the portfolio, GPs often fall in love with their own cooking and ignore obvious signs of a downward trajectory. A number of factors—ego, saving face, good capital following bad—can stall this process and become a sinkhole. As David Cowan says, "Just focus on your top five—the rest is distraction." The harder part of the investor's discipline is to know when to quit.

A seasoned practitioner, Seth Rudnick of Canaan Partners, points out that risk is inherent in this business and calls for disciplined balance that any LP would expect. "Despite all the foresight and hindsight that you can muster, you can still go wrong. And that is the difficulty of being in this business. The environment can get you, markets can get you, technology can get you, regulatory agencies can get you. You have to constantly scan all of those things and be willing to adjust your own sense of what's a reasonable outcome and move the company into a position where it has the maximum chance to succeed. And that is a lot of work. If you see a portfolio company consistently struggle and stumble, as a board member you may feel compelled to continue to work on that company. But as a venture investor you may ponder 'I can't make this work anymore and should let it die. I should rather turn my efforts to something I can make work.' And that's hard for practitioners. The intrinsic belief to throw a little more energy and a little more time into it may not necessarily save the company.'"

- *Time is your enemy*: Portfolio companies always take twice as much capital and twice as long to exit. Early-stage companies rarely meet milestones as planned and always burn cash faster than anticipated. If the capital markets are frozen and no exit is foreseen, raising additional capital can be difficult. Most early-stage investors are wary of "future financing risk" where they have lost preferences and ownership position in portfolio companies. External factors and market conditions are bound to augment this risk. Establish a contingency plan. LPs seek real-life experience where GPs were able to protect their investment in such circumstances. Have a realistic estimate of capital needs for each company to reach break-even. For a $20 million fund, the maximum investment per company would be capped at $2 million. Thus, the investment strategy of such a fund should describe how the capital flows into an opportunity would be staged. Staging and prudent management of reserve capital ensure that milestones are met and the overall ownership is preserved right up to the exit point.
- *And finally, not all exits will be equal*: Not all exits are going to be IPOs, as much as you wish. Staged investments minimize risk but also reduce the potential returns. See Tables 2.11 and 2.12, which demonstrate how the returns and dilution vary by stage of investment. In Table 2.12, the investors' ownership dropped from 30 percent to ~10 percent while value moved upward. This was in a frothy market so it is prudent to down rounds, expect higher dilutions when markets are not supportive.

"The portfolio is your strategy in action: you can touch the portfolio, taste it, and see it. I spend a lot of my time visiting portfolio companies.

TABLE 2.11 Target Returns for Various Stages of Investment: Exit Value of $100 Million

Round	Typical Investment Amount	Target Multiple	Required Ownership at Investment	Required Ownership at Exit	Implied Pre-Money	Implied Post-Money
Series A	$2 million	10X	43.5%	20%	$2.6 million	$4.6 million
Series B	$6 million	5X	39.5%	30%	$9.2 million	$15.2 million
Series C	$12 million	2X	24%	24%	$64 million	$76 million

Source: Adapted from Dr. David Brophy, University of Michigan Business School, Center for Venture Capital and Private Equity Finance.

I can tell when something is going well, and the portfolio companies share the value of VC and how it is actualized. This is the prism: I see the whole symphony being played out, and hopefully it is a harmonious interplay of the various elements" says Chris Douvos of TIFF.

Lisa Edgar of Top Tier Capital Partners summarizes the art of portfolio management succinctly: "As experienced LPs, our decision-making process relies upon pattern recognition in order to identify the characteristics of success and of failure—something GPs should be able to do, too. What I'm looking for is the fund manager's view of which companies look like winners and which companies aren't quite cutting it, so that they can manage the portfolio to support only those that deserve additional capital. I understand this is an extremely difficult exercise—especially for very early-stage companies or when the outcome is truly binary, like with many health care investments. I would suggest that picking the winners from the

TABLE 2.12 Dilution over Rounds: A Seed Investor Could Be Diluted as Much as 3x to 6x by the Time of Exit

Round	Pre-Money Valuation ($M)	Amount Invested ($M)	Post-Money Valuation ($M)	Dilution of Equity for Seed Investor	Cash-on-Cash Return
Seed	4.6	2.0	6.6	30.3%	284.4X
Series A	17.0	8.0	25.0	19.5%	75X
Series B	69.4	10.1	79.5	16.3%	23X
Series C	135.1	21.0	156.1	13.2%	12X
IPO	1,802.7	73.5	1876.2	10.2%	N/A

Source: "Valuing pre-revenue companies," Angel Capital Education Foundation (ACEF), Kauffman Foundation, accessed February 6, 2011, www.angelcapital association.org.

losers—and more importantly, effectively managing the fund's capital—is specifically the role of the GP (and for which the limited partners pay a management fee)....I want to know how the VC's micro views on each company and macro view of the exit environment is directing overall capital allocation. That's what we call 'portfolio management,' and to LPs, effective portfolio management is one of the core criteria we use to evaluate managers."[65]

FIT WITHIN THE LP's CURRENT PORTFOLIO

Any institutional investor manages a number of portfolio relationships. Capital is allocated in various asset classes to balance risk and returns. In *Beyond the J Curve: Managing a Portfolio of Venture Capital and Private Equity Funds*, authors Thomas Meyer and Pierre-Yves Mathonet point out that institutional LPs typically follow either a combination of a top-down approach or a bottom-up approach.[66] In a top-down approach, an LP would start with picking a sector (technology or life sciences), geographic region (Silicon Valley, Beijing, Israel), fund style (PE, VC, buyout), and stage (early, mezzanine, multistage). A bottom-up approach is opportunistic and starts with identifying suitable funds, conducting a thorough analysis, performing due diligence, and completing the investment. Most LPs tend to blend these two approaches. "We look at every prospective deal in two ways: first in isolation, to see that it stands on its own merits; and secondly we see how the deal fits in the context of our existing portfolio. We obviously do not want to load the portfolio with a lot of [GPs] pursuing the same strategy, but there are areas where we are actively seeking greater levels of exposure," Peter Keehn, head of alternative investments, Allstate Investments, managing $120 billion in assets, once stated in an interview with AltAssets.[67]

The matrix of relationships is vast and intricate, as seen in Figure 2.11; thus, any GP ought to qualify a target LP vis-à-vis his or her current portfolio. While no LP publicly discloses their portfolio, Van Heel suggests a simple approach: "We are trying to build our relationships, like everyone else. If I get an e-mail asking whether we are looking to invest in early-stage technology funds, I would have little hesitation in responding with candor."

Bob Clone, who managed a PE portfolio at a $50 billion state pension fund, noted, "We design our portfolio but in general, we have always found room to accommodate a good opportunity. We have a top-down approach with subgroups within private equity such as venture, buyout, mezzanine, distressed debt, and growth equity. When we add a new fund, my allocation moves from 9 percent to 10 percent so it does not make a significant

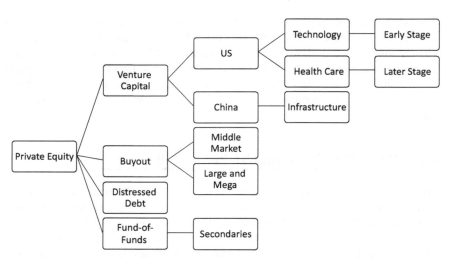

FIGURE 2.11   Sample LP's PE Portfolio—A Crowded Dinner Table

difference. But if we are overweighted, say, I have eight biotech firms, we are not going for the ninth, obviously. We do watch allocations within each subgroup but ensure we are balanced."

Chris Douvos points out the challenges of new entrants in any LP's portfolio: "All my GPs are like my children: I love them all, but they all keep me up at night for different reasons. But I have a limited amount of money. At my dinner table, I can ladle out only so much soup. If you want to come for dinner, I have to send one kid off to college or juvenile hall—my table is a crowded one. If you are doing the same old thing, it's not compelling. What is it about your voodoo that would make me send one of my kids packing?"

Any LP invests a considerable amount of time in building a portfolio of GP relationships. "LPs have invested the effort, completed the due diligence, and committed to the marriage," says Gus Long. The easier thing for any LP to do is to commit additional capital to an existing relationship: a re-up. A new manager means more work, more risk, and more uncertainty for any LP. Thus, for most GPs, the competition is not from other new funds competing to get in, but from the existing relationships—or, as Douvos puts it, a crowded dinner table. In a 2010 survey, Preqin polled 100 leading institutional investors across the globe and only 44 percent of the LPs stated they would consider new GP relationships. In all likelihood, these LPs would have sent some of their GPs packing, either due to performance or alignment of interests.

WHY LPs TERMINATE EXISTING RELATIONSHIPS

Catherine Crockett, founder of Grove Street Advisors, a $6.8 billion fund-of-funds, says, "Terminating a relationship is the hardest part." Crockett and her team screen over 500 PPMs and deploy $500 million in any given year. "The primary reasons for terminating a relationship are performance, partners' motivations, and fund size."

- *Fund performance:* When performance falters, the decision is easy. No re-ups; it is an easy good-bye.
- *Partners' motivations and alignment:* As partners become successful, they lose their motivation—bloated senior partners with decreasing appetite should stay on the couch, not in the PPM. They are not an asset in this business. Ensuring that the rewards are shared with all investment committee and junior members is important. Finally, partners need to stay current with the market and technology developments.
- *Fund size:* Successful funds grow too big too fast. LPs worry that with bloated funds, finding the right investment opportunities and generating returns will be harder. Small is beautiful, indeed. While success breeds success, and as more LPs try to kick down the doors, the smarter LPs quietly exit through the side doors.

In a dynamic world, markets change and the ability to generate returns changes. "If the three variables: investment team, investment strategy, and the market environment are static, it is easy to make re-up decisions. But these are in a state of perpetual flux," adds Lisa Edgar.

SUMMARY

While there are no barriers to entry, raising a venture fund is not for the fainthearted. If the partners have a strong investment, entrepreneurial, or operational background, and can develop a compelling investment strategy, and, most importantly, launch the fund in a supportive market, the friction can be minimized.

Fund-raising is an extremely competitive exercise. Consider the fact that more than 460 VC funds were on the road in 2010 seeking aggregate commitments of $80 billion.[68] LPs will eventually invest only about a third of that, or $25 billion. What are your differentiators that will ensure you are in this chosen pool?

First-time funds have limited probability of raising funds with institutional investors, but are looked on favorably by some funds of funds. History shows that fund managers who started small, raised capital from high-net-worth individuals and local foundations, and built a track record were able to achieve liftoff. Their performance helped them raise their next fund.

GPs love those entrepreneurs who invest their own capital in start-ups. LPs love when GPs demonstrate such behavior themselves. It is called alignment of interest. A GP sure should make money, but the LP comes first. And if a GP brings its own capital to the mix, preferably more than 1 percent, all the better.

A new fund is always scrutinized to the highest degree. The amount of diligence is an order of magnitude higher: track record, references, and such. "We put every piece of relevant information in the data room and let the LPs slice it any way they want," says Ravi Mohan of Shasta Ventures. "We did not pick a list of references but rather said, here are *all* the people we worked with. We did not cherry-pick—we let them decide who to call." In the end, it paid off. Shasta raised its Fund I in six months. The fund was oversubscribed.

The LP courtship process is a long and slow dance: As most LPs say, introductions are the best way to start. The role of a placement agent can be critical. And for new managers, the typical time line from the first touch to an LP commitment is about 12 months or as long as three years.

If you choose to get too clever on that attribution or find creative ways to squeeze yourself into the top quartile rankings, do so at your own risk. Rather, just offer the data and let the LP do the analysis. After all, your LP is smarter than you are, just like every venture capitalist is smarter than the average entrepreneur.

Finally, good GPs work hard to generate returns—for the subsequent funds, their performance drives the business and LPs come knocking at their doors. KPCB Fund I returned about 40x; Benchmark Fund I generated a 92x return. I am positive their Fund II raise was much easier. Aim for returns in that range—LPs will come to you in droves.

CHAPTER 3

Terms of Investment: The Limited Partnership Agreement

Terms are important but seldom the primary drivers of investment decisions. As they say, terms never make a poor firm look good nor make a good firm unattractive.
—Kelly Williams, managing director and head, Customized Fund Investment Group, Credit Suisse Fund of Funds

The terms of an LP-GP relationship primarily revolve around alignment of financial interests—ensuring the GPs are focused on the larger goal of generating returns for LPs.

A typical fund offering document, called the private placement memorandum (PPM), will include the fund's investment strategy, the GP's background and expertise, and market opportunity. In successful firms, these elements combine to create a compelling investment opportunity for LPs. The fund's limited partnership agreement (LPA) is the legal document that contains legal terms that describe the control, management, financial investment, and distribution of returns.

Howard J. Beber is a partner at Proskauer Rose, one of the leading international law firms that has built a strong brand based on representing sponsors of private investment funds as well as LPs that invest in alternative assets. Having spent over 13 years representing private investment funds and institutional investors, Beber has reviewed many of the top investment funds on behalf of both GPs and LPs. This experience translates into valuable insights in forming funds, understanding fund terms, drafting partnership and GP documents, negotiating with investors, and advising on internal GP and management issues. With respect to investors' appetite for VC, Beber reports, "Despite the challenging market conditions, a number of LPs are still interested in VC as an asset class. While recent 10-year returns lag behind comparable asset classes, many view historic returns over a longer time span as attractive. LPs view continuing innovation and value creation, particularly in technology and life sciences sectors, as primary drivers to stay in this asset class."[1] Beber also notes that the industry is contracting, and for those firms fortunate enough to survive, the LPs are exerting their ability to negotiate terms aggressively. After all, the supply-demand relationship has tilted back in the favor of the LPs for any VC firm other than those in the very top tier of the asset class.

In the sections that follow, Beber shares his insights on the various terms commonly negotiated between GPs and LPs. Needless to say, none of what appears here is legal advice; rather, please view it as an expert's insights and observations.

SAMPLE TERMS IN A FUND'S PPM

The various terms in any GP-LP relationship are structured to meet the objectives shown in Table 3.1.

A short summary of key terms is usually included at the beginning of a fund's PPM. The terms attempt to balance various issues that may arise between GPs and LPs during the course of business. Beber points out that for managers who are just starting out, the "middle of the fairway" is usually the best approach.

General Partner

ABC Ventures, a Delaware limited partnership (the "General Partner"), whose General Partner will be ABC Management, LLC.

Comments: Tax, regulatory, and legal issues typically dictate the fund's jurisdiction. Delaware is a standard choice for domestic funds. For funds investing outside the United States, the Cayman Islands, Channel Islands, and Luxembourg are popular jurisdictions of formation.

Investment Objective

To achieve superior investment returns from investments in equity and equity-related securities in companies in the [sector] and [sector]-related companies.

Comment: This is typical boilerplate language.

TABLE 3.1   Terms in a Fund's PPM

Objective	Terms
Describe the basic financial structure	Fund size, term, management fees, minimum contributions, and GP commitment
Describe the flow of investment capital and any restrictions	Drawdowns, reinvestments, investment limitations, defaults, co-investments
Determine how investments are made	GP Investment Committee
Describe the flow of returns from the GP back to the LP	Allocation of profits and losses, distributions, GP clawback
Describe the management and governance of the fund	Key person event, investment period termination or suspension, no-fault divorce or GP removal, for-cause termination or GP removal, transfer of LP interests and withdrawal, reports, parallel funds and successor funds, audit
Other legal, taxation, and regulatory matters	Liability of LPs, indemnification, employee benefit plan regulations, public disclosure issues, tax-exempt investors, non-U.S. investors

Offering

The partnership is seeking $100 million of capital commitments from limited partners ("Capital Commitments"), with a maximum of $150 million in Capital Commitments. The General Partner will invest an amount equal to at least 5 percent of the total Capital Commitments of all partners on the same schedule as the limited partners of the Fund (the "Limited Partners").

Comments: LPs view the fund size in conjunction with fund investment strategy and the size of the investment team. For example, a fund focused on investments in the drug discovery/pharmaceuticals sector needs more capital per investment as compared to a software/technology-focused fund. The stage of investment matters as well.

Financial Commitment of GPs: While the industry norm has historically been 1 percent, LPs are now seeking higher investments, especially from unproven GPs. This ensures alignment of interest or "skin in the game." "It is no longer 'yes, it's 1 percent—check the box and move to the next term.' LPs are demanding that the commitment be a meaningful portion of the GP's net worth. A 3 to 5 percent commitment usually gets it over the threshold," says Beber, but LPs also need to be sensitive and recognize that the situation for each GP may be different. There is no cookie-cutter approach, as each GP comes from a different background.

LPs are also concerned if GPs try to roll in their management fees as part of the GP commitment. "You cannot play with the house money before the game has begun," as one LP remarked.

Maximum size of fund: In times when fund-raising is easier, GPs may wish to raise larger funds, but LPs have a valid concern as to whether a fund manager can properly manage an oversized fund.

Multiple funds: If the GPs manage an existing fund, LPs may seek to understand the existing fund's investment period, commitments, fees, and its impact on the proposed fund's fees. It is typical for GPs to be permitted to raise a new fund when an existing fund is about 70 percent invested.

Minimum Investment

The minimum investment is $3,000,000 from institutions and $500,000 from individuals, provided that the General Partner may accept subscriptions for smaller amounts at its sole discretion.

Comment: Percentage of investment: Typically, if in the enviable position to be able to select LPs, GPs prefer to cap any LP's position to no more than 10 percent to 15 percent of the fund to ensure LP diversity.

Institutional Limitations

To minimize the number of relationships, several LPs have a floor—a minimum investment amount—due to the size of the assets under management (AUM). For a $50 billion pension fund, a $5 million investment is inefficient due to the amount of work involved to perform due diligence on the investment. To make the fund-raising process efficient, GPs need to target appropriate LPs and consider their AUM.

Drawdowns

Drawdowns may occur on an as-needed basis with a minimum of 10 days' notice, provided that the initial drawdown may be required upon five business days' notice. No more than 35 percent of the capital may be called in any 12-month period.

Timing: Once a GP finds a suitable investment opportunity, a "capital call" is made that alerts the LPs to wire transfer their pro-rata share to the fund.

The GP's portfolio construction plan and investment period are to be taken into consideration alongside this clause. On average, a GP projects to invest about 15 to 20 percent of the total committed capital each year over an investment period that lasts for three to five years.

Amount: Due to cash flow considerations and to ensure vintage year diversity, some LPs prefer that a ceiling be placed on the maximum amount that will be "called" or invested in any given year.

Eligibility

Accredited investors only.

Comments: Each LP would sign an accredited investor form stating that it conforms to the SEC guidelines governing accredited investors and understands the risks involved with the investment. As required under the securities laws, this clause protects "that little old lady" from buying a security she does not understand. As one LP advised a GP, "Try not to be on the SEC's speed dial list."

Management Fees

An annual Management Fee will be paid quarterly in advance by the Fund and shall equal 2.50 percent of Capital Commitments commencing upon the initial closing. Beginning on its sixth anniversary, the Management Fee shall be reduced in each future year of the Fund by 10 percent. The Management Fees are reduced by the cost basis of the securities sold, distributed, or written off.

Comments: *Percentage:* 2.0 to 2.5 percent in venture is standard; 2.0 percent is typically the maximum in private equity, with lower percentages for larger funds.

Duration: LPs prefer that these fees ratchet down each year after the investment period. GPs try to establish a minimum floor percentage to make sure there are adequate fees to support the ongoing efforts toward the end of the life of the fund.

Other considerations: LPs typically insist on language stating that fees be reduced when a successor fund is formed. The fees are also typically reduced if any compensation or fees are received by the GP from portfolio companies.

Beber points out that alignment of interests is key. "Management fee streams from multiple funds have always caused some LP heartburn."

As shown in Table 3.2, the amount of investable capital varies as the structure and timing of fees vary. None of these scenarios take into account any exits or write-offs, which typically impact the fee amounts.

TABLE 3.2 Fund Management Fee Vesting Scenarios

Year	1–5	6	7	8	9	10	Total GP Fees ($M)	Investable Capital ($M)
Scenario 1	2.5	2.5	2.5	2.5	2.5	2.5	25.00	75.00
Scenario 2	2.5	2.25	1.75	1.5	1.25	1	20.25	79.75
Scenario 3	2.25	1.8	1.44	1.15	0.92	0.73	17.30	82.70
Scenario 4	2.5						12.50	87.50

In Scenario 1, the fees stay flat at 2.5 percent of the committed capital. This is unlikely—a GP dream scenario—but is presented for illustration.

In Scenario 2, the fees drop by 10 percent after year 5, or the investment period.

In Scenario 3, the fees start at 2.25 percent and drop by 20 percent after year 5.

In Scenario 4, the fees drop to zero after year 5. This example is atypical and is extracted from a single LP (government-sponsored) fund PPM.

Seth Levine, managing director, The Foundry Group, a leading technology fund based in Colorado, says, "Good GPs think of management fee as a loan against carried interest. Carry is paid on the full fund value, not net of fees. Any fees you take out are effectively loans against future performance." For the Institutional Limited Partners Association (ILPA) members, such expressions can be music to their ears.

Allocations

The cumulative net income and gains of the partnership will be allocated 80 percent to all partners in proportion to their contributed capital and 20 percent to the General Partner. Cumulative net losses, if any, generally will be allocated to all partners in proportion to their contributed capital. For this purpose, cumulative net income, gains and losses, will include unrealized profits and losses on securities distributed in kind, and all partnership expenses attributable to portfolio investments (which expenses shall include the Management Fee, but will not include income, gain, or loss from temporary investments of idle cash). Income, gain, and loss from such temporary investments will be allocated to all partners in proportion to their contributed capital.

Comments: Percentage: Industry standards have established that 80 percent of profits will be paid to LPs and 20 percent to GPs. The "A" funds in the VC industry sometimes command a higher carried interest in the 25 percent to 30 percent range. In the long run, the LP's perspective is that it would rather pay a premium carry to GPs that "earn money for them" than pay lower carry to managers that do not perform.[2] Beber points out that some firms that can no longer convince LPs to pay a premium (over 20 percent) carried interest are moving to a variable carry structure: If the return threshold exceeds, say, 2x or 3x committed capital, then the carry adjusts to 25 percent or 30 percent.

Tax Distributions

The Fund intends to make tax distributions to each partner in amounts intended to enable taxable partners to defray their income tax liability attributable to their participation in the Fund.

Comments: Any gains realized would result in taxes for both GPs and LPs. (Some LPs—for example, state pension funds—may not have tax liability due to their status.) It is common for GPs to have the authority to make "tax distributions" to partners in the event of taxable income in a calendar year that is not accompanied by a corresponding distribution. Several underlying factors affect this section and are beyond the scope of this book (e.g., fund accounting procedures, tax calculations for each LP, etc.). Suffice it to say that GPs need to be prepared to make distributions and thus plan the cash outflows.

Discretionary Distributions

Distributions of available cash from sources other than portfolio investments generally will be made to the partners in proportion to their respective contributions. Distributions of available cash from the disposition of investments in portfolio companies, as well as distributions of securities in kind, generally will be made as follows:

- First, to all partners in proportion to their respective contributions, until each partner has received an aggregate amount of distributions equal to its contribution; and
- Thereafter, in the amounts and proportions necessary to ensure (1) that the General Partner has received, as "carried interest," an amount equal to 20 percent of the Fund's cumulative net profits and (2) that all remaining amounts have been distributed to the partners, in proportion to their respective contributions.

Limited Partners may be required to return distributions previously made to them to satisfy certain Fund obligations.

Comments:

- *Amounts:* Typically for VC funds, LPs receive all their contributed capital back first, then the GPs receive 20 percent of profits, and the remaining 80 percent goes to the LPs. Other options are a total return of committed capital to LPs before the GP receives carry or a more aggressive deal-by-deal waterfall where profits from each deal are distributed 80/20.
- *Timing of distribution:* GPs may choose to distribute stock quickly if they believe the value may fall or hold it longer if the value can go up. After all, all GPs seek better IRR.

Employee Benefit Plan Regulations

The GP will use its reasonable best efforts to manage the business and affairs of the partnership so that the partnership will qualify as a venture capital operating company (VCOC) within the meaning of the Final Regulation.

If equity participation in the Fund by "benefit plan investors" is "significant" (each within the meaning of the U.S. Department of Labor regulation relating to the definition of "plan assets" under ERISA[3] (the "Plan Assets Regulation")), the General Partner will use its reasonable best efforts to manage the business and affairs of the Fund so that the Fund will qualify as a VCOC within the meaning of the Plan Assets Regulation.

Comments: If GPs receive commitments from pension funds governed by ERISA, certain regulations apply. In a nutshell, the GP needs to ensure that requirements for meeting the VCOC test are met, or commitments of such ERISA LPs should be less than 25 percent of the total fund commitments.

Tax-Exempt Investors

The General Partner will use commercially reasonable efforts to avoid causing the Fund to make any investments that would cause any tax-exempt Limited Partner to realize "unrelated business taxable income" (UBTI). Such commercially reasonable efforts will be deemed satisfied with respect to a Portfolio Investment if tax-exempt Limited Partners are given the opportunity to hold their proportionate share of the Fund's investment in such portfolio company through a blocker corporation.

Comments: This clause protects LPs that are tax-exempt institutions, such as foundations or endowments. Such LPs are subject to taxes on any income that arises from "unrelated business." GPs need to exercise caution that the fund does not conduct certain types of transactions that would generate UBTI for such LPs.

Initial Closing and Additional Closing

An initial closing will be held as soon as practicable. Thereafter, the Fund may accept additional subscriptions until the one-year anniversary of the initial closing date (the "Final Closing Date"). Any Limited Partners who are admitted at closings subsequent to the initial closing date will pay their pro rata share of any capital contributions ("Contributions") previously called down by the Fund, plus an interest equivalent amount from the date such funds were called down.

Comments: Timing: GPs are eager to conduct the "first close" so that they can start investing as well as drawing fees. It is in the mutual interest of both the GPs and the LPs to raise the full target amount in a timely manner so that the fund strategy can be executed effectively and the GPs can devote their attention to investing rather than fund-raising. A one-year fund-raising period is typical, although recently many GPs have gone back to the LPs seeking extension of this period in any challenging fund-raising environment.

Investments made prior to the final closing may act as an attractive hook for later LPs who can get a pro rata share of the investment at a later date. As the time value of money comes into effect, a nominal interest charge is often sought from LPs who invest after capital has been drawn.

Investment Period

The Fund may call capital to fund new investments from the Initial Closing Date until the fifth anniversary of the Final Closing Date (the "Investment Period"). At the end of the Investment Period, each Limited Partner will be released from any further obligations with respect to unfunded subscriptions, except to the extent necessary to (i) cover the Fund's operating expenses; (ii) complete investments in process at such time; and (iii) make follow-on investments.

Comments: LPs expect that investments will be made during a reasonable investment period (typically five to six years), after which follow-on investments are typically permitted. After the investment period, GPs are expected to harvest investments and work toward liquidity exits.

Term of the Fund

Ten years from the Final Closing Date, subject to up to two one-year extensions at the General Partner's discretion to effect an orderly liquidation of the Fund's investments.

Comments: Ten years is the standard term for a VC fund. Since management fees are typically payable during the full term, LPs generally insist on a 10-year term. Most fund terms are ultimately extended if investments remain in the portfolio. Management fees during extensions are typically negotiated.

"A joke in the industry is that the average life of a 10-year partnership is 13 years. In my experience, I have not seen a 10-year partnership end in 10 years," Beber says.

Leverage

The Fund does not intend to borrow money, other than on a short-term basis. Short-term borrowing will not exceed 10 percent of the aggregate subscriptions of all partners to the Fund ("Fund Commitments").

Comments: Leverage at the fund level is not common in a VC fund, as opposed to hedge funds that often use significant leverage.

Reinvestment of Capital

The Fund may reinvest proceeds of disposed investments, provided that the acquisition cost of all portfolio investments in portfolio companies ("Portfolio Investments") will not exceed 110 percent of Fund commitments.

Comments: Unlike hedge funds, when VC funds liquidate investments, they typically distribute proceeds to LPs. A minimum amount of "recycling" allows the GP to either withhold proceeds or distribute and recall proceeds for future investments.

Seth Levine of the Foundry Group views this clause as an opportunity where GPs can make the LPs whole with respect to management fees. "In order to actually invest your full committed capital, you have to generate returns. To me, it further reinforces that the management fee really is just a loan against profits!" To illustrate Seth's point, consider a $100 million fund with a 2 percent management fee. The GPs will generate $10 million in fees during the initial five-year investment period, leaving the investable capital at $90 million. However, the carry (and return) is calculated on the total committed capital of $100 million. Recycling allows the GP to take $10M in proceeds generated by the sale of companies and reinvest it. "So if you sell a company and generate $20 million in returns in year 5, the GP returns only $10 million to LPs and invokes the recycle provision for the other $10 million," says Seth.

Capital Contributions

Contributions generally will be drawn down from all partners pro rata based on unfunded subscriptions on an as-needed basis to fund investments and expenses of the Fund, including the Management Fee, with a minimum of ten business days' prior written notice.

Comments: This is a self-explanatory clause.

General Partner Clawback

If, after the Fund has made its final liquidating distribution, the General Partner has received aggregate distributions with respect to its carried interest in excess of 20 percent of the Fund's cumulative net profits, the General Partner will return to the Fund the amount of such excess, provided, however, that in no event shall the General Partner be required to return to the Fund an amount in excess of the aggregate distributions it has received with respect to its carried interest less income taxes attributable thereto. The underlying obligations of the partners of the General Partner with respect to such payment will be several and not joint and for each partner will be proportionate to such partner's respective share of the aggregate carried interest distribution.

Comments: One of the heavily negotiated provisions, clawback is critical to LPs to ensure that the ultimate economic deal between the GP and LPs is respected. When carry is distributed early in the life of a fund and followed by later losses, GP clawbacks are necessary to ensure that LPs get their 80 percent profits for the full portfolio at the end of the fund term. It is impossible to predict what the overall portfolio returns and fund profits will be at the end of the term. Overdistribution to GPs is likely to occur if the early successes are offset by later failures. Thus, an LP can "claw back" the shortfall amounts from GPs at the final liquidation.

GPs must take great care to plan for clawback possibilities. "I have known of GPs that have to sell their houses due to clawbacks," says Kelly DePonte of Probitas Partners. "This is a Damoclean sword that hangs over every GP's head."[4] LPs prefer that an escrow account be established combined with joint and several personal guarantees from all carry recipients.[5] Other options include annual assessments/adjustments or reduction of fees.

The clawback conditions on taxes are obvious in that LPs shall not seek to claw back the income taxes paid by the GP on the carry earned.

Naturally, neither party looks forward to triggering this clause, but it is a necessary clause for protection. An escrow account is often a suitable middle ground, where a portion of distributions are set aside for such situations.

Within GPs themselves, suitable agreements need to be established. If clawback liability is joint *and* several among the carry recipients, one GP can end up paying back another GP's profits. Ouch!

Expenses

The Management Fee will cover overhead and normal operating expenses of the Management Company, including salaries and employee benefits, office expenses, entertainment, office and equipment rental, and bookkeeping. All other expenses of the Fund, including without limitation, legal, auditing, custodial, insurance, Limited Partner Advisory Board (the "Advisory Board") expenses, annual meeting expenses, the Management Fee, and all other expenses associated with investigating and evaluating investment opportunities and with the acquisition, holding, or disposition of investments (whether or not such acquisition or disposition is consummated), will be paid from the assets of the Fund.

Comments: Note the difference between this clause (Expenses) and the following clause (Organizational Expenses). Certain operating expenses are borne by the management company or the GPs, while other expenses, including setup of the fund (or Organizational Expenses) and the legal fees thereof are borne by the fund.

Organizational Expenses

All Fund organizational expenses will be paid or reimbursed by the Fund. Such expenses are not expected to exceed $500,000.

Comments: These expenses, borne by the fund, as seen in Table 3.3 typically include the legal accounting and audit expenditures. LPs typically seek a ceiling on the amounts and types of organizational expenses borne

TABLE 3.3 Sample Expenses Split

Expenses Borne by the Fund or LPs	Expenses Borne by the Management Services Company or GPs
Organizational expenses	Operating expenses of the partnership
Legal fees, audit and accounting fees, portfolio-related expenses, liability insurance, annual meeting expenses, other extraordinary expenses (such as litigation)	Salaries, rent, and such

by the fund. The fees paid to placement agents are not usually borne by the fund, but rather borne by the management company or GPs:

Key Person Event

If, prior to the end of the Investment Period, fewer than [number of] Key Persons are devoting substantially all of their business time to the Fund and the portfolio companies, the GPs shall notify the LP Advisory Committee. Upon occurrence of a Key Person Event, all investment activities will be temporarily suspended and the GP shall have 180 days to present a plan for continuing the Fund's investment activities, including admission of an additional Key Person. If the LP Advisory Committee approves the plan, the investment activities shall resume. If the plan is not approved, then upon the vote of $66^2/_3$ percent in interest of the LPs, the suspension will become permanent and the Investment Period will terminate.

Comments: This is another heavily negotiated clause. The LPs' perspective is that if there are any changes in the core investment team, the LPs should have the right to suspend the fund's investment period or terminate the fund. The GPs, on the other hand, have an interest in continuing the entity and investment activities and may present alternate options. Some points to consider:

- Who are the "Key Persons?" What subset of partners is considered more important to execute the strategy? Are the LPs in agreement with the selection? Beber advises it is critical for LPs to identify the key persons and have adequate remedies if they are no longer managing the fund. If one or a group of key persons leaves the firm, this section comes into play.
- What is defined as the trigger for such a clause? Death, disability, and failure to devote appropriate time to the fund are standard conditions.
- After trigger, is the investment activity automatically suspended? Is the fund shut down? LPs prefer the suspension to be automatic after a triggering event, unless a plan is approved to move forward, according to Beber. They would certainly like to have a say in the replacement for the key person(s).

Investment Restrictions

The General Partner will not, without the prior approval of the Advisory Board, (i) invest more than 15 percent of Fund Commitments in the securities of any single issuer; (ii) invest in portfolio companies domiciled outside of the United States or Canada; or (iii) invest in securities that are issued by companies that, at the time of the Fund's initial investment, have any securities traded on a public securities market.

Comments: A prudent risk management and mitigation strategy, this provision prevents strategy drift and forces portfolio diversification.

Defaults

Failure by any Limited Partner to fund any portion of a subscription when due or otherwise make a payment when due will result in such remedies and penalties as the General Partner may pursue or impose on such Limited Partner on behalf of the Fund as set forth in the Fund Agreement, including the forfeiture of all or a substantial portion of such Limited Partner's interest in the Fund.

Comments: A GP-friendly term that ensures the LP will respond to capital calls or face the consequences. Rarely have GPs taken strong legal action against defaulting LPs, as doing so jeopardizes the future prospectus and creates reputational risk. Typically, GPs have the right to charge interest, assess default penalties, or sell the defaulting LP's rights to another LP.

Time and Attention Requirements

Prior to the earliest to occur of (i) the date on which at least 70 percent of Fund Commitments have been invested, expended, committed, or reserved for future investments in existing portfolio companies or reasonably anticipated Fund expenses; (ii) the end of the Investment Period; or (iii) the date of the Fund's dissolution (the earlier of (i), (ii) or (iii), the "Full Time Period"), the Principals will devote substantially all of their business time to the affairs and activities of the Fund and related entities unless otherwise approved by the Advisory Board. Subsequent to such time, the Principals will devote such business time to the Fund as may be reasonably necessary to manage its affairs and activities.

Comment: This LP-friendly term ensures that GPs stay focused on generating returns for LPs and do not wander about to other sources of income.

Transferability of Interests and Withdrawal

Limited Partners will be restricted in their ability to withdraw from the Fund except in limited instances to comply with laws or regulations specifically applicable to a Limited Partner. A Limited Partner may assign, sell, exchange, or transfer its interest in the Fund only with the consent of the General Partner.

Comments: Allows LPs to transfer interests with GP consent—not much debate here. On the contrary, LPs typically negotiate for significant restrictions on ownership transfers of the GP's interests.

Exculpation and Indemnification

In general, none of the General Partners, the Management Company, the Principals, the members of the Advisory Board, or any members, partners, employees, directors, officers, agents, or affiliates thereof (the "Indemnitees") will be liable to the Fund or any partner for any act or omission by it, except for acts or omissions that are not committed in good faith and not reasonably believed to be in the best interests of the Fund or constitute gross negligence, fraud, or willful malfeasance. In general, the Fund will indemnify each Indemnitee against any loss, damage, or expense incurred by it on behalf of or in connection with the affairs of the Fund, except to the extent that the underlying act or omission is not committed in good faith and not reasonably believed to be in the best interests of the Fund; constitutes gross negligence, fraud, or willful malfeasance; or is criminal in nature and such Indemnitee had cause to believe beyond a reasonable doubt that such conduct was unlawful. The General Partner may have the Fund purchase, at the Fund's expense, insurance to cover any indemnification obligation.

Comment: A GP-friendly clause designed to protect the GP from legal issues.

Parallel Funds

The General Partner may establish one or more parallel limited partnerships ("Parallel Funds") to address the needs of certain investors or to address tax, regulatory, or other issues, including compliance with the Investment Company Act of 1940, as amended. If any such Parallel Funds are established, such partnerships and the Fund generally will operate in parallel, participate proportionately in all investment opportunities, and share proportionately in all investment expenses.

Comment: Parallel funds are sometimes established to meet legal or tax needs of certain investors.

Successor Fund

Without the prior written consent of a majority in interest of the Limited Partners of the Fund and the limited partners of any parallel funds collectively, neither the General Partner nor any principal will begin investing on behalf of another investment fund with investment objectives substantially similar to that of the Fund (other than a Parallel Fund) until the end of the Full Time Period.

Comment: LPs seek to ensure that the GPs cannot invest from a new fund until substantial capital commitments, say, about 70 percent of the current fund, have been deployed.

Reports

The General Partner will provide Limited Partners with (i) quarterly reports, including unaudited financial statements and the balances in partners' capital accounts, after the end of each of the first three quarters in each fiscal year; (ii) an annual report, including audited financial statements, after the end of each fiscal year; and (iii) tax information necessary for the preparation of U.S. federal income tax returns after the end of each fiscal year. Limited Partners will be required to keep such reports and all other Fund information strictly confidential.

Comments: This is boilerplate language. Quarterly reports, annual reports, and meeting and capital account statements are ways a limited partner tracks how the fund is performing. In some situations, the LPs rarely meet with the GPs: They solely rely on the quality of reports. As one LP quipped, "The best form of GP communications are large and frequent distributions of cash. Most other forms of communication are superfluous."[6]

Advisory Board

The Fund will have an Advisory Board comprised of three representatives of the Limited Partners. The Advisory Board will meet with the General Partner periodically to discuss the Fund's investments and strategy. The Advisory Board will also have the authority to approve transactions involving conflicts of interest and to approve waivers of certain investment restrictions.

Comments: This is an LP-friendly clause to keep the GPs in check and to help resolve potential conflicts of interest. Larger LPs are typically invited to serve on advisory boards. Advisory boards rarely get too involved except when a special situation arises: for example, Fund II seeks to make investment in a company that received an investment from Fund I.

Tax Matters

The Fund will be organized with the intention that it will be treated as a partnership for U.S. federal income tax purposes. Each prospective investor is advised to consult with its own tax advisor regarding the income tax considerations applicable to an investment in the Fund.

Comment: Partnership structures are designed to minimize the tax impact and avoid any double taxation.

Effectively Connected Income

The General Partner will use commercially reasonable efforts to manage the Fund so as to avoid causing any non-U.S. Limited Partner to realize income effectively connected with a U.S. trade or business for U.S. federal income tax purposes. Such commercially reasonable efforts will be deemed satisfied with respect to a Portfolio Investment if non-U.S. Limited Partners are given the opportunity to hold their proportionate share of the Fund's investment in such portfolio company through a blocker corporation.

Comment: Protects non-U.S. LPs from certain tax situations.

Risk Factors and Conflicts of Interest

An investment in the Fund involves a high degree of risk. Prospective Limited Partners should carefully review the matters discussed under "Risk Factors" and "Potential Conflicts of Interest."

Comment: This boilerplate language protects GPs from liability.

Securities Law Matters

The LP Interests are not being registered under the U.S. Securities Act of 1933, as amended, and must be acquired for investment purposes only and not with a view to the distribution thereof. Offers of LP Interests will be made only to qualified investors under applicable law.

Comments: This is more boilerplate language. Advises LPs that certain legal constraints exist on securities.

OTHER LP-GP TERMS

Other LP-GP negotiations include:

No-fault divorce: LPs can terminate the relationships with the fund without any particular reason or "fault" on either side. This certainly tilts the axis of power. Depending on the terms of the partnership agreement, the fund can thus be dissolved, the investment period can be stalled, and/or the GP can be replaced. While LPs have not misused this power, it creeps up when issues such as GP misconduct or breach may have occurred. The devil is always in the details, of course. Tax/regulatory matters, felonies, bankruptcies, negligence, and breach of agreements by GPs can trigger this clause. "In my experience, a 75 percent to 80 percent LP vote is typical for a no-fault termination of the fund," says Beber. LPs suggest that the lower the bar, the better, but most LPs are reasonable.

Side letters: All LPs are equal, but some LPs are more equal than others. Side letters provide additional clarity or describe the specific agreement (above and beyond the standard terms) between the GP and the LP. LPs know that side letters are a common theme in the business. To avoid debates regarding the GP fee calculations, one LP proposed an elegant side letter asking, "The auditors have reviewed and ascertained that the GP fees have been calculated correctly."

Strategy drift: In several LP interviews, strategy drift was brought up as a minor irritant. Strategy drift occurs when GPs claim to make investments in a certain sector and stage but later shift away from the agreed upon strategy. While most GP-LP agreements allow for up to 10 percent of capital to be invested in such "opportunistic" investments, LPs start to feel uncomfortable when a larger amount of capital starts to move into other categories. One LP chuckled, "You will be amazed what was being passed off to us as a clean-tech opportunity." Another said, "When the best returns for a GP come from the 'other' investment categories and not the primary investment thesis, it makes us wonder."

Co-investment rights: Unlike private equity investing, co-investments are not standard in venture deals, according to Beber. Even so, LPs may negotiate co-investment rights to have the ability to cherry-pick investment opportunities and invest more capital in promising companies. In doing so, LPs also gain insights into how the GP chooses the opportunities, structures investments, and adds value as a board member. The process and timing of responses needs to be managed effectively by the GP: It is likely that the LP may not have the ability to conduct due diligence, invest in follow-on rounds, or respond within the allocated time frame. However, if an LP can bring some strategic insights to the company, it is often worth the time and effort for both parties. GPs also need to be cautious in that such an investment from an LP, especially a corporate LP with industry knowledge, does not scare off acquirers and impair the exit potential and value.

Public disclosure: Certain LPs, such as state pension funds and university endowments, are subject to Freedom of Information Act ("FOIA") guidelines. FOIA is an information disclosure statute that encourages accountability through transparency and ensures an open government. While FOIA laws vary from state to state, generally, in the VC context, certain information reported by a GP to a public plan limited partner can be the subject of a FOIA request. A newspaper journalist could submit a FOIA request to a public plan limited partner and subsequently publish sensitive fund or portfolio company information. To date, many states have modified their laws to protect portfolio company information from public disclosure. GPs also seek to limit details of fund investments in portfolio companies from becoming public as they could impact future financing and valuations. Thus, GPs vigorously try to protect the information. A variety of remedies exists, including limiting information to such LPs or, in extreme cases, barring such LPs from future participation in funds.

Attempting to balance these varying GP-LP terms is no mean feat, one that keeps Timothy Recker, chairman of the Institutional Limited Partners Association (ILPA) busy. The ILPA represents 240 organizations that collectively manage over $1 trillion of private equity capital. As the managing director of private equity for the University of California Regents, Tim manages a portfolio of various VC and private equity funds.

As the chair of the ILPA, his larger goal is to ensure that the interests of LPs and GPs are aligned. "The ILPA has diligently worked to address a number of issues that make the GP-LP relationship stronger," he says.[7] The ILPA has developed best practices that focus on the following three areas:[8]

- Alignment of interest
- Governance
- Transparency

These practices are governed by the terms shown in Table 3.4.

A cause of heartburn for LPs is the way GPs calculate fees. "Take for example, the calculation of carried interest. Carry should be calculated on the basis of net profits, not gross profits," suggests Recker.[9] Recall Seth Levine's comments stated earlier on how good GPs treat fees as a loan. Industry terms in VC have certainly leaned toward net profits.

TABLE 3.4   ILPA Best Practices vis-à-vis GP-LP Terms Summary

Driver	Terms
*Objective: **Alignment of interests.** The GPs should focus on profit maximization and not live off management fees.*	
Does the GP have skin in the game?	Is the GP commitment significantly above or below industry standards? What is the GP's commitment with respect to their net worth?
Are the management fees structured appropriately?	Do the management fees adjust when successor funds are raised? How are the fees adjusted after the investment period?
Are there opportunities where a GP-LP conflict of interest may arise?	Can the GP co-invest its personal capital in select cherry-picked opportunities? Will this create a fundamental conflict in the portfolio? As one LP asks, "Why should a manager have side-bets and other businesses?"
Is the GP-LP profit sharing structure designed appropriately?	Waterfall distribution and clawback
Are all the GP management team members motivated to succeed?	Compensation, GP distribution of carry within its team, resources to operate the fund
What is the investment strategy?	Investment limitations by company, sector, pace of drawdowns, reinvestments, investments from multiple funds in same opportunity
*Objective: **Governance:** Good governance practices are adopted by the GPs and LPs.*	
Does an LP advisory committee exist? What are the roles and responsibilities of such a committee? Do the LPs have adequate information?	LP advisory committee size, responsibilities, and frequency of meetings Reports, annual meetings, valuation guidelines
Standard of care: Does the GP allocate substantial time and attention to building and managing the portfolio?	Is the fund a GP's primary activity? Does the GP have other income streams, investments, or interests?
Do the LPs have options to limit the downside or exit the relationship?	No-fault divorce, key person event, key person insurance, termination of investment period, transfer of LP interests, and withdrawal

TABLE 3.4   (*Continued*)

Driver	Terms
Objective: **Transparency:** *Does the GP demonstrate sufficient transparency in the relationship?*	
Transparency of GP income streams, portfolio quality	Fees and carried interest calculations, valuation and financial information, other relevant GP information, and protection of proprietary information

---

EXAMPLE: CARRY CALCULATION: NET PROFITS VERSUS GROSS PROFITS

To illustrate the difference between net profits and gross profits, consider the following table:

Carry Calculated on the Basis of Net Profits and Gross Profits

	Net Profits ($M)	Gross Profits ($M)
Profits	$125	$150
LP Returns at 80%	$100	$120
GP Carried Interest at 20%	$25	$30
GP Fees + Carry =	$50	$55

For a $100 million fund, assume a management fee of 2.5 percent flat over a 10-year period. Typically, management fee steps down after the investment period, but for simplicity of calculations, let us assume a flat rate. Thus, $25 million in fees is paid to the GPs, which leaves investable capital of $75 million. Assume GPs double this to $150 million. The difference between net profits and gross profits can be substantial. LPs look at the "gross" profit calculations unfavorably, especially for larger funds.

Separately, Preqin surveyed leading LPs in 2010 and found that 13 percent of LPs will certainly not invest in any funds that ignore the ILPA Private Equity Principles, and another 58 percent may not, and will lean in the conservative direction.

TABLE 3.5 Most Negotiated Terms in Order of Priority: LPs and GPs

LPs—Most Negotiated	GPs—Most Negotiated
1. Key person	1. Clawbacks
2. Waterfall	2. Key person
3. Management fees	3. Management fees
4. Clawbacks	4. Carry
5. Side letters	5. Side letters
6. Indemnification	6. Waterfall
7. Carry	7. Indemnification

Note: Survey included 97 LPs and 117 GPs.
Source: Center for Private Equity and Entrepreneurship, Tuck School of Business at Dartmouth.

WHAT MATTERS MOST

In a survey conducted by the Center for Private Equity and Entrepreneurship at Dartmouth's Tuck School of Business, about 100 GPs and LPs were asked to rank the most negotiated terms.[10] For GPs as well as LPs, the primary tension arises around the overall economics of the fund. As Table 3.5 displays, key person provisions, clawbacks, and management fees were among the top negotiated terms.

Separately, in a Preqin survey of 50 institutional investors, LPs ranked the relative importance of various terms. By far, the largest issue for any LP is the calculation of carry—is it calculated "deal by deal" or "fund level"? Needless to say, LPs prefer fund level calculation of carry, which allows them to recover their capital first before any carry split.

SUMMARY

Understanding key Limited Partner Agreement (LPA) terms and knowing what to negotiate can help a GP accelerate the fund-raising process. Kelly Williams, head of Credit Suisse Customized Fund Investment Group, a fund-of-funds, remarked that it is in the GP's interest to understand these terms thoroughly. Selecting fund attorneys to develop an appropriate negotiating plan is equally critical. "Choose your service providers wisely—the wrong choice can damage your prospects," she says. "We have seen some very good first-time funds but their legal counsel behaved poorly and it did not help the cause."[11] A good attorney knows the market trends on GP-LP terms, understands the value of attracting an institutional LP, and proceeds to guide the GPs accordingly. Wisdom and tact is better than brute force, especially when negotiating with LPs, who can make or break a fund. In one example, a \$30+ billion institutional investor complained that a mature venture firm, now raising Fund IV, had picked a small-town attorney with very little experience in negotiating LPAs. "We were utterly flummoxed" says this LP, "and wondered—were the GPs trying to save the fees? I mean, this inexperienced attorney created much angst at our end. They used improper terminology, did not know the market standards ... it reflected very poorly on the GPs. In fact, nowadays, the first thing we look at in an LPA is the name of their legal counsel. If this is an experienced firm, well versed with private equity, it shows that the GP knows what they are doing."[12]

LPs seek to ensure the alignment of interests. The fees carry, and other restrictive covenants, safeguard their investments and focus the GP toward long-term profit creation. Should the fund face challenges, LPs may have remedies, such as key person provisions or "cause" or "no fault" fund terminations or GP removal provisions, but these remedies are rarely exercised and are of limited utility other than to provide one side with negotiating leverage over the other.

Most industry veterans agree: LPs do not invest in funds based on terms (but they may choose NOT to invest if terms are too GP favorable). Rather, LPs make investment decisions based on the full package including projected returns. As one GP remarked, "Show me an established firm with consistent top quartile returns and I will concede on most terms."

The following chapter addresses the structure and operations of a venture firm.

CHAPTER 4

Fund Structure, Governance, and Operations

Style and Structure are the essence ... great ideas are hogwash.
—Vladimir Nabokov

his chapter describes the steps leading to incorporation of various fund entities. Any fund includes the following framework of entities, as seen in Figure 4.1:

- The fund: an entity, structured as a limited partnership (LP). Investors, or limited partners, commit to investing as much as 99 percent of the capital in this entity via the limited partnership agreement (LPA). The LPA governs the following:
  - Admission of investors, or limited partners
  - Capital allocations and contributions
  - Distributions
  - Withdrawals and dissolution
  - Governance, reports, and audits
- The general partner (GP): an entity, typically structured as a limited liability company (LLC).
- The management services entity, governed by an operating agreement, employs the various investment and operational individuals and provides all administrative services to the fund. The services entity charges an annual management fee, typically 2 percent of the committed capital, to the fund. In certain situations, two separate LLCs are formed—one as a passive investment vehicle wherein the partners contribute their 1 percent capital commitment to the fund, and another as a services entity.

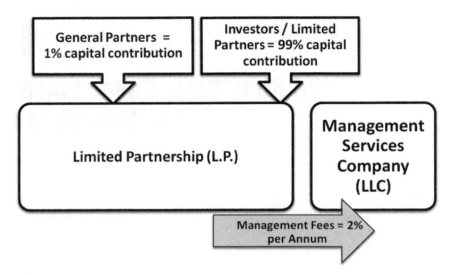

FIGURE 4.1 Fund Structure

This chapter covers basics of fund structures and management. As with most entities, the two key elements are *economics* and *control*. We will see this theme recur in Chapter 10 "Structuring Investment Transactions".

KEY CONSTITUENTS OF THE GP TEAM

In any venture firm, the cast of characters includes the GPs (also known as managing directors or managing GPs), vice presidents, principals, associates, and analysts. These primary investment professionals are responsible for generating returns. Venture partner and entrepreneur-in-residence positions are created to host proven entrepreneurs or operational executives who may eventually help source or create companies that fit within the fund's investment strategy. Recall Table 2.6, which describes the complementary skills of an investment team.

Newer titles have evolved as fund operations have become more focused. For example, in larger funds, roles such as director of business development or head of deal sourcing have emerged. The administrative team, also re-ferred to as the back office, is responsible for the day-to-day operational aspects. This team includes, depending on the size of the fund, an office manager, chief financial officer, chief operating officer, and others such as legal counsel, marketing, and human resources.

The primary responsibilities of the investment team differ along the lines of seniority. On any typical day, the GPs would juggle a number of activities:

negotiating terms for investment opportunities, participating in boards of current portfolio companies, responding to any LP/investor requests, and putting out a few fires along the way. On a rare day, exit negotiations may occur.

An entry-level analyst is expected to source investment opportunities and conduct the first screening of due diligence. At the other end of the spectrum, the partners keep a close watch on portfolio construction, governance, exits, and strategy and timing of the next fund. The typical compensation package includes a salary, annual performance bonus, and a share of the profits, called "carry," which stands for carried interest.

A position description for a venture capitalist would read as follows:

- *Key Tasks and Responsibilities:* Participate in and contribute to all aspects of the investment process with responsibility for all quantitative and qualitative analysis of portfolio companies and funds
- *Analysis:*
  - Qualitatively and quantitatively evaluate potential transactions, including performing detailed sector and company research and analysis
  - Conduct due diligence and assist with deal execution and transaction management
  - Carry out portfolio company analysis including valuations and financial modeling
  - Prepare materials for investment committee and other internal meetings
  - Interact with external consultants and advisers as required regarding analysis
  - Assist with closing administration
- *Deal Sourcing, Marketing, and Fund-Raising:*
  - Conduct desk research for marketing, deal sourcing, and fund-raising.
  - Build strong relationships with GPs/investors/consultants/advisers
  - Undertake warm/hot calling and cold calling (focused on a specific geographic area, industrial sector, or transaction type)
- *Structuring and Execution:*
  - Participate in the development of appropriate deal structures to meet sellers' and/or managers' needs in close liaison with legal team
  - Work with the deal team and legal team to prepare and coordinate the execution of nondisclosure agreements, offer letters, purchase agreements, and other legal and transaction documentation
  - Postinvestment monitoring
  - Familiarity with board member roles and corporate governance

- o Keep up-to-date on portfolio performance and address any specific requests for action or approval
- o Prepare returns forecasts, commentary, and other investment information for LP meetings
- *Skills:*
  - o Deep knowledge of relevant sector (e.g., health care, energy, technology)
  - o Transactional experience and analytical abilities
  - o Advanced financial, business modeling, and writing skills
- *Competencies:*
  - o Is results driven, ambitious, and highly motivated
  - o Possesses strategic and commercial acumen
  - o Has an entrepreneurial approach, takes the initiative, and adapts
  - o Is a team player with a strong work ethic
  - o Is well informed on market trends and key players
  - o Has excellent networking skills
  - o *Qualifications:* MBA or equivalent with some experience at an Associate level (five years related experience) within a relevant industry including:
    - Private equity/funds of funds/pension funds/family office investment expertise
    - Corporate finance/leveraged finance
    - M&A or transaction services/corporate finance

Hiring Stars of the Future

Famously, Union Square Ventures recruited a two-year rotational analyst position by not seeking resumes but asking for "web presence." Union Square defined web presence as "anything accessible via a URL. It could be a blog, a social networking profile, a portfolio, a company, a social bookmarking archive ... it is whatever you think best represents who you are online."[1] At the entry-level position, differentiators can be few and competition fierce. Any job posting could very quickly lead to flooded inboxes and cold calls from eager beavers.

Take the example of a pre-MBA analyst position posted at Bessemer Venture Partners, one of the longest-standing VC firms in the country (the firm started in 1911). More than 650 resumes, 42 first-round interviews, and 7 second-round interviews later, one offer was made. That's about 0.15 percent odds for an entry-level position! Such odds are daunting for any aspirant, and for the GPs the process can be long and exhausting.

Brant Moxley, managing director at Pinnacle Group International, an executive recruiting firm that focuses on private equity career opportunities, says, "The demand is staggering—there are ten times the number of applicants for every job opening in the venture capital arena. Applicants who are successful have differentiated experience, skills, and are not perceived as a commodity. The ones who have been successful in landing positions were strong on operating experience and demonstrated technical and financial skills. Experience in the investment banking business may also be a badge of honor at the entry level—it shows a candidate can survive the intensity and the demands of this business. What I find fascinating is while everyone wants to get in the business of venture capital, not many understand what it takes to stay in the business." A pre-MBA position is, by design, established for two years. "Ninety percent of the time, these positions are not partner tracks. At best, an analyst would stay with the firm for three years, instead of the usual two," declares Brant. C. Richard Kramlich of NEA, once remarked, "Below the surface there's a huge amount of turnover."[2]

Bessemer has had six full-time analysts, and five have been involved in entrepreneurship in one way or another. Sarah Tavel of Bessemer writes, "People who do tend to rise to the top during the selection process [do so] because of their passion not just for venture capital, but for the entire ecosystem."[3] Rajeev Batra, partner at the Mayfield Fund, can testify to that. "When I was finishing up my MBA at Harvard, I was approached by a few venture firms. I did not even realize I was being interviewed till we met for the third time." Rajeev had done all that Sarah talks about—besides his evident passion for this career path, he had been involved in a few entrepreneurial gigs. A PhD in electrical engineering demonstrated his domain knowledge. Rajeev was a bit skeptical of jumping in too soon in the venture business. "Starting a company while at the business school, my third start-up, sounded like much more fun," he says. But Rajeev, standing at the crossroads of start-ups and finance, turned toward the VC profession. "In my B-school essay, I had written that eventually, I wanted to be a venture capitalist when I grow up," he says.[4]

SPOTTING TALENT

Mary Lemmer attended her first VC conference at the age of 17. Eager to understand the nuances of this business, she networked extensively, pushing without being obnoxious and all along, maintaining an appropriate stance.

After she finished her BBA, she was spotted by Marc Weiser, founder of RPM Ventures. Marc had become aware of Mary when she won an award he had instituted at the university—RPM Entrepreneur of the Year Award. At a course Marc conducts at the University of Michigan, he could see Mary's energy and intellect. Six months later, Marc assigned a project to Mary. She passed with flying colors and now is a full-time analyst at RPM Ventures. "In any given day, I am juggling with four functions: portfolio management, screening new opportunities, managing investor relations, and finally administrative stuff." It is the full gamut, an advantage at a smaller firm where she is one of three active professionals. "What surprised me most about this business was that in business school, the rules were crisp and clean—but the real world is ambiguous. There is no black or white," she says.*

While Mary exhibits a strong passion for the business of VC, equally interesting is how Weiser was able to spot her and attract her to the firm. In a business where hiring mistakes can be expensive, and irreparably damage a firm's reputation, the relationship at the business school worked in RPM Venture's favor.

---

*Mary Lemmer (RPM Ventures) in discussions with the author, February 2011.

Campus Recruitment

Meet Matthew Garratt, a thoughtful, soft-spoken MBA graduate. As soon as Matt finished his MBA, he landed at Battery Ventures, a Silicon Valley-based VC firm with over $3 billion under its management. After responding to an advertisement, he was interviewed *only* about 11 times. "I was skeptical of even getting a response to my application," says Matt, responded to a campus advertisement. Matt had interned at another early-stage VC firm. I had the chance to watch Matt hone his skills at this firm. "The interview questions were designed to understand my technical expertise and my entrepreneurial background."

Matt's focus on the energy sector shaped his career path into VC. He had completed an internship in Ghana, where he evaluated the financial, environmental, and social performance of various clean energy enterprises for E+Co, a nonprofit public purpose investment company. Before enrolling in the University of Michigan, Matt had worked in the new product design and development group at a Fortune 500 company, Alcoa, where he led efforts to commercialize advanced materials for the aerospace and transportation sectors. As a member of Alcoa's sustainability team, he had developed a business strategy for product development with an emphasis on environmental sustainability.

To hone his start-up skills, he participated aggressively in various business plan competitions and represented his school at the Social Venture

Capital Investment Competition. Separately, his team won a business plan competition for conceiving an energy-friendly building supply company. And of course, with the growth in cleantech investments, Matt was at the right place at the right time. His master's degree project aimed to understand how renewable energy policy environments influence the cost and overall availability of private financing for renewable power projects. "By distilling the perspectives of capital providers and others familiar with the project financing process, we aim to deliver insight to policy makers on lowering the cost of capital needed to finance new renewable power projects," he wrote. During his career progression, Matthew ensured he had a strong understanding of the energy sector, was aware of start-ups, and had interned with an early-stage VC firm in Ann Arbor, Michigan. He was approaching the VC business with a strong footing.

AN BFHUIL SE FLUIC, AMACH?

Terry McGuire, a venture capitalist of 25 years and chairman emeritus of National Venture Capital Association, is the co-founder of Polaris Ventures, a firm that manages $3 billion and has invested in over 100 companies.

After college, he spent a year in Ireland on a fellowship and learned to speak Gaelic. At his first job interview, the interviewer, who spoke fluent Gaelic, muttered, "An bfhuil se fluic, amach?" which is Gaelic for "Is it wet outside?" Terry promptly responded in Gaelic. The two hit it off, and Terry landed the job.*

But was it just a stroke of luck? It certainly helped that Terry was the president of the Harvard Business School Venture Capital Club. "It's a combination of training, network, and opportunity that presented itself," says Terry. Terry co-founded Polaris Ventures after a seven-year stint at a Chicago-based venture firm. If you know Gaelic, it might be a good start, but knowing Gaelic is neither a necessary nor a sufficient condition—it is just an opportunity that meets a prepared mind.

---

*Terry McGuire generously granted me an interview, but this quote comes from Steve Arnold, Jonathan Flint, and Terrance McGuire, "Polaris Venture Partners," in *Done Deals—Venture Capitalists Tell Their Stories*, ed. Udayan Gupta (Boston: Harvard Business School Press, 2000), 281.

Proactive Searchers: Those Who Kick Down the Doors

Those who want to get in the business do not necessarily wait for job openings, but will come knocking at your doors—and it's best to find a way to integrate such bright minds, for these are indeed the ones who are driven by their callings.

"I remember cold-calling Brook Byers, founder of Kleiner Perkins Caufield & Byers, about a hundred times ... I was always interested in venture capital," says Robert ("Bob") Nelsen. Nelsen went on to be the co-founder of ARCH Venture Partners, which has now grown to manage $1.5 billion in assets. In his 20-year investment career, Bob has led nine companies to valuations of $1 billion or more. Bob's entrepreneurial streak started early. He sold gerbils at the age of 7, got his first Social Security statement at age 9, and started investing in stocks by age 11. By the time he got into college, he had stashed away more money than his parents. And Bob's dad was a doctor, so what Bob had earned by the age of 19 was a significant amount. "Venture capital was my first career choice. I got a guide—this *Pratt's Guide to Venture Capital Sources*—to find out about this business," he says. In his first year of business school, Bob read about the launch of ARCH and approached the founder, Steve Lazarus. Bob recalls, "I told Steve I would work for him for free." Nelsen started with ARCH as soon as he finished college.[5]

John Doerr, one of the leading practitioners at the preeminent VC firm Kleiner Perkins Caufield & Byers (KPCB), once remarked his journey to VC began with "luck, a fascination with innovation and entrepreneurs, and ambition.... I cold-called Silicon Valley's venture groups, hoping to apprentice myself to one."[6] His cold-calling efforts did not get him a job at KPCB, but eventually, after five years at Intel, John would land at this firm. Byers, who had asked John to get some experience, famously invited John Doerr for a 5:30 A.M. jog to see how motivated he was. John was at the track the next morning and the rest is history.

Like Bob and John, David Cowan of Bessemer Venture Partners was able to kick a few doors down. "Back in the 1980s, I heard once that all venture capitalists operated from 3000 Sand Hill Road," he says. The ultimate Mecca of any wannabe venture capitalist, Sand Hill Road is a small strip that houses venerable names in the venture business: Kleiner Perkins, NEA, Sequoia, Draper Fisher Jurvetson (DFJ), Battery Ventures, and Canaan Partners. Entrepreneurs eagerly flock here to find the fuel for their dreams. David, who had a brief two-year stint at Oracle, was eager to explore possibilities in the venture universe. One fine afternoon, he drove to Sand Hill Road and walked unannounced into one of the venture firm's offices. The lady at the front desk was firm: "No, we don't have any openings."

But David has never taken "No" for an answer. "I am sure you know a few firms who would be looking." The lady pulled out a copy of the Western Association of Venture Capitalists directory and circled a few names. "I wrote letters to five firms. Two of the five offered me a position," recalls David, who is ranked as one of the top investors in the world.[7] In his two decades at Bessemer Venture Partners, David has built an enviable track record of 37 exits, of which 19 companies are publicly listed, and the rest were acquired. But cold-calling a VC firm rarely works—especially in the modern day. "I don't think that approach will work today—the business is much more complex and competitive," warns David.[8]

Networking could well be the proven approach to find the best candidates. In the largest study ever conducted on VC success factors, Geoff Smart, founder and CEO of management assessment firm ghSMART, surveyed 145 VC investors. Leading firms such as Accel Partners, Benchmark Capital, KPCB, Greylock, New Enterprise Associates (NEA), and Norwest Venture Partners participated in the survey. Geoff summarized that *most enter the business through personal contacts.*[9]

Leading firms have found their future talent at the Kauffman Fellows Program—a two-year hands-on training program designed by the VCs for the VCs.

The Kauffman Fellows Program

Bryan Roberts, a partner at Venrock, found his mentor and career in venture capital thanks to the Kauffman Fellows Program. Venrock, one of the country's leading investment firms, has invested $2.5 billion in over 400 companies and celebrated over 250 exits via initial public offering (IPO) or acquisitions. Bryan has been named to the *Forbes* Midas list of leading venture capital investors in the country on multiple occasions. "I liked science and business and wanted to explore the intersection of these two fields—venture capital seemed interesting. I called HBS's career office as I was finishing my PhD in chemical biology, and I was told about the Kauffman Fellows Program." Bryan was invited for a match-making event where 30 finalists were competing for 10 opportunities. "Tony Evnin, who started health care investing at Venrock over three decades ago and one of the first investors in the arena, showed up there and at the end of the day, offered me a job," recalls Bryan. "I didn't know anything then.... I was really lucky that I landed with a good person and a good firm." Evnin may have picked his protégé well. Of the first four investments led by Bryan, three companies went public and the fourth was acquired for $1.1 billion. Good for Venrock, good for Bryan!

For Punit Chiniwalla, getting into VC was all he wanted. He pursued the coveted Kauffman Fellows Program, eventually landing him smack in the center of the hypercompetitive venture universe: Sand Hill Road. Punit, a mild-mannered MBA student, would participate in the Venture Capital Investment Competition (VCIC), a competition for business school students where their skills as VC professionals are tested. Student teams act as venture capitalists and are judged for their skills and abilities in identifying an investment opportunity and negotiating a terms sheet. Pitched by three companies, each venture team has to pick one company for an investment, negotiate a terms sheet, and convince the judges that they made the best choice. As one of the judges, I was to watch for a variety of soft and hard skills, including analytical, relationship building, and negotiating skills. Punit's team won the competition at the university level and went on to win third place in national competition that year.

Punit also interned at a local venture firm and eventually found his break with the University of Michigan-based Frankel Fund, a seed fund designed to be a learning opportunity for MBA students—except that this was no play money! Opportunities originating from the technology transfer offices received a higher priority for assessments. Punit was intrigued by a new laser technology: This technology had the "power of 10" potential. A term investors often use, the power of 10 demonstrates that it is 10 times faster, better, or cheaper.

Laser beams are used in a variety of industrial cutting applications: a single beam of laser light acts as a knife to elegantly slice sheets of metal. To meet the growing demand to slice thicker metal sheets, the laser power needed to be amplified proportionally. This increase in power would, in turn, blur the edges of the beam, and the finesse of the cut would be compromised. Users had to be content with the trade-off between a fine cut on a thinner material or a blunt cut on a thicker material. But as Punit could see, the inventor had found an elegant solution to this problem. By combining three beams in a circular, coupled design, the limits of current technology could be pushed—you could increase the power without compromising the quality of the cut—and this technology could be used in several new applications. With his PhD in polymer science combined with four years at IBM Research, Punit knew how to assess the scientific claims of this new technology.

The technology was the basis for the formation of Arbor Photonics, a fiber laser technology that combined beam quality and optical power to expand the limits of performance of current laser technology. "If applied successfully, these lasers can enable dramatic improvements in throughput and processing speed in microelectronics manufacturing, solar cell processing, and industrial materials processing applications," Punit wrote in his Frankel Fund investment memorandum. Arbor Photonics landed a small investment from Frankel Fund and eventually went on to attract $3 million within a year from venture capitalists. A CEO with deep expertise in the laser industry was recruited. Punit's first investment was progressing nicely, even before he had graduated from B-school. This experience enabled Punit to land in the Kauffman Fellows Program. The much-sought-after program, whose mission is to "identify, develop, and network emerging global leaders in venture capital,"[10] is a near-guaranteed entry ticket into the world of VC.

While working full-time at a VC firm, each Kauffman Fellow engages in a 24-month hands-on apprenticeship that includes professional coaching in seven modules, mentoring by seasoned venture partners, and triennial sessions of industry and leadership curriculum. The program claims that the fellowship's value can be measured along three axes of investing: apprenticeship, leadership development, and being a part of a global network. Each year, about 20 to 30 fellows are picked from a pool of about 200 applicants. The application process is a two-step dance, which is rigorous by any measure. The written application and the interview—reviewers include leading venture capitalists—look for a prior track record of accomplishments that are significant. Entrepreneurial background trumps operational background, in fact it trumps everything else.

At the interview stage, the universe of 200 applicants narrows down by about a third. Candidates fly in to one of the two hot spots, Silicon Valley or Boston, and are grilled by panels of four to five venture capitalists. The next stage is the finalist stage, where candidates who cross the finish line are then matched with firms who are seeking to bring on fresh talent. If a finalist is not picked up by any firm, the process ends. For those selected, the sponsor VC firm pays the $60,000 tuition in addition to the salary for the two-year internship. These would-be Fellows are assigned mentors from established venture firms who, over the course of a two-year period, would provide insights and formal training into the art and science of venture investing. The fellowship itself has evolved with the changing times. As a firm, if you have your eyes set on a candidate, sponsoring her could be one way to further her career and augment your firm's team.

Biographical profiles of the Fellows from previous classes (14 batches with about 20 Fellows each) show that practitioners came from varied backgrounds. The Kauffman Fellows' web site points out that common characteristics of Fellows include "a bias toward entrepreneurs; deep scientific, technology, or business domain expertise; demonstrated leadership strengths; an aspiration to contribute to the building of companies, either as a building investor or as a startup leader; an appetite for risk, ambiguity, and unstructured environments; and humility, empathy, a sense of service, and unquestioned integrity."[11]

Corporate Venture Capital

Similar to Bryan Roberts and Punit Chiniwalla, Christopher Jones earned a PhD in chemical engineering, but Chris's career trajectory in VC differs. When I first met Chris several years ago, he was shadowing Dr. James ("Jim") Plonka. Jim was then the Vice President, Venture Capital, for Dow Chemical. In the early 1980s, Dow had formed a corporate VC arm to seek strategic investments that would further Dow's understanding of market trends and opportunities. Across various sectors, corporate venture capital (CVC) has been launched by companies like Dow, Intel, Siemens, Johnson & Johnson, and Eli Lilly, to name a few. In a given year, about 6 to 8 percent of all VC investment in the country comes from CVC. Besides a financial return, corporations invest in start-ups to gain a view of the newest new thing. Accessing novel technologies can enhance revenue streams and amplify a corporation's competitive position.[12]

Jim had launched this internal business unit 14 years earlier within Dow, managing a $500 million evergreen fund and leading investments in a range of companies that operated in sectors such as health care, devices, materials, and energy. What's more, Jim had also positioned Dow as a strategic investor, or an LP-of-choice with leading venture funds, building deep relationships in the United States, Europe, Israel, and Japan. Studies show that about 60 percent of corporations invest in venture funds as LPs and 90 percent of CVCs invest directly in start-ups. Jim had found a way to do both.

With his breadth and depth of experience, combined with a patient, nurturing approach, Jim had a lot to offer, and Chris was quietly taking it all in. Shadowing Jim had its own advantages: Jim's prior protégé, Ken Van Heel, was now the global head of Dow's pension fund, managing $10 billion in assets. "Subject matter or domain expertise is a good starting point—essential elements for a good venture capitalist," says Jim. With a doctorate in chemical engineering, Chris started his career with Dow in the annals of research and development seven years ago. Jim, a PhD himself, had started in a research and development function and had spent 24 years in various operational roles within Dow.

It didn't take superior forecasting skills to see that Chris's career path was being cast. Jim had found his next protégé in Chris, and the grooming had begun. Time would tell whether Chris's career would accelerate into a trajectory like that of Kenneth Van Heel. "Look at Kenny," Jim says fondly, describing the quiet man. "Several years ago when he started, he wasn't unlike Chris." Sizing people up and starting to shape their venture careers speaks of an artistic ability that Jim innately exhibits. Ken Van Heel started with Jim and would go on to head the $10 billion pension fund for the Dow Chemical Company. Succession is a significant challenge in the venture business, and Jim has a good start on his next protégé. "In this business, being smart and hungry is a lethal combination, and Chris shows a good mix of both these qualities," Jim comments.

Like most practitioners, Jim agrees that the venture business is an apprenticeship—possibly a lifelong one. Having grown up in a blue-collar family in Clinton, Iowa (population: 26,000), Chris grasped the philosophies of listening and learning from his parents, a farmer and a nurse who taught him the values of seeding, nurturing, and caring. "And most of all, my parents would remind me to stay away from hubris and any get-rich-quick schemes," he remembers. His first job after his graduation was at Dow Chemical in Midland, Michigan, where his first seven years were focused on various process technology developments. His interest in VC was piqued when he spent a year in Dow's New Products R&D group. "I led the Opportunity Identification Team, where we performed early-stage project analysis." Here, Chris learned the nuances of looking at the crystal ball with a rational lens. This step sowed the seeds for his next leap: A word-of-mouth discussion with a colleague led him to Jim Plonka's Dow Venture Capital group, where he started as an analyst. "At the new products group, we looked at the development process, its hurdles and path to commercialization. Tying my chemistry background with the business process and milestones gives me an edge—if I can minimize the risks, I can win at this profession," remarks Chris.

Jim did not conduct a classic interview to understand Chris's strengths, but rather relied on the feedback of trusted people who knew Chris. "In a large corporation like Dow, you will find plenty of smart people who are smart but unknown. I made a few calls to people I trust and found that Chris had a strong foundation." Unlike Matthew Garratt, Chris did not go through 11 interviews. But his domain expertise, combined with an appetite for launching new products, helped him to gain a foothold in the VC arena. And with a mentor, his path becomes much easier. "A good mentor in this business can be a huge asset," advises Brant Moxley. "But realize that in a firm, the senior partners do not have all the time to mentor juniors. A junior is like a remora—they just have to find the right feeding ground," he adds with a chuckle.[13] Brant, an avid big-game hunter and traveler, manages placements for a number of venture funds, funds of funds, and related asset classes. "It's okay to be a remora," he says.[14]

FINDING SUITABLE PARTNERS

While the various sources of talent pools have been described, individuals who have deep trust and confidence in each other's abilities often form the primary partnership. When Jan Garfinkle decided to start Arboretum

Ventures, she had placed an advertisement in a leading venture capital publication. "I needed someone who has investment experience to complement my operational expertise," she recalled. She placed an advertisement in *Venture Wire* and launched a national search, but a close friend would introduce her to Tim Petersen, who lived half a mile away. Jan would soon realize that venture partnerships occur serendipitously.

Frank Caufield, or the "C" in KPCB, met with Tom Perkins, or the "P," through a mutual friend. Frank, who had made up his mind early on in his career to dive into venture capital, had snagged an interesting opportunity that called for relocation to Silicon Valley. "As a part of the relocation, I had a deal with my boss—after one year, I will leave. In fact, he agreed to help me find an opportunity and sure enough, a year later, he lived up to his word," he says.[15] Frank's boss introduced him to Tom Perkins and the rest is history.

In a parallel universe, Tim Petersen would come on board at Arboretum and bring his investment expertise. Tim managed a portfolio of investments for Wolverine Venture Fund. The fund, based at the University of Michigan, made seed and early-stage investments in university-based spinouts. Tim, whose entrepreneurial background was well established, had played a leadership role at the Wolverine Venture Fund and carefully constructed the portfolio, but was eager to break away from the academic environment. The two launched Arboretum Ventures, and have gone on to raise Fund III. The multiple exits from Fund I and Fund II have certainly helped, but at its core, the partnership is complementary in skills, personalities, and long-term goals.

FUND GOVERNANCE AND ECONOMICS

The limited partner advisory committee (LPAC) may lead the fund level, or LP governance, while the GPs manage the services entity. It typically includes some of the larger investors in the fund. Bob Clone, who manages a portfolio of investments for a pension system in Indiana, says, "In designing LPAC, while being one of the largest investors in a fund, we would always look for the interests of the smallest investor. At times, we would insist that the GPs invite at least one representative from the high-net-worth group to participate on the LPAC."

It is typical to have three to five LPs serve as members of the LPAC. A balanced LPAC has representation of various constituents by size of investment or type of constituent (pension funds, endowments, HNWs, et al.). Responsibilities of the LPAC include, but are not limited to:

- *Valuation matters:* LPAC adopts guidelines and weighs in on markups or markdowns of portfolio company valuation.

- *Conflict of interest matters:* Can the founders cherry-pick and make a personal investment in a portfolio company? For example, Jim Bryer of Accel Partners personally invested $1 million in Facebook at the time of its Series A investment.
- *Investment matters:* Can the Fund III make an investment in a Fund II portfolio company? Under what circumstances will the investment be referred to LPAC for approval?
- *Carry interests offered to advisory committees:*
  - Percentage offered to each member: In certain cases, technical advisory committee members receive a modest carry of say, 0.1 to 0.5 percent of the total pool.
  - Vesting period: The vesting period can be a straight-line vesting over the investment period, or some variation thereof.

GOVERNANCE OF MANAGEMENT SERVICES GP LLC

The governance of the GP LLC primarily rests on the shoulders of the co-founders, or the managing directors. Thus, prior to formalizing a partnership, the fund's co-founders need to agree on the various operational matters. These include details such as names of the individuals who will be the members of the GP LLC and decision-making guidelines for all operational matters, such as:

- Employee matters: Compensation, hiring and firing processes
- Investment committee composition
- Selection of venture partners and entrepreneurs-in-residence
- Service provider selection: attorneys, accountants/audit firms, marketing and PR related activities
- Budgetary allocations

The GP LLC can also develop guidelines for:

- Guidelines on operations, ethics, and confidentiality matters
- Process of admission and selection of investment committee members
- Guidelines on board participation:
  - Best-suited member versus one who sourced the opportunity
  - Participation on conflicting company boards
  - Public boards participation

GP Membership Admission, Withdrawal, and Termination

While a firm attracts individuals who perform various investment functions, not all members are considered partners eligible for sharing profits (termed *carry*), unless you are with Benchmark Capital. While some are elevated to a partner level eventually, others rise to claim ownership in the GP LLC—the management services company. Within this context, the founding partners would establish guidelines that would ascertain how the following decisions will be made:

- How are new individuals admitted or terminated from the GP membership?
  - Majority vote of number of current members
  - Majority vote by percentage of carry allocation
- Will carry or economic interest of existing members be diluted
  - Proportionally?
  - Selectively (only a few existing members take a hit while others do not get diluted)?
- Under what conditions can a member withdraw, or be terminated?
  - Cause: negligence, breach of conduct, fraud, SEC or tax matters, personal financial situation such as bankruptcy
  - Membership withdrawal in challenging circumstances—disability or death
  - Voluntary withdrawal
  - Under each of the conditions above, the withdrawn member
    - Retains carry interest as is and is liable for clawback.
    - Retains carry in existing investments but no new carry is offered.
    - Forfeits carry completely.
    - Is liable for pro rata share of capital contributions.
    - Stays/resigns from portfolio boards.
- Investment committee structure, decision-making criteria, and votes
- Unanimous decision to invest, exit, and invest additional amounts

Salaries and Expenses

To better understand the economics, take the example of a $100 million fund. The GPs of the fund would invest this capital in, say, about a dozen companies and after building value, aspire to exit the investments, meaning to sell the ownership. Should these investments generate profits, the investors (or LPs) keep 80 percent of the profits, and the GPs take home 20 percent. The carry of one-fifth profits evolved from the time of Phoenicians, who in AD 1200 commanded 20 percent of profits earned from trade and shipping merchandise.[16] In addition to the carry, the LPs also pay the GPs an annual management fee, typically 2 to 2.5 percent of the committed capital per year. Thus, for a $100 million fund with a predetermined life of 10 years, annual fees of 2 percent yield $2 million for the firm. The fees provide for

TABLE 4.1 Typical Compensation ($000)

Title	Salary	Bonus	Carry	Total
Managing GP	700	350	101	1,151
Partner	350	130	20	500
Principal	206	75	6	287
Venture Partner	185	40	12	237
Analyst	100	10	0	110

Compensation is tied to the size of the fund. Data as of April 1, 2009.
Source: Venture Capital and Finance of Innovation, Second Edition by Andrew Metrick and Ayako Yasuda. Reprinted with permission of John Wiley & Sons. Original data from Holt Private Equity Consultants, Private Equity Analyst-Holt Compensation Survey.

the day-to-day operations of the firm and are used to pay for salaries, travel, lease, and legal expenses. The responsibilities and compensation packages are determined by the professional's responsibilities and experience.

The primary expenses in any fund are salaries. The majority of this budget is allocated to investment professionals (general partners and members of the team, which could include associates and analysts) and the rest of the world (comptroller, operations, and back office). The budget also includes fees (legal, audit, and in some cases, specialized due diligence), travel, and miscellaneous operating expenses. The typical compensation package, as seen in Table 4.1, includes a salary, bonus, and a share of the profits, termed as carry or carried interest. A word of caution to a freshly minted MBA: salary varies by size of the fund and, thus, a venture partner in a $20 million fund may not necessarily attract $200,000 per annum.

Carried Interests

Allocation: How is carry distributed and what is the rationale? Some LPs do not accept the *Benchmark Model* (described here) of equal carry for all members. In their perspective, not all partners are created or can be equal. Others feel that if members are not incentivized with a meaningful portion of the carry, they will not stay. Carry split, described in Table 4.2, can occur on the basis of

- Investment expertise
- Entrepreneurial/operational expertise
- Ability to raise a fund

TABLE 4.2 Sample Carry and Vesting Schedule

	Carry	Y1	Y2	Y3	Y4	Y5	Y6–Y10
Managing Director 1	8%	20%	15%	15%	15%	15%	20%
Managing Director 2	7%	20%	15%	15%	15%	15%	20%
Principals, Associates, and Staff	5%	20%	20%	20%	20%	20%	

Notes on vesting:

Pace of vesting is tied to investment period of fund. Typical investment period is four to six years.

Vesting schedules can match investment period on a straight-line method vesting yearly in equal shares.

A 20 percent withholding released at final dissolution of fund induces professionals to remain engaged throughout life of fund.

Vesting clawback for cause, death, or disability occurs per standard industry practices.

An average cash value of carry is highly speculative and very few firms have actually seen carry profits in the past decade.

COMMUNISM, CAPITALISM, AND PARTNERSHIP OF EQUALS

"At Benchmark, we are a partnership of equals. Matt Kohler, 31, who joined Benchmark in 2008, gets an equal share of carry as does Bob Kagle, who founded the firm 15 years ago. This philosophy fosters a team-oriented approach to the business—internal competition is removed and we function together as a united team" says Mitch Lasky of Benchmark Capital.*

When this structure was announced by Benchmark in 1995, an industry veteran protested that such behavior is tantamount to "communism." Bruce Dunlevie of Benchmark promptly pointed out that the guy who said that "must have been a senior partner."† Touché indeed! But in a business where the stakes are high, hero worship prevails, and few claim to deliver returns, such a refreshing approach has yet to be widely adopted.

---

*Mitch Lasky (Benchmark Capital) in discussions with the author, Jan 2011.
†Randall E. Stross: *eBoys: The first inside account of venture capitalists at work* (Crown Business, 2000), 89.

Carry split percentage allocations and vesting timelines: Of the 20 percent pool, typical carry at the general partner level would be, say, 5 percent, while at the entry level, an associate's share of carry would be less than 0.5 percent, if any. In some cases, firms allocate carry by each portfolio company. The lead partner who is on the board of a portfolio company may get a predetermined percentage of the carried interests.

Economics beyond carry: Note that members not only share a percentage of carried interest but also potentially share any LLC fee income that is not turned over to the Fund.

Administration and Operations: The Back Office

Back- and middle-office operations are critical to a fund's success. Investors are paying more attention to the details; poor or insufficient back-office administration is often a reason for investors to forgo making an investment in the fund. Georganne Perkins of Fisher Lynch Capital, a fund-of-funds puts it bluntly: "If the GPs are equipped to handle other people's money, it can be a positive." Put another way, a suitable investment opportunity with the requisite financial talent (a CFO) and financial controls is attractive to any GP, and the same goes for any LP. "Well designed back- and middle-office operations provide fund principals and investors with confidence that the data they are receiving is correct—data integrity—and may be used to base decisions on," says Harry Cendrowski, author of *Private Equity: History, Governance and Operations*.[17] Harry is also the founder of Cendrowski Corporate Advisors, a back-office services firm that offers financial, taxation services, and investor relations to a number of PE and VC firms. According to Harry, a back office can offer the following:

- *Financial reporting:* Fund and portfolio company financial reporting for limited partners and fund managers, monitoring of portfolio company performance.
- *Accounting:* Accounting services are a critical component of the back- and middle-office operations. Fund principals rely on the information generated in the accounting system for decision making (e.g., how much cash should be distributed to investors? what are the cash needs of the fund for future expenses?), inspiring investor confidence (are capital accounts properly stated and communicated timely?), and their own economic interests (are management fees properly calculated? are incentive allocations properly calculated?).
- *General accounting:* Bookkeeping functions, posting journal entries, account reconciliations, preparation of financial statements, management

of operating cash, maintenance of the general ledger, including posting of all transactions, is necessary for proper financial and tax reporting.

- *Capital accounting:* Tracking cash intake, basis in entities, maintenance of investor capital accounts, calculation of distributions.
  - Maintenance of investor capital accounts is a critical function, as this is the primary measure that investors rely on in assessing their investment. It represents the investor's economic interest in the fund and is often the key component in determining distributions as well as profit and loss allocations.
  - Components of investor capital accounts include the proper computation and documentation of capital calls and distributions. Computation and documentation of capital calls allows the fund to meet its obligations and commitments for fund expenses and portfolio investments. Computation and documentation of distributions is critical to investor confidence by indicating that fund principals are abiding by the terms of the operating agreement. In addition, fund principals need to know how much capital has been committed, how much has been called, and how much has been returned to investors.
  - The proper allocation of economic and taxable profits and losses is another reason why proper maintenance of capital accounts is critical. Economic income affects the investors' right to distributions.
- *Tax services:* Preparation of tax returns, tax consulting for portfolio companies and the fund, tax representation.
- *Business valuation:* A back-office interfaces with fund principals with respect to the valuation of portfolio investments. GAAP basis financial statements must reflect investments at their fair value rather than historical cost. The back- and middle-offices may provide assistance in the valuation process and must ensure that the proper value is recorded in the general ledger. ASC 820 (formerly FAS 157) compliant mark-to-market portfolio company valuations for fund return calculations are essential.
- *Preparation of investor communications:* Fund return calculations, investment reports, capital call notices are included in communications.
- *Audits:* A back-office coordinates the annual financial statement audit of the fund and is the primary contact with auditors. It is the source of all the information the auditors will be assessing in their examination. As such, it is critical that the back office not only is able to provide the necessary information in a timely manner but also is able to provide explanations and answer questions with respect to the information on the auditor's request.
- *Taxes:* The back office is usually involved in the preparation of fund tax returns and investor K-1s. While some back-office operations will

actually prepare the necessary tax returns and investor K-1s, every back office has a hand in the preparation process through the provision of accurate financial information. In addition, the back office is responsible for calculating and documenting tax basis—the fund's tax basis in its investments as well as the investors' tax basis in the fund.

■ *Principal tax planning:* Some back offices extend their services into offering consultative services in principals' tax liabilities and goals, develop a plan to minimize tax liabilities, and/or enhance after-tax return on investment.

Transferring responsibility for these activities to an independent third party reassures limited partners that they are receiving timely and accurate information. Administrative resources at the fund level are freed up, permitting managers to focus on scouting, screening, and harvesting deals. Costs to the firm are further decreased, as these operations are typically borne by the fund, not the general partners. Thus, it is in any GP's interest to establish strong business systems. John Alfonsi, managing director at Cendrowski Corporate Advisors, points out that the back office can allow the GPs to focus on what they are good at—sourcing, investing, and managing the portfolio. Any outsourced back office creates these advantages:

■ Permits fund managers to focus on core operations—investments.
■ Provides timely gathering and recording of necessary information for fund managers, reducing the need to chase information.
■ Increases investor confidence in financial reporting and portfolio company valuation.
■ Can easily increase or decrease with demand throughout the fund's life.
■ Services are performed by licensed industry specialists.
■ Facilitates third-party control on movement of funds.
■ Middle office operations are a relatively newer concept that interfaces with both the back office and front office (fund principals). Their functions generally include risk management, calculation of profits and losses, and investor communications. In many organizations, there is relatively little distinction between the back-office and middle-office operations; everything but fund-raising and portfolio investments is grouped into back-office operations.

Investors are also direct beneficiaries of well-designed and implemented accounting systems in the back- and middle-office operations. Accounting systems with a documented and enforced internal control environment provide protection from the misappropriation of investor monies as well as the misstatement of results of operations and investments. Timely communication of the operations through regular capital account reporting, financial statements, and portfolio company updates provides investors with comfort that the monies entrusted to the fund principals are being used as intended.

Back- and middle-office operations should include all services that are necessary to support the fund principals' investment activities. Administrative services should include a review of the fund documents with an understanding and possible modeling of the waterfall—the priority in which money is returned on an investment. Maintenance and storage, preferably in a secure cloud, of fund documents, investor data including subscription documents, and portfolio company investments to ensure that permanent documents are safeguarded and may be referred to as needed. Back- and middle-office operations should allow fund principals increased time to focus on the fund's core investment business rather than on fund administration. "Whether the back- and middle-office operations are outsourced or staffed internally, the design should be based on employee qualifications and capabilities, integrity, and confidentiality," says Harry Cendrowski.

SUMMARY

While establishing the legal entities is easy, attracting suitable talent to the firm, building a team, and defining the culture of a firm requires adequate care. Establishing the underlying fabric of economics, ownership, and culture requires a diligent approach. For many first-time funds, the fund-raising activity often commences prior to formal establishment of structures. Once the first close is on the horizon, the attorneys can put the legal structures in place promptly. But it is getting to the "first close" that matters.

CHAPTER 5

Getting to the First Close

It is useless to be a creative original thinker unless you can also sell what you create.
— David Ogilvy, "Father of Advertising"

Having reviewed the universe of investors, their investment criteria, terms, and fund structure, we look at getting to the finish line—getting the fund to a close—the process of admitting investors into the fund. Most funds have a two-step closing process—a first close followed by the final close. Unless of course, you are Andreessen-Horowitz, where you can raise $1.1 billion in 22 months across three funds. After the fund has closed, the exhilarating or exhausting process of raising capital comes to an end. We conclude this "Raising the fund" section with this chapter and in the following section, we look at the investment process.

The process of closing, or the first close, as depicted in Figure 5.1 can occur typically at about 40 to 70 percent of the size of the fund. For example, a $20 million fund can conduct its first close at $10 million or higher. The final close occurs ideally within 12 months of the first close. Conducting the first close allows a GP to start making investments and collecting fees. But it is human nature to stall when it comes to firming up the commitment. Several GPs have often been frustrated with LPs making verbal commitments and backing off at the time of executing documents. Consider how William Draper nudged a potential LP, who was firmly perched on a fence, to take the leap. "Maybe you're just not ready for venture capital," says William Draper III, to a potential LP, debating over a $10 million commitment. "Oh, no, no, no," the LP said. So all of a sudden, the cards turned and he signed it.[1] The LP committed, and Draper Gaither Anderson did not ever call the entire $10 million. They invested $6 million and returned $750 million to

Prepare	Soft Launch	First Close	Final Close
• Assemble team and develop strategy • Draft initial pitch deck • Identify target universe of LPs • Warehouse investment opportunities	• Meet with lead LPs to test-drive the concept • Seek inputs and feedback —avoid hard sell • Soft circle at least ~25 percent from lead investors	• Aim to complete first close at 50 percent of the fund size • Beware of long cycles— maintain momentum • Invest in first portfolio company	• Wrap up fund-raising after 12 months of first close • Find that 10X exit in three years—raise Fund II • Repeat

FIGURE 5.1   Steps to Fund Closing

their happy investors. I am sure that was one happy LP who would not have attained nirvana without that ever-important nudge.

When sufficient financial commitments have been gathered, the attorney sets a closing date. Prior to closing the following preconditions must occur:

- *Private placement memorandum (PPM):* Finalize PPM and supplements and circulate to all closing investors.
- *Subscription agreements:* For each investor, the subscription agreement is reviewed to ensure accuracy, completeness, and compliance with securities laws. The aggregate capital commitments are established for the first close.
- *Limited partnership agreement:* All negotiations with the LP universe are completed and the final draft is circulated to all investors.
- *General partner agreement:* The GP LLC agreement, which is internal to the fund managers, is completed and circulated to all fund managers.
- *Side letters:* Any side letters that may have been negotiated must be completed and circulated with relevant investors.[2]

The steps to a close are typically led by an attorney/law firm and after all LP Agreements have been executed by limited partners, the Certificate of Good Standing is obtained by attorneys. This date of "good standing" becomes the closing date. Fund managers execute subscription agreements and accept closing subscriptions. Wire transfers are then completed and at times are held in escrow by attorneys until the full amounts are received from all LPs. The fund managers would execute the GP LLC agreements.

This process requires much orchestration of several different elements and a good attorney will offer a checklist at least 60 days ahead of closing. Such a checklist can help a GP to coordinate all the moving parts effectively. And don't forget the champagne!

BUILD YOUR TARGET LIST OF INVESTORS

Screening and targeting potential limited partners (LPs, outlined in Chapter 1) in a systematic manner can significantly improve the GP's ability to successfully raise a fund. Some questions to consider while screening LPs are:

- *Affinity for emerging managers versus established managers:* A delicate question to ask, especially if you are in the emerging manager category. While some funds of funds have dedicated emerging manager programs, others would not engage.
- *Size:*
  - Assets under management: If the target LP is too large, for example, a $50 billion pension fund, a smaller fund of, say, $100 million in size may have a harder time convincing the LP to invest $10 million. Typical investment size for such a pension fund would be ~$50 million or higher.
  - Minimum investment size: Larger LPs seek to avoid a number of smaller transactions and thus, improve internal efficiency in managing their portfolios.
- *Affinity to your stage of investments:* Some LPs have found middle-market buyout to be a suitable strategy; conversely, others have found early-stage venture to be appropriate.
- *Sector of investments:* Is the LP looking to build a technology portfolio? Or cleantech?
- *Past investments activity:* Has the target LP invested in similar funds? Average amounts? A caveat for emerging managers—if an LP has not invested in this asset class, be prepared to invest in a long education process. And frequently, after you educate the potential LP, you might find that this LP has decided against investing in this VC asset class. Or worse, to invest in another, likely better performing fund. At least you earned some karma points from that LP!

Various customer relationship management (CRM) vendors, such as Salesforce.com, offer a customized tool for venture capital funds. These can be used to track and manage the fund-raise process. A sample LP contact log can be seen in Table 5.1. Depending on the brand, performance,

TABLE 5.1 Sample LP Contact Log

Organization Type	Contact Person (Name)	AUM	Average Investment Size	Status	Next Steps
State Pension Fund	PE Portfolio Manager	$30B	$50M	E-mailed executive summary	Follow up in March.
University Endowment	Chief Investment Officer	$10B	$10M	Awaiting introduction	
Fund-of-Funds	Vice President – Fund Investments	$800M	$20M	Initiated due diligence	Expected to finish due diligence in 4 weeks. Discuss LPA post due diligence.
Family Office	Director of PE	N/A	$1M	Soft commitment	Execute LPA.
Strategic Corporate Investor	VP, Corporate Development	N/A	TBD	Met with CFO and CEO	Awaiting response.
HNWI	Ms. Wendy C	N/A	$500,000	Soft commitment	Execute LPA. Request for additional contacts.

and market conditions, the process takes anywhere from a few months to 18 months. (See Figure 5.2.) The market indicators are clearly downbeat when you consider Figure 5.3. In Figure 5.4, the LP outlay variation can be seen by size of funds. Note that in a $20 million early-stage fund, the population of HNWIs is significantly large.

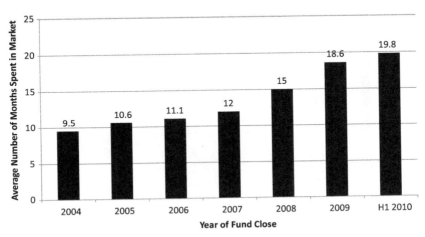

FIGURE 5.2 Fund-Raising Time Lines: The Uphill Crawl
Source: Preqin, 2010.

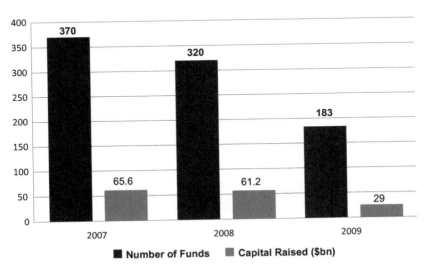

FIGURE 5.3 VC Funds Raised: Darwin at Work?
Source: Preqin, 2010.

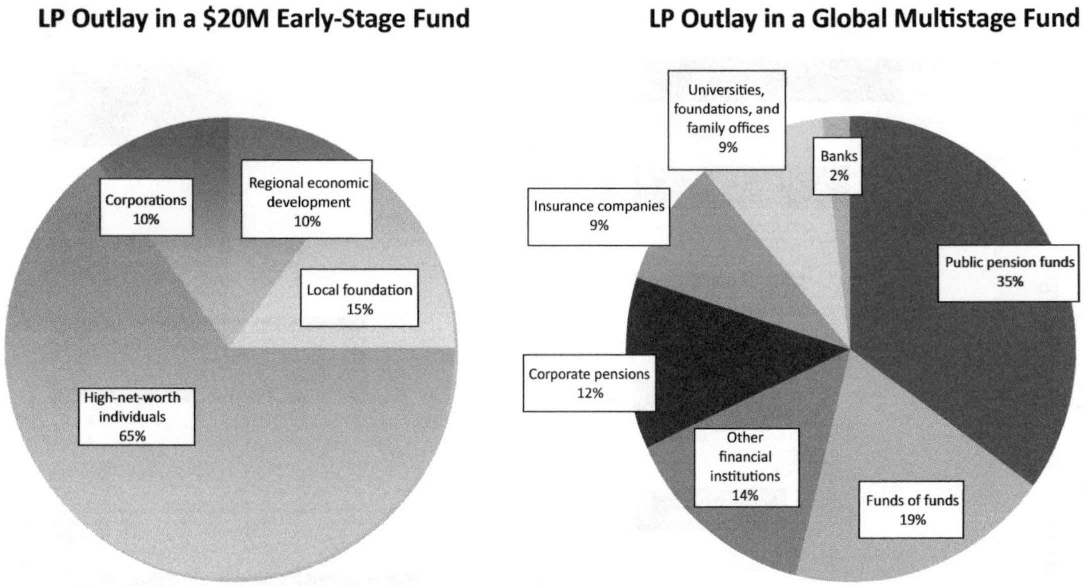

LP Outlay in a $20M Early-Stage Fund

Regional economic development 10%

Local foundation 15%

Corporations 10%

High-net-worth individuals 65%

LP Outlay in a Global Multistage Fund

Public pension funds 35%

Funds of funds 19%

Banks 2%

Universities, foundations, and family offices 9%

Insurance companies 9%

Corporate pensions 12%

Other financial institutions 14%

FIGURE 5.4 LP Outlay Varies by Type of Fund

"We wanted to attract 20 LPs which would include a healthy mix of Fund-of-Funds, Foundations, Family Offices, Pension Funds. Eight months and 200 meetings later, that is exactly where we ended up" says Ravi Mohan, Shasta Ventures. Shasta's Fund I target size was $175 million and closed at $210 million in approximately seven months.

FUND MARKETING MATERIALS

Not every fund has the luxury of raising capital without a private placement memorandum (PPM), but the Foundry Group, investors in Zynga, closed their most recent fund at $225 million without a PPM. Most funds do not have this luxury and have to prepare a private placement memorandum (PPM), a rough equivalent of a business plan. Besides a PPM, a succinct presentation slide deck and a two-page executive summary are helpful tools as well. Any good PPM will have, at the minimum, the following key sections:

- Management team—general partners' background
- Investment strategy
- Prior track record
- A brief summary of terms and conditions of the investment opportunity

These sections are critical, while other supporting sections, such as Investment Process and Investment Summaries of prior portfolio, are a welcome addition. However, these do not hold high importance in the decision-making process. Other mandatory sections include Risk Factors; Tax and Regulatory Matters; and Foreign Securities Laws, which are boilerplate texts of pure legalese and placed to protect both the investors and the general partners.

While the PPM is the backbone, an executive summary (ES) and a slide deck (PPT)—both drawn from the PPM—are used as opening gambits with potential investors. According to Wilson Sonsini Goodrich and Rosati, a leading California-based law firm, omitting information can be just as damaging as affirmative misstatements.[3] Other issues to look for in any PPM include:

- *Team*: Overstatement of qualifications of the team, time commitment, track record and prior experience, education and other attributes.

- *Financial information*: Failing to distinguish between gross and net investment returns, valuations, complete listing of all investments as opposed to mere highlights.
- *Other material information*: Failure to disclose adverse facts related to lawsuits, regulatory actions, conflicts, disputes, and other adverse facts.

The PPM averages about 50 pages to 75 pages in length and includes the following:

- Executive Summary (3 to 5 pages): The primary reasons—the headliners—why any LP should invest in the fund:
  - Market opportunity
  - Background (history and performance) of the firm
  - Management team
  - Investment focus areas
  - Summary of terms (1 page)
- Market Opportunity and Investment Strategy (5 to 8 pages)
- Investment Process (3 to 5 pages)
- Organization and Management Team (5 pages)
- Selected Transactions/Investment Summary (5 to 8 pages, one page per transaction)
- Investment Terms (10 pages)
- Risks and Regulatory Considerations (20 pages)

The bulk of the PPM—about 30 pages—is weighted heavily with investment terms and legalese. Any potential investor's attention needs to be drawn to the team, performance, and strategy sections. GPs should take extra care to ensure that the marketing documents are packaged elegantly without heavy emphasis on visual sizzle, sans any errors. "I have seen several PPMs or PPTs with typos—it is not a good starting point," one Midwest-based LP pointed out. As the PPM version goes through any changes, it is a normal practice to date the PPM cover (month and year). PPMs are also serially numbered and tracked, a practice strongly recommended by attorneys to minimize legal challenges.

PRESENTATION SLIDES

A fund presentation is no more than 12 to 14 slides encapsulated for a 15 to 20 minute presentation. By all means, avoid any adjectives and resist the urge to overindulge in self-praise. Let the actions (numbers, outcomes) speak for themselves. Key points to highlight in a presentation would include:

- *Team*: Demonstrate expertise (number of investments, returns), strong interrelationships (cohesion), and complementary skills.
- *Investment strategy and market opportunity*: Demonstrate a compelling thesis that explains how this team, combined with the stated strategy and market conditions, is a well-timed opportunity.
- *Prior and new investments*: Demonstrate that the GPs can source at least 6 to 8 good opportunities and syndicate these in the first five years. Note to GP: To invest in 6 to 8 opportunities, a flow rate of 100x needs to be demonstrated.
- *Returns*: The team has the track record and/or the ability to make investments and generate superior returns. Demonstrate that you can find opportunities and invest at favorable terms leading to step-ups and strong exits.

Following is an outline of a fund presentation:

Slide 1	Summary highlights: Describe fund (strategy, size, and focus), overall team's expertise, past performance, and ability to generate returns. Highlight GP contribution if it is substantially more than typical 1 percent commitment.
Slide 2	Management team overview: individuals, backgrounds, their investment/domain expertise.
Slides 3 and 4	Management team details: provide background and details of each investment professional.
Slide 5	Market opportunity: Macro-level trends and pockets of opportunity.
Slides 6 and 7	Portfolio construction strategy: size of investment, number of companies and stage of investment, exit horizons, and capital needed to reach exit points.
Slide 8	Case studies/summary of target companies.
Slides 9 and 10	Conclusion: Why is this fund/team better suited to generate superior returns? Why now?
Appendix	Pipeline of warehoused opportunities; syndicate VC relationships, size of their fund and sector expertise.

MAKING THE PRESENTATION PITCH: DRINK YOUR OWN KOOL-AID

GPs should consider approaching LPs from a customercentric view—the LPs should clearly see the benefit in investing in you. "VCs demand of the portfolio companies that the value proposition should be very customer focused. But I find that GPs seldom approach LPs with a value proposition. If a GP can make it in the interest of that LP, they may actually want to invest in the fund. This simple perspective seems to be lost on a fair number of GPs," laments Chris Rizik, who raised two venture funds as a GP and now manages Renaissance Venture Capital Fund, a fund-of-funds.

Really, that is your elevator pitch! That is a common reaction after LPs have suffered lengthy, boring presentations where GPs get into self-aggrandizing mode. Slide after slide of ennui where GPs get into "and let me tell you about this company..." mode has gotten many LPs to wringing their hands. Note to GPs: LPs really don't care that much about how great you are. So instead of sucking up all the oxygen in the room, start by asking how the LP would like to best use this time. If given a chance to present your pitch, drink your own Kool-Aid. Remember when you chastised entrepreneurs about their presentations being long-winded and off point. Your pitch should be no more than a dozen slides and 15 minutes. "This is so basic, but rarely happens. A GP should approach the LP exactly the same way they want an entrepreneur to approach them. I have been surprised how few GPs can actually eat their own cooking when it comes to making presentations," says Chris Rizik. A lengthy 40-slide presentation, macro trends, and off-point information do not further your cause. Having lived the life on the other side as a VC, Chris is sympathetic about the challenges faced by any GP. Igor Rozenblit adds, "The goal of the meeting is for the LP to collect information from the GP. The GPs should not spend time telling us about their value-add to the portfolio. In my opinion, most LPs do not believe that GPs add any value—thus, GPs are better off focusing the time on LP questions during the meeting."

ATTRACTING THE LEAD INVESTOR: YOUR "NUT"

Many GPs start the fund-raising process by looking for the lead investor, a limited partner who can make the first significant commitment for the fund. If the fund managers are relatively newer to the game, this can be a significant challenge. Certain institutional LPs, particularly pension funds and funds of funds, seldom consider investing in funds with limited track records.

Endowments and foundations may be open to looking at the opportunity, but it all depends on the sophistication, nuances, and appetite of each LP.

SNAGGING THAT LEAD INVESTOR: LESSONS FROM RICHARD KRAMLICH, FOUNDER OF NEW ENTERPRISE ASSOCIATES (NEA), WITH $11 BILLION UNDER MANAGEMENT

"So, let me get this straight. You're talking about us putting up a million dollars, right?"

Kramlich: "Yes, sir."

"You're talking about not telling us how you're going to invest it, is that right?"

Kramlich: "Yes, sir, that's correct."

"And you're telling me this money is going to be illiquid for twelve years, is that right?"

Kramlich: "That's correct."

"You're telling me, you all, as a group, have no track record, and you're not promising any rate of return, is that right?"

Kramlich: "Yes, sir, that's right."

So finally, this LP says, "Well, if you all feel comfortable taking the risk, I'll support you."

This LP invested $1million in NEA Fund I.

Source: C. Richard Kramlich, "Venture Capital Greats: A Conversation with C. Richard Kramlich," interviewed by Mauree Jane Perry on August 31, 2006, in San Francisco, California, National Venture Capital Association, Arlington, Virginia.

Consider ARCH Venture Partners' ability to find a lead investor for their Fund I circa 1980. On a Saturday afternoon, Steven Lazarus, founder of ARCH, was able to pitch a vice chairman of an insurance company. This potential LP took a break during his tennis game and committed $4 million by the end of the hour-long meeting. "I had my nut and from that point the money rolled in," Lazarus would say.[4] ARCH raised $9 million for its Fund I. But that was in the early 1980s—in current times, newer funds are better suited in targeting a larger number of smaller investors, such as high-net-worth individuals and family offices.

When it comes to fund-raising, the top quartile firms, of course, have a problem of meaningful allocations. In the brief windows of fund-raising cycles, the problem of excess prevails—how to choose from all those LPs kicking down the doors and ensure that a meaningful share is allocated to each LP. A problem that the mediocre firms would love to have! Recall that larger LPs, who typically have billions in assets under management, would be underwhelmed with a tiny share of a top quartile fund. And if the top quartile fund doubles this capital in 10 years, the overall impact it has on the pension fund returns is minimal. A drop in the bucket doubles to two drops—still a minor variation. All LPs are waiting for that top quartile bucket to overflow. And once funds reach that stature, the fund-raising cycles become shorter and shorter as existing LPs tend to stay put and the new LPs compete to get in. "We have little to no churn in our LPs," says Mitch Lasky of Benchmark Capital. On the other hand, several subpar or below-average firms are able to sucker in newer LPs at every fund-raising cycle.

A good lead investor can act as a source of other introductions, be a powerful reference, and greatly improve your chances of raising the fund. GPs should focus their early efforts on attracting such a king maker. But finding someone who will take a leap of faith with a newer GP team is not as easy.

Once a lead investor is snagged, the GPs ought to continue to attract those fast followers, and finally those laggards, who will come in days before the final close. The only proven way to attract these is to communicate effectively.

COMMUNICATE, CREATE, AND MAINTAIN MOMENTUM

The process of managing multiple relationships effectively and leading these to a closing point where they are ready to make a commitment is fraught with uncertainties and challenges. GPs who were successful pointed out that they followed some simple guidelines:

- *Communicate:* Any potential investors with whom you met would like to know how you are progressing with your fund-raising efforts. A steady flow of meaningful communication, timely but not excessive overload, can help a GP to gain ongoing mind-share with LPs.
- *Create momentum:* The ability to create momentum with LPs is an art form, akin to rolling a snowball downhill and making sure that it arrives at its destination in one piece. Tying momentum and communication together, an example could be, "In the past 90 days we have added commitments of an additional $10 million, raising our total commitments to $25 million. These commitments include a family office, several HNWIs, and a strategic corporate investor."

Take the example of .406 Ventures Fund I that attracted $167 million in the tough economic environment of 2008. "About 90 percent of our fund was raised from institutions. It took one year to get it done from first close, 18 months from start to finish. LPs tested us at every step. We were politely persistent and created momentum. It is a lot of work and not for the faint of heart," says Liam Donohue, co-founder and managing director of .406 Ventures.

OFFERING SWEETENERS TO ATTRACT LPs: A DOUBLE-EDGED SWORD

Several GPs offer sweeteners to make the fund attractive to potential LPs, and some even attempt to create a sense of urgency.

Liam Donohue offers a good example of a sweetener. "We pooled our own capital, invested in five companies and offered to contribute this portfolio of five investments to the fund *at cost*. LPs got a sense of opportunities we can attract and realized that we were serious about getting in the business. We believed that this is a small price to pay. We could demonstrate we understood how to build a portfolio that aligns with our strategy. LPs know that it is easy to write about strategy in an offering document, but having actually 'walked the talk' and done it as a first-time fund, that level of thoughtfulness and sophistication allowed us to demonstrate that we can walk the talk," he says. When one of the portfolio companies, HealthDialog, a health care analytics company, was sold for $775 million, the LPs received 2x in less than seven months.

Examples of sweeteners that have not yielded positive outcomes include offering portfolio companies from previous funds that may not have made any meaningful progress. In one example, Fund III offered at least half a dozen companies from Fund II to LPs at cost. This can irritate existing Fund II LPs who have borne significant risk. Future Fund III LPs who may also wonder how they might be treated when it comes time to raise Fund IV.

THE ROLE OF PLACEMENT AGENTS IN FUND-RAISING

Who are the placement agents and what do they exactly do? In general, the roles of placement agents are multifaceted and complex. They not only advise venture capital funds seeking advice and capital in raising a new fund, but also broker much of the crucial interaction with institutional investors and key players in the private equity community. Placement agents provide a necessary service for venture capital firms—expanding and bolstering the investor base and aiding in fundraising efforts.[5] Emerging managers as well as more established firms look to placement agents to gain access to new institutional investors and to streamline the logistics of the fund-raising operations. Beyond opening new doors for funds, they also influence fund terms with investors and offer advice on market conditions.[6]

Investment banks like Credit Suisse and UBS have divisions that offer placement agent services. These global entities, operating from many offices with dedicated staff handling multiple accounts for their private equity customers, can access a larger pool of investors quickly. In addition to investment banks, there are also other global investment placement and advisory firms that focus on providing placement agent service. Unlike investment banks, though, these large independent entities often work exclusively as placement agents. Smaller boutique independent firms also provide placement services, often focusing on a sector or geographical niche (e.g., the Middle East) or a select circle of investors. They may also specialize in specific types of funds (e.g., funds of funds and venture capital funds). "The big houses like Credit Suisse or UBS typically send institutional LPs a book of deals in the market. You can pick a few and ask for more details. The good placement agents research extensively and listen carefully. More so, even before they sign up a client they know who they will market it to," says Bob Clone, who manages a PE portfolio at State of Indiana Retirement Systems.

The right placement agent can make a significant impact during the fund-raise process. "We spend tremendous amount of time getting materials ready, presentations and rehearsals to ensure consistency of communication. Getting an hour with a leading LP is difficult but when you do get it, we make sure that the GP can make the best use of it," says Gus Long of Stanwich Advisors. Kelly DePonte of Probitas Partners points out the critical roles that a placement agent plays in supporting venture capital funds:

- *Market intelligence and social capital:* Placement agents offer connections and a solid base of contacts for their clients, but they are much more than a glorified Rolodex or phone book of investors. Rather than serving as a static database of names for private equity funds, the best placement agents are aggressive trackers, watching the shifts in personnel, sniffing out sector trends, and monitoring investment appetite in the allocations of private equity. In hiring placement agents, funds gain more efficiency in their fund-raising efforts, by benefiting from the agents' targeted approach rather than relying on shallow leads and marketing plans.[7] Agents keep a constant check on the pulse of the market, honing long-term insight and an instinctual know-how on what relationships work or don't work. Placement agents also provide access to new investors and sources of capital. Sentinel's David Lobel has noted the role a placement agent plays, "When [managers] want new investors, or to raise a larger fund, one is left with the task of speaking to strangers, and a placement agent can be helpful with that."[8]

A VC WHISPERER

Doug Newhouse, a managing director with Sterling Investment Partners, notes that placement agents allow them to "focus on [their] core competency—deal making."[9] Placement agents save a fund from being distracted on the lengthy and painful process of fund-raising—a necessary but often periodic step. "You only raise funds every four, five, six years, [so] you can't do it as well as a professional," said Newhouse.[10] Placement agents are key strategists in determining the details of a fund-raising campaign, such as a target fund size, investor expectations on staffing and professional backgrounds, selection of the right legal team, and other launch details that might be overlooked even by more experienced fund managers or fund managers overseeing multiple funds. They also play an indomitable role in marketing, giving advice on putting together a scalable mix of investors in the United States and abroad who not only are willing to commit, but have the resources to do so given a difficult market. With their close contacts, they often have a better sense of the investor market than does a venture capital fund manager. Also, in taking a lead negotiator role in interfacing with investors, placement agents can advise on the right timing for a launch, gauging the strengths and handicaps of investors. More importantly, placement agents can sustain the momentum in a marketing or fundraising campaign. By moving swiftly in these areas, a fund is brought to a close much faster and avoids languishing and being dubbed unimportant or irrelevant by investors faced with a wide range of opportunities. "The fund-raise process is a step function—the objective of the first meeting is not to get signed subscription documents—the objective is to get the LP to do more work—the next step is for them to come on site for due diligence. The objective is always to move to the next step—for some it's three steps and for some it's twenty steps—but you have to be ready at every step. A qualified team without form and delivery can kill the investment. There are groups that should get funded but do not because they cannot communicate their story effectively . . . that part of our preparation process is often painful, but that's where we make the biggest impact," says Gus Long.

■ *A guide on fund terms and trends:* Finally, placement agents offer value to venture capital firms by keeping fund managers informed about fund terms and conditions before going to market. What is the latest on distribution waterfalls, no-fault divorce, and clawback provisions—a placement agent can guide you. From their interactions with investors, placement agents can predict how the investment market will react to fund terms and conditions as well as adapt to shifting economic and governance provisions. Venture capital fund managers should look for placement agents who demonstrate the range of abilities addressed previously, possessing intimate knowledge of the investment community and the experience in conducting rigorous due diligence, preparing marketing and fundraising campaigns, and exhibiting integrity and professionalism in bridging partners and investors.[11] On the other side of the coin, as institutional investors become increasingly selective about the funds they invest in, the placement agent's role becomes more critical than ever in smoothing communication between general and limited partners, particularly for emerging funds. While many limited partners want to invest in safe bets and brand-name funds, they are also willing to invest in new funds if an accomplished placement agent brokers the deal. Placement agents are particularly supportive of new venture capital funds run by managers with a track record. Commenting on the deals between general partners and limited partners, Jeffrey Stern, a managing director with Forum Capital Partners, has said that new funds with experienced leaders are the kinds of firms that "make LPs perk up," and that "it's [the placement agent's] job to scout these firms for the LPs"—striking the right balance between the positive return and inherent risks for investors.[12]

Igor Rozenblit, who represented a $2.5 billion European financial services company seeking investments in venture capital and private equity funds, would frequently interact with some of the top placement agents such as UBS, Credit Suisse, Lazard, and Park Hill. He says: "Some GPs may not be good at exaggeration but the placement agents are gifted at it. Placement agents would usually puff things up—and the top worn-out clichés of placement agents ignored by most LPs include:

We have soft-circled about two-thirds of the fund. . . .
This is the hottest fund to date . . .
It's going to be oversubscribed—we are closing tomorrow. . . .

And the final close is never the final close—there will always be room for one more LP. Often, we were able to reserve a spot—in one case, we closed one month <u>after the final close.</u>"

CAVEAT EMPTOR

Incidences of abuse in the placement service industry—often from political insiders using their political affiliations, contacts, and celebrity reach to broker deals between investors and funds have caused much headache to the legitimate entities. Orin Kramer, head of New Jersey's Investment Council, has commented on some placement agents as "politically connected intermediaries ... who are not really in the financial business," which causes a multitude of thorny ethical issues.[13] According to various news sources, New York, New Mexico, Florida, and Massachusetts have seen a rise in civil complaints regarding the management of pension funds and the use of placement agents with political connections and financial self-interest in brokering deals with investors. For example, the Los Angeles Department of Fire and Police Pensions was shocked over the $150,000 fee received by Henry Morris, a former New York political advisor, who worked as a placement agent from Quadrangle Group LLC, for roping in $10 million for their investment fund. In New Mexico, firms that employed Marc Correra, son of a supporter of New Mexico Governor Bill Richardson, earned $15 million on investments to the state's endowment and teacher pension fund.[14]

While taking advantage of political affiliations for private gain isn't necessarily a criminal offense, these examples illustrate how former politicians, campaign operatives, and other public officials are getting into the business and may raise legal issues. In 2010, California passed a bill to restrict the use of placement agents by requiring anyone who solicits investments from CalPERS and CalSTRS—the California state public retirement systems (with $274 billion in assets under management as of July 2010) to register as lobbyists. This effectively prohibits agents from receiving compensation from investment deals in state funds. Legislators pushed the bill in light of the case of a former CalPERS board member who garnered placement fees of more than $47 million from the state investment managers.[15] Other private equity firms, such as Carlyle, became embroiled in a fund-raising controversy.[16] In 2009, the New York Attorney General and the SEC accused Hank Morris, a placement agent hired by Carlyle and many other firms, of hatching a scheme that involved kickbacks from investment firms seeking allocation deals with the state's public pension fund.

Some placement agents will continue to function as hired guns for private equity funds. Others play a legitimate role and reduce friction in an industry where constraints on time are high and the demand-supply ratio of capital is perpetually tilted.

SUMMARY

Getting to the first close for any emerging manager is easy—all it takes is the ability to indulge in self-flagellation, listen to a thousand no's, and eventually find a lead investor. By rudimentary estimates, less than 10 percent of first-time funds reach the finish line while the other 90 percent abandon their plans and try their hand at something else.

LPs are much more responsive when a GP aims to be customercentric (as in "What is in it for them?") and concise. Offer middle of the road terms. And know that the right placement agents can play a vital role in accelerating the fund-raise process.

This wraps up the fund-raise section. In Part Two, we look at the investment cycle: sourcing, due diligence, structuring, and exits.

Two

The Investment Process

Whereas Part One covered the aspects of fund-raising, in Part Two we look at the steps of the investment process:

- Any venture firm's investment process starts with sourcing—the art of finding opportunities that fit within a fund's investment criteria. Chapter 6 covers the best practices in the art of sourcing opportunities.
- The next phase involves screening and due diligence where risk and potential upside are assessed. In a business where a practitioner reviews a large volume of opportunities to make a small number of investments, screening starts with the ability to say "No" to virtually most opportunities. The due diligence phase, where the trade-offs are assessed, is reviewed in Chapter 7.
- Structuring prudent investments results in a term sheet that balances the elements of economics and governance/control provisions. Several newcomers in the business describe the term sheet as "dense legalese"—a put-off. In describing terms, the approach in Chapters 8 through 10 has been to simplify ownership, cap tables, valuation, and terms.
- The real fun begins after the term sheet—post-investment monitoring, where your mettle is tested as you support the CEO to meet and exceed the predetermined milestones. Chapter 11 describes the roles and responsibilities of a VC as a board member. This chapter is based on the foundation built by Pascal Levensohn of Levensohn Venture Partners, a board member of National VC Association.

■ Finally, the process culminates with an exit where the investment yields a return. In Chapter 12, we look at the basics of how exits occur. This book will self-destruct after your first successful exit. The last chapter sums up the attributes and attitudes of successful practitioners.

CHAPTER 6

The Art of Sourcing Investment Opportunities

Good GPs and funds magnetize good entrepreneurs. I have found sourcing to be a differentiator, a huge advantage, much more than what I was trained to see.
—Chris "SuperLP" Douvos, Co-Head of Private Equity Investing at The Investment Fund for Foundations (TIFF)

Kevin Efrusy of Accel Partners is fast approaching the "God" category of venture capitalists. After all, he sourced, or found, this great investment opportunity called Facebook for Accel Partners. Efrusy, who had served two separate stints as an entrepreneur-in-residence at Kleiner Perkins Caufield and Byers (KPCB), had joined Accel in 2003, and his primary directive was to find the next big thing in social and new media applications. While Efrusy was on the hunt, he found his target two years into his career at Accel. Chi-Hua Chien, a graduate student doing research for Accel, pointed out this opportunity to Efrusy, who never gave up till he trapped this elusive beast.

"Social networks had this dirty name," he said in *The Facebook Effect*.[1] But as soon as he saw Facebook, he could smell the potential. Here was an opportunity for marketers to reach a much-wanted demographic during their most impressionable years. This was 2004, when the number of Facebook users was fewer than 1 million. Efrusy called and e-mailed relentlessly—and was stonewalled or turned down. "We will move heaven and earth to make this a successful company," Efrusy once told Mark Zuckerberg. But Facebook was not interested in talking to venture capitalists. "He was hounding us," one Facebook executive would recall.

Finally, Efrusy decided to walk over to Facebook's offices and into a chaotic scene, where remnants of the previous night's liquor party were strewn all over. One person, struggling to assemble a DIY table, had blood oozing from his forehead. Efrusy promised Zuckerberg, who was nibbling on a burrito: "Come to our partners' meeting on Monday. We'll give you a term sheet by the end of the day, or you'll never hear from us again."

Over the weekend, Efrusy did some intense calling around to find out more about the Facebook phenomenon. On Monday morning at 10 A.M., Zuckerberg, wearing his flip-flops, shorts, and a T-shirt, showed up at Accel's offices with two cohorts. They didn't bother bringing any slides. Five days later, after much song and dance and pleading, Accel had closed on a $12.7 million investment, owning a 15 percent stake in Facebook. Efrusy did not get a board seat. "It hurt my feelings," he would say. "But I understand."

Efrusy displays all attributes essential to source a good investment opportunity: rapid assessment, proactive contact, tenacity, and shamelessness. But it is not just Efrusy's qualities that count—the firm also matters. Accel's capital, track record, and the stature of Jim Bryer (who is firmly established in the "VC God" category) had an overall impact on completing the investment. But even more interesting is the fact that James Swartz, founder of Accel Partners, speaking prophetically of investing in new technological waves, once said, "The older generation . . . better just get the heck outta the way, or if you want to stay in the game, get a kid and let him do his thing."[2] Little did Swartz know that this Efrusy kid was already at work in sourcing the next big thing for Accel. Hany Nada, co-founder of GGV, a $1 billion venture fund boasting of investments in Chinese giants like Alibaba, agrees. "I am 42 years old and I find that it is better to bring in the newer generation—they understand emerging technology trends better than I do." Nada demonstrates the same realistic approach of Swartz—know your limitations.

While the hypercompetitive universe of the Silicon Valley demands such Efrusy-like attributes, the rest of the geography functions differently. Typical sources of investment opportunities lie embedded within the network—the social fabric woven over time that yields consistent quality referrals. Serial entrepreneurs or peer venture practitioners are the most qualitative and reliable sources. Other sources include attorneys, angel networks, banks and nonbank financial institutions, incubators, and technology transfer offices. Figure 6.1 depicts the overall investment process, which commences with sourcing. Table 6.1 outlines these options in more detail.

This chapter describes the various sources of investment opportunities for venture investments. As a rule of thumb, investors look at

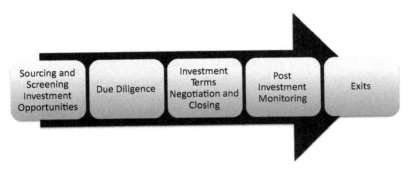

FIGURE 6.1 A Venture Fund's Investment Process

1,000 investment opportunities before they invest in any one. Consider the statistics in Figure 6.2 representative of typical percentages of investment.

THE BEST SOURCE: THE NETWORK

In any business, it's primarily relationships that matter. But in the venture business, relationships can make or break a practitioner. For the handful of venture firms that have established brands, opportunities may arrive from a vast matrix of relationships: serial entrepreneurs, peer venture investors, attorneys, investment bankers, and service providers. Brad Feld of the Foundry Group had a 15-year relationship with Mark Pincus, the founder of Zynga. Feld and Union Square Ventures led the first round of investment in this start-up in 2007 and by 2011 the company's valuation was well over $5 billion. Or consider Pierre Omidyar, founder of eBay. While seeking the first round of capital, Omidyar had a term sheet, which offered at least 2.5x higher valuation, but he still chose to go with lower valuation offered by Benchmark Capital. Pierre knew Bruce Dunlieve, a GP at Benchmark who had invested in his prior company, and trusted the relationship. And Benchmark netted $2.5B on its $5M eBay investment.[3]

Networks function well within certain geographies. "Northern California is very network-centric, and it's relatively uncommon to find really high-quality investment opportunities in the straightforward way of going to conferences and having people submit things on your web site. The really good deals go through a network because it's an extremely well connected, low-friction community," says William Elkus, managing partner of Clearstone Venture Partners, who counts PayPal and Overture among his past investment successes.

TABLE 6.1 Sources of Investment Opportunity

Category	Source	Advantages
Financial	Angel networks	Minimized technology and market risk. Watch for nonmarket terms and misaligned expectations.
	Peer investors/other venture practitioners	Possibly same terms, speedier due diligence, trusted relationships. Watch for lame horses being parlayed as great opportunities.
	Attorneys/accountants/ consultants	Can provide some level of prescreening based on fund criteria and fit. Caveat emptor: All clients who pay $300 an hour look great!
	Banks/venture debt providers	Can mitigate risk; may have skin in the game.
Social	Serial entrepreneurs	Well-vetted ideas, ability to attract teams, recognition of challenges. The best source, by far!
	Government/economic development/nonprofit professionals	Volume, access to a larger network. Quality may be suspect.
	Business plan competitions and venture forums	Prescreened and vetted, this may be a good source of opportunities for early-stage investors. Watch for students who participate for the sake of participating and winning—not building a business.
Technology	Incubators, university tech transfer offices, federal research labs	Diamond in the rough! May need to invest time to build the business strategy and team. Watch for technology in search of an application.
	Corporate IP	Potential for joint development, co-investments, beta customers. Pharma VCs are suited to benefit from the inherent challenges in the biotech sector.

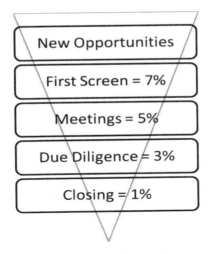

FIGURE 6.2 Typical Sourcing, Screening, and Investment Ratios

WHEN OPPORTUNITY MEETS THE PREPARED MIND

One evening, Don Valentine, founder of Sequoia Capital, was dining at a restaurant when he saw Steve Jobs and Mike Markkula together and sensed what was being discussed. He dispatched a bottle of wine with a note: "Don't lose sight of the fact that I'm planning on investing in Apple."

Valentine invested $150,000 shortly thereafter in Apple at a $3 million valuation.

Source: Michael Moritz, *Return to the Little Kingdom: Steve Jobs, The Creation of Apple and How It Changed the World* (New York: Overlook Press, 2009), 237.

For the rest of venture practitioners, the sourcing process is executed in the good old-fashioned way: by attending industry conferences, reading various publications, and initiating contact with company executives to build trust and initiate due diligence. Brent Ahrens of Canaan Partners summarizes the business of venture capital elegantly: "This business is about deal flow and cash flow—if you can generate a quality deal flow or raise cash from LPs, you are good."[4]

The business calls for the perpetual development of the art of honing sourcing abilities. Regional venture conferences blend company presentations with the wisdom of reputed venture practitioners. While it is rare to find truly novel and groundbreaking opportunities at such events, this is fertile ground for most venture practitioners. However, LPs are seldom impressed to hear that your firm's sourcing strategy consists primarily of attending conferences. LPs often wish to know whether you have any unfair advantage or competitive threats in sourcing opportunities. Chris Douvos, co-head of private equity at TIFF, says, "Some of the brand name funds have a deep network, which is very hard for new GPs to replicate. This network can be a significant advantage—you can validate ideas, launch products, and even engineer exits at the right time."[5]

HOW TO SAY NO TO AN ENTREPRENEUR

"My best opportunity ever in my 30 years of investing experience came from an entrepreneur I had turned down. He referred another entrepreneur to our fund, and we made an investment that turned out to be our best performer ever. I guess when we said no, we must have done it in a thoughtful way."

—Jack Ahrens, TGap Ventures, in discussions with the author, December 2010.

When Rick Thompson, who sold Playdom to Disney for over $700 million, started his next company, Wild Needle, he invited Shasta Ventures to invest $2.5 million. He did not need the money, but he wanted access to Shasta's managing director, Robert Coneybeer. When a successful entrepreneur reaches out to you and asks you to participate in his next big thing, you have arrived. That sourcing advantage can be immense. As Chris Rizik says, "What is it about you that acts as a magnet to entrepreneurs? Dumb money is found aplenty, everywhere."[6]

THE FOUNTAINHEADS OF ACADEMIA AND RESEARCH

The top 25 universities in America invested $25.18 billion in research activities in 2009.[7] According to the Association of University Technology

Managers (AUTM), about 300 institutions invested $53.9 billion in research in 2009. Granted that a fair amount of this would be in basic research, the data indicates that the universities are fertile domain for sourcing opportunities. In 2009, 596 new companies were spun out from universities in the United States.[8]

When it comes to mining universities, Robert Nelsen of ARCH Venture Partners may have mastered the art of sourcing opportunities within university labs. When Bob met Mark Roth, a cellular biologist at the Fred Hutchinson Cancer Research Center, Mark was working on suspended animation—a technique to induce a hibernation-like state in animals by cutting off their oxygen supply. Most venture capitalists would flee such a discussion. Not Bob, who worked with Mark patiently for five years. Steven Lazarus, founder of ARCH and now its managing director emeritus, would say of ARCH's investment strategy, "This was not seed capital. In our case, we were identifying science literally at the site of inception, assessing whether it had commercial potential and then erecting a commercial entity around it—it was virtually [starting] from scratch."[9] As a result, Ikaria was formed with a $10 million investment from ARCH, Venrock, and 5AM Ventures. Today, Ikaria has over 400 employees and $200+ million in revenues. A suitable IPO candidate indeed! And Mark Roth, the scientist who could have easily been passed off as a "mad scientist," went on to win the MacArthur Genius Award after the company was launched. ARCH has several such hits to boast of.

Several other venture funds have focused on these fertile grounds. One, Osage University Partners, has developed the fund's investment thesis on university-based technologies or start-ups and recently closed its $100 million fund.

But it is not only the science that translates to opportunities—the talent and the brain trust can lead to greater opportunities. Consider this fact: K. Ram Shriram bumped into two young kids called Sergey and Larry in an elevator at Stanford University. He went on to invest $500,000 in their start-up (called Google), which catapulted him onto the list of Forbes billionaires.

CORPORATE RESEARCH

R&D spending by U.S. companies is at least four times that of university expenditures. Corporations invested $233.92 billion in 2008 according to the National Science Foundation. According to Booz & Company, a consulting firm, the top 1,000 companies invest $500 billion each year globally.[10]

While these territories may seem fertile, most R&D investments occur to further productivity and profitability. Corporations have little expertise or motivation in spinning start-ups that eventually become venture backed. As such, corporations have a reason to be threatened by such activity, and rather than promote start-ups, corporations tend to relinquish rights to a valuable IP. Xerox is one example that comes up often, in view of missing the opportunity on the graphic user interface (GUI), which was monetized by Apple. To that point, it was Bill Gates, founder of Microsoft, who once famously called on Steve Jobs, "Hey Steve, just because you broke into Xerox's store before I did and took the TV doesn't mean I can't go in later and steal the stereo."[11]

A similar example of a missed opportunity originates from the merger of Pharmacia-Upjohn, two pharmaceutical giants. After the merger of Pharmacia and Upjohn, David Scheer, a venture catalyst who blended his knowledge of science and venture capital, was hired to scour some back-burner projects for potential development or divestiture. A compound caught David's attention. "Apo-I Milano protein was the most interesting," Scheer recalls. "We had vision that this project deserved a platform as the next frontier in the cardiovascular arena."[12] Scheer partnered with Roger Newton, the co-discoverer of Lipitor, the world's most successful cardiovascular drug, and launched Esperion Therapeutics. Esperion went public in five years and was acquired by Pfizer for $1.3 billion. Timothy Mayleben, the chief operating officer who led the company through multiple venture rounds to IPO, says, "Every investor in every round made strong returns." That includes leading venture firms like Canaan, Alta, Domain, Oak, and Healthcap, to name a few.

In the biotech sector, spinout activities have occurred more frequently as compared to other sectors. While larger companies are sources of talent and know-how, limited start-up and venture activity of merit has evolved from larger companies. In select cases, and especially in the pharmaceutical sector, corporations can be a rich source of opportunities.

TAPPING INTO CORPORATE R&D: YET2.COM

Yet2.com, an online technology marketplace, brings buyers and sellers of technologies together and offers companies and individuals the tools and expertise to acquire, sell, license, and leverage intellectual assets. Companies like Microsoft, Siemens, Honeywell, and Boeing use yet2.com to commercialize their technologies. Yet2.com is backed by Venrock Associates. But for most practitioners, this is "just technology" and lacks the key ingredient necessary to build start-ups: management teams.

VENTURE EVENTS AND TRADE CONFERENCES

Venture conferences, where entrepreneurs pitch their businesses, and trade conferences, where the cutting edge of developments can be seen, are rich sources of opportunities for seeking investments.

Pitch Events

On a late summer afternoon, at 650 Page Mill Road, Palo Alto, the law firm of Wilson Sonsini is getting ready to host a VC pitch event. In nervous anticipation, an entrepreneur waits in his car, rocking back and forth in his seat. Memorizing his business pitch, he will shortly present it in no more than two minutes to a panel of leading West Coast VCs, including Khosla Ventures, Mayfield Fund, Lightspeed Venture Partners, and Intel Capital, to name a few.

Across the country, such pitch sessions have become customary pegs in any technology ecosystem. Equivalent to a beauty pageant, entrepreneurs walk the ramp in 10 minutes or less, the VCs show the scorecard of a 5 or an 8 ("Never a 10, one VC told me—that would mean I would be hounded by the entrepreneur"), the audience claps and moves on to the next pitch. Eleven such entrepreneurs will pitch their businesses today to five venture practitioners. They all will have mere two minutes followed by a five-minute question-and-answer session. As the pitches roll by, the practitioners offer their feedback. "Sounds like a Swiss knife," they say to one idea. A Swiss knife is a technology with 23 or more features, very difficult to manufacture, and in VC jargon translates to "you are trying to do too much—let's get focused here." One entrepreneur who could barely scratch the surface in two minutes, protests, "I have a lot more to say here..." but is gently ushered along into the Q-and-A session. "I applaud you for trying to change the world," says one VC. An older lady in the audience, oblivious to all this, is doodling on a sheet of paper. Ninety minutes later, the panel having shared its observations, the entrepreneurs leave the room with lots of advice and no cash. But for practitioners across the country, such events are a tactical mechanism of looking at opportunities. Any practitioner worth his expertise is invited to feature on such panels, where entrepreneurs seek attention and capital, not necessarily in equal parts. And then there are entrepreneurs who will stop at nothing at such events to get a VC's attention. "Someone started to whisper in my ear at a urinal—bad idea!" says Rick Heitzmann of FirstMark Capital.[13]

These events offer prescreened opportunities to investors who may choose to follow up after these events, and dig deeper into the investment thesis. Ask Rajeev Batra of the Mayfield Fund, who was featured on a panel called "Hand us the next killer Cloud App, and we will hand you $100,000." The event, organized by Salesforce.com, the leading customer relationship management (CRM) company, invited 40 companies to present to a VC panel, with leading practitioners from firms like Sequoia Capital and Bessemer Venture Partners. Such pitch sessions are ideal opportunities to build your brand as a practitioner as well as land the next big thing. Consider how William Draper III came across LSI Logic, a semiconductor company. Wilfred Corrigan, then CEO of Fairchild Semiconductor, was itching to do something new and met with Draper at a convention and expressed his desire to start a new company. Draper invested, and LSI Logic went public two years later. At the time, NASDAQ billed it as the largest technology IPO.[14]

Trade Conferences

Arthur Rock, one of the early investors in Apple, once went to a computer show in San Jose when nobody really had a computer to show, but parts of computers. And while other booths were empty, there was a long line at the Apple booth. Arthur would recall, "Jesus, there's got to be something here."[15] Leading investors walk the halls of trade shows to assess industry trends and direction, meet with the technical thought leaders, and explore investment opportunities. Start-ups that may have achieved a certain stature or size are often exhibiting their wares at industry trade shows.

"A combination of factors is at play—attending conferences, listening to the keynote speakers present new ideas, and looking at the new products helps us to understand the problems these smart people are trying to solve. We take that into consideration and try to define what really makes sense for us to invest in," says Lip-Bu Tan of Walden International. "Ideally, for a new market, there are no conferences. We find many of our most interesting opportunities in tiny conferences, where there are 30 or 40 vendors, and we're the only VC firm that's at the conference," says John Jarve of Menlo Ventures.[16]

But while attending conferences is one way of seeking opportunities, Tim O'Reilly, who organized such conferences frequently, had a head start in sourcing when he partnered with Bryce Roberts to raise a venture fund. "Tim is one of those rare businesspeople who not only takes the longest and broadest possible view," the *Linux Journal* wrote of Tim O'Reilly, who has launched a series of publications and conferences around technology and innovation.[17] After hosting O'Reilly Media's first Open Source event in 1998, O'Reilly garnered national publicity and since has held summits on peer-to-peer technology, Web services, geek volunteerism, and Ajax. These summits forge new ties between industry leaders, raise awareness of technology issues, and crystallize the critical issues around emerging technologies.

And of course, they are a fertile ground for investment opportunities. O'Reilly Media describes itself as "a chronicler and catalyst of leading-edge development, homing in on the technology trends that really matter and galvanizing their adoption by amplifying 'faint signals' from the alpha geeks who are creating the future."[18] Chris Douvos says, "Tim is the Obi-Wan Kenobi of the tech space ... a great ecosystem exists around him and entrepreneurs are attracted to this guru and the ecosystem."[19] So when Tim and Bryce Roberts decided to raise a fund, O'Reilly Alphatec Ventures (OATV), Chris jumped in with both feet and invested. OATV has a significant sourcing advantage, a first look at many new opportunities even before they become opportunities.

Practitioners can benefit from conferences primarily via gathering industry trends and interacting with thought leaders. Consider these as educational sessions. Every now and then, an opportunity might pop up that will merit an investment.

THE ROLE OF MEDIA IN SOURCING

Jim Armstrong of Clearstone Venture Partners, CA, once complained to a *Business 2.0* journalist that he had $1 million to invest in an instant messaging company but could not find any good opportunities. The journalist penned a brief column describing what Jim and Clearstone were seeking. Within a few weeks, Armstrong was sitting on 20 solid business plans. He griped that he could not decide which of the top three he should invest in.

Source: Michael Copeland, "The $50 million giveaway," *Business 2.0,* March 13, 2006.

VENTURE FARMING

"Incubators" have waxed and waned with economic times—the term creates visions of tall buildings, teeming with young entrepreneurs and their BMW convertibles. But from a practitioner's sourcing perspective, venture farming could be an interesting approach where entrepreneurs share their ideas and you decide whether these are worthy of an investment. Two models that stand apart from those real estate models include TechStars and Y Combinator.

TechStars and Y Combinator: Mentor Capitalists at Work

TechStars is a mentorship-driven seed stage investment program. The average program lasts for three months and is in four cities in United States. Of the hundreds that apply, only about 10 companies per city are chosen each year. These companies receive up to $18,000 in seed funding, three months of intensive mentorship from leading VCs, and the chance to pitch to angel investors and venture capitalists at the end of the program. In its first three years of operation, 70 percent of the 39 companies received funding from angels or venture capitalists. Five were acquired, and another five failed.[20] Brad Feld of the Foundry group is one of the co-founders of TechStars, but the Foundry Group does not boast of a sourcing monopoly: The fund has invested in only three "TechStar" graduate companies. "TechStars was not designed so that the Foundry Group could cherry-pick opportunities. It was meant to be a mentorship and training ground for entrepreneurs," says Brad, who has co-authored a concise book for budding entrepreneurs: *Do More Faster—TechStars Lessons to Accelerate Your Startup,* with David Cohen.

Y Combinator, an established mentor capital firm, focuses on technology start-ups and offers mentoring in an intense boot-camp environment. Both Y Combinator and TechStars offer start-ups modest funding amounts in exchange of 5 to 7 percent equity: There must be something magical about that $18,000 number. Y Combinator is based in California, while TechStars started in Boulder, Colorado, and has spread its wings to Boston, Seattle, and New York.

At Y Combinator, the most recent batch had 36 start-ups. For both, the cycle culminates in an event at which the start-ups present to an audience of investors. At Y Combinator the nurturing approach includes helping entrepreneurs figure out what to do or where to begin. Paul Graham, founder, and three other partners advise start-ups. Paul's partner, Jessica Livingston, has authored a fascinating book for entrepreneurs, *Founders at Work: Stories of Start-up's Early Days.* Graham writes, "Since there are a large number of points on the perimeter of most existing technologies at which one could push outward to create a quantum blister, what to build first is one of the most important questions we talk about." About halfway through each cycle, the sourcing dance begins. Sequoia Capital's partners meet each start-up over a casual conversation. Sequoia does this, obviously, to get an early look at the start-ups, and the start-ups find the partners' advice useful.[21] As sourcing of opportunities gets competitive and heated in the venture world, aggressive investors are beginning to see the value of staying connected with these venture farmers.

Sourcing Competition

In 2010, Y Combinator raised over $8 million. Sequoia Capital led the investment.[22] Y Combinator usually accepts an average of 6 percent equity in the start-ups and has invested in over 200 start-ups since 2005. In 2011, Silicon Valley über-angel Ron Conway and Russian investor Yuri Milner (of Digital Sky Technologies fame—investors in Facebook, Zynga, and Groupon) announced that every Y Combinator start-up would get a $150,000 investment as a convertible note (with no cap on valuation, nice!). Michael Arrington of TechCrunch wrote, "It's the most entrepreneur friendly investment that I can think of, short of just handing people money as a gift." Of the 43 start-ups, 39 had accepted this offer in a matter of days.

What's more, the investors did not conduct any due diligence, but rather invested on the basis of Y Combinator's stamp of approval.[23] "Every venture capitalist will tell you that good deal flow is the biggest competitive advantage an early-stage investor has. Milner may have just bought his way into this game for the low price of $6 million," TechCrunch reported.[24]

ANGELS AND PLEDGE FUNDS

Fertile territories for opportunities for venture investors, angel funds, and affiliated forms of seed capital provide an early access to investment opportunities. Over 550 angel groups exist worldwide,[25] nearly 300 of which are based in United States.[26] Angel investor groups are composed of wealthy individuals or high-net-worth individuals (HNWIs) who pool resources and investment expertise. Angels typically target early-stage entrepreneurs who need $100,000 to $1 million in equity financing. The number of active angels in the United States is reported to be upward of 125,000; of these, between 10,000 and 15,000 angels are believed to belong to angel groups.[27]

- An average angel group invests $1.9 million in approximately seven opportunities. About 42 members compose a typical group.[28]
- The macro data for angel investing is promising: In a given year, angels invest approximately $20 billion. In H1 2010, total angel investments were $8.5 billion in 25,200 start-ups.[29] Compare this with approximately $10 billion invested by venture capitalists in the same period, and you can see why this is serious business.
- The investment ratios are similar to venture. According to David Rose, CEO of Angelsoft, the Internet platform used by most of the world's angel investment groups to manage their deal flow, the percentage of

funding applications that result in a completed investment has averaged between 2 percent and 3 percent per year from 2005 through 2010.

■ Stage: Twenty-six percent of angel investments are in the seed and start-up stage, while 56 percent are post-seed/start-up investing. The balance is scattered in various other stages.

■ Sectors: Health care services/medical devices and equipment accounted for the largest share of investments, followed by biotech and software.

■ Returns:[30]
  o The average return of angel investments is 2.6 times the investment in 3.5 years—approximately 27 percent the internal rate of return (IRR).
  o Fifty-two percent of all the exits returned less than the capital the angel had invested in the venture.
  o Seven percent of the exits achieved returns of more than 10 times the money invested, accounting for 75 percent of the total investment dollar returns.

Angel groups have limited cash resources for administration and management. Before you build in-roads to any angel investor network, consider the following.

■ Understand the overall process and the strength of the network:
  o Does the network have good opportunities in the pipeline?
  o How is the prescreening conducted? Who conducts the due diligence?
  o Does each angel invest one-off on his or her own, or do they pool their investment and negotiate as a group?[31]
  o Are there standard terms of investment? What, if any, sectors are preferred over others? Have the angels made any follow-on investments?
  o Have there been any "up-rounds" or syndications with venture capitalists? Any exits?
■ Limited bandwidth: Angels have limited resources to invest, and an angel can lose interest fast after a few investments turn into tax write-offs. A measure of activity is the number of investments made in the past 12 months.
■ Limited sector expertise: If an angel has expertise within a certain sector, that's a good start. Make sure you spend time with those who have domain knowledge and can share their experiences.
■ Get to know the big dog: Every angel group has a big dog—the "center of this universe" or the smartest guy with the deepest pockets. In Silicon Valley, that would be Ron Conway. The big dog is essential to the longevity and cohesion of a group: Many angels typically follow the

investment rationale of a big dog. Big dogs make a lot of investments and are astute in managing their portfolios and risks. By the same token, be wary of passive angels and tire kickers: Many angels sign up as members but are rarely active. For example, 65 percent of the memberships in angel groups are latent angels: individuals who have the necessary net worth yet have not made an investment. Either they are too busy or just not interested or they are tire kickers, entertaining themselves at the cost of entrepreneurs. Avoid these unconscionable devils at all costs.

- Standardized terms: Angel investment terms can be nonstandard: In one survey, 78 percent of VCs said the number one reason that makes an angel-backed company unattractive to VCs is overly high, unrealistic valuations. Fifty-eight percent of the respondents said angels' involvement had made a company unattractive. Angels also complicate negotiations and are viewed by venture capitalists as generally unsophisticated.[32] Opportunistic angels can stick an entrepreneur with investment terms that hurt both parties in the long run. In another study, it was evident that angel funding was helpful in survival of a company per se, but was not central in whether a company obtained follow-on financing.[33] Despite this, at least 49 percent of the venture capitalists co-invest with angels on most opportunities.[34]

- Quality of the portfolio: Are the investments progressing toward an exit? The ultimate test of any investment activity is future rounds from venture investors or, better still, exits. Only 45 percent of angel groups had co-investment with venture capital firms. As we saw earlier, only 7 percent of investment opportunities returned 10 times the capital—or as they say, venture-like returns.

A Network of Angel Networks

When Steven Mercil launched RAIN Source Capital, an angel network in St. Paul, Minnesota, he had no elaborate visions of grandeur or dominion. Today, 23 RAIN Funds, each with a commitment of approximately $1 million, are up and running in six states, including Idaho, the Dakotas, Montana, and Iowa. Over 70 companies have been financed by these RAIN Funds, with 450 individual investors in this network. Each network has a minimum of 20 angel investors and a commitment of $1 million of investable capital. The central hub, managed by Steven and his team, offers best practices and templates and provides guidance and decision-making assistance. It's a franchise model, if you will. A set of investor tools, streamlined legal and due diligence processes, along with entrée to fund syndication, a high quality of investment opportunities, and sharing of expertise and resources have been some of the key drivers of growth.

Each RAIN Fund, structured as a limited liability company (LLC), aggregates a minimum of 20 angel investors. Investors commit $50,000 each, which is invested over a three-year period. A governance structure is established at each network, which includes a chairperson, a treasurer, and a secretary. Investment criteria, process of screening, due diligence, and investment approvals are also established locally with guidance from Steven. Opportunities are selected by simple majority vote of members. Each franchisee fund pays RAIN Source a 2 percent management fee combined with 20 percent of carry. "Our expertise, tools, and capital have provided much needed value to investors and companies in regional communities," says Steven, who traces his career back to a humble family retail business. "Our primary challenge has been leadership in communities—if any region has an interested individual, networks take off. When institutions such as universities or economic development entities attempt to launch angel networks, we have seen mixed results," Steven explains.[35] That has not deterred RAIN Source Capital's ambitious plans: The company is planning to create 100 angel investment funds in the next five years, which may well be potent source of opportunities for practitioners based in middle America.

Pledge Funds

An extension of the angel network model, a pledge fund seeks a commitment, or a pledge, from investors who pay an annual fee to review investment opportunities. The opportunities are presented based on predetermined criteria and investors choose the ones that provide the maximum opportunity for returns. The pledge fund manager collects the annual fee and at times may negotiate a carry. In exchange, investors get access to prescreened investment opportunities. The fund manager also negotiates the investment terms with the company based on feedback from investors.

Several venture funds started off as pledge funds. For example, when Jim Dugan began investments along with several former partners, he launched OCA Ventures Pledge Fund in Chicago. The OCA Ventures Pledge Fund made investments in nine companies, raising capital on a deal-by-deal basis. Two years later, Duggan launched OCA Ventures I, hired two professionals, and deployed capital in 12 companies. As the fund was launched, the team honed the fund's investment strategy with respect to stage, industry, and business models. OCA Ventures syndicated with more than 26 different institutional investors. Its portfolio of 12 companies went on to raise over $100 million from other investors—a testimonial to the quality of investments being made by Dugan and his team. Subsequently, Dugan launched OCA Ventures II, which is two and a half times the size of OCA Ventures I and includes institutional capital.[36] Similarly, General Atlantic, with

$15 billion under management, is rumored to have started under such a structure.[37]

BUSINESS PLAN COMPETITIONS

For business school students across the country, participating in and winning a business plan competition is a badge of honor. MIT claims that its competition, which offers a $100,000 prize, has facilitated the birth of over 130 companies that have received $770 million in venture capital funding.

The Rice University Business Plan Competition claims to be the world's largest and richest graduate-level business plan competition. For example, in 2011, 42 teams from around the world will compete for the top cash award of over $250,000. Venture capitalists from around the country volunteer their time to judge the competition, with the majority of the 250+ judges coming from the investment sector. Ninety-seven past competitors have gone on to successfully launch their own business and have raised in excess of $223 million in funding.

Several start-ups have been funded and launched successfully—thanks to such competitions. Todd Dagres of Spark Capital found his Akamai opportunity when he was mentoring a team at the MIT $50,000 competition. Dagres, then at Battery Ventures, invested in Akamai, which is now a publicly traded company with $800 million in revenues.

When Jayant Kulkarni and Adam Regelman started Quartzy, a company dedicated to solving inventory management solutions for scientific laboratories, they participated in the Olin Cup—a business plan competition at Washington University at St. Louis. After winning the competition, the duo attracted two term sheets and closed a seed round shortly thereafter. Quartzy went on to win Startup 2011, another competition in New York City, leading to even more attention from eager VCs.

For Scott Hanson, founder and CEO of Ambiq Micro, winning the DFJ-Cisco business plan competition was a pleasant surprise. He shook his head in disbelief. "Unbelievable," he muttered as he posed with Tim Draper, founder of DFJ Ventures, for photo ops and TV cameras in the heart of the Silicon Valley. Scott had just beaten 16 teams from around the world to win a $250,000 seed investment. Ambiq Micro is developing next generation energy-efficient microcontrollers. Reducing energy consumption in phones, computers, and other computing devices by a factor of 5 to 10 times tipped the scale in his favor. Six months after the award was announced, Ambiq raised a $2.4 million round led by DFJ Mercury. Draper said every single plan had a strong case to be the winner, and it was exceptionally difficult to choose just one. As a result, DFJ started due diligence on the six runner-up teams. Draper has a reason to be a big believer in business plan competitions—after all, these winners could become the proverbial 10-baggers for the fund.

COLD CALLING

While this may be the most painful part of any analyst's job, cold calling is now an essential mechanism in hypercompetitive markets. "I had barely started, but we were expected to cold call and source at least 25 opportunities each month," says an analyst at a leading Silicon Valley multistage venture fund. While some firms have found cold calling to be tactically advantageous; others have relied primarily upon their networks.

Most practitioners I talked to did not share stellar examples of opportunities sourced as a result of cold calls. In fact, many shrugged their shoulders, and one muttered, "I just need to make these calls . . . my senior partners say it builds my character, but it's just a waste of time. I know that if anything comes from it, it will be a pleasant surprise." Even the legendary investor of yesteryear, Arthur Rock cold-called 35 companies—from airplane companies to battery manufacturers—and got turned down by all of them.[38]

YOU WIN SOME, YOU MISS SOME

As successful as some of these venture capitalists may be, every practitioner misses a few good investment opportunities. Bessemer Venture Partners and OVP Venture Partners are venture firms that have created the "anti-portfolio" showcasing their missed opportunities. The Bessemer anti-portfolio lists the investment opportunities that the firm missed—one of the few venture firms to make light of its opportunities lost, which include Google, Apple, and other legendary barn-burner investment opportunities.[39]

OVP Venture Partners, a venture firm based in Portland, Oregon, missed its opportunity to invest in Amazon.com. "If you are in this business long enough, you'll see some great deals walk through your door. If you are in this business long enough, you'll show some great deals the door. We try to limit our self-flagellation to one deal per fund."[40] OVP's Gerry Langeler suggests that "it takes a certain personality, one that many venture firms lack, to publicize your fallibility. . . . It indicates you're not some stuffy, highfalutin' group that's going to lord over your entrepreneurs," Langeler writes. "Business is fun . . . you may not be able to laugh on most days, but if you can't laugh, find another line of work." And for the limited partners who invest in OVP, such acts build "credibility that comes from candor and self-disclosure."[41] Rare qualities indeed, humor and candor are not hallmarks of this business.

Legendary investor Warren Buffett admired Bob Noyce, co-founder of Fairchild Semiconductor and Intel. Warren and Bob were fellow trustees at Grinnell College, but when presented, Warren passed on Intel, one of the greatest investing opportunities of his life. Warren seemed "comfortably antiquated" when it came to new technology companies and had a long-standing bias against technology investments.[42]

Peter O. Crisp of Venrock adds his misses to the list: One "small company in Rochester, New York [came to us and one of our junior guys] saw no future [for] this product . . . that company, Haloid, became Xerox." They also passed on Tandem, Compaq, and Amgen.[43]

ARCH Venture Partners missed Netscape—that little project Marc Andreessen started at the University of Chicago. An opportunity that, according to Steven Lazarus, would have been worth billions! "We just never knocked at the right door," he would say. Eventually, ARCH decided to hire a full-time person to just keep tabs on technology coming out of the universities to "make certain we don't miss that door next time."[44]

Deepak Kamra of Canaan Partners comments on his regrets: "Oh, God, I have too many . . . this gets me depressed. A friend of mine at Sun Microsystems called and asked me to meet with an engineer at Xerox PARC who had some ideas to design a chip and add some protocols to build what is now known as a router. The drivers of bandwidth and Web traffic were strong market indicators, and he was just looking for $100,000. I really don't do deals that small and told him to raise some money from friends and family and come back when he had something to show."[45] That engineer was the founder of Juniper Networks. He got his $100,000 from Vinod Khosla. Khosla, then with KPCB, added an IPO to his long list of winners. Juniper slipped out of Kamra's hands because it was too early. And of course, those were frothy times when everyone was deluged with hundreds of opportunities each day.

KPCB missed an opportunity to invest in VMWare[46] because the valuation was too high: a mistake, according to John Doerr. Draper Fisher Jurvetson (DFJ) was initially willing but eventually passed on Facebook (ouch!), as the firm believed the valuation was too high at $100 million pre-money.[47] KPCB, not wanting to be left out of an opportunity like Facebook, invested $38 million at a $52 billion valuation.[48]

Tim Draper of DFJ, who earned his stripes with opportunities like Baidu (the Chinese version of Google), Skype, and Hotmail, turned down Google "because we already had six search engines in our portfolio." K. Ram Shriram almost missed his opportunity to invest in Google when he turned the founders away. "I told Sergey and Larry that the time for search engines has come and gone but I am happy to introduce you to all the others who may want to buy your technology."[49] But six months later, Ram Shriram, who had once turned Google down, now invested $500,000 as one of the first angel investors.

SUMMARY

Sourcing is a critical component of any fund's investment strategy and longevity. LPs are eager to find out if you have any unfair advantage in sourcing opportunities. When capital is available aplenty everywhere, why would entrepreneurs or syndicate partners call you?

Good practitioners develop a simple tracking tool, where opportunities are logged and a pipeline is tracked. This pipeline is not substantially different from any sales pipeline—if it is thin, you will be in trouble sooner or later. The tracking tool also helps to assess the forest—patterns of missed opportunities, strong sources, and more.

Proprietary relationship is a tired and overused term found in every fund document. LPs abhor it—use it at your own risk and only when you can substantiate your unfair advantage in sourcing. "I give a lot more importance to sourcing, even more than the value-add claims of VCs as board members," says Erik Lundberg, chief investment officer of University of Michigan Endowment.[50]

The opportunities you attract are an indicator of the quality of your brand and network. As Goldman Sachs' eighth commandment goes, "Important people like to deal with other important people. Are you one?"[51] If your networks are poor, you will attract subpar opportunities. "The ability to attract the best opportunities is closely tied to a brand—the aura of the venture firm, which is a by-product of historic performance. You originate deals based upon the reputation of the firm—that's recursive. The better deals you've done, the better your reputation and the easier it is to find people willing to approach you. The reputation of your firm depends upon your success in marketing, but more important, it fundamentally depends upon the quality of the people. It's a complex set of dynamic variables," says William Elkus of Clearstone Venture Partners. Any good practitioner develops the art of getting to the crux of the opportunity quickly—and say "No" often to those who do not fit within the investment criteria of the fund. As it is often said, a fast no is better than a slow yes. And consider the qualitative aspects of sourcing. If you are not fishing in the right pond, as Warren Buffett says, you could end up with a lot of frogs in your portfolio.

Any GP needs to ask, "Can I find an opportunity that can grow or generate 10x within five years?" If not, your next fund may be in jeopardy.

As we will see in the following chapters, sourcing is only a small part of the puzzle. Negotiating terms and closing in on the investment are equally important. As one GP quipped, "If sourcing was like dating, closing the investment is like a marriage—it is a commitment."

CHAPTER 7

The Art of Conducting Due Diligence

Conrad was a speculator ... a nervous speculator ... before he gambled, he consulted bankers, lawyers, architects, contracting builders and all of their clerks and stenographers who were willing to be cornered and give him advice. He desired nothing more than complete safety in his investments, freedom from attention to details and the thirty to forty percent profit, which according to all authorities, a pioneer deserves for his risks and foresight...."
—Sinclair Lewis, *Babbitt* (1922)

Most venture practitioners would agree that "a pioneer deserves 30 percent to 40 percent profit ... for his risks and foresight," although they may not necessarily agree with Conrad's style of due diligence. Due diligence is the art of sizing up an investment opportunity—its potential and risk. Mitch Lasky of Benchmark says, "I almost hesitate to use the word due diligence because it implies a certain methodical rigor—rather we ask, what are attributes of successful venture investments." For Mitch, due diligence includes:

- *Quality of the entrepreneurs:* Do they have a sparkle, a sense of enthusiasm, penetrating intelligence, and courage—even if they have not done it before, these qualities are essential.
- *Market:* Does this opportunity create disruption and outsized returns?

Note that early-stage investors seldom start with valuation or financial projections. "Valuation is down the list," Lasky says. And what about financials? Most practitioners, especially at the early stage of investing, seldom get caught up in the projections. It is certainly important to understand the highlights: capital needed to accomplish major milestones or reach break-even, year 5 revenue projections or exit multiples. But the two criteria—management and markets—trump the financials by orders of magnitude. The proportion of this due diligence mixture is odd, outcomes are unpredictable, and there is no magic formula. At Venrock, the underlying question asked of every opportunity is, "Is there a glimmer of greatness in here?" Kleiner Perkins seeks "people, unfair advantage, clarity on risk, and home run swings."[1] Warren Buffett summarizes his due diligence process with four simple criteria:[2]

1. Can I understand it? Buffett defines 'understanding a business' as 'having a reasonable probability of being able to assess where the company will be in ten years.'[3]
2. Does it look like it has some kind of sustainable competitive advantage?
3. Is the management composed of able and honest people?
4. Is the price right?

If it passes all four filters, write a check.

This chapter establishes the framework for conducting due diligence efficiently. Venture capital due diligence focuses on three key aspects: management, markets, and technology. Investment decisions are made using a combination of these three parameters.

WHAT IS IMPORTANT: JOCKEY, HORSE, OR MARKETS?

In any investment opportunity, most venture capitalists concur that management, or the jockey, matters more than any other criteria. Others believe that a large, growing market is the primary criteria. Studies show that underlying business or technology platform, or the horse, is what really matters. While this remains a much-debated subject, practitioners gravitate toward a combination of the three, and it all starts with a growing market.

Give Me a Market First, Please

John Doerr of Kleiner Perkins postulates the value of management and sees the role of a venture practitioner as a glorified recruiter. Don Valentine, founder of Sequoia Capital, takes a contrarian view. For those who want to back smart people, the proverbial A team with a B market, Valentine has stated tongue-in-cheek, "I continue to encourage them in that direction."[4] Valentine's position I: "Give me a B idea with a huge market and I will find the best people. But give me the market first. *Please.* I think choosing great people is much more difficult than picking great markets because we have always understood the technology and understood the markets. Picking great people is a less than 50 percent proposition and if you are right 52 percent of the time, they ought to build a statue to you."[5]

The legendary Warren Buffett's observation mirrors the philosophy of picking the right market. "Good jockeys will do well on good horses, but not on broken-down nags. Managers are never going to make progress while running in quicksand."[6] Buffett goes on to point out that to the extent he has been successful, it is because he concentrated on identifying one-foot hurdles that he could step over, rather than attempting to clear a seven-footer.[7] "The market, like the Lord, helps those who help themselves," notes Buffett.[8]

But how does one spot the direction of the market? "A good practitioner needs to be a student of the market: one who can perceive where the market is going, the trends. Hidden here may lie an opportunity—you have to sniff it out. There's no single source for that information—it's generally drinking in, reading and talking to smart people. And as a venture capitalist, a lot of people come to you. If you see something's happening and you can put it together, you can sense a trend. The trick is to find a company that is an emerging leader in an emerging sector. You have to catch the opportunity before it's obvious," says Todd Dagres, Founder, Spark Capital, and investor in Twitter. Lip-Bu Tan of Walden International agrees: "You have to identify a big market that you can go after and systematically look for opportunities that would allow you to enter the market." Tan has evolved from making investments over the past two decades in the electronics sector to semiconductors to energy: His first investment was in a company called Mouse Systems, which made a handheld mouse for a personal computer. Today, Walden International manages over $1.6 billion and ranks among the top venture firms with a presence in the Silicon Valley and China.

The right way to gather the data points is to be a student of the market—be on the street. Market reports produced by leading research firms are only good for macro-level trends. Take the simple example of four research firms, each of which predicted the first year unit sales for the iPad: iSuppli Corporation predicted 7.1 million units; Piper Jaffray predicted 5.5 million. Forrester Research was more conservative at 3 million units and Kauffman Brothers predicted a meager 2.5 million.[9] Steve Jobs beat all these projections handily, as Apple sold a staggering 15 million iPad units in the first year of its sales.[10]

ATTRIBUTES OF THE JOCKEY

The attributes of strong management teams, or the proverbial jockey, start with integrity. Other important factors include the ability to attract a team of high performers and execution skills.

Integrity

In selecting the jockey—the top executives—Warren Buffett's views are relevant and appropriate "Somebody once said that in looking for people to hire, you look for three qualities: integrity, intelligence, and energy. And if they don't have the first, the other two will kill you. Think about it; it's true. If you hire somebody without the first, you really want them to be dumb and lazy.[11]

When assessing the management team of an early-stage start-up, integrity ranks first. Integrity boils down to the sum total of honesty in words and actions, an ethos that defines any individual. But there is no easy way to assess this attribute. Practitioners spend a substantial amount of time investigating business skills and technical expertise of entrepreneurs. The process is imprecise and involves referencing—multiple discussions with people who have interacted with the entrepreneurs in the past. It is usually during this process that one can discover the mind-set of any entrepreneur. It is easy to spot those who are at the bookends of the spectrum—the strong, high-integrity individuals and the ones who are mired in sleazy dealings. It is the ones in the middle—those who manage to stay above the law but hide beneath a web of lies and inconsistent behavior—these are the ones who always get you! As Buffett says, those who do not have integrity but have intelligence can kill you!

Consider the case of Entellium. Based in Seattle, Washington, this developer of customer relationship management (CRM) tools raised $50 million in venture investments over its eight-year history. But the CEO and CFO were cooking the books faster than they were raising venture capital. They overstated revenues by as much as three times for three consecutive years. An employee stumbled upon the actual revenue data while cleaning out a former employee's desk and discovered the fraud. The lead venture fund had invested as much as $19 million in Entellium. Fraud may be a rare occurrence in the VC arena, but it can be crippling.

Integrity and honesty are fundamental qualities of any management team but are much harder to assess. Practitioners are quick assess whether the team is hungry, has technical expertise, or business acumen. But if you see any shades of gray, try not to justify the investment and consider walking away from the opportunity. Pete Farner of TGap Ventures says, "I use a simple test in assessing potential CEOs we would back—would I trust them enough to look after my own kids." Such a high bar would eliminate the vast majority of riffraff quickly.

Team Building

Besides integrity, what are the other qualities in any management team to look for? "Do they understand their own limitations and weaknesses? Are they able to attract a team, and eventually, can they recruit their own CEO and replace themselves?" asks Lip-Bu Tan of Walden International. These qualities are fundamental but rare—after all, human beings suffer from insecurities. If they attract team members who are highly accomplished, they might end up looking like dwarves. Or get sidelined! And very few can overcome this innate and primal urge—most gravitate toward looking smart in a land of dwarves as opposed to looking stupid among giants. But every once in a while, you will find entrepreneurs who know that great companies are built on the shoulders of giants—a strong team.

Consider William Shockley, who won the Nobel Prize for co-inventing the transistor. Despite being a brilliant physicist, Shockley had no people skills and successfully alienated his two co-inventors, thanks to his brash and abrasive style. His staff was subjected to lie detector tests, and he publicly posted their salaries. He was even passed over for promotion at Bell Labs. When he died, he was completely estranged from most of his friends and family—his children read about his death in the newspapers.[12]

When eight of Shockley's researchers, termed as the Traitorous Eight, resigned to start Fairchild Semiconductor, all he did was write "Wed 18 Sept—Group Resigns" in his diary.[13] His communication skills certainly did not impress anyone.

> Besides being a poor manager, Shockley's presentation skills were terrible. He read all his speeches in a monotone, was a poor writer, and "flogged metaphors" mercilessly. Larry L. King wrote of Shockley that he "made such an inept presentation that he could not have instructed us how to catch a bus."[14]

Joel Shurkin, Shockley's biographer, writes, "If Shockley had been a better manager, he'd be one of the richest people in the world today. He would have been the match for Bill Gates. He is the father of Silicon Valley; he knew more than anybody in the world the importance of these machines, these transistors; he knew that he was revolutionizing the world; he knew that if his company could control the direction that the transistor should go toward, that he would be very rich. Unfortunately, he was a terrible manager and he never had the chance."[15]

Shockley's inability to build teams is evident—despite being a brilliant technologist and a Nobel Laureate, he could not get over his fear and insecurities. An investor needs to watch for traits where the founders or the core management team are able to attract star power. Most management teams will be replaced, either by choice or by sheer exhaustion in the travails of the start-up journey. Team building can make an investment opportunity stronger. A simple question to consider: Is this person honest and bold enough to replace him- or herself at the right time and even become redundant?

Execution

Defined as the fine art of getting things done, execution abilities are one of the top criteria of management assessment. In an early-stage company, execution would be quite simply "the ability to define and meet value creation milestones using optimum resources." In his *New York Times* bestselling book *Who: The A Method for Hiring*, author Geoff Smart asks, "What types of CEOs make money for investors?"[16] Smart, who has frequently interacted with the VC world, grew up in a family in which psychology was discussed at the breakfast table. "My father was an industrial psychologist. So when I interned at a VC firm, I asked the partners what it takes to be a successful venture capitalist. And they said, it's all about management," he says. But Geoff found that despite all the emphasis on management, there was no clear methodology of assessing people. "If people are so important, why is it that we spend all of this time doing Excel models or market analysis?" he would ask. But Smart was told that the people part is intuitive and that there is no way you can evaluate people accurately. "Had I not had the contextual background of psychology, I would have taken everything that venture capitalists told me at face value."[17] Smart was not about to take anything at face value and wrote an entire dissertation on the subject dedicated to his father: "Pop."

Later, Smart launched his own company to focus on these human capital selection issues. To assess CEO traits, he teamed up with Steven Kaplan, a noted scholar on entrepreneurship and finance at the University of Chicago. The team went on to conduct the largest study of CEO traits and financial performance. The results were compelling and controversial. Data from 313 interviews of PE-backed CEOs were gathered and analyzed. Taking these assessments, the authors matched the CEO assessments with actual financial performance. The *Wall Street Journal* ran a half-page article on the findings. Smart points out that investors have a tendency to invest in CEOs who demonstrated openness to feedback, possess great listening skills, and treat people with respect. "I call them 'Lambs' because these CEOs tend to graze in circles, feeding on the feedback and direction of others," he says. And he concludes that investors love Lambs because they are easy to work with and were successful 57 percent of the time. But Smart found that the desirable CEOs are the ones who move quickly, act aggressively, work hard, demonstrate persistence, and set high standards and hold people accountable to them. (He called them "Cheetahs" because they are fast and focused.) "Cheetahs in our study were successful 100 percent of the time.

This is not a rounding error. *Every single one of them* created significant value for their investors," writes Geoff.[18] He and his coauthor conclude that "emotional intelligence is important, *but only when matched with the propensity to get things done.*"[19]

Separately, Steve Kaplan's research leads to the same conclusion. In the study "Which CEO Characteristics and Abilities Matter?" the authors assess more than 30 individual characteristics, skills, and abilities.[20] Surprisingly, the study showed that success was not linked to team-related skills and that such skills are overweighed in hiring decisions. *Success mattered only with CEOs with execution-related skills.* The study asserted Jim Collins's "Good to Great" description of Level 5 CEOs who have unwavering resolve, are fanatically driven, and exhibit workmanlike diligence.

The essential lesson we derive from this study and from the Shockley example is that while technical expertise is important, marrying technical skills with short-term milestones and rapid execution are critical. As Peter Drucker says, effective executives "get the right things done"[21] —and at the right time, as any venture practitioner worth his internal rate of return (IRR) would expect.

SERIAL ENTREPRENEURS VERSUS FIRST-TIME ENTREPRENEURS

A study conducted to assess the performance of serial entrepreneurs concludes that, all things equal, a VC-backed entrepreneur who has taken a company public has a 30 percent chance of succeeding in his next venture.[22] A failed entrepreneur is next in the pecking order with a 20 percent chance of success and a first-time entrepreneur has an 18 percent chance. Researchers assessed the cause of success and point out that successful entrepreneurs know how to launch companies at the right time—before the markets get crowded. Market timing skill is important in entrepreneurs as well as investors. Consider the fact that 52 percent of computer start-ups founded in 1983 went public. In contrast, only 18 percent of those started in 1985 went public. The world had changed in 24 months by a factor of three!

Interestingly, the same entrepreneurs who were able to time the market in 1983 were able to time the market in their next start-up as well. Conclusion: Success breeds success. Find the smart entrepreneurs and stay with them over multiple start-ups, if you can. However, with successful entrepreneurs, the hunger level may drop with financial gains. Or worse, arrogance may set it.

Recycling is good for the environment, but it's even better in the world of investments. Consider Jeff Williams, who had taken a company public in his prior life. Jeff stepped in as a CEO of HandyLab, a University of Michigan microfluidics start-up backed by a number of venture firms in the Midwest. Five years after Jeff's arrival, HandyLab was sold to Becton Dickinson (BD) generating strong returns for the investors. No sooner had Jeff sold HandyLab, the venture firms practiced the art of recycling this proven CEO. They encouraged Jeff to join another portfolio company, Accuri Cytometers. One year later, Becton Dickinson acquired Accuri, generating ~5x return for early investors. Jeff would joke that among other considerations, he had to plan for capital gains taxes, or else he could have sold Accuri much faster. Performance persistence indeed!

WHAT ABOUT CHARISMA?

In an interview with Sally Smith Hughes, Arthur Rock recalls a meeting with Steve Jobs and Steve Wozniak:

> *Jobs came into the office, as he does now, dressed in Levi's, but at that time that wasn't quite the thing to do. And I believe he had a goatee and a moustache and long hair—and he had just come back from six months in India with a guru, learning about life. I'm not sure, but it may have been a while since he had a bath.* . . .
>
> *And he was very, very thin—and to look at [him]—he really belonged somewhere else. Steve Wozniak, on the other hand, had a full beard and he's just not the kind of a person you'd give a lot of money to.*[23]

Nevertheless, Rock invested in Apple. Why? Because Jobs was very articulate.

How often are we swayed by soft signals? A study conducted by two MIT researchers, Sandy Pentland and Daniel Olguin, predicted with 87 percent accuracy who would win a business plan competition.[24] But get this—neither of the researchers had read the plans or heard their pitches. So how did they predict with such high accuracy? Pentland gathered what he calls "honest signals" from these executives. Honest signals are defined as nonverbal cues—gestures, expressions, and tone. In an interview with *Harvard Business Review*, Pentland said, "The more successful people are energetic. They talk more, but they also listen more. . . . It's not just what they project that makes them charismatic; it's what they elicit. The more of these energetic, positive people you put on a team, the better the team's performance."[25] Pentland's research did not indicate which pitch will be best—it just indicated who will win, irrespective of the quality of the idea or the pitch. Venture capitalists look for buzz and enthusiasm, "but they also need to understand the substance of the pitch and not be swayed by charisma alone," he added.

MANAGEMENT TEAM DUE DILIGENCE: HOW TO ASSESS THE JOCKEY

Management due diligence is easy; just be prepared to invest, say, two to three hundred hours in the process. In "The Art and Science of Human Capital Valuation," Geoff Smart assessed the styles of conducting CEO due diligence and its outcomes. GPs from storied firms such as Accel, Bessemer, KPCB, Greylock, New Enterprise Associates (NEA), Sequoia, and Mayfield Fund shared information on how they assessed management teams of 86 portfolio companies.[26]

For example, William Hunckler III of Madison Dearborn Partners invested 322 hours over six months. Hunckler invested more than 50 hours interviewing nine categories of references leading to detailed assessments of the team. Geoff Smart describes this approach as the "airline captain approach" who checks every parameter to ensure that a plane is safe to fly. Hunckler focused his attention principally on prior work assessment. Smart says, "The approach is common sense, but fewer than 15 percent of venture capitalists actually use this approach."

Eugene Hill of Accel Partners, another participant in the study, said, "Evaluating the management team properly and backing the right people is the difference between success and failure in this [venture capital] business."[27] Hill has a track record of accuracy that ranks him at the 92nd percentile. In total, he spent 126 hours on human capital valuation, spread systematically across various methods. He "spent 21 hours in reference discussions with people from 11 different categories of references. This was the highest number of different categories of all venture capitalists in the study. He said his analysis was based on 'mostly data' rather than gut intuition," wrote Smart.

Why the Airline Captain Approach Matters

Various styles of assessing human capital include the airline captain approach, the art critic, the sponge, and the prosecutor. Of these, the airline captain approach, as Hunckler used, yielded a median internal rate of return of 80 percent. A high level of systematic and disciplined data collection and analysis of the management team members characterize this approach. In contrast, as seen in Figure 7.1, the three primary alternative approaches

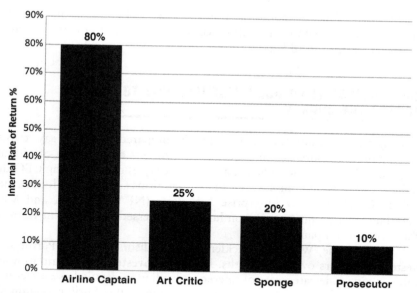

FIGURE 7.1 IRR and Due Diligence Styles
Source: Geoffrey H. Smart, "The Art and Science of Human Capital Valuation."

achieved internal rates of return under 30 percent. While airline captains tend to achieve close to 90 percent accuracy in human capital valuations, art critics are lucky if they hit 50 percent. If you're an art critic, one of two CEOs will crash and burn. Recall Don Valentine, founder of Sequoia Capital, who once remarked that if you can select people 52 percent of the time correctly, they ought to have a statue for you. The moral of the story, the author concludes, is that gut checks are good, but a diligent checklist approach will avoid the plane crash.

- *Airline captain*: This method of assessing CEO candidates "resembles the way an airline captain assesses his or her plane prior to takeoff to decide whether it is safe to fly." It is the most effective method for yielding top results, but it is also time-consuming and intense.
- *Art critic*: An art critic glances at a painting and within a few minutes can offer "an accurate appraisal of the value of the work." But art critics in VC can be ineffective, especially when trying to value human capital. They "think that their years of business experience equip them to achieve an accurate assessment of people in a very short amount of time—that a person's human capital is as visible in its entirety as a painting on

the wall," wrote Smart. "Art critics talk a lot about intuition, gut feel, and 'shooting from the hip.' Unfortunately, they also talk a lot about inaccurate human capital valuations and deals in which they lost 100% of their investment."

- *Sponge*: "Sponges are like art critics who need a little more data before making an assessment. Sponges do not perform a human capital needs analysis, but 'soak up' data through multiple methods of human capital valuation—and then synthesize the information in their gut. As one sponge said, he does 'due diligence by mucking around.'" The sponge is proven as effective as an art critic.
- *Prosecutor*: "Prosecutors act like prosecuting attorneys." As they walk into the room to conduct an interview, they will indulge in theatrics, such as slamming a fist on the table, pointing a finger, and waving their arms. According to the study, "They aggressively question managers and attempt to 'pull the truth out of them.'. . . Prosecutors talk about 'testing' management on what they know. The problem with this method is that prosecutors only collect data on present behaviors—how managers respond to questions in the present, live, right now. In comparison, *past* behaviors are more indicative of future behaviors," concluded Smart. One of the least effective methods for CEO selection, this method is best used where it belongs—to conduct depositions and interrogate Guantanamo cell mates.

According to Geoff Smart, VC practitioners typically conduct interviews based on the following categories:

- *Work sample:* This is the most heavily used means of interviewing: typically, venture capitalists spend over 60 hours per deal in work samples with management.

  In these direct interactions, venture capitalists quiz the management team on various issues related to the business. They are called work samples because they allow the venture capitalist to view samples of how the managers think and work firsthand. The time that venture capitalists spent in work samples was positively related to the accuracy of the human capital valuation in early-stage deals but negatively related to accuracy in later-stage deals. Why the difference? In early-stage deals, these discussions are more probing and often personal. In later-stage deals, formal presentations by managers coached by investment bankers can be as misleading as they are informative. The evidence suggests that work samples are not sufficient for achieving accurate human capital valuations.

- *Reference interviewing:* "Reference interviews are discussions with people who have observed the behavior of the target managers. There are several possible sources of reference interviews: personal references, supervisors, coworkers, industry players, current employees, suppliers, customers, lawyers, accountants, bankers, or other investors."
- *Past-oriented interviewing:* "Whereas the work sample relies on present or 'hypothetical' behavior, past-oriented interviews rely on *past* behavior." "This method," branded by Smart as the top-grading interview, "is based on the notion that past behavior is the best predictor of future behavior. Therefore, during past-oriented interviews, venture capitalists talk chronologically with individual managers about their entire career histories. This interviewing format has emerged as the most effective personnel assessment method in industrial psychology within the last five years."

THE TOP THREE LESSONS FROM THE ART AND SCIENCE OF HUMAN VALUATION, BY GEOFF SMART

What venture capitalists were seeking to assess in CEO candidates of early-stage companies:

1. Technical knowledge
2. Industry knowledge
3. General management/operations

What they failed to assess:

1. Lack of general management/operations experience
2. Cannot work well with others
3. Sales/marketing skills

Top three reasons given by venture capitalists for bad hiring decisions:

1. Speed: Sign that term sheet quickly and get the deal done. Pressure to invest due to competition or co-investors.
2. Halo effect: What a rock star—great past performance or great technology! We just ought to be grateful to be a part of this investment.
3. Too many cooks: A number of syndicate partners, other team members, and no head chef.

Source: The Art & Science of Human Valuation, Geoff Smart.

As venture practitioners, there is seldom enough time to understand the abilities and creative elements of any candidate. For a practitioner, the biggest challenge is assessing the intangibles in a very short time. Smart's approach, assessing skills with respect to the demands of the position, may be one technique that can be meaningful.

A number of other personality tests exist, each of which have a varied set of inputs and outputs, all aimed at establishing the window in a person's emotional and intellectual construct. A few that are noteworthy include the Myers-Briggs Type Indicator (MBTI) and the Caliper Test.

The MBTI is a Jungian personality test that qualifies people into one of 16 types based on how they focus their attention, analyze information, make decisions, and orient themselves into the external world. For example, an "ESTJ" = extraversion (E), sensing (S), thinking (T), judgment (J) person would be defined as "practical, realistic, matter-of-fact. Decisive, quickly moves to implement decisions. Organizes projects and people to get things done, focuses on getting results in the most efficient way possible. Has a clear set of logical standards, systematically follows them. Forceful in implementing their plans."[28] While the MBTI output paints a picture, it doesn't offer clarity as to whether an ESTJ is suited to be a venture capitalist.

For that reason, Don Walker, a senior partner at a Midwest venture firm, uses the Caliper Test for almost all hiring decisions. Caliper believes equating a person's interest with a person's ability is a flawed approach. You have a lot of wannabe CEOs, but do they have the requisite abilities? Most tests are also eminently fakeable, according to Caliper. Obviously, if you ask the true-false question "I am a responsible person," the probability that anyone would select false is near zero. But Caliper Tests are structured to eliminate these challenges with a more sophisticated test design. Further, the test recognizes that desirable qualities for certain positions may be handicaps for others: for example, impulsiveness and originality can be seen as evidence of weakness or instability. Keeping the perspective of the person as a whole and not his or her parts and not relying on past experience as a prime qualification are two essential ingredients of a good test design, but what tips Caliper over the edge to the more reliable side is its ability to match the person to a role.

Caliper has developed four categories and over 25 criteria that assess a person's ability to influence, build relationships, solve problems, make decisions, and organize. The test applies these criteria to specific job functions that determine whether the best match can be crafted. For example, a manager and a salesperson need varying degrees of certain skills. Caliper uses the term "ego drive" to define how much a person needs to be able to persuade others and gain satisfaction from the successful persuasion. The test also uses the term "ego strength" to refer to the degree a person likes himself or herself. Described another way, ego strength is an individual's ability to keep pushing when everyone says no. It is a strong sense of self: A CEO has good ego strength when he or she can take no for an answer yet keep moving in the right direction without flinching. Such events do not destroy the self-image but rather make a good leader hungrier for the next opportunity. This is the key to resilience. People who take rejections personally lose steam very quickly: Afraid of rejection, they find that it's better to not make the next call—they invite rejection, or worse, potential conflicts. On the other hand, "ego drive," the *ability to persuade* coupled with the intense *need to persuade*, can yield a highly productive person.

Caliper concludes that just drive is not sufficient to make a good salesperson. To be a good executive, you need to have a strong blend of these two criteria ... a strong sense of self *and* the ability to persuade. In any early-stage company, the CEO will hear a lot of the word "no" from potential investors, customers, and partners. It's not personal, just business! Of these three approaches, ghSMART, Caliper, and MBTI, ghSMART's approach may be more relevant, thanks to Smart's contextual background in VC.

ANDREESSEN HOROWITZ ON THE ART OF CEO SELECTION

Ben Horowitz, who launched companies like LoudCloud and Opsware with Marc Andreessen, now manages over a billion dollars across three funds. The art of CEO selection according to Horowitz can be summarized in three words: direction, execution, and results.

Direction: Does the CEO know what to do?
Strategy and decision making: Does the CEO know what to do in all matters all of the time? Can the CEO tie the strategy to a story—how is the world a better place, thanks to this company? A CEO can most accurately be measured by the speed and quality of her decisions. Great decisions come from CEOS who display an elite combination of intelligence, logic, and courage.

Execution: Can the CEO get the company to do what he or she knows?
Execution and team building: Once a vision is set, does the CEO have the capacity, and can the CEO execute? Horowitz points out that capacity translates to having

world-class, motivated talent. Building a world-class team and ensuring the quality of the team stays strong is important.

Effectively run the company: Very few CEOs get an A and fail to scale because the skills required to manage a well-run organization are wide-ranging from organizational design to performance management, incentive, communication, the whole gamut. The key question to ask is, "Is it easy for the employees to get their job done?"

Results: Did the CEO achieve the desired results against an appropriate set of objectives?

Were appropriate objectives established? Too low or too high? Horowitz warns against setting objectives for early-stage companies, as no one really knows the size of the opportunity. Finally, the size and the nature of opportunities vary across types of companies: some are capital intensive, while others have measured growth and market adoption. CEOs will perform better on a test if they know the questions ahead of time.

Source: Ben Horowitz, "How Andreessen Horowitz Evaluates CEOs," Ben's Blog (blog), May 10, 2010, accessed February 6, 2011, http://bhorowitz.com/2010/05/30/how-andreessen-horowitz-evaluates-ceos/.

But in most venture-backed start-ups, while attracting top-level talent may be important, the stability of teams is entirely unpredictable. Churn of top-level talent occurs due to a number of reasons—the pace, the pressures, low cash positions, missed milestones—and thus, practitioners need to realize that while management teams are important, no one can predict when teams run out of steam and hit the bottom—or give up! I once had an opportunity to watch an entrepreneur pitch an idea to Tim Draper, Founder of Draper Fisher Jurvetson. Over an informal lunch in Palo Alto, Tim listened to the idea for this new-new thing, fully engaged. "And what will you do if the idea does not take off?" asked Tim. The young entrepreneur-making said, "I will try something else—maybe find a job" At which point Tim said, "Entrepreneurs never give up." One significant risk every practitioner faces is when the CEO throws in the towel. On the other hand, CEOs are replaced at a fairly regular pace as companies evolve.

Professor Steven N. Kaplan of the University of Chicago Graduate School of Business studied 50 venture-backed companies that evolved from business plan to IPO and found that management turnover is substantial. Kaplan concludes that investors in start-ups should place more weight on the horse, as in the business, and not the jockey. And all the hoo-ha about "quality of management" may be important in the early stages, but it declines rapidly: Only 16 percent of the companies stress the importance of management expertise at the time of the IPO. Founders get slayed quickly along the way: Only 49 percent of the VC-backed founders stayed until the IPO. Kaplan concludes: "Human capital is important, but the specific person appears less so. A business with strong non-people assets is enduring."[29] He asserts: "The glue holding the firm together at a very early stage is composed of the patents, the stores, and the processes. Except, perhaps, for raw start-ups, VCs should bet on the horse. We see the jockeys changing, but we don't see the horse changing."[30]

THE IMPORTANCE OF CONDUCTING BACKGROUND INVESTIGATIONS

Many venture capital (VC) funds perform detailed due diligence of potential portfolio companies prior to investments. Background checks of key portfolio company personnel are often a component of this due diligence analysis. However, while background checks will detect some issues with potential portfolio company managers, an in-depth background investigation, performed by an experienced professional, will yield a more detailed analysis of potential portfolio company managers, and serve to verify the assertions and representations these individuals have made to the VC funds.

Background investigations include significantly detailed analyses of potential portfolio company managers. These investigations examine individuals' work history, board service, educational background, community involvement, criminal background, and, in some instances, assets. While this level of information may seem excessive, it is a necessary component of the due diligence process and serves to mitigate future issues a VC fund may encounter with an executive at a later date. Moreover, the reasons for conducting an in-depth background investigation as opposed to a cursory background check of a potential portfolio company manager are myriad.

Recent studies indicate that roughly 50 percent of job candidates misrepresent their job credentials, although the level and degree of misrepresentation varies widely.[31] Candidates might wish to maintain the lifestyle they had before the 2008–2009 economic crisis caused their asset values to plummet; thus their selection might supplement their current income with significant remuneration. In other instances, these individuals might seek to revitalize a lagging career.

Furthermore, misrepresentations are made by candidates applying for jobs at all levels of an organization's hierarchy, including its board of directors. For example, in 2004, Smith & Wesson Holding Corporation chairman James J. Minder resigned when a newspaper report revealed he spent up to 15 years in prison for various armed robberies and a bank heist. Minder maintained he did not cover up his past. Instead, he stated that no one on Smith & Wesson's board asked about his criminal record. A background investigation of Minder could have prevented the embarrassing revelation and allowed the company to better evaluate Minder as a job candidate.[32]

Background investigations can not only verify information presented by job candidates, they can also provide insight into their personality. For example, they may potentially reveal a candidate has been a party to numerous lawsuits, a corporate or personal bankruptcy, a personal drug habit, or had an extramarital affair. While some information revealed in the background investigation may be of a highly personal nature, personal issues may soon impinge on a candidate's ability to successfully perform his or her job, thus putting a portfolio company, and the entire PE or VC fund's portfolio, at risk.

Although events with portfolio company executives may seem rare, this is often due to the fact that many PE and VC funds do not want the events publicized. In reality, even the most successful PE and VC funds experience issues with portfolio company executives. For example, consider the case of a Kleiner Perkins-backed portfolio company and its CEO, an episode Managing Partner Tom Perkins described as "one of the most bizarre episodes" of his career.[33] After a period of successful tenure, the CEO started to demonstrate paranoia, claiming his office was bugged and that he was being followed. In time, Perkins discovered the CEO's cocaine habit, and the executive was removed. However, by the time of his removal, the CEO had already exacted significant damage on the portfolio company and it soon failed. While the CEO may or may not have possessed an addictive habit when he was first hired, a background investigation conducted prior to his hiring might have revealed personal information about the CEO suggesting a predisposition toward the use of drugs.

In this manner, the best way to mitigate issues with portfolio company personnel is to detect them through a background investigation conducted at the start of the portfolio company due diligence process. Performing this activity early in the process can minimize wasted activities in the event unfavorable information is revealed. In another example from the VC industry, several venture partners interviewed a potential CEO over a period of 10 weeks. Immediately prior to presenting a final letter of employment, a background investigation was conducted. This investigation revealed that the CEO did not have the Harvard MBA he claimed to possess. The VC fund had to restart the process of interviewing CEO candidates; 10 weeks of work could have been saved had the background investigation been conducted at the start of the interviewing process.

In addition to conducting a preliminary background investigation, experienced investigators state that PE and VC funds should not only perform investigations prior to hiring an individual; investigations should also be conducted periodically throughout the individual's career. Periodic investigations maximize the possibility of detecting issues that may arise after an individual is hired and help minimize potential damage caused by an unscrupulous employee. For instance, one experienced investigator related an experience where she discovered Interpol was chasing a number of shareholders of a tiny start-up, as they were the target of a fraud investigation overseas. One of the shareholders was hiding in Switzerland, but all documentation he provided as a candidate stated he resided and lived in the United States. In another situation, the investigator alerted venture capital partners of the fact that a company founder had conveniently transferred assets to his partner's spouse to avoid paying federal taxes as there were numerous tax liens levied against him.[34]

In summary, background investigations are an essential component of the due diligence process. While they are more costly than a background check, an investigation might yield a significant piece of information unknown to those at the PE or VC fund. This information might cause the PE or VC fund to select a different executive in the hiring process, or help detect a potential future issue with the executive.

ASSESSING THE MARKET

Successful investors know that a good idea is not necessarily a good opportunity. "Market demand is the key ingredient to measuring opportunity," writes Jeffry Timmons. Key characteristics of a market include:

- Is the market emerging, mature, or fragmented? Is there an unmet need, a pent-up demand, a potential market pull for the products? Market adoption rates differ for various technologies.
- What is the growth potential? Can the given opportunity reach a target market share quickly?
- What is the competitive advantage of the opportunity? How does it fit within the current state of competition?

■ Are there any existing barriers to entry? Is there freedom to operate? Is there an existing structure of market players? Warren Buffett says, "It's no fun being a horse when a tractor comes along or the blacksmith when the car comes along." But if the blacksmith lobby is strongly represented in Washington, DC, it could attempt to ban the car—or subject it to disparagement, criticism, and ridicule. The question a practitioner needs to ask is, "Who is going to suffer the maximum pain when this product arrives in the market?"

WHEN BEING TOO FAST IS A BARRIER TO ENTRY: GOOGLE

In a keynote speech at the Michigan Growth Capital Symposium (Ann Arbor, MI, 2007), K. Ram Shriram recounted his initial meeting with Sergey and Larry co-founders of Google. He suggested that as the time for search engines had come and gone, they sell their technology to the existing search engine companies like Yahoo!, Inktomi, and Lycos. Sergey and Larry demonstrated their search engine to several existing search engine companies, but nobody wanted to buy the technology. They called Shriram with the feedback: "None of them want to buy us.... They said that because our engine is brutally efficient, it would hurt their current businesses—it would cut their banner ad revenues by half...."

Shriram promptly wrote a small check that led to the first $500,000 angel round. "I still did not believe that this would succeed," he said. He cautioned, "You are up against heavy odds."

Menlo Ventures, one of the leading venture firms, uses a process called systematic emerging market selection (SEMS) for every investment. Via this process, Menlo tracks four aspects: market size, team, unique technology, and stage of product development (beta, shipping). Of these four, Menlo concluded that market size and the product's stage of development mattered the most. Seasoned practitioners at times create a market for products or services—a good surfer at times has to go a bit farther instead of waiting for the tide to come!

Case Study: Role of Venture Capitalists Creating a New Industry: Retail Clinics

A busy parent with a sick toddler has two options: Call the family doctor and hope to grab an appointment or head over to CVS, Target, or

Walmart to visit the local retail clinic. As the debate on the Health Care Act in Washington heated up with House Republicans threatening to submit a bill to repeal the landmark legislation, as well as worsening unemployment, many Americans cut back on doctor and hospital visits, using fewer medical services.[35] In fact, according to some estimates, 18 million Americans opted for a higher deductible plan in 2010, up from 13 million in 2009.[36] The sluggish economy and persistent unemployment have made physician visits costly. Cash-strapped consumers who now have higher out-of-pocket spending may be drawn to more affordable retail clinics.

An Alternative Health Care Venue: How the Retail Clinic Works   While the business is still evolving, the retail clinic is essentially a model based on providing affordable and convenient primary care services to consumers.[37] Clinic operators exist in three forms: as retail-owned operators, independent operators, or hospital-owned operators. Most are of the first variety, residing inside big retail pharmacies such as Walgreens or CVS or in discount stores like Target[38] Clinics are also more accessible, open seven days a week, and open late into the evening hours, compared to traditional doctors' clinics, which require appointments and hold irregular hours. They often treat routine conditions like colds, sore throats, and other minor ailments, though many chains are now expanding to offer a broader range of services, including specialized injections for chronic conditions, such as asthma, and treatment for more serious injuries, such as sprains, minor wounds, and skin conditions. Some retail clinics are rolling out pilots offering cutting-edge treatments and infusions of biotech drugs.[39] They are generally staffed by nurse practitioners and host no extensive paper medical records, with most data stored electronically.[40]

First to Market: The Front-Runner Becomes a Leader   MinuteClinic started in 2000 under the name QuickMedx with a mission to provide quality urgent care and family practice medicine for the treatment of common ailments. It pioneered the model for other retail clinics and led the retail clinic boom as consumers shifted their demand from the traditional doctor's office visit to visits to convenient retail clinic outlets.

Ten years later, MinuteClinic is now one of two operators (along with Take Care), dominating the market with a 72 percent market share. Since its inception, it has treated almost 2,000,000 patients and earned a satisfaction rating of 99 percent, saving patients, employers, and insurers time and money.[41] Under the MinuteClinic model, most visits cost around $25 to $45 and require no appointments. While most people who go to MinuteClinic pay out of pocket, most health insurance plans also cover its services. In fact, some insurers offer no co-pay options for retail clinic visits, noting that it is often cheaper for them when beneficiaries head to the clinics instead of the emergency room.

Striking While It's Hot: Investing at the Right Time　MinuteClinic started raising capital in 2002. Key venture capital firms, such as Boston-based Axcel Partners, Bain Capital Ventures, HQ Investments, Quinstar Ventures and TGap Ventures were early investors. Jack Ahrens of TGap Ventures says, "The market drivers were clear. Attracting the right CEO also helped the company to grow at a rapid pace." In a second investment round in 2004, MinuteClinic raised $15 million, giving the fledging company the critical funding to expand to major metropolitan areas outside its locations in Minneapolis-St. Paul and Baltimore.[42]

The initial vehement opposition by those in the medical community is also fading with many hospitals getting in on the retail clinic game. Hospitals were key players in 2009 and 2010 in supporting and financing the expansion of clinics through the recession. For example, Aurora Health Care in Wisconsin, CoxHealth in Missouri, and the Christus Medical Group partnered with Walmart to provide retail clinic options for consumers.[43] According to Bruce Shepard, who heads health business development at Walmart, hospital partnerships have the potential to jump-start growth, pointing out that hospitals could shore up initial financial losses as part of an overall marketing strategy focused on access to care.[44] Clinics could act as feeders into the hospital care system, sending new patients to primary care physicians. MinuteClinic established a partnership with CVS in 2005 and it was a good start.

Exit Drivers, and Returns　In late 2006, four years after the first investment, TGap and other investors debated whether MinuteClinic should raise additional capital and continue to build. "When we modeled the capital needs, tied to the number of clinics, revenues, and competitive pressures, the answer was clear. The returns would be much better if we sold the company," says Jack Ahrens.

In 2006, when CVS acquired MinuteClinic for $170 million (roughly $2 million per clinic), it was considered the pioneer of the retail clinic model, operating in 12 states.[45] At the time of acquisition, 73 of its 83 clinics were already operating in a CVS pharmacy location. Did the CVS partnership crimp the exit value or make the negotiations tricky? "Not really," says Jack. "We managed the relationship with CVS well but our primary goal was to generate returns for our LPs." Jack, a seasoned negotiator with over 30 years of investment experience, adds, "Let's just say both parties walked away with a win."

By mid-2008, MinuteClinic expanded to 520 clinics and quickly made plans to expand to 2,500 clinics over the next five years.[46] CVS's Dave Denton pointed out how a shortage in health care providers to meet the increase in baby boomers will continue to boost the retail clinic industry. "There will be a gap in the number of providers available in an already constrained system.... Our MinuteClinics are a very nice complement to that environment. We will easily double the number of clinics and maybe even more than that."[47] According to Merchant Medicine, which monitors retail clinic operators, growth trends may lead to 4,000 retail clinics by 2015.[48] MinuteClinic stands to benefit and hopes to operate more than 1,000 clinics in 100 markets in 2015.[49]

Exits Are All about Timing   Consider a what-if scenario. Instead of exiting, let us assume that MinuteClinic investors choose to put in more moolah. Heck, why not—the market is growing and so are the clinics, patients, and revenues. This where a savvy practitioner's expertise outplays his own greed. The opportunity would have become overripe leading to market pressures on margins, me-too's, and this could impact the exit dynamics. In 2008 through 2009, succumbing to arrival of incumbents and recessionary pressures, the retail clinic market growth decelerated from its high point of 350 percent in 2007 to 30 percent in 2008, trending negatively in the first half of 2009, causing many people to liken the fallout to the dot-com bubble.[50] In 2009, MinuteClinic closed 104 struggling clinics, citing low consumer demand. The clinics later reopened in response to seasonal flu traffic.[51] MinuteClinic cited that visits were up 36 percent in the second quarter of 2010, reflecting the steady growth in this new demand for alternative venues for health care outside the hospital or doctors' clinic setting.[52]

But while the industry's growth prospects going forward remain positive, many analysts and investors are still cautious. While bouncing back from the recession, growth in the retail clinic industry is set to be slower in 2011 and beyond. According to Paul Keckley of the Deloitte Center for Health Solutions, "the capital markets have said this is a promising sector, but it needs to define its business model better."[53] Tom Charland, CEO of Merchant Medicine, argues that many VC investors left too early because "the path to making money [from retail clinic investments] was longer than they could tolerate."[54] Not for TGap and MinuteClinic! While many smaller chains will probably struggle, bigger players in the market like MinuteClinic will probably drive the growth for CVS Corporation.

TGap Fund I had invested nearly $1.7 million in MinuteClinic over multiple rounds. In four years, the investment yielded a near-triple-digit IRR. As Jack Ahrens of TGap Ventures rightfully pointed out, "As an investor, you derive immense satisfaction in helping create the 'retail clinic' industry—a simple solution to a complex problem."

EVALUATING THE IDEA OR PRODUCT

While conducting due diligence for products or technology, consider the following factors:

- *Primary value proposition*: Quite simply put, does the stated solution offer a significant advantage—a significantly quantifiable improvement over the current solution? Is it faster, better, or cheaper? Terry McGuire of Polaris Ventures says, "Early on in my career, I found every technology fascinating—my reaction would be 'You can do that, really!'—but over time, I found that you need healthy skepticism. Believe that the world can be changed but ask all the right questions"[55]
- *Development stage*: Where is the idea in development? Is it a mere idea on a napkin, is it in the beta stage, is it already shipping, or are the first customers at hand?
- *Can it be protected?* How easy is it for another entrant to jump in? Is this an execution play, where better execution could lead to more market share? Or is it a secret sauce, where the patents, processes, or intellectual property can be used to build a moat around the business?
- *Market acceptance and adoption rate*: Several points of friction may come into play as the new technology/product tries to penetrate the market. While this is harder to analyze, the challenge is to ascertain the market pain and reasons for adoption. Are the needs of early adopters—the first customers—and the mass market aligned?
- *Growth potential*: What percentage of growth can be achieved in the first five years, and how does that compare with the size of the overall market? What is the effective mechanism to reach such potential? What are the points of friction in growth? Is the sales cycle long? What distribution channels exist?

Intellectual property (IP) due diligence requires some additional points:

- Ownership, title, assignments, and license agreements
- Claims and scope of protection (technical and geographic)
- Noninfringement—does the core IP address the company's primary products? Does the company have freedom to operate? Are there any blocking patents?
- Can the IP be invalidated in a litigious environment? Is any threatened or pending litigation foreseen?

It is important to consider the product in conjunction with the timbre of the entrepreneur. In a study, Saras Sarasvathy finds that *"starting with exactly the same product, the entrepreneurs ended up creating companies in 18 completely disparate industries!"*[56] As the French writer Antoine de Saint Exupéry wrote, "A rock pile ceases to be a rock pile the moment a single man contemplates it, bearing within him the image of a cathedral."[57] Sarasvathy builds a theory of effectuation where given means can lead to several imagined end points. The means in any entrepreneurial environment are meager: personal traits, expertise, and social networks. There is no elaborate planning—to the contrary, the plans are made and unmade, recast on a daily basis as entrepreneurs uncover new information. Seasoned entrepreneurs know surprises are no deviations from the path but are the norm from which one learns how to forge a path.

Take the example of a company that had six different changes in its business plan—the last iteration was PayPal.[58] Formed on the premise of developing cryptography software for handheld devices, the model evolved to transmitting money via a handheld PDA. The final evolutionary step in the business model was web-based payments, which allowed for rapid traction and acted as a de facto tool for processing web payments. One of the co-founders, Max Levchin, exhibited the energy and technical acumen of a typical Type A entrepreneur who goes down the wrong path on several occasions but iteratively corrects those missteps by asking the right questions. To start with, Levchin partnered with Peter Theil, a hedge fund manager who invested initial capital and complemented Levchin's technical acumen. Peter bought into the premise that there is demand for cryptography and that it is a relatively untapped and poorly understood market. "The assumption was that the enterprises were all going to go to handheld devices ... as a primary means of communication. Every corporate dog in America will hang around with a Palm Pilot or some kind of device." These assumptions were accurate, except that the timing was wrong—too early by about a decade. "Any minute now, there'll be millions of people begging for security on their handheld devices," Levchin would recall. But pretty soon, they realized that the market was not ready. It was a nightmare that every venture practitioner dreads—a technology in search of a market. "It's really cool, it's mathematically complex, it's very secure, but no one really needed it," Levchin would say. The battle between inertia versus changing direction and adapting flexibly to meet the market's needs paid off handsomely. Levchin started experimenting with questions like "What can we store inside the Palm Pilot that *is* actually meaningful?" and "Why don't we just store *money* in the handheld devices?" And while most venture practitioners would wring their hands at these questions and promptly kick the entrepreneur out, the early investors took a supportive approach, returns of which may have been significant. Four years from its inception, PayPal was acquired by eBay for $1.5 billion. Peter Theil went on to be the first angel investor in Facebook.

REVIEWING THE BUSINESS MODEL

The term *business model* is often misunderstood. When asked, "What is your business model?" seldom do entrepreneurs offer a clean, crisp one-line answer. As Ron Reed, Managing Director, Seneca Partners, says, "The question behind the question is—How are you going to make money?"

A business model defines how value is created and monetized. It succinctly addresses the who (target customer), the how (distribution strategy), leading to how much (gross margins!) and how soon (revenue growth!). The set of choices any company makes differentiates their business and establishes its costs and gross margins. Examples of business model jargon include "bricks and mortar" model, "razor blade" model, and "freemium" model, to name a few. In the example of HP versus Dell: One sells direct, while the other uses distributors. Or Amazon and Borders: Both sell books, but one is direct, while the other is via stores.[59]

The pattern is the same with Netflix, which offers movies via online streaming, and Blockbuster, which offers archaic store-front (bricks and mortar) rentals of DVDs with a significantly higher cost of goods. Within the universe of movie rentals, Netflix, Blockbuster, and Coinstar compete in different ways to achieve the same end result. Coinstar operates a network of DVD vending machines that allow customers to book DVDs online and pick these up at a local vending machine.

The business model determines the efficiencies of meeting the customer needs and ergo impacts the margins and costs for operating. Consider the software industry, where the products were once distributed in shrink-wrapped cases complete with manuals. Today, the cloud prevails, where no disks, installations, or manuals are necessary.

However, at the very early stages of any company, the business model may not be clear. In an interview with NBC, Eric Schmidt, former CEO of Google, recalls his first meeting with Larry and Sergey and subsequently his challenges with the business model. "Larry and Sergey were sitting there . . . they looked like children to me. I certainly did not see the success of the company and thought it was a terrible risk. I did not understand the advertising business at all and thought it was a joke. I thought there was something wrong in the cash position . . . they could never be making so much money as they claimed. My first act was to investigate the books to make sure this was legit. . . . I asked to see the money was coming in to prove that the people were actually paying for these adwords. . . . I overheard that a customer who was not getting their reports was screaming at one of the sales executives! I asked our Google sales executive, why is he screaming at you and she said, 'You don't understand Eric, their business needs cash every day and *we* are their business.' And then all of a sudden, I got it!" he recalled.[60] Schmidt joined Google in 2001 and took the company public in 2004 when the company was valued at $23 billion. At the time of his departure, in 2011, Google's market capitalization was over $180 billion.

Today, Twitter might be in the same league, where its business model is unclear but the users are hooked. While the market demand and users exist (think Twitter and its 150+ million users who send 50 million tweets per minute), the monetization of the business did not occur for the first few years and is an ongoing work in progress. According to Todd Dagres of Spark Capital, the rationale to invest was clear: "The team was great and the product seemed compelling. Our main concern was how broadly the product would appeal. When we invested, the traction was largely among early, techie adopters. We thought the appeal would spread from the tech community to the general population so we invested. We were also concerned about the competitive market but became comfortable when we decided that Twitter had the potential to be the category leader. *We were not obsessed with monetization when we invested.* The main issue was viral growth and engagement. We felt comfortable that monetization would follow if Twitter could build a large and engaged community,"[61] he remarked. As any investor in Twitter will tell you, not obsessing over monetization prematurely is better.

CONSIDERING THE FINANCIAL PROJECTIONS

At the very early stages of venture investment, practitioners rarely debate the financial projections. Rather, shrewd venture practitioners test the assumptions and capital required to achieve value inflection. "What are the milestones that this financing will achieve? How far are you from being cash-flow positive (in both time and money)?" are the questions Khosla Ventures team would ask of any entrepreneur.[62] As the company progresses to maturation with Series B or Series C rounds and starts to generate some revenues, the financial projections are analyzed in greater detail.

Finally, any practitioner would seek to understand the amount of capital needed to reach break-even. This is important from the perspective of reserving capital over multiple rounds for future investments. But it is foolish to expect precision when you are in this cloud of ambiguity. As Aristotle remarked, "for it is the mark of an educated man to look for precision in each class of things just so far as the nature of the subject admits; it is evidently equally foolish to accept probable reasoning from a mathematician and to demand from a rhetorician, scientific proofs."[63]

WEIGHING THE IMPORTANCE OF BUSINESS PLANS

Practitioners do not put much emphasis on business plans, but use them effectively to understand aspects of the business. A business plan is more like a resume—it is used to get an interview, or in this case, a meeting with an investor. Beyond that, it becomes a fluid or at times completely irrelevant document. "I don't care much for business plans," says Brad Feld, managing director of The Foundry Group. Or consider Arthur Rock's example: When he raised the first round of capital for Intel, he "wrote the business plan myself, just two-and-a-half pages, double-spaced, which said nothing! ... Normally I don't write business plans—the companies write a business plan. But in this case, I just felt that the investors were already there and all we needed to do was give them a little sheet of paper they could put in their files."[64]

In an interesting study of over 100 ventures, researchers concluded there was "no difference between the performance of new businesses launched with or without a written business plan. The most widely dispensed advice for would-be entrepreneurs is that they should write a business plan before they launch their new ventures."[65] Courses are taught, business plan competitions pit universities against each other, and writing the plan takes about 200 hours. But unless a would-be entrepreneur needs to raise substantial start-up capital from angels or institutional investors, there is no compelling reason to write a business plan, aside from its use as a good strategic planning tool.

For passive investors, the business plan is a starting point, assessed by a junior analyst and eventually debated by senior partners. However, for investors who have deep domain expertise, the business plan is not of much consequence. And Jeffry Timmons rightfully argues that the business plan is obsolete the instant it emerges from the printer.[66]

THE DUE DILIGENCE CHECKLIST

The following checklist (see Table 7.1) can be used as a simple outline to assess any opportunity and develop the investment thesis.

TABLE 7.1 Due Diligence Checklist

Criteria	Description
Product or service	The product or service is described completely and concisely. The need for the product or service is evident. The stage of development—prototype, first customer, multiple customers—is identified. A development road map is included.
Customers, revenue, and business model	The customer value proposition is quantifiable, high, and recognizable. The market need is established and the customer has an urgency to act. The product price points are identified, along with gross margins and costs.
Market size	The current target and addressable market size is estimated. It is a large and growing market, quantifiable to a certain degree.
Management	The key team member(s) have the expertise and skills needed to run this type of business. Clarity on additional hires and timing of recruitment? What are the significant holes in the team?
Competitors and competitive advantage	The product or service is better than the competition based on features and/or price. Is current and future competition identified and evaluated for weakness or significant barriers?
Capital efficiency and value creation	A reasonable milestone event chart with value drivers, date, and capital needs is identified.
Financials	Are plans based on realistic assumptions with reasonable returns? Does it contain reasonable, justifiable projections for 2 to 3 years with assumptions explained?
Exit assumptions	Is there a reasonable exit time frame? Some clarity on target universe of buyers?

Source: Adapted from Ann Arbor SPARK Pre-seed fund.

Table 7.2 a generic checklist; that elaborates on key checkpoints by stage of company.

TABLE 7.2 Key Due Diligence Questions for Consideration by Stage

	Seed Stage	Early Stage	Growth Stage
Management	Founder's expertise and understanding of the market pain. Ability to let go and attract smarter people at the right time.	Based on market needs, can the management team take a prototype and develop a commercial product? Technology development? Sales? Financial?	Can the team achieve high growth, high margins? Explore geographic expansion? Manage resources—people and cash—effectively? Board dynamics?
Market	Is there a need in the market? Is it a growing market? Will the market expand to accommodate breakthrough products?	Gauge ability to cross the chasm from early adopters to mainstream market.	Arrival of me-too's; competitive pressures.
Technology	IP assessment. Freedom to Operate. Laboratory scale data. Can you make it once?	Features and alignment with market needs. Market/customer level data. Can you make it many times?	Deployment and operational efficiencies. Can you make it consistently, with high quality while maintaining costs?
Financials	Shot in the dark. Look for milestones and capital needed to reach value creation.	Test pricing and revenue assumptions, gross margins.	Margin erosion. Ability to improve or sustain gross margins? Assess detailed financial analysis of past (a) income statement, (b) balance sheet, and (c) cash flows.

Practitioners can focus on most important criteria of due diligence by stage of the investment opportunity. It is pointless dissecting detailed financials for a seed stage company. A document checklist is presented here:

Due Diligence Document Checklist
- ☐ Corporate charter and by-laws
- ☐ Founders and management agreements and stock option plans
- ☐ Capitalization table
- ☐ Property (IP)—review patents, trademarks, ownership, license and royalty agreements, and financial considerations. Infringements, if any?
- ☐ Property (Real): Review lease agreements and any significant personal property
- ☐ Financial records/statements for the past three years, including all tax returns. Credit/loan agreements, any security agreements and guarantees. Investor agreements, warrants and equity-related matters, and all investor communications
- ☐ Material contracts, distribution, and supplier agreements
- ☐ Litigation or contingent liability matters
- ☐ Insurance, regulatory, or compliance matters

SUMMARY

James R. Swartz, founder of Accel Partners, once said that good venture capitalists can size up an opportunity in five minutes—"they have situational awareness. They can walk into just about any kind of meeting and, in about five minutes, figure out who's doing what to whom and exactly what the issues are, sort of cut through it and figure out what's going on.... You sort of look at a given situation and project its trajectory reasonably well."[67]

Good due diligence process helps a practitioner find the top risks and the upside of any opportunity. Steeped in shades of gray, any due diligence process offers some answers, but not all: practitioners need to be comfortable with some degree of ambiguity. If you had all the answers, the opportunity would cease to exist. Practitioners should be wary of analysis-paralysis and respect an entrepreneur's time—not make incessant irrelevant demands. Rather, a practitioner needs to ask: What are the top three risks associated with this opportunity, and can I make an investment decision based on addressing these risks effectively? As Jim Plonka of Dow Venture Capital says, "For any opportunity, I can get as much as 85 percent of the information needed to make a decision in 14 days or less."

And should a practitioner care about exits? While it is essential to ascertain a broad universe of potential buyers, and the reasons why these players would buy a start-up, it is futile to sweat the details. In an ever-evolving arena, where technologies and markets are in a constant state of flux, it is difficult to predict how two vectors will intersect. As Rick Snyder, former venture capitalist and now governor of Michigan, once famously remarked, "Forget exit strategy, most of these start-ups need an entry strategy."[68]

Once the due diligence steps are completed, the structuring of an investment—the deal outline—commences. The structure and terms of investment are discussed in the following chapters.

CHAPTER 8

The Basics of Corporations, Ownership, and Control

I wasn't a founder in the sense that I contributed anything scientifically but in the sense that I signed the corporation papers and owned founder's stock.

—Arthur Rock, early investor in Apple, Intel

Nowhere is the desire for ownership more heightened when you consider blazing new companies like Facebook, Zynga, or Twitter. For a rookie practitioner, it is important to understand the basics of ownership and control. Assume Jack and Jane decide to form a start-up called NewCo. Jane's idea promises to be the next big thing and Jack, with his proven skills and expertise, is eager to help execute that vision. He quits his $250,000-a-year job to join NewCo. The two shake hands and split the ownership 60:40.

The first step is to agree on how business decisions will be made, and the second step is to incorporate the company. The control feature comes into play with the business decisions. The economic feature relates to shares and cash—the value of the enterprise, share price, preferences and classes of shareholders, and how the cash spoils, if any, will be distributed. As simple as it may seem, it is easy to confuse ownership and control: A shareholder who owns shares of Google is eligible for the economic spoils (the ability to buy low and sell high, to receive dividends, and to take advantage of stock splits) but does not decide how the company is operated. On the other hand, a COO may have control of the operating decisions but have little or no ownership in the company.

The two documents that must be drafted when any company is being formed are:

1. *The Certificate of Incorporation:* Filed with any state, this is a license to establish the entity.
2. *The Articles of Incorporation (or corporate bylaws):* The Articles are generally the supreme governing document of any company and contain the most fundamental principles and rules regarding the nature of the company. The Articles regulate the form, manner, and procedure in which a company should be run. At the time of formation, a corporation's founders execute the Articles, which generally cover topics such as how directors are elected, how meetings of directors (and shareholders) are conducted, and how officers are elected and should carry out their duties. Typically, the Articles cannot be amended by the board of directors; instead, a supermajority vote of all the shareholders, such as a two-thirds vote, is usually required for amendment. The rights of shareholders, and how these differ from those of the board, are discussed here.

Let's assume Jack and Jane choose to form a C Corporation and domicile it in Delaware. In the United States, a Certificate of Incorporation is filed with a state government division; in Delaware, it is filed with the Delaware Division of Corporations.[1] The state division needs to know the name of the entity, the location of the registered office, the number of authorized shares, the par value, and the name of the incorporator.

Jack and Jane choose to establish a pool of 100,000 shares of stock. Note that this is an arbitrary number. It could be 100 shares or 1 million shares. Two aspects come into play while selecting this number of shares. First, human psychology—it is better to own 60,000 shares than, say, 60 shares. The smarter ones focus on percentages, but I have been surprised how many times this "small number" has become an issue. Second, some states tax entities on the number of authorized shares, their par value, or a combination thereof. Called the franchise tax, each state has its own method for calculating this madness. In Delaware, for 100,000 shares, the franchise tax is $825. If the founders had authorized 5,000 shares, they would have paid only $75 in franchise tax[2] (and would likely have had to deal with the psychological issues).

At the point where investors come in, two events will occur. Initially, the Articles of Incorporation will be amended to describe the board's structure and composition (see Figure 8.1). These define the control aspects. The number of authorized shares would increase and the classes of

FIGURE 8.1 Rights and Responsibilities of a
Corporation Are Shared between Various Stakeholders

shareholders may change, which would define the economic aspects of the investment.

My creativity is clearly lax when it comes to names—Jack, Jane, and NewCo—but the objective of this chapter is to help a reader understand the basics of ownership and how capitalization tables are constructed.

AUTHORIZED SHARES AND ISSUED SHARES

At the time of incorporation, NewCo is established with a predetermined number of shares. This is an arbitrary number determined by the founders. These shares, called *authorized shares*, are quantified in the company's articles of incorporation. At the time of formation, there will likely be only one class of shares: common. Investors typically seek preferred shares, and I will discuss the differences between the two classes in due course.

From the pool of authorized shares, all shares issued to founders, investors, or other parties are called issued shares. Issued shares are also termed *outstanding shares*. From the preceding, it is obvious that the number of authorized shares will always be equal to or more than the issued and outstanding shares. Treasury shares, not as pertinent to start-ups, are shares that have never been issued and do not have any voting rights.

Preferred Shares versus Common Shares

To understand the preferences of preferred shareholders, consider a balance sheet of a corporation, which lists assets, liabilities, and equity. Notice in Table 8.1 the overall context of risk, target returns, and the position of the preferred shares. At the top of the balance sheet is the secured lender, say a bank, which has first rights to collateral for the value of the secured debt. As the bank is "senior" to all and secured, its risk is considered the lowest. Thus, the rate of return expected by a secured lender is a much smaller percentage as compared to the unsecured lenders or stockholders.

Suppliers/payables are clubbed under unsecured debt. Stockholder preferences create a pecking order, especially with respect to liquidation preferences. Series B or later-stage investors have lower risk relative to Series A and thus target a lower rate of return. Common stock holders are at the bottom of the proverbial totem pole and are last to receive any liquidation proceeds. Management and founders are typically in this category.

Investors will seldom accept common shares, the lowest form of security with no significant control provisions. The two preferences all major investors seek are: economics and control. "If both investors and founders are at the same level of ownership and hold common shares, a problem exists," writes Dr. David Brophy,[3] who heads the University of Michigan Center for Venture Capital and Private Equity.

"The use of common shares bestows not only 50.1 per cent of the economics [for the founders], but also 50.1 per cent of the control of all aspects of the firm's management. With this voting majority, the founder 'wins all votes' and effectively controls the company. Both parties, however, may argue that some or all of the control should rest with the investor in order to mitigate the management risk. Usually, failure to accommodate this demand by the investor would be a 'deal-breaker,'" writes Dr. Brophy. The answer: convertible preferred shares. Preferred shares are a separately established class in the articles of incorporation that enjoys control and financial preferences above common shareholders. The convertible feature allows the preferred shares to convert to common under certain conditions, ideally at the time of an exit when risk is minimized.

Ownership Dynamics and the Capitalization Table

A capitalization table, or a cap table, lists the ownership of shares by name, class of ownership, percentage, and number of shares. It allows the investors and the company to understand the ownership structure. Consider Table 8.2, which demonstrates a cap table of a newly formed company with two founders. Let us term this as Phase I of the company. As we progress,

TABLE 8.1 Balance Sheet, Preferred and Common Stockholders

Assets	Liabilities	Remarks	Risk	Target Annual Returns (%)
Cash	Debt			
Receivables	Secured debt	Debt holders have priority lien on assets of the company. As the collateral decreases, risk increases, and target returns increase.	Lowest risk	6
Long-term assets	Unsecured debt		Medium risk	12
Intellectual property	Subordinated and convertible debt			14
	Equity			
	Preferred stock—Series B Preferred stock—Series A	Preferred stock enjoys higher economic benefits via liquidation and antidilution; it behaves like debt in early stages and converts to common stock as risk is reduced and eliminated.	Higher risk—typical structure for venture investments	20 30
	Common stock	Only minimum economic benefits of dividends	Highest risk— typical structure for founders	

TABLE 8.2 Phase I—Founders Only: NewCo Capitalization Table

Name of Shareholder	# Shares	Price	Paid-Up Value	Percent Ownership
Jane	60,000	$0.001	$60.00	60
Jack	40,000	$0.001	$40.00	40
Issued and outstanding shares	100,000	—	$100.00	100

note that while the ownership is negotiated in percentages, the subsequent calculations lead to the number of shares and per-share prices.

The price per share is established at a nominal value of $0.001, as the enterprise has little or no value at the time of its launch. The paid-up capital is thus $100.

Let's now move into Phase II of this company's growth, where a CEO is invited to join the team. Ms. CEO negotiates a 10 percent ownership in the company. Table 8.3 shows the resulting capitalization and ownership.

In this situation, we can see that the number of shares owned by the founders, Jack and Jane, remains the same, but the percentage of ownership changes. The company has now increased its pool of authorized shares to 111,111. Both the founders have tasted dilution—a dreaded word in entrepreneurial jargon. However, as we will see, dilution is acceptable so long as the enterprise value increases with every step of dilution.

In Phase III, a Series A investor is eager to invest. The investor and the founders agree to a premoney valuation of $1.0 million. The investor seeks preferred shares—a new class of shares. Consider Table 8.4 with certain assumptions. Two scenarios are presented where the amount of Series A investment is $500,000 for one scenario and $900,000 for another.

If the amount of investment increases, it causes further dilution for the founders. Investors and entrepreneurs need to balance the capital infusion and ownership with due caution. Investors are motivated to buy low. However, the amount of capital invested should be based on reasonable

TABLE 8.3 Phase II—Hiring of CEO: Dilution of 10 Percent

Name of Shareholder	# Shares	Price	Paid-Up Value	Percent Ownership
Jane	60,000	$0.001	$60.00	54
Jack	40,000	$0.001	$40.00	36
Ms. CEO	11,111	$0.001	$11.11	10
Issued and outstanding shares	111,111	—	$111.11	100

TABLE 8.4 Phase III: Impact of Series A Investor

Assumptions:

Premoney enterprise value established (A) =	$1,000,000	$1,000,000
Amount of investment (B) =	$500,000	$900,000
Postmoney enterprise value = (C) = (A + B)	$1,500,000	$1,900,000
Percentage ownership to Series A Investor =	$500,000/	$900,000/
(B) / (C) =	$1,500,000	$1,900,000
	= 33%	= 47%

Name of Shareholder	Paid-Up Value	Percent Ownership	Paid-Up Value	Percent Ownership
	$500,000 Investment		$900,000 Investment	
Jane	$60.00	36	$60.00	28.4
Jack	$40.00	24	$40.00	18.9
Ms. CEO	$11.11	7	$11.11	5.3
Series A investor ownership	$500,000	33	$900,000	47.4
	$500,111.11	100	$900,111.11	100

assumptions of milestones and should be sufficient to create a value inflection for the company. Compare the four scenarios in Table 8.5.

While the example is highly simplistic, the objective of the exercise is to demonstrate that (1) dilution occurs as newer entrants arrive and (2) dilution is good so long as the value of enterprise increases at every stage of dilution.

Let us assume a $900,000 investment and add a layer of employee option pool to this mix of ownership. Further, let us assume the investor and the founders agree to set aside a 10 percent option pool to attract future management. Table 8.6 shows the modified capitalization table.

TABLE 8.5 Impact of Dilution at Various Stages

	Founders and Management		Series A Investment	
	Founders Only	Founders and CEO	Amount $500,000	Amount $900,000
Jane	60%	54%	36%	28.4%
Jack	40%	36%	24%	18.9%
Ms. CEO		10%	7%	5.3%
Series A			33%	47.4%
Enterprise value	$100	$100	$1,500,000	$1,900,000

TABLE 8.6 Impact of Employee Option Pool Creation: Before and After Financing

	Founders and CEO	Option Pool Created Prior to Financing	Option Pool Is Diluted Post-financing	Option Pool as 10% of Postfinancing Capitalization
Jane	54.00%	48.60%	25.76%	22.90%
Jack	36.00%	32.40%	17.17%	15.26%
Ms. CEO	10%	9.00%	4.77%	4.24%
Series A Investor			47.60%	47.60%
Option Pool		10.00%	4.70%	10.00%
Total	100%	100%	100%	100%

By adding the option pool *postinvestment*, the investor's ownership was diluted as well. Thus, option pools are negotiated premoney (the equity for the option pool comes from the founders' pockets and not the investors' pockets) and agreed on prior to closing but come into effect postfinancing. It is customary to add language to the term sheet that states that *"the company will create an option pool so that it composes 10 percent of the postfinancing capitalization."* This avoids dilution for investors. For founders, it is customary to negotiate the size or percentage of the pool. The effective valuation for the investors drops by the percentage of the pool and investors should ensure that entrepreneurs are aware of this impact.

As Mark Suster, who has sold two companies and is now a partner with GRP Ventures, writes:

> *When I was raising capital as an entrepreneur, I had several term sheets and I thought I knew every term ... somehow I still got a bit duped. One of the leading term sheets had an option pool of 40 percent in it. I couldn't understand why until a friend pointed out that this just lowered the true pre-money valuation. Nowhere on the term sheet could I find the true pre-money or effective pre-money ... that was left for me to calculate.[4]*

While each shareholder owns a certain percentage, if the options were exercised to their maximum 10 percent, each shareholder would be "fully diluted." Fully diluted ownership is defined as the ownership after all options and any warrants would be exercised. Thus, in Table 8.6, the far right column, "Option pool as 10% of postfinancing capitalization," indicates fully diluted ownership. If options stay in the pool and are not fully utilized, and an exit was to occur, founders and Series A investors could find themselves with a bit of a bounty. A simple way to sort this out is to offer the unutilized portion back to the founders. After all, it came out of their pockets.

SHAREHOLDER RIGHTS

Shareholders generally enjoy the following rights, which are *distinct from the powers of the board of directors*:

- Shareholders must approve any changes made to the corporation as a whole. For example:
  - The articles of incorporation would be amended when any investment is made and additional shareholders are authorized.
  - A change to a corporation's bylaws would affect the shareholders. In one case, a simple oversight in bylaws led to undue inefficiencies. The bylaws of a company did not specifically mention that shareholder communication could be conducted via e-mail or that shareholder meetings could be conducted remotely. The start-up had to endure pain as it printed books, shipped them, and waited patiently to receive the signature pages. This was eventually corrected via a modification of the bylaws—an expensive and time-consuming oversight.
  - Acquisitions: All shareholders have rights related to the assets of the corporation and thus must approve the transfer of assets.
  - Stock/transfer of stock: For example, a board may authorize creation of an employee option pool; however, all shareholders would approve such a creation.
- Shareholders can sue the corporation for wrongful acts by the directors and officers of the corporation. This is lost on many rookie venture capitalist board members. This is the reason why director and officer (D & O) insurance exists and why indemnity clauses are important.
- Shareholders have the right to inspect the records and books of the corporation.
- Shareholders have the right to receive dividends as declared by the board of directors of the corporation.
- Shareholders have the right to approve or disapprove corporate transactions where some directors have a conflict of interest.

ROLE OF THE BOARD

The board is responsible to and primarily represents *all* shareholders (not just investor A or B). A venture-backed board member is responsible for ensuring that shareholder value is sustained and enhanced. The board is also primarily responsible for assessing CEO performance and assisting in recruitment, transition, and succession planning. Additionally, the board must establish good governance practices.

SUMMARY

In summary, the corporation as an entity is owned by its shareholders, governed by a board of directors, and managed by the CEO. The board members act as representatives of all shareholders and are legally bound by duties of care and loyalty. The corporation's ownership varies as depicted in the capitalization table dynamics.

The goal of this chapter was to provide a simple overview of the ownership dynamics and its impact of the capitalization table. Let us proceed to valuation, that voodoo art of prescribing a tangible number to the dreams of two guys in a basement with a PowerPoint presentation.

CHAPTER 9

Valuation Methods and Other Voodoo Arts

The price was way too high but sometimes that's what it takes to do the deal.

—Jim Bryer, on Accel's $12.7 million investment to acquire 15 percent of Facebook at ~$100 million premoney valuation.[1]

While valuation is one of the important terms for the entrepreneur as well as the investors, no simple method exists to calculate valuation at the seed and early stage of investments. "Sounds about right" is often an expression used by practitioners when numbers are tossed around. Depending on the stage of the company, valuation can be a simple back-of-the-envelope calculation, net present value calculation, or comparable transactions, called "comps." This chapter briefly covers the approaches to valuation. However, the emphasis is more on the subjective art at an early stage, rather than formulaic net present value (NPV)/discounted cash flow (DCF) approach.

Valuing an early-stage company is a nebulous exercise—an art form at best. Aswath Damodaran, author of "The Dark Side of Valuation," writes, "There can be no denying the fact that young companies pose the most difficult estimation challenges in valuation. A combination of factors—short and not very informative histories, operating losses and the ... high probability of failure—all feed into valuation practices that try to avoid dealing with the uncertainty by using a combination of forward multiples and arbitrarily high discount rates."[2]

HOW TO VALUE INTEL: LESSONS FROM ARTHUR ROCK

Bob [Noyce] called me one day and said, "We're thinking of leaving {Fairchild Semiconductor} to form a company," and I asked him how much money they thought they needed to get started, and they said, "$2.5 million." And I said, "Okay. You got it." No—first, I think we first discussed the terms—how much of the company they would be willing to give to investors for putting up $2.5 million, and we agreed on 50 percent. Then I said, "Okay, you're covered," and went about raising it.

Source: Arthur Rock, interview by Sally Smith Hughes, 2008–2009, "Early Bay Area Venture Capitalists: Shaping the Economic and Business Landscape," accessed February 10, 2011, http://digitalassets.lib.berkeley.edu/roho/ucb/text/rock_arthur.pdf.

THE DRIVERS OF VALUATION

By aligning the valuation drivers with the prior steps of the due diligence, we can see that in order of priority, the valuation will tend to be higher when all the following criteria are met:

- The opportunity serves an *attractive market* with higher *growth potential.*
- The opportunity has *an established competitive position* via patents or market share or leadership.
- A *strong team* is in place or, as Rob Hayes of FirstMark Capital puts it, it has "an execution machine."
- The opportunity may demonstrate *capital efficiency* (needs lower amounts of capital to achieve financial independence), revenues, gross margins.
- A meaningful *exit potential within the target time frame* can be achieved: There is a universe of strategic buyers that is large, accessible, and seeks growth opportunities via acquisition.
- Finally, the state of the market frothiness, or excessive capital supply, can often elevate valuations across the board and trounce all of the above criteria.

THE SIMPLIFIED FORM OF THE VC METHOD OF VALUATION

Harvard Business School Professor William Sahlman's VC method of valuation begins with the end in mind. Consider Table 9.1. Current market trends of 2009 state that if you are investing $800,000 in a seed stage company, your ownership will be in the 26 percent range. This rule of thumb works well when you are dealing with very early-stage companies with little or no meaningful comparable data. Also, consider data trends in Figures 9.1 and 9.2.

Starting with some data, we know that:

Median time to liquidity via an acquisition = 5.5 years

Median premoney valuation of seed round = $2.3 million

Median amount of investment at seed stage = $800,000

Imputed VC ownership at the time of investment = 26 percent

To generate a target IRR of, say, 106 percent, you need to retain, or preserve ownership to, as much as 20 percent. On the lower end of the spectrum, with a 36 percent IRR, you would be expected to retain at the minimum of 5 percent. Thus, the simple exercise should allow any practitioner to assess whether the investment opportunity can realistically help reach the target IRR by preserving ownership until an exit point is reached. Preservation of equity depends on a number of variables, and not all can be predicted. Thus, while negotiating valuation, any practitioner keeps the following three variables in perspective: Timing of exit, Ownership at Exit and Target IRR. Lets expand on these:

1. The timing of the exit depends on several factors, both internal and external.
   a. Internal factors:
      i. Resources, including management team quality and cash resources: Any rapid churn in the management team, unforeseen uses of cash, and changes in the burn rate will significantly affect the timing and value of the exit.

TABLE 9.1 Example of Simplified Valuation Method

Scenarios	Home Run	Not Bad	Phew
Estimated value of VC ownership at exit, assuming dilution from 26%	20%	5%	2%
Estimated value of company at year 6	$150 M	$75 M	$25 M
IRR	106%	36%	4.5%
Cash-on-cash multiple	37.5	4.68	1.25

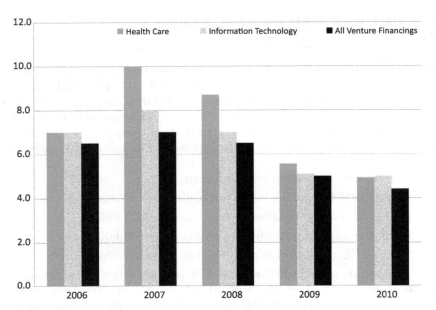

FIGURE 9.1 Median Equity Financings for U.S. Venture-Backed Companies
Source: Dow Jones VentureSource.

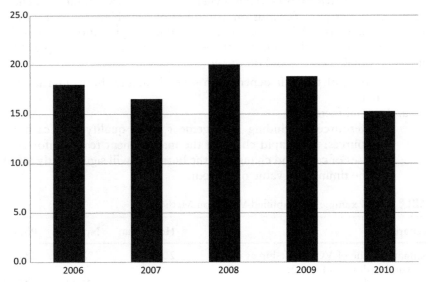

FIGURE 9.2 Median Premoney Valuation for U.S. Venture-Backed
Companies
Source: Dow Jones VentureSource.

      ii. Ability to execute and meet milestones

      iii. Strategy and business model

      iv. Investor's desire to force an exit: Many practitioners need to show exit activity to allow for future fund-raising success.

   b. External factors:

      i. Competitive threats

      ii. Acquirer industry dynamics

      iii. Public market/macroeconomic conditions

2. The estimated VC ownership at exit: Ownership at exit depends on value creation vis-à-vis burn rate. All practitioners aim to minimize future dilutions. Some common sources of nondilutive capital infusion include:

   a. Strategic relationships: Joint development agreements within the pharmaceutical sector are common. The start-up gets access to a funding stream in exchange for exclusive distribution rights.

   b. Venture debt: When Facebook wanted to raise $3 million, right after raising $12.7 million, Western Technology Investment offered venture debt. This form of financing reduces the overall cost of capital for start-ups and preserves equity for current owners. Venture debt is a hybrid form of financing available to certain types of venture-backed companies. As it is considered higher risk, venture debt financiers usually seek collateral, a higher rate of return, and warrants to sweeten their rate of return.

   c. Federal and state grants: A range of options are available, but restricted to technology-intensive companies for conducting research and development activities. The Small Business Innovation Research (SBIR) and Small Business Technology Transfer (STTR) federal funding programs offer grant opportunities each year. While these depend on funding availability for agencies and are hypercompetitive, several start-ups have opportunistically gained traction with such grants.

3. The exit value of the company: While this value can be guesstimated, as most practitioners say, focus on building something of value, and exits take care of themselves. Practitioners typically target a minimum threshold of IRR, say 35 percent, for each opportunity and, based on projections and exit probability, choose to invest or pass on opportunities.

In summary, the valuation economics boil down to (1) minimizing dilution and (2) maximizing exit value. Some practitioners alleviate all these concerns and try to squeeze as much equity as possible at the early stage, that is, maximum ownership at the lowest valuation. But this approach can come back to bite you. As Rick Heitzmann, managing director, FirstMark

Capital, says, "Valuation matters. But you cannot get too focused on it. You get a sense of people when they fight for the last nickel—this is a like a marriage and the goal is to keep the big picture in mind. Entrepreneurs do not always take the highest offer but select the best partner, and we have found that the combination of our experience and networks creates a far superior value proposition to just offering money."[3]

COMPARABLE VALUATIONS OF SIMILAR INVESTMENTS (COMPS)

In the comparable valuation or "comps" method, valuation is determined by comparable transactions in the marketplace. Consider Table 9.2, which shows a typical range of values. The revenues and the acquisition price are estimated, as these may not be declared or available publicly. A median and mean multiple is calculated that indicates a range of multiples that could be deployed in such a scenario.

In Table 9.3, the universe of publicly traded companies is assessed. While the data is available, critics argue that the method does not factor in several risks such as technology, market adoption, and liquidity risks. Further, the growth rates and gross margins for each company are different.

TABLE 9.2 Sample Comparable Method (Private Companies)

Company	Acquisition Price	Date of Acquisition	Estimated Revenue	Multiple
Accio Energy, USA	$550M	Jan 2013	$50M	11×
Premier Solar, Germany	$225M	July 2012	$28M	8×
Gemini Global, USA	$155M	Dec 2010	$26.2M	5.9×
Pantera Premier, Spain	$40M	June 2011	$2M	20×

TABLE 9.3 Sample Comparable Method (Publicly Traded Companies)

Company	TTM Revenues	TTM EBITDA	Market Cap	Enterprise Value	Enterprise Value (X Rev)	Enterprise Value (X EBIT)
General Energy	670	73	1,640	1323	2.0	18.1
Second Solar Group	433	99	1776	1220	2.8	12.3
Avalon Energy	1229	114	4440	3600	2.9	31.6
Sapphire Technology	225	45	800	990	4.4	22.0

While this method is used broadly in later stage companies, it has its own set of fair challenges:

- *The universe of comparable transactions may be broad*: As they say, with a large dataset, you can draw any conclusion you desire. When entrepreneurs present comparable transactions, and when investors dig the dataset, valuations can be surprisingly different.
- *Lack of transparency*: While the only data available is the premoney valuation, the data does not depict the finer nuances of strengths and risks embedded within. For example, valuation skews toward the positive when an experienced entrepreneur may be leading an opportunity. Other factors that may affect value are the quality of technology estate and its attractiveness to customers or existing partnerships—these factors may be invisible from the comps dataset.
- *The comparable dataset in a frothy environment may create a lemmings effect*: In the year 2000, the median premoney valuation at first round was $8 million. By 2010, it had dropped to $4 million.

VALUATION AND THE ART OF GETTING A SEAT AT THE TABLE

Early-stage investors can seldom predict whether an opportunity will grow, gain momentum, and generate returns. A classic investment approach is to invest a small amount and gain a seat at the table. "You are buying an option to invest in future rounds," says Jim Plonka of Dow Venture Capital. And if the company begins to grow, investors could maintain or build up their ownership position by investing additional amounts in future rounds. Consider when Sabeer Bhatia, founder of Hotmail, met with Draper Fisher Jurvetson (DFJ) to pitch his idea. Like most entrepreneurs, he asked for valuation in nice round numbers: $3 million. That was the heyday of the dot-com boom, and neither DFJ nor Bhatia would have the time to debate comps, develop intricate financial models, and craft the correct "ask" amount. Rather, DFJ followed the classic move of buying a seat at the table and putting in enough chips.

Tim Draper asked, "How much money do you need just to prove to us that you can do this—that it's even possible to make e-mail available on the web?" Draper asked for 30 percent of the company for $300,000; Bhatia pushed back and they agreed on 15 percent, with an implied postmoney valuation of $2 million.

DFJ was able to invest a small amount and test the hypothesis as well as the team's mettle. DFJ invested additional capital in future rounds and 20 months later, Hotmail was acquired by Microsoft for approximately $400 million.

Source: Adapted from Jessica Livingston, Founders at Work: Stories of Startups' Early Days (Berkeley, CA: Apress, 2007), 20.

DISCOUNTED CASH FLOW METHOD

If you have a master's in business administration, the DCF valuation technique would have been drilled into the depths of your cranium. If you do not have an MBA, you could review the following techniques, but like most highly academic techniques, the DCF is irrelevant for early-stage VC on a number of counts. For one, at an early stage of any company, you really do not have comparable data and the rest is projections—thus, I have seen entrepreneurs conjure up projections and use extensive DCF models to develop precise valuation, a healthy exercise, but at the end of the day, value is what can be transacted upon. A great model with multiple Excel spreadsheets is helpful, but if a transaction cannot be consummated, what good is all this idealism?

To calculate valuation of a firm using DCF, we estimate growth rate—the percentage of growth and the number of years of such growth. (Therein lies caveat #1.) The entrepreneur's estimates and practitioners' estimates can vary significantly. But let us assume that the two come to some mutual ground. The second variable is free cash flows (FCF) available during such a period. FCF seems like a novel concept when we discuss start-ups and early-stage companies. Finally, we assume a discount rate—you consider the terminal value and those FCFs, and pull them all together to the present date. That rabbit you pull out of your hat is called Net Present Value (NPV)—a formula that is an amalgamation of four different projected variables—the rate of growth, the time period of growth, the cash flows, and the cost of capital. The closest I can come to assessing, on any given day, is that just one variable equals the cost of capital. But the rest seems like voodoo to me. Allow me to humor you for a bit longer:

Value of firm = value of operating and nonoperating assets + cash

Or, put another way, Value of equity = Value of a firm − Value of debt

When all is said and done, you are trying to establish a value for the existing assets and future growth. The approach is well suited for more mature companies. Start-ups have little or no revenues, no customers, and at times, operating losses. Even those young companies that are profitable have short histories, and most young firms depend on private capital, initially owner savings, and VC and PE later on. As a result, many of the standard techniques we use to estimate cash flows, growth rates, and discount rates either do not work or yield unrealistic numbers.

In addition, the fact that most young companies do not survive has to be considered somewhere in the valuation. Researchers studied the survival rate of 8.9 million firms over a seven-year period (1998–2005) and concluded that only 38 percent of businesses survived over a five-year period. See Table 9.4, which shows the survival rate of technology companies (clubbed under "Information"), which is substantially lower than health services.[4] At least two-thirds of technology companies die in five years, a higher mortality rate as compared to health services.

Damodaran suggests that besides using "a combination of data on more mature companies in the business and the company's own characteristics to forecast revenues, earnings, and cash flows," we should "adjust the value for the possibility of failure."[5] Value is based on future revenues on the assumption the business survives. Hence, the possibility of failure needs to be factored into the equation. He further points out that multiples of valuation should be considered at the point of exit, rather than present-day multiples. If the revenue of a start-up after year 5 were to drop to a compound annual growth rate (CAGR) of 10 percent, the multiple should reflect this growth as opposed to, say, 50 percent CAGR in earlier years. This would create an interesting conundrum where, besides revenues, practitioners would try to project the exit multiple five years down the road.

While this may not be adopted as easily, most practitioners use a rule of thumb to assert valuation while considering risks of technology failure, management churn, financing risk, and illiquidity premium. As one GP pointed

TABLE 9.4 Survival Rate of Firms

Sector	Year 1	Year 5	Year 7
Health Services	86%	50%	44%
Information	81%	31%	25%
Financial Activities	84%	44%	37%
Business Services	82%	38%	31%
All Firms	**81%**	**38%**	**31%**

out, "I expect each of my portfolio companies to generate 10X returns and make the fund whole—getting caught up in discount ratios and valuation techniques does help. I seek the best in class and work hard to make them the *numero unos* of their category." As Michael Moritz of Sequoia Capital once remarked, "We are in the business of creating a large bonfire with a small matchstick."

SUMMARY

Establishing a price for an illiquid security, with significant risk (management risk, market risk, technology risk, follow-on financing risk) is nebulous activity. At the early stages of investment, practitioners have honed the valuation process to an art form, a subjective technique at best. For most practitioners, the ability to generate returns is what matters. And for each investment, seasoned investors seek 10x or higher returns. "I want each of these to have the potential to be a 10-bagger and make my fund," one GP remarked. Should the valuation debate become prolonged, consider using a blended approach with others terms. An interesting approach that diffuses valuation—called springing warrants—is discussed in the following chapter. As most agree, valuation is just a small part of the overall structure.

As far as Jim Bryer goes, he may have felt the investment was expensive at $100 million premoney valuation, but ought to be comforted by the fact that Facebook is valued at $50 billion and the numbers keep getting higher. Accel's investment has grown at least 50x in six years—not too shabby, eh?

CHAPTER 10

Structuring Investment Transactions

For many entrepreneurs, reading a term sheet is no more interesting than reading the latest volume of the Federal Register.
   And most lawyers will tell you what the terms mean but not how they can be used to screw you, how to negotiate them, and what is the "norm."
                           —Mark Suster, General Partner, GRP Partners[1]

Much has been written about term sheets, including line-by-line analysis of terms. A line-by-line analysis is helpful, but it is akin to looking at trees when the perspective of the complete picture or the forest is critical. My own struggle with term sheets was the legalese: the jargon that was a completely different language. Newbie practitioners describe standard term sheets as "incredibly dense" and often hesitate to tackle these. The goal of this chapter is to simplify, prioritize, and focus on the key terms that help complete a transaction. Investment structure is the framework that describes the flow of capital from the investor to the company and back.

THE SPIRIT OF THE TERM SHEET

After due diligence, investors propose a set of investment terms that define the transaction. At the heart of it, both the entrepreneurs and investors agree upon the following underlying spirit of the term sheet:

■ The investment opportunity and market conditions are ripe for rapid growth.

- Both parties bring a unique set of elements—technology and capital—to create value.
- Together, these elements can help catalyze and create value faster.
- Both parties agree to collaborate for a meaningful period of time, ideally until exit do us part.
- Both parties understand that financial success is critical for both parties, as is the timing of returns.

While this credo can be established, there can be several points of creative tension or stress between the two parties.

NEGOTIATION STRESS POINTS

The potential stress points in any negotiation can occur around the economic or control factors. Table 10.1 identifies these stress points and the relevant terms that address them.

Types of investment structures include debt, convertible loan, and preferred stock. A simplest form of investment, a debt would be governed by some basic parameters, such as the principle, interest rate, collateral, and schedule of payments. Debt may be secured by collateral such as assets and/or receivables, or it may be unsecured. An unsecured debt acts as a quasi-security. In this chapter, convertible note and preferred stock structures are presented. The preferred stock is the most commonly used investment structure in venture capital investments.

But at the heart of it, investment structures are designed with two key parameters: economics and control. As Brad Feld of the Foundry Group points out, terms sheets can be simple if we focus on what matters:

1. *Ownership and economics:* Buying a meaningful slice of the company at the right price is the first step for any investor. But most savvy practitioners know that while valuation is important, the potential of the opportunity in the long run, as well as other investment terms, matters. In some investments, such as distressed real estate, the philosophy that "you make money when you buy" may be true; with VC investments, that may not necessarily be the case. A premoney value of $8 million or $10 million is not that significant when the opportunity could potentially offer a billion-dollar exit. The price-based debate creates undue tension at the point when a relationship is being established.
2. *Governance and control:* Also described as protection or control aspects of an investment, these rights minimize risks, protect against any downside, and thereby potentially amplify the upside. Governance is established by the board of directors, which typically appoints the CEO and approves an annual plan, budget, and major business decisions. The

TABLE 10.1 Differing Goals of Entrepreneur and Investor

	Entrepreneurs Want …	Venture Capitalists Want …	Relevant Terms That Come into Play
At point of entry	Maximize valuation Adequate capital to meet and exceed milestones Avoid loss of control	Minimize risk and valuation; potential for up rounds and target returns Capital efficiency; reach breakeven/financial independence rapidly Ensure that the team, strategy, and vision are aligned	Price per share and amount of investment leading to valuation Amount of investment, use of proceeds Employment agreements, vesting of founders' stock, structure of board, independent board seat choices
Between entry and exit	Venture capitalists bring strategic value, domain expertise, and connections Venture capitalists can help with future financing Stay in control and experiment despite inefficiencies	Ensure that execution is as agreed on and that business strategy and plans are sound If opportunity grows rapidly, maintain pro rata ownership If it doesn't grow as well and leads to the "living dead" category, have the ability to liquidate	Board and governance matters; milestone-based financing Preemptive rights or right of first refusal Antidilution, redemption, or liquidation, drag-along rights and tag-along rights
Exit	Can be patient; may choose to delay/avoid an exit	Speed to exit is critical	Redemption, dividends, liquidation preferences, and registration rights
Exit Drivers	Self-actualization	Highest IRR	

board is controlled by investors and establishes certain protective provisions to ensure that the management does not jeopardize the security interests of the investors.

Let us start with the convertible loan, a simple investment structure that is used more often by angel investors and early-stage investors.

Convertible Loan

A convertible loan starts with senior position on the balance sheet and drops down, or converts to equity, when the company meets certain milestones. Primarily used as a risk mitigation tactic in the early stages of the company, a convertible note allows the investor to claim the assets of a start-up if it fails. Alternatively, in certain conditions, the note holder can call the note. Used in situations where establishing valuation is cumbersome, a convertible note postpones the pricing of equity until a suitable event occurs. The key parameters that come into effect with convertible notes are principle, interest rate, and conversion trigger points. After the conversion, the interest payments are terminated and appropriate changes on the balance sheet (the liabilities are shifted to the equity section) are duly recorded. Typical convertible note terms include:

- *Interest rate*: Depending on the risk investor's appetite, interest rates vary from 3 percent upward to as much as 10 percent; it is normal to accrue interest for most convertible notes.
- *Term*: Typical terms are one year, but notes can be as much as two years or higher.
- *Conversion triggers*: The note would convert to preferred stock upon raising a predetermined amount in a Series A round.
- Improving the returns: Investors frequently add a few other aspects in the mix to improve the risk-reward ratio.
  - *Discounts*: For example, a 20 percent discount to the share price established at following series.
  - *Warrants*: Warrants would act as sweeteners and help aggregate a higher ownership via additional shares at a lower price point.
- Capped valuations: A capped convertible note establishes a cap on valuation for the next round; for example, a cap at $2.5 million premoney indirectly establishes the valuation of $2.5 million at the next round. Mark Suster warns, "Make no mistake—this IS a priced round." A sword that can cut both ways, a convertible note with cap, could hurt the entrepreneur, he points out. "It basically sets your maximum price rather than your actual price. Example: If you do a convertible note raising $400k at a $3.6m premoney, your ceiling is that you've given

away 10 percent of the company ($400k/$4m postmoney). But your actual next round might come in at $2 million premoney. You might have been better just negotiating an agreed price in the first place. Not always, but sometimes."[2]

For angels and early-stage investors and entrepreneurs, the valuation debate can be postponed by using a convertible note. Generally speaking, savvy investors resist any structure where the value is to be ascertained by a third party at some point in the future. Entrepreneurs find the convertible note easier to digest as the valuation can be built to their advantage, speedier to negotiate, with limited legal expenses.

JUST DON'T F— IT UP . . .

Peter Thiel, an investor who made his money in PayPal, was one of the first angel investors in Facebook. He invested $500,000 as a loan that would convert to equity if Facebook achieved its milestone of 1.5 million users. "Just don't f— it up," Thiel said to Mark Zuckerberg at the time of investing.

    Facebook did not meet the milestone, but Thiel converted his loan to equity and joined the board. Thiel's $500,000 got him 10.2 percent equity, implying a valuation of $4.9 million for the company. In six years, Facebook's value has grown to an estimated $50 billion. Thiel's investment has grown by a mere 10,000x in six years!

Source: David Kirkpatrick, *The Facebook Effect* (New York: Simon & Schuster, 2010), page 89.

Bridge Loan   Similar to a convertible note, a bridge note is raised to meet certain short-term needs of a company. Typically used between financing rounds, a bridge loan bridges a company between its existing cash and a future financing round. Terms are similar to a convertible note. Investors are leery of a bridge to nowhere and may build in a stair-stepped interest rate, warrants, or incentives. Thus, if the bridging event does not occur as predicted, investors gain additional ownership as a result.

Equity: Preferred Stock

In Chapter 8, we discussed preferred stock and how this class of shares enjoys control and financial preferences over and above the common shareholders. Table 10.2, summarizes these various aspects of a term sheet. If the value

TABLE 10.2 Summary of Key Investment Terms: Preferred Stock

Term	What It Means	Importance to Investors	Key Negotiation Variables
Economic Terms: Those That Impact Financial Outcomes for Investors			
Valuation	Establishes value of a company	Project potential IRR	Percentage of ownership, price per share
Liquidation preference	Creates a waterfall of distribution—who gets paid first and how much—when a liquidity event occurs.	Improves returns at exit, protects investment at lower exit values	Multiple (1x, 2x), participating preferred, cap/no-cap
Antidilution	Prevents dilution of investors' ownership when down rounds occur.	Minimizes downside/protects ownership	Weighted average/full ratchet
Dividends	Allows investors to declare dividends	Improves potential returns	Percentage, cumulative/noncumulative
Preemptive rights/right of first refusal (ROFR)	Allows investors to buy additional shares in future rounds	Allows for increasing ownership if opportunity gets stronger	Time frame for decision, pro rata share
Redemption of shares	Allows investors to redeem their ownership/shares after certain time frame. Ensures that investors are able to	Allows for exits; redemption is especially important when the company has minimal upside potential.	Time period (number of years), fair market value.
Registration rights, conversion to common at public offering, piggyback rights, drag-along rights/tag-along rights, co-sale agreements	trigger the timing and conditions of an exit; drag-along and tag-along rights allow one party to sell his or her shares if the other party is able to find a seller.	Registration rights depend on the strength of the company and state of the public markets.	These are exit-related provisions and savvy practitioners do not waste much time negotiating these boilerplate terms.

Governance Terms: Those That Impact Control of the Company

Board composition	Number of seats for Series A, common, and independent shareholders	Allows for control and protection of security	Number of seats, how the board structure can be changed, rights of preferred shareholders vis-à-vis the rest
Board approval items	Board approves hiring of executives, employment and compensation agreements, issuance of stock options, annual operating plan, and incurrence of debt obligations or contracts above a certain financial limit	To protect the ownership and equity, board would approve key business decisions that may impact the operations or the equity structure of the company.	David Cowan of Bessemer Venture Partners says, "As long as the ink is black—if the company is doing fine—I don't care much about control provisions."**
Protective provisions	Allows for protection of security interests	Preferred shareholders will approve all changes to securities, board structure, mergers, redemption of stock, and amendments to articles of incorporation	Most of these terms are standard and very few practitioners open these up for negotiation.
Employment and vesting for management	Keeps management team focused on building the business	Aligns interests of founders and investors	Employment agreements, stock vesting, restrictions on co-sale, creation of option pool, key man insurance, noncompete provisions

*David Cowan (Bessemer Venture Partners), in discussions with the author, December 2010.

of preferred stock grows, the ability to invest additional amounts of capital, such as with preemptive rights, helps investors maintain or build their position in a growing company. If it sours, the ability to gain control (via management changes), minimize the impact of downsides (via antidilution), and attempt to salvage the remains of the day is important. In reality, most practitioners agree that if any opportunity teeters, not much can be done to resurrect the remains. In any portfolio, at least a third of the investments will likely end up as write-offs.

Warrants   A warrant is a right to buy a security at a fixed price: the "exercise" or "strike" price. Typically, warrants are issued in conjunction with an existing investment—a security, such as a convertible note or venture debt. For investors, warrants provide the ability to increase the overall return. Investors can improve their ownership positions at a suitable point in the future, as the opportunity matures.

A typical warrant would include terms such as:

- Percentage of investment or amount of investment:
  - Percentage of investment: If an investor issues a $500,000 convertible note with 10 percent warrants, the warrant allows the investor to invest $50,000 in the future.
  - Amount of investment: The warrant allows an investor to purchase shares worth $100,000.
- Strike price:
  - Nominal value: Established at, say, $0.001 per share. An investor-friendly term, this would allow an investor to increase ownership at a certain point in the future.
  - Share price of the next round: A company-friendly term, this allows an investor to double up or increase the ownership position.
- Term:
  - Time: Term could be any time, say, up to 10 years; the longer the duration, the better for the investors.
  - Event-based triggers: Reduce the life of the warrant upon certain trigger conditions, such as future financing or value creation milestones. Such milestones reduce the overall liquidity that would affect the founders.

Springing Warrants   At the point of entry, valuation debates are the primary cause of tension. Founders believe that the value of the company should be as high as possible. Its technological marvel—future revenue and growth projections are just a matter of time. For practitioners who have heard ample stories and burnt their capital, the skepticism is obvious.

TABLE 10.3 Springing Warrants Can Be an Effective Way to Diffusive Valuation and Performance-Related Challenges

Revenues	2012		2013		2014	
Baseline Revenues	$5M		$12M		$23M	
Upside case revenues	$7M	$9M	$15M	$18M	$27M	$30M
Additional equity granted to founder for meeting upside targets	3%	5%	3%	5%	3%	5%

For John Neis of Venture Investors, the answer was simple—the middle path. When the founders of Tomo Therapies came up to discuss an investment opportunity, Neis was intrigued, but like most practitioners, he looked at the financial projections with a degree of healthy skepticism. Typically, the struggle between the buyer and the seller is evident, as each side tries to extract the maximum value up front. Not in this case—Neis developed a structure of springing warrants.

In this structure, quite simply, the venture fund's ownership decreases as the founders and entrepreneurs meet their projections and milestones. A representative example is presented in Table 10.3. It is an elegant model to balance the ownership struggles and provide adequate rewards if the founders meet their goals. The springing warrants are issued to founders and these are exercisable (at a nominal exercise price) at certain milestones. The founders would thus acquire additional shares of common stock based on a predetermined formula. In the example in Table 10.3, if the founders believe they can generate revenues of $30 million in 2014, while the investors think it would be more like $23 million, the two parties can converge the valuation today with the assurance that as founders create value, investors relinquish a portion of their equity.

Tomo Therapies (Nasdaq: TOMO) grew to $200 million in revenues in four years of commercial launch. For Neis and Venture Investors, the largest shareholders, this investment was a barn burner—a 10x return or higher. As a result, Neis was listed in the Forbes Midas list, the first Midwesterner to be featured in this coveted club of who's who of successful venture capitalists. In his modest style, he says, "Tomo's technology saves lives—and bringing that to market was the important goal for all. The financial returns are always a welcome by-product of our efforts to change the world."

Options The typical recipient of a stock option is an employee. A typical recipient of a warrant is an investor. This is the primary difference beyond which the mechanics are more or less the same. It is important for any practitioner to understand the impact of an option pool on the investment structure. When exercised, options will dilute ownership for all stockholders. Employee stock options are offered as incentive tools to attract and retain talent. Incentive stock options are used for vendors, consultants, and the like. The tax implications for each need to be considered—these are beyond the scope of this book. Typical option agreements include:

- Number of shares
- Strike price
- Term and vesting
- Buyback provisions

MILESTONE-BASED FINANCING: RISK MITIGATION OR DISTRACTION

Staged financing is used in seed and early-stage investments, and the primary reason is to de-risk the opportunity. Completion of a prototype and customer validations are a few examples of milestones that are typically used to structure investments. Recall Peter Thiel, who agreed to invest in Facebook with the precondition that his note would convert to equity after they reached a certain number of users. Staged financings can provide incentive for the teams to perform and move faster, and entrepreneurs can be assured that the tranches of capital will arrive as the milestones are completed. But is it that simple?

"Milestone-based financing forces the management to either declare victory too soon, or worse, it distracts them from a potentially bigger opportunity—in an evolutionary stage, milestones can push the founders in the wrong direction," says Jack Ahrens of TGap Ventures. If you choose to use milestone-based financing, consider the primary question: "Can you disengage if the milestones are not met?"

Further, the caveats are:

- *Definition of milestone:* Avoid ambiguity and insist on measurable and simple definitions. Instead of a broad, complete beta, it would be prudent to identify the top three key functions that the technology should meet.
- *Amount necessary to reach milestone:* If an entrepreneur prepares the budget, a practitioner needs to ensure that the resources, amounts, and line items are vetted. On the flip side, if you squeeze the amount down, be prepared to accept the blame: A common excuse from entrepreneurs can be "We couldn't meet the milestones because we did not have enough money to start with."

As with most terms, flexibility, speed, and simplicity are the keys to a successful start.

STRUCTURING TERMS TO GENERATE TARGET RETURNS

A good investment structure allows an investor to double up and invest higher amounts as the opportunity progresses—or minimize the risks if it craters. Structure starts with valuation primarily, followed by liquidation and antidilution preferences (used to protect ownership), dividends, and rights of first refusal. These terms combined effectively can help any investor (a) establish an ownership position and (b) build up ownership as the opportunity progresses.

Liquidation Preference

The second most important term after valuation is liquidation preference, writes Mark Suster of GRP Ventures.[3]

Liquidation preferences, often seen as an opportunity to juice up the returns, are rights to receive a return prior to common shareholders. These preferences come into play at the time of liquidating the assets of the company. Liquidation occurs under two scenarios: a sale via acquisition (presumably a good outcome if the sale price is right) or shutting down the company (and calling it a dog).

From a negotiation perspective, liquidation preferences have the following variables:

- *Liquidation multiple:* Defined as multiple of the amount invested, practitioners set a multiple of, say, one time the value of the original investment. This essentially translates to investors recovering the amount invested. The multiple is an indicator of market dynamics, and while one time is the standard norm in a healthy market, at times the multiple has scaled up to as much as 10 times. In the third quarter of 2010, 85 percent of the transactions had a multiple of one to two times.
- *Straight convertible preferred or nonparticipating:* In a nonparticipating liquidation preference, investors are entitled to the amount they invested and dividends, if any. That is it: They do not get anything more. Under certain circumstances where an earn-out amount has been offered upon achieving certain milestones, investors can get a higher return when the preferred shares are converted to common. Thus,

practitioners should ensure they have the option to choose the greater of the two scenarios.

- *Participating preferred (or, as entrepreneurs call it, a double dip):* In this scenario, investors first recover the amount invested, dividends, and the multiple agreed on. The double dip occurs when they participate—a much kinder term—which means the preferred shareholders get to enjoy the spoils with the common shareholders on an as-converted basis. Market trends indicate that about 50 percent of the transactions conducted fall in this category.
- *Capped participation:* A smart entrepreneur may have invented this term, which essentially caps the return any investor can get. A typical cap would be, say, 2.5x of the original amount invested. Typically, about 40 percent of participating transactions are capped.

As Table 10.4 illustrates, liquidation preferences can have a significant impact on the rate of return. But it is primarily a downside protection mechanism for investors. At larger exit values, these preferences do not demonstrate a significant impact on the common shareholders or the IRR.

Assumptions:

- Acquisition value for company = $4 million
- Investment = $900,000
- Time to exit after initial investment = 3 years
- Dividends at 8 percent per annum, noncumulative

TABLE 10.4 Liquidation Preference and Its Impact on IRR and Common Shareholders

	4x	2.5x No Cap	2.5x Capped	1x
Liquidation Multiple (A)	$3,600,000	$2,250,000	$2,250,000	$900,000
Dividends (B)	216,000	216,000	216,000	216,000
Balance (C = A − B)	184,000	1,534,000	1,534,000	2,884,000
As Common (D = 47% of C)	86,480	726,631	726,631	1,366,105
Total to Investors (A + B + D) =	3,902,480	3,192,631	2,250,000	2,482,105
IRR to Investors	63%	52%	36%	40%
Balance for common shareholders	$97,520	$807,369	$1,750,000	$1,517,895

Stacking of Liquidation Preferences over Multiple Rounds

If you are a Series A investor and a Series B investor arrives and stacks on his or her preferences on top of yours, the scenario could get more complex due to the misalignment of interests between the various parties (two separate classes of preferred shareholders and common shareholders). Brad Feld of the Foundry Group writes in his blog:

> *As with many VC-related issues, the approach to liquidation prefer-*
> *ences among multiple series of stock varies (and is often overly com-*
> *plex for no apparent reason). There are two primary approaches:*
> *(1) The follow-on investors will stack their preferences on top of*
> *each other: series B gets its preference first, then series A or (2) The*
> *series are equivalent in status (called pari passu…) so that series*
> *A and B share pro-ratably until the preferences are returned. De-*
> *termining which approach to use is a black art which is influenced*
> *by the relative negotiating power of the investors involved, ability*
> *of the company to go elsewhere for additional financing, economic*
> *dynamics of the existing capital structure, and the phase of the*
> *moon.*[4]

Higher Liquidation Preferences = Demotivated Founders and Employees

Excessive liquidation preferences benefit only the investors and reduce the potential outcomes for common shareholders, including management and founders. When those who are working hard to create value see that all they would get is W-2-like returns, the desire to perform and create significant value diminishes. Brad Feld explains: "The greater the liquidation preference ahead of management and employees, the lower the potential value of the management/employee equity. There's a fine balance here and each case is situation specific, but a rational investor will want a combination of 'the best price' while insuring 'maximum motivation' of management and employees. Obviously what happens in the end is a negotiation and depends on the stage of the company, bargaining strength, and existing capital structure, but in general most companies and their investors will reach a reasonable compromise regarding these provisions."[5]

An elegant solution to protect the founders could be the founder's liquidity preference. Although rarely used, it is a creative approach to address the challenges wherein the founders can washed out completely. "Creating a special class of common stock for the founders with a special liquidation preference is not typical, but it is an option that offers investors a great deal of flexibility and creativity," writes attorney Jonathan Gworek. Gworek recommends a win-win approach where a founder's liquidity preference creates a financial threshold for the founders, especially if they have invested significant capital prior to any outside investments. Such a clause allows for the founders to retain a floor, a minimum position for value created by the entrepreneurs.[6]

Professors Colin Blaydon and Fred Wainwright, who head the Center for Private Equity and Entrepreneurship at the Tuck School of Business at Dartmouth, write that "risk-reducing mechanisms were seen to be counterproductive—an attempt to 'close the barn door after the horse was gone.'" Blaydon and Wainwright conclude, "the continued prevalence of a participation feature in deal structures today indicates that the VC community either has less confidence in the potential growth of portfolio companies or a lower appetite for risk." Further, they point out that participation "sets a precedent for terms in subsequent financing rounds" and that the "VCs who funded the earlier rounds . . . will now have to transfer some of that hard won value to the new investors."[7] It becomes a karma thing, as a Series A investor tries to squeeze the entrepreneur; when the Series B investors come in, they love to jump in and do the same. Ahrens of TGap Ventures says, "It is best to avoid any multiple preferences and clever terms—it becomes a rat's nest and does not do anybody any good." At the early stage of investment, simpler is better. "You are betting on the market and the CEO—let's not get too tied up in preferences and such legalese when there are no revenues and no product," says Rick Heitzmann, FirstMark Capital.[8]

Consider the typical trends of liquidation preferences.

- In 2010, an average of 40 percent of financing uses senior liquidation preferences. As the series scale up to Series C and D, senior liquidation preferences grow, from 30 percent (at Series B) to 60 percent (at Series E or higher). Naturally, the later investors are risk-averse and want to have the exit prior to the other investors, and thus demand better preferences.
- At least 20 percent of the financings have multiple liquidation preferences. As much as 85 percent of the Series A financings have a multiple of 1x to 2x, with the rest being 2x to 5x. In certain market conditions, when capital supply shrinks, or if the company may have struggled, a 5x preference was observed.

    At Series A, about 50 percent of financings were participating preferred. Of these, about 25 percent to 50 percent had no cap. The rest were capped anywhere from 2x to 5x.

Antidilution Protections

Antidilution protection is a downside protection mechanism that protects existing investors when a company is forced to accept a down round, which is a lower share price compared to what the previous investors have paid. Existing investors receive additional shares, and their position is adjusted based on the price of the down round. The common shareholders, typically the management and founders, endure the maximum pain in such circumstances. An investor-friendly term, it forces the management team to retain value, execute on its milestones, and ensure value is created in an effective and timely manner. However, down rounds can occur with changes in burn rates (as unanticipated issues occur). Poor market conditions could significantly affect a company's ability to raise future rounds of capital.

Antidilution provisions fall into three categories:

1. *Full ratchet*: An investor-friendly provision, this has the largest impact on the common shareholders. The full ratchet converts the price of *all* the previously sold shares down to the price of the current round irrespective of the amount raised or the number of shares issued.
2. *Broad-based weighted average*: A company-friendly provision (well, a true company-friendly provision = no antidilution provisions), this clause has the least impact of all on common shareholders as it is based on the weighted average of the outstanding shares, including options and warrants.
3. *Narrow-based weighted average*: Same as broad-based, but eliminates the options and warrants and thus has a lower impact on common shareholders.

The norm is weighted average (either broad-based or narrow-based), and thus practitioners are better off staying in the middle of the road.

As Table 10.5 illustrates, the impact of antidilution on Series A would have been significant if there were no protective provisions. This is illustrated in the line "Additional ownership due to antidilution protection." The full ratchet offers maximum additional ownership, while the weighted average drops the ownership proportionally. Notice the significant drop in ownership for common shareholders.

Assumptions:

Series A price per share = $9
Number of Series A shares sold = 100,000
Series A amount raised = $900,000
Series B price per share = $4.50
Number of Series B shares sold = 250,000
Series B amount raised = $1,125,000

TABLE 10.5   Impact of Antidilution Provisions on Ownership

	Full Ratchet (%)		Weighted Average—Broad (%)
	Series A	Series B	
Series B Preferred		42.6	44.5
Series A Preferred	47	17	17.8
Additional Ownership Due to Antidilution Protection		17	13.2
Common	43	18.9	19.8
Options	10	4.4	4.6

Frank Demmler, who has participated in over 200 investments, points out that if Series A antidilution leaves little ownership for common/management, the Series B investors will have a due concern. Often, Series B investors will drive renegotiation between Series A and management to find a satisfactory middle ground. "The bottom line is that under most circumstances, full ratchet antidilution protection will be completely waived, while weighted average is likely to be accepted."[9]

So why negotiate for something that will potentially be renegotiated anyway? In 2010, over 93 percent of the financing rounds used weighted average antidilution.[10] These percentages vary slightly as capital supply and demand conditions vary. Advice to rookie practitioner: stick with weighted average antidilution.

Dividends

While most early-stage practitioners know that dividends are neither expected nor declared by the board, the provision is included in the term sheet. The investor-friendly language is to seek cumulative dividends to juice up returns at the time of an exit. The 2010 data trends indicate that about 40 percent of Series A financings seek cumulative dividends. In 2005, as much as 80 percent of Series A financings sought cumulative dividends.

As we can see in Table 10.6, liquidation preferences, combined with the antidilution provisions, impact the overall economics significantly.

Pay-to-Play

Usually, this clause comes into effect when several investors have joined the club, say at Series B, Series C or later. The provision tries to keep the

TABLE 10.6 Key Economic Terms and the Middle Path

Economics	Investor Friendly	Middle of the Road	Company Friendly
Liquidation preferences	2x or higher, no cap, participating preferred	1x participating preferred	No liquidation preferences
Antidilution preferences	Full ratchet	Weighted average— broad	No antidilution preferences or weighted average— narrow
Dividends (as and when declared by the board)	12% cumulative	8% noncumulative, as and when declared	None

Source: Adapted from Alex Wilmerding, *Term Sheets & Valuations: An Inside Look at the Intricacies of Term Sheets & Valuations* (Boston: Aspatore Books, 2003).

syndicate together and ensure that all investors continue to participate in future rounds, especially when times are bad. As venture funds of varying shapes, sizes, and motivations join the syndicate, it is likely that Fund A will not have as much ammunition as Fund B. Or views of Fund A may differ with Fund B on the company's exit potential, execution plan, or business strategy. The pay-to-play provision would mean that if Fund A is unable to invest more capital in the following rounds for any reason, it will no longer play. Fund A gets kicked out of the playground wherein its ownership is converted to common stock, resulting in the loss of preferences and any substantial economic upside.

Preemptive Rights/Right of First Refusal

Seed and early-stage investors seek a right of first refusal (ROFR) to ensure that they can maximize their upside. Thus, when a company is ready to offer additional securities, the first call would be placed to existing shareholders. In some situations, ROFR allows investors to purchase any founders stock that may be up for sale. This tactic is used by early-stage investors who place a smaller amount of capital and as the opportunity matures, they are able to increase their ownership and take advantage of the potential upside.

GOVERNANCE AND CONTROL: PROTECTING YOUR SECURITIES

All governance and control aspects in any term sheet are designed to protect the ownership interests of investors. Security ownership can be challenged due to internal performance issues (poor performance leads to cash challenges or lower valuation) or external financings (down rounds, debt obligations). An investor attempts to manage these conditions by controlling the board, via governance and control mechanisms.

Consider the Series A investor in NewCo, who owns a 47 percent interest and thus is a minority ownership from a control perspective. But special voting rights and preferences allow such an investor to exercise control over key aspects of the company. As described in Table 10.2, typical board approval items include:

- *Officers and management hiring, firing, and compensation*: These provisions allow the board to select the CEO, and if necessary replace him or her if performance is lax.
- *Stock option programs*: These have a dilutive impact on the overall shareholders if an option pool is not established. Establishing an option pool may require shareholder approval. If an option pool is established, the board would approve grant of options to key executives.
- *Annual budgets*: As the annual budgets are directly related to the direction of the company and spend rates, the board typically approves all major budget items.
- *Debt obligations*: Any secured debt creates a lien on assets of a company, and can be a drain on the cash. Under the right circumstances of growth, venture-backed companies raise debt. The board would approve any debt obligations to ensure they are aligned with the CEO/CFO's plans and performance.

Protective provisions included in the term sheet would minimize any impact to the value or preferences of the security:

- *Ownership/shares*: Any issuance of stock would impact the ownership, and dilute current owners. Furthermore, the pricing of stock, the amount being raised, and the type of investors are all approved by existing investors/board members.
- *Mergers/acquisitions and co-sale*: Investors and all shareholders would approve such moves, as these impact ownership and economics.
- *Changes to the certificate of incorporation, voting, and bylaws*: Any changes in the corporate structure are typically approved by all shareholders and can impact the powers of the board.

- *Changes to board or election procedures*: Existing board members typically approve any changes to the board structure (additions of seats, observers) that occur as newer investors come to the table. Investors control the board dynamics closely, especially in the early stages of the development and growth.

EXIT-RELATED PROVISIONS

These provisions come into effect at the time of the sale of the company. As very few companies go public, savvy investors do not invest too much time and effort splitting hairs around these terms. For the most part, these are treated as boilerplate language. A brief description of the terms follows.

Redemption

Certain practitioners are tempted to sell the stock back to the company and redeem their investment at, say, the sixth anniversary. This provision is typically triggered when the company has made modest middle-of-the-road progress, but is not going to be a significant exit for investors. Unkind expressions address these as the living dead. This provision implies that the investment is more a debtlike instrument and attempts to recover some or all of the investment.

Drag-Along Rights/Tag-Along Rights and Co-Sale Agreements

These rights allow investors to "drag" the shareholders to an exit. The dragging comes in when a specified percentage of shareholders wants to sell the company when another group, typically, the founders or common shareholders, refuses to sell. The price may not be right, or they may see a bigger, better opportunity in the future. The investors may have given up on the opportunity and choose to get what they can. Drag-along provisions allow investors to sell the package as a whole—if any investor is unwilling to sell, it could block an exit, and this provision allows the sale to occur. In tag-along provisions, also called co-sale agreements, the founders or management either give up or find a third party to whom they can sell their shares. The tag-along rights allow investors to tag along with the founders and offer their shares for sale as well.

Conversion to Common at Public Offering, Registration Rights, and Piggyback Rights

In the rare event a portfolio company is ready to file for an IPO, all securities convert to one class: common stock. This allows for smoother marketing and share price establishment. Thus, the preferences established will vanish. In *Venture Capital Due Diligence*, Justin Camp writes, "Convertible instruments allow investors to take full advantage of the protections offered by preferred stock ... until they are no longer necessary, and then allow them to forgo such protections. When investors invoke registration rights, they push the company to register the stock or piggyback on other registrations. Once registered, venture capitalists are able to sell their stock in the public markets."[11] Investors can demand registration, although several factors come into play, primarily the revenues, growth rate, and state of the public markets. Piggyback rights obligate companies to let investors piggyback on the registration.

OTHER TERMS

These terms fall neither in the economic nor the governance category but are important to align the interest of investors and management.

Employment-Related Terms

All founders and key management team members should execute employment agreements. Other important terms such as stock vesting, restrictions on co-sale, key man insurance, and noncompete provisions are included to ensure management teams are aligned with the long-term goal of value creation.

Employment agreements clearly state a founder or manager's roles, responsibilities, and deliverables. These agreements incentivize the team to stay with the company, especially through tough times, and to create value. Stock vesting for founders is often negotiated aggressively to ensure that after the investment is made, the founders remain and continue to add value to the company. A separate "Stock Option Plan" is typically created postinvestment and governed under the auspices of the board. This plan determines the dynamics of the employee stock options. Should an employee be terminated, his or her ability to exercise the balance of options will lapse.

THAT WAS ONE EXPENSIVE PARTY ...

Sean Parker, one of the founding board members of Facebook, was arrested and charged with cocaine possession. He was pushed out of Facebook and lost his unvested stock options. These lost options would grow to approximately $500 million in value over a four-year span.

Source: David Kirkpatrick, *The Facebook Effect: The Inside Story of the Company That Is Connecting the World* (New York: Simon & Schuster, 2010), 146–148.

Vesting can occur on a quarterly basis over a three- to four-year period. Acceleration of vesting upon acquisition is considered suitable to reward management for having created value. The contention is amplified when founders quit or are fired: The vesting debate can create a fair amount of distraction and hence needs to be addressed in employment agreements.

The restrictions on co-sale have been seen in a new light, especially when founders are allowed to take significant portions of their stock and liquidate them prior to a sale or IPO. Key man provisions are methods of ensuring that investors are protected if key management team members were to become unavailable due to death or disability.[12] Noncompete provisions can be enforced in certain states, but not all. The duration (number of years) and scope (geography, sector) of the noncompete needs to be negotiated diligently.

Closing Conditions

The following miscellaneous conditions are prescribed in the term sheets:

- *Exclusivity and no-shop clause:* To ensure entrepreneurs do not use the opportunity to get an auction going or to find better terms of investment by "shopping" the term sheet around.
- *Closing date and conditions:* To ensure that all parties, legal counsel for both sides especially, are prepared to complete the transaction on a certain date and meet any conditions prior to closing
- *Nondisclosure, press/media:* To ensure confidentiality until the parties are ready to make any announcements

TOWARD A SIMPLER TERM SHEET FOR SMALLER INVESTMENTS

When Silicon Valley lawyer Ted Wang decided to simplify the standard hundred-page term sheet, he started with Mahatma Gandhi's quote: "First they ignore you. Then they laugh at you. Then they fight you. Then you win." Three years later, when Mark Andreessen adopted Wang's simplified term sheet, the victory was clear. In his uncommonly modest style, Wang wrote, "I hesitate to use a quote from one of the greatest people ever to grace planet earth, and certainly the question of how to structure early-stage investment is a laughable cause as compared to the rights that Gandhi (also a lawyer) fought to advance. That said, I think this quote accurately captures the life-cycle of creating a simple set of documents for early-stage investment."[13]

The motivation: "Start-up company lawyers are under an intense pressure to keep our fees low on these deals and we find ourselves struggling to meet our clients' expectations around pricing," wrote Wang, who represents companies like Facebook, Dropbox, and Twitter.[14] "The result is that these small Series A deals have become a source of unwanted tension between us and our clients."[15]

Wang's simplified documents are relevant to the seed stage investors as well as succinct. And he may have had a lot of unlearning to do, as he eliminated language that had been a part of term sheets for 20 to 30 years. The simplified term sheet, about 30 pages in all, eliminates antidilution, registration rights, and closing conditions. Even more so, it reduces the time and expenses for completing the investments.

"The big reason we are doing it is that we think for these early-stage round, bashing over these terms does damage only brings mistrust," Mark Andreessen was quoted as saying. "VCs who do angel rounds should be acting like a VC in a VC round and acting like an angel in an angel round. The problems come when VCs act like VCs in angel rounds."[16]

Separately, the law offices of Wilson Sonsini have developed an online tool that generates a venture financing term sheet based on inputs/responses to an online questionnaire. Fifty years ago, in 1954, Roald Dahl, popular writer of children's fiction, wrote a short story, "The Great Automatic Grammatizator"—in which a mechanically minded man concludes that the rules of grammar follow mathematical principles. He creates a mammoth grammatizator—a machine that can write a prize-winning novel in 15 minutes. Wilson Sonsini has developed such an engine, a term-sheetizator if you will, that takes a few inputs and develops fascinating term sheets. The WSGR term sheet generator has an informational component, with basic tutorials and annotations on financing terms. This term sheet generator is a modified version of a tool that the firm uses internally, which comprises document automation tools that the firm uses to generate start-up and venture financing-related documents. Because it has been designed as a generic tool that takes into account a number of options, this version of the term sheet generator is fairly expansive and includes significantly more detail than would likely be found in a customized application. Worth a look—see www.wsgr.com/wsgr/display.aspx?sectionname=practice/termsheet.htm.

SYNDICATING INVESTMENTS

An analysis of over 2,000 venture transactions shows that syndication was found to be highest in biotechnology investments (in over 60 percent of investments) and lowest in the software sector (with only 37 percent of investments). Syndication was least at the seed stages and increased in later stages.[17] Risk does bring investors together, especially in biotech sectors where capital intensity is significant.

Whether seeking syndicate investors or being asked to be one, the simple rule applies: Does the combined intellectual and financial acumen allow for the better outcomes of the investment opportunity? When inviting syndicate investors into opportunities led by Walden International, Lip-Bu Tan follows a blended approach of the heart and the head: "I look for complementary skill sets in syndicate investors so that the combined power of the board is higher in terms of value add. I am also very picky, so the core philosophy of building a company for the long term rather than the short term is important. Mutual respect is important, as is the willingness to come up with a solution that is best for the company. No ego trips!" Tom Perkins, while seeking the first round of funding for Tandem Computer, wrote about his experiences: "I showed our business plan, which I had mostly written myself, to all the local potential investors with no luck. . . . The investors' rejection was based solely on general worries over the companies in the field. . . . They had little understanding of the technical breakthrough we had achieved and how difficult it would be for those competitors to duplicate our effort and circumvent our patents. . . . These were financiers . . . who maybe were clever with money but who had no . . . confidence in technology, the kind of investors who relied on hired experts to tell them what to think."[18]

Practitioners need to conduct due diligence on each other with the same rigor they would apply to looking at new opportunities, but add a few other parameters to the mix: What are the motives of the syndicate investor? Is it a true partnership? Are their interests aligned? Do they have the ability to withstand the tremors?

Ideally, smaller funds would invite larger funds to participate with the optimistic outlook that as the capital needs for the company grow, the larger funds will be able to lead the future rounds. If a small fund invites a larger fund to come in as a syndicate partner, it creates a win-win situation for both funds. A smaller fund generates the opportunity and acts as a feeder to the larger fund. In turn, the larger fund can invest substantially higher amounts as needed by the company. The smaller fund needs to consider how anti-dilution and pay-to-play provisions could affect the smaller fund if the opportunity does not progress as desired. The loss appetite also differs with the size and the stage of the fund.

"It took me 15 years to crack into the inner circle of the Silicon Valley venture network. To be invited to co-invest in opportunities with the likes of John Doerr, Promod Haque, and other established practitioners takes time—you have to earn their respect as a value-add partner," says Tan.

Syndication caveats include choosing your partners with care. As one practitioner pointed out, "keeping a bad venture capitalist is worse than the first time bad entrepreneur."[19] Syndicate with the ones you trust—you know how they will react in bad situations. Partnership of unequals can be challenging. As a practitioner remarked, "I would hope that we would get an equal ownership, but if Sequoia says they want 75 percent and we keep 25 percent, we'd be happy with that."[20]

THE CLOSING PROCESS: AFTER THE TERM SHEET

To approve the investment, any company would follow these steps:

- Board approval of the investment via formal resolution
- Majority of shareholders consent via vote
- Execution of final documents: Once the term sheet is executed, attorneys draft detailed documents that include:
  - Share purchase agreement or subscription agreement including purchase details, company's representations and warranties, board composition, and voting matters
  - Investor rights agreement (IRA) including information rights, preemptive rights, registration rights, and affirmative and negative covenants[21]
    - Affirmative covenants (or actions the company should take) include maintaining the existence of the corporation, paying taxes,

maintaining insurance, complying with key agreements, maintaining accounts, and allowing access to premises
- Negative covenants (or actions the company should avoid) include changing the business, amending the charter, issuing stock, merging the company, conducting dealings with related parties, making investments, or incurring debt or financial liabilities
  ○ Modifications to the certificate of incorporation to allow for the new shareholders to be recognized as well as ensure that the company does not take any actions that are not aligned with preferred shareholders' rights
  ○ Issuing of share certificates to shareholders/investors

SUMMARY

Structuring a simple terms sheet is an art form as well as a science. The goal is to grasp the risks inherent within the opportunity and develop a set of conditions that would allow the investor to generate target returns. At the very early stages of an investment, savvy investors invest small amounts and get a seat at the table—as the opportunity grows, they double up. It is prudent to establish these terms as middle-of-the-road. Any exotic elements would cast a practitioner in an unfavorable light.

The lead investor, the one with the maximum investment, typically sets the terms. As goes the golden rule—he who has the gold makes the rules. The other syndicate investors have a choice—to accept those terms or not—but seldom have significant negotiating leverage. In anticipation of future financing, existing shareholders, at times and without much reason, will attempt to bump up the value significantly. If the bump-up is not justified, this creates the illusion of progress and can cause more harm than any benefit in the long run.

Everything that can be renegotiated will be renegotiated. In as much as 30 percent of subsequent financing, new investors renegotiated terms established at previous rounds. The most commonly renegotiated terms are (1) automatic conversion price, (2) liquidation preferences, (3) redemption maturity, and (4) funding milestones, vesting provisions, or performance benchmarks.[22]

As follow-on rounds occur, it is typical for the new lead investor of the follow-on round to set the valuation and terms. Down round financings are normal occurrences in the business of venture capital—companies often miss milestones and run low on cash. The only valuation that matters is the one at the time of exit.

The entire philosophy of term sheets is summarized in Steven Kaplan and Per Stromberg's words: "The elements of control: Board rights, voting rights and liquidation rights are allocated such that if a firm performs poorly, the venture capitalists obtain full control. *As performance improves, the entrepreneur retains/obtains more control rights. If the firm performs very well, the venture capitalists retain their cash flow rights, but relinquish most of their control and liquidation rights.* [italics added]"[23]

CHAPTER 11

Behind Every Successful CEO Stand a Few Good Board VCs

No school teaches a venture capitalist how to be a good board member.

—Pascal Levensohn, Levensohn Venture
Partners and member of the board,
National Venture Capital Association

In a narrative account of a business, there is usually only room for one hero. When we look at the plucky start-up or entrepreneurial business venture, the company founder or CEO is deified as a visionary who forges a groundbreaking idea into reality against all odds. In this account, the CEO is described as a captain of industry, creating with mighty volition a brilliant management team that works tirelessly to craft the idea into a viable business. Cast into a secondary supporting role is the venture capitalist. Despite this more marginal role, the venture capitalist's critical contributions, such as providing the capital and financing—the lifeblood of a firm—and access to a plethora of resources, from networks and contacts to mentoring and strategic guidance, can be invaluable.

Giving entrepreneurs the opportunity to cultivate an idea with the benefits of professional management and strategic guidance is a potent formula that fast-tracks ideas and products to the market. As the gatekeeper to this highly sought-after funding, a venture capitalist is someone in the business of providing financial capital and advisory assistance at every stage of development, including by serving as a board member. At the most basic level, board members are expected to adhere to duty of care and loyalty. In a venture-backed company, these duties extend to:

- Value identification
- Value creation
- Sustaining value
- Asserting value via an exit/liquidity event

No corporate governance textbook can prepare someone for the challenges of the boardroom. However, the basics seldom change. Thus, the goal of this chapter is to help understand and appreciate the protocols and practices of board meetings.

THE NEED FOR DIRECTOR EDUCATION

In a survey of over 300 participants, the National Association of Corporate Directors (NACD) Private Company Governance Survey concluded that the three weakest areas of board effectiveness are director education and development, board and director evaluation, and CEO succession planning. Interestingly, these areas of weakness were consistent over multiple years. Put a different way, while the weaknesses have been identified, no action has been taken to address these challenges. Rightfully so, good board members tend to be in high demand, are spread thin over multiple boards, and are at times reactive. Boards have little or no time to indulge in the luxury of education, development, and self-evaluation. When time is the most critical resource, no director is going to raise his hand to take on any additional tasks. Lindsay Aspegren of Northcoast Technology Investors says, "When I was finishing up my MBA, I should have taken that Board Directorship class at Harvard. But on a more serious note, as board members, we are charged to make decisions amidst a dynamic and fast changing microcosm. We have to manage change effectively. So it is not only understanding this role, but having the skills and the experience to do this job well." Aspegren has sat on boards with some of the most successful investors, like Promod Haque (Norwest), Bruce Dunlevie (Benchmark), and Bill Davidow (Mohr-Davidow), investors who can be mercurial and at times, intimidating. "There is much emphasis on the front-end, the deal, in our business, but not enough on the postinvestment plan."

While this is not necessarily a healthy precedent for a rookie venture practitioner, self-orientation is a good starting point. In early-stage companies, the business, its goals, and its challenges, complete with its cast of characters, are visible. The following pointers covered in the due diligence process are listed here to initiate steps into self-orientation and education. In addition to possessing a thorough understanding of the history and evolution of the company, any practitioner needs to consider the following:

- Develop a thorough 360-degree understanding of the business, including suppliers, customers, competitive threats, and replacements. The practitioner needs to understand the cycle of cash and friction therein: This is critical.
- Understand a company's strategy and key goals. Over the next 12 months and three years, how do you see your contribution vis-à-vis issues and challenges facing such a company? ("What would keep the CEO awake at night, and how can I help?")
- Ensure you have relevant expertise to affect the stated strategy. Prepare to impact the company's challenges and demands in a disciplined and consistent manner.
- Be aware of people and cash related challenges. Does the team need to be augmented? What are the cash position, burn rate, and timing of next financing rounds, if any?
- Understand the current board structure and how you fit in this context
- What are the board's external and internal challenges? Examples may include:
  - *External:* Compliance with tax, civil, criminal, and employment laws, any legal matters or shareholder actions
  - *Internal:* Emotional and power dynamics between board members, excessive churn of board members or CEO, strategy du jour, product development and market adoption challenges, burn rate and cash situation.

ROLES AND RESPONSIBILITIES OF A BOARD MEMBER

It is well known that venture capital is the financial fuel that kick-started many great companies in the past decade, but there is less familiarity with what venture capitalists do once they sit on a company's board. Beyond financing, what kinds of support do they provide to start-ups? How do they use their investment muscle to attract and win more capital? Recruit a star management team? How do they winnow and champion the most promising drivers from the rest? "As a board, you role is to prove the business plan," says Aspegren, "and your only two control levers are the CEO and the budget."

The boardroom is where the venture capitalist wields the greatest influence on a company's future growth. Typically, a company board is a group of people who meet periodically and provide advice and guidance on the direction of the firm. For many start-ups and younger firms, venture capitalist board members are selected based on their influence and knowledge of the industry to help companies to make a clear footprint on the market. Venture capitalist boards therefore do a lot: They attract, recruit, and retain an excellent management team and fellow board members; mentor and manage the executive team; provide advisory services and expertise outside the purview of the management team; and oversee adherence to fiscal, legal, and ethical governance standards. Brad Feld, managing director of the Foundry Group, points out the simple role of any board member: "With the exception of really two decisions, I'd like to think that we work for the CEO of the company. The two decisions we really make are, one, the capital allocation decision (Do we want to keep funding the company?), and two, whether we keep and support the CEO."[1]

Key Roles of a Board Member
The primary role of any board member boils down to:

- *Shareholder value:* Create, sustain, and enhance shareholder value.
- *CEO selection and assessment:* Evaluate CEO performance, transition, assist in recruitment, succession planning.
- *Governance:* Manage risk via business strategy, finance, management, market insights, and legal compliance.

The board expertise, attributes, and roles of the board members shift as the company matures. Table 11.1 demonstrates the minimum attributes required as the company evolves over time.

Summary of Legal Requirements of Board Service

"The Basic Responsibilities of VC-Backed Company Directors," a white paper developed by the Working Group on Director Accountability and Board Effectiveness[2], provides a framework of responsibilities and duties of VC board members. Any board member must discharge his or her actions in good faith and in the best interest of the corporation at all times. The fiduciary duties —a legal relationship between the director and the corporation of confidence and trust—are described here.

Duty of care: Requires a director to act with the care that an ordinarily prudent person in a like position would exercise under similar circumstances.

TABLE 11.1 Arc of Value and the Attributes of Board Members

	Seed and Early Stage	Growth Stage	Path to Liquidity
Management goals	Product development	Sales	Management of growth
Key metrics of the company	Burn rate, time to launch	Revenues, break-even	Growth, profitability, and gross margins
Evolution of management team attributes	Technical/product development, intellectual property	Operational, sales and marketing, finance, HR	Management, investor relations, legal
Minimum board attributes	Relevant technical expertise	Business/financial expertise	Public company-like corporate governance
Number of board members	Three	Three to five	Seven or more
Culture of the board	Experimentation, nurturing, and openness	Expansion	Control and efficiencies
Governance via committees	Establish financial reporting and financial threshold levels; approval of key legal and shareholder agreements	Establish compensation and audit committee, name formal board chairman, and perform additional financial and risk reporting	Name lead director, establish public company-like internal controls and practices, and conduct Section 404 planning
Examples of board's role in value creation	Provide access to scientific and technical luminaries, identify product development guidelines, attract first beta sites, and assess/identify development partners	Advise on sales efficiencies, accelerate customer access, provide channel partnership insights, position competitively, provide access to future rounds of capital	Maintain the course and develop regulatory and financial standards, practices, and policies

Source: Adapted from "A Simple Guide to the Basic Responsibilities of a VC-Backed Company Director," a white paper on director accountability and effectiveness" developed by a working group of leading venture capitalists.

Requires directors to:

- Obtain information they believe is reasonably necessary to make a decision
- Make due inquiry
- Make informed decisions in good faith

Duty of loyalty: Requires a director to act in the best interests of the corporation and not in the interest of the director or a related party. Issues often arise where the director has a conflict of interest.

- Where the director or a related party has a personal financial interest in a transaction with the company (e.g., the inherent conflict between venture capitalists as directors and as representatives of their fund's interests)
- Where the director usurps a corporate opportunity that properly belongs to the company
- Where the director serves as a representative of a third-party corporation and the third-party corporation's objectives conflict with the company's best interests
- Where the director abdicates his or her oversight role or does not act in good faith

Examples of not acting in good faith:

- Consciously or recklessly not devoting sufficient time to required duties
- Disregarding known risks
- Failing to exercise oversight on a sustained basis
- Failing to act in good faith can have serious adverse consequences to a director, such as being exposed to personal liability for breaches of the duty of care or losing coverage under indemnification provisions or insurance policies. Generally, state corporate laws have procedures for handling interested transactions and corporate opportunities, such as requiring full disclosure and disinterested director approval.

Confidentiality and Disclosure

- *Duty of confidentiality:* A subset of the duty of loyalty. Requires a director to maintain the confidentiality of nonpublic information about the company.
- *Duty of disclosure:* Requires a director, pursuant to the duties of care and loyalty, to take reasonable steps to ensure that a company provides its stockholders with all material information relating to a matter for which stockholder action is sought.

- *Business judgment rule:* Creates a presumption that in making a business decision, the directors of a company acted on an informed basis, in good faith, and in the honest belief that the action taken was in the company's best interests. The business judgment rule helps protect a director from personal liability for allegedly bad business decisions by essentially shifting the burden of proof to a plaintiff alleging that the director did not satisfy his or her fiduciary duties. This presumption and the protections afforded by the business judgment rule are lost if the directors involved in the decision are not disinterested, do not make appropriate inquiry prior to making their decisions, or fail to establish adequate oversight mechanisms.

BOARD COMPOSITION AND ORIENTATION

Let us assume that a board of a venture-backed company is populated with five members: three investor representatives and two management team members. "Great boards are relatively small, generally not more than five or seven people, who understand finance and technical areas," says Seth Rudnick of Canaan Partners.[3] While in the early stages of a company's evolution, board composition may be driven by the largest shareholders, it is critical to structure the board with expertise necessary for the company's growth. "The board should have one expert each at the minimum from sales, strategy, industry expertise, and marketing areas. This allows for a balanced contribution and the CEO can reach different experts as needed," says Rick Heitzmann of FirstMark Capital.

While board-member orientation is critical, it happens in a fairly ad hoc manner in most venture-backed companies. An orientation is essential to ensure that members understand their role and that they align their agenda with the overall mission. Members may have differing agendas: Investors may seek exits at varying times, while the management team may have a desire to build the company.

A typical orientation meeting would include:

- Introduction of the company and the management/current board members, if any
- Key goals and challenges of the company
- Board structure and goals
- Review of materials: handbook, policies, evaluation, and committees

The following orientation materials can be offered to a new board member:

- Company Handbook
  - Company overview/business background
  - Management team and organization chart
  - Directors' bios, listing, and contact information
  - Financial reports and projections
  - Capitalization table
- Board Policies
  - Conduct
    - Frequency of meetings
    - Establishment of committees: audit, compensation, governance
    - Decision-making procedures
    - Policy on observer roles
    - Legal responsibilities
    - Liabilities and insurance coverage
    - Indemnification
  - Confidentiality
  - Conflict of interest matters and resolution
  - Media and press
  - Term and nomination process of new members
- Board self-evaluation process
  - Skills, knowledge, expertise of each board member
  - Membership on various committees
  - Attendance and performance
- Committees
  - Description (audit, governance, compensation committees are typically formed)
  - Chaired by, purpose, and authority
  - Composition/names of members

Board Self-Evaluation

Self-evaluation of boards, while it seldom occurs, is a critical exercise. Venture-backed company boards tend to be smaller in size, and are more interactive. Thus the formal self-evaluation may never occur. Nevertheless, several CEOs of venture-backed companies express the challenges of time and attention. Quotes such as "He learned how to be a director. We paid the tuition," or "My strategy is to minimize the value subtracted"[4] are indicative of fundamental challenges that exist in the boardroom. In the white paper "A Simple Guide to Basic Responsibilities of a VC-Backed Director"[5] guidelines for an annual self-review suggest the following criteria:

- Preparedness
  - Reviewed all board materials prior to meetings
  - Aware of key challenges for the company: both short-term and long-term
  - Communicated with other board members between meetings
  - Completed any assignments in a timely and thorough fashion
- Alignment
  - Aligned with other board members and CEO with respect to key performance indicators and challenges
  - Ensure other board members are aligned with CEO and supportive, as well.
  - Raise any challenging issues related to performance and conflicts, which are not to be ignored or brushed under the carpet
- Attention
  - Attended all board meetings, engaged in thoughtful manner without cell phone or e-mail distractions
- Contribution
  - Proactively seeks ways of assisting the CEO to meet or exceed her goals. The CEO is the hero and a VC's role is to be supportive, staying behind the scenes as much as possible.

BOARD PRACTICES

Any good board would establish the following practices.

A. Annual calendar: frequency of meetings, including an annual strategy session where you can "go deep" and assess the company's progress and prepare a road map for the next 12 months.
B. Management ensures board materials are distributed ahead of time. Materials include:
  1. Agenda
  2. Minutes of the last meeting
  3. Business overview: The primary focus is on key milestones and business aspects. Depending on the stage and evolution of the business, an overview could include the following:
     a. Progress against key milestones: highlight delays and develop countermeasures

    b. Product development: completed alpha, beta, pilot customer trials

    c. Sales and marketing:

      i. Pipeline

      ii. Actual sales versus budget and its impact on cash situation

      iii. Gross margins

      iv. Competition

      v. Customer feedback

    d. Financial status highlights: cash position and burn rate, including an income statement, balance sheet, and cash flows

    e. Any significant issues to be considered

  4. Resolutions

C. The secretary records the minutes of any board meeting. Generally, minutes are brief, factual statements that briefly state the resolutions and outcomes.

D. Records: Board books, minutes, and resolutions are available for reference in legal and acquisition-related discussions.

In a McKinsey study of 586 corporate directors, respondents pointed out that they would like to double their time on strategy and spend at least five times their time on talent management.[6]

HOW TO AVOID DEATH BY BOARD MEETING

In his blog aptly titled "Death by Board Meeting," Nick Sturiale, partner, Sevin-Rosen Funds, points out that superior board meetings follow three simple rules:

1. The agenda focuses on a few key questions: Instead of a blow-by-blow account of each department, the emphasis is on conversation around solving the top one or two challenges.
2. The board steps up to solve problems, not just take the pulse of the company: The board is aligned with the company's metrics and is aware of the progress using dashboards. The CEO has the trust of the board and shares all challenges without feeling threatened.
3. The board members do their homework assignments and come prepared: The ability of the board members to assist the CEO and be supportive has been emphasized time and again. Has the board ensured that the CEO knows the strengths of each

of the board members and deploys these effectively? If not, the board has to take active steps to build a culture in which the CEO can rely upon the "biggest weapons in the arsenal," writes Sturiale.

Ineffective board meetings can be a challenge for the venture practitioner as well as the CEO. The behavioral dynamics in the boardroom are like that of a family, and as Leo Tolstoy said, happy families are all alike and every unhappy family is unhappy in its own way.

Source: Nick Sturiale, "Death by Board Meeting," Venture Beat (blog), October 2, 2007, http://venturebeat.com/2007/10/02/death-by-board-meeting/.

GET THAT GAVEL: OVERVIEW OF ROBERT'S RULES OF ORDER

Robert's Rules are a set of rules for conduct at meetings that allow everyone to be heard and to make decisions without confusion. It's a time-tested method of conducting business at board meetings. These rules can be adapted to fit the needs of a company.

Organizations using parliamentary procedures usually follow a typical order of business. For example:[7]

- Call to order
- Quorum/roll call
- Approval of minutes of last meeting
  - Minutes should include resolutions adopted
  - Agreements/reports that need to be evidenced are enclosed as a part of the exhibits
- Officers' reports
- Committee reports
- Special orders: important business previously designated for consideration at this meeting
- Unfinished business
- New business
- Announcements
- Adjournment

Types of Motions

The method members use to express themselves is by presenting motions, which are proposals for the entire membership to take action upon. Individual members can:

- Call to order
- Second motions
- Debate motions
- Vote on motions

Motions are divided into four types, albeit in early-stage venture-backed companies, it is unlikely that all of these would come into effect.

1. *Main motions:* The purpose of a main motion is to introduce items to the board for consideration. Main motions cannot be made when any other motion is on the floor, and they yield to privileged, subsidiary, and incidental motions.
2. *Subsidiary motions:* A subsidiary motion is used to change or affect how a main motion is handled, and is voted on before a main motion.
3. *Privileged motions:* A privileged motion is called to bring up items that are urgent about special or important matters unrelated to pending business.
4. *Incidental motions:* An incidental motion provides a means of questioning procedure concerning another motion, and must be considered before the other motion.

Board Action Items: Presenting a Motion The procedure of making a motion and seconding it, followed by approval of the chairperson, is as follows.

- Make a motion: "Ms. Chairperson, I move that we accept and approve the proposed business budget and plan for forthcoming annual year."
- Wait for someone to second your motion. If another member does not second your motion, the chairperson will call for a second. Note that technically, if there is no second to your motion, it is lost.
- If there is a second, the chairperson will restate your motion. "It has been moved and seconded that we...."; thus, the chairperson places your motion before the board for consideration and action. The board then either debates the motion or may move directly to a vote.

- Expand on the motion.
  - Technically, early-stage companies will seldom have much protocol and fanfare. Motions will be presented, debated, and voted on in no particular order.
  - The mover is always allowed to speak first.
  - All comments and debate must be directed to the chairperson.
  - The mover may speak again to offer counterpoints only after other speakers are finished, unless called upon by the chairperson.
- Approving a motion
  - The chairperson asks, "Are you ready to vote on the question?"
  - If there is no more discussion, a vote is taken.

Voting on a Motion   The method of voting on any motion depends on the situation and the bylaws or policies of each company. There are a few methods used to vote:

- *By voice:* The chairperson asks those in favor to say aye and those opposed to say no. The secretary may record the number of ayes and nays.
- *By roll call:* Each member answers yes or no as his or her name is called. This method is used when a record of each person's vote is required.
- *By general consent:* When a motion is not likely to be opposed, the chairperson says, "If there is no objection...." The board members show agreement by their silence; however, if one member says, "I object," the item must be put to a vote.

Two other motions are commonly used that relate to voting:

1. *Motion to table:* This motion is often used in the attempt to kill a motion. The option is always present, however, to take a motion from the table for reconsideration.
2. *Motion to postpone indefinitely:* While this is unlikely to occur in venture-backed companies, it is often used as a means of parliamentary strategy and allows opponents of a motion to test their strength without an actual vote being taken. Also, debate is once again open on the main motion.

In an early-stage venture-backed company, it is unlikely that an elaborate parliamentary procedure may be followed. Formal board meetings are conducted to approve and record key action items, especially those that affect all shareholders. Therefore, it is essential for a rookie board member to understand the procedure by which a motion is proposed, voted on, adopted, or debated. Examples of motions of an early stage company board member may include:

- Approve to adopt an annual operating plan, financials, and goals.
- Approve granting CEO additional stock option.

VALUE CREATION: HOW TO SUPPORT YOUR PORTFOLIO COMPANY'S CEO

A lot of VCs have a playbook of how they are going to add value. They end up in a Socratic mode—always asking for information—constantly probing and pushing but never turning around and saying—let me help you solve that problem. It becomes a very time-consuming affair for the CEO, and it's a very selfish act on the part of the venture capitalists.

—Brad Feld, The Foundry Group[8]

To ensure that as a practitioner you are on the "assets" side of the board's balance sheet, you must understand the company's short-term value drivers. For early-stage companies, the immediate drivers may be product development, calling for technical acumen. As the product gets ready for launch, access to beta sites or first customers takes priority. Risk mitigation is interwoven at all stages with ongoing threats from competitors or substitutes. As the company grows, access to financial resources and growth management techniques comes to bear. Finally, the exit negotiation requires the ability to align all stakeholders and ensure positive outcomes. Several variables affect this complex interplay, including the stage of the company, the present and future constitution of the board, skill sets, and investor alignment and preferences.

Generally speaking, a practitioner can support the CEO of an early-stage company via following value creation steps:

- Product development
- Sales and growth of revenues
- Improved profit margins

"The only reason top-tier venture capitalists invite you to co-invest is because of your ability to add value—be it your domain expertise or your network of contacts. You have to win their respect and gain confidence to be invited to participate in the future deals," says Lip-Bu Tan of Walden

International. A board becomes a stage where relationships are forged.[9] How a practitioner engages with the company determines the strength of those relationships.

PricewaterhouseCoopers conducted a study of over 350 companies that had received seed or first-round financing.[10] The three value creation metrics were:

1. *Strategy:* market size, competitive position, and business model.
2. *Resources:* cash flow, investor value contributed, and strength of management team.
3. *Performance:* product development, channels/alliances, and customer acquisition.

The study concluded that a company that experienced a successful IPO had successfully attracted customers, built a distribution channel, achieved good cash flow, and seized a strong competitive position very early. On the other hand, a company that experienced acquisition had a smaller market and gradual progress on product development, customer acquisition, and channel development.

Good Governance as the First Step toward Value Creation

A McKinsey survey of over 2,500 directors and officers concluded that institutional investors are willing to pay a 14 percent premium for shares of a well-governed company.[11] On the flip side, poor governance translates to failed investments and even worse, lawsuits.

Depending on the stage of venture investments, the role of directors is amplified in areas such as value identification, value enhancement, sustaining momentum, and risk mitigation. The concept of value is unique to each company's stage of evolution. Exploring the fit between the company's needs and the practitioner's expertise starts with the primary driver: capital. A practitioner "buys his board seat" and attempts to ensure value enhancement by displaying his wares: intellectual and social capital.

THE CEO's PERSPECTIVE ON VENTURE CAPITALIST VALUE ADD

In an informal study, a sample of presidents and founders of VC-backed companies were asked to value the contributions of their venture capitalist counterparts.[12] The top three areas of contribution reported were:

1. Financings, advice, and introductions
2. Strategic focus
3. Recruiting and hiring senior management—CEOs and VPs

On the flip side, the areas where venture capitalists were least valued include:

- Selection of professionals, law, patent, accounting
- Strategic relations with other companies
- Functional advice in marketing, engineering

The challenge around functional advice on marketing, especially when practitioners do not have entrepreneurial background, is widespread. "I have seen situations where relatively junior VCs get too caught up in what-if analysis and demand that the CEO prepare these unnecessary scenarios—what is a meteorite hits the earth and such," says Rick Heitzmann of FirstMark Capital.

Another survey of over 300 participants of PE-backed companies shows that the best value a board member can offer is to assist with future financing. On the flip side, the CEOs surveyed said that industry knowledge and time commitments were identified as the top two weaknesses of boards. This survey sample includes PE-backed companies, and the challenges for a VC-backed company board may marginally differ. However, the study is indicative of the need for ongoing assessment of VCs and their alignment with the CEO's expectations.

Consider the views of Dave Robbins, CEO of BigFix—a VC-backed company that was acquired by IBM. When Keith Benjamin of Levensohn Venture Partners sourced BigFix and led the investment for his venture fund, he did not build Excel models of the exit values and IRR. Rather, he rolled up his sleeves and stood by the CEO until the day he lost his life in an untimely event. Keith would have been proud of what came of this fledgling start-up.

Setting the Direction: Shift from Consumer to Enterprise

The history of BigFix is anything but smooth—fraught with challenges of any technology company caught in a down economic cycle. Founded in 1997 by a statistician and an operations research expert,[13] BigFix started with its initial focus on consumers, building products for individuals who could download them for modest pricing. "The primary strategy shift occurred when we moved from consumer to enterprise markets—this was a harder shift, as will be for any CEO," explains Dave Robbins, its CEO. During the shift, Keith offered his time and efforts to help Dave develop a clear strategy to penetrate the enterprise markets. "I am shocked they never sent me a bill—they must have invested over a thousand hours and provided tons of market research—it was incredibly invaluable. A profound partnership," says Dave of Keith and his venture firm.[14]

The company was successful in shifting its direction and provided security management solutions for large companies. It offered an operations platform that enabled real-time visibility and control of globally distributed desktop, mobile, and server computers, enabling "big" enterprises to "fix" or continuously enforce IT security anytime and from anywhere. E-commerce enterprises prone to cyber attacks were protected through a platform that automatically detected system vulnerabilities and proactively fixed them across networks. The technology monitored thousands of critical security updates, service packs, and hardware and software updates and proactively scanned all computing devices on the network to detect which needed a particular fix. Once found, the system alerted the IT administration and identified problematic computers via a console, which allowed them to target and deploy a fix with a single action to only those PCs that needed it. It was able to identify and correct security holes in every network installation, even those that were previously thought to be secure.[15] At a time when companies were moving toward improved security, BigFix's technology found a viable solution to a significant bottleneck in the industry. It offered an easily deployable, controllable, and cost-effective tool.

Rapid Execution: Customer Acquisition Gets Analysts' Attention

Soon, BigFix's customer base ballooned to more than 900 customers in industries that included banking, financial services, manufacturing, government, education, and health care, with notable accounts such as Deutsche Bank, Pitney Bowes, Stanford University, SunTrust Bank, Miami Dade County Schools, and the U.S. Department of Energy, among others. Corporate clients willingly adopted this technology because it was affordable and because it was able to effectively automate security and compliance features in an efficient manner. BigFix could cut costs consistently and better than its competitors.[16] Environmentally conscious large-scale organizations such as the Miami Dade County Schools also found significant savings in energy consumption, which even reduced its carbon footprint by as much as 34.3 million pounds of CO_2.[17]

Referring to BigFix, Peter Firstbrook, an analyst at the Gartner research firm, has said "it is an innovation leader" because it possesses an easily scalable and expandable security patch management system to other diverse ends such as power conservation.[18] This was a perennial problem that even the goliaths in the field, such as Symantec and McAfee, were not able to address in a cost-effective manner in the scale that the BigFix solution was able to.

Great Businesses Survive, No Matter What the External Environment

BigFix arrived at a time when the clamor for slashing overhead costs and tightening security on all endpoints was at its peak. The company had a unique set of offerings that made it easy to attract venture capitalists who were willing to support its business goals and invest much-needed funding. Early investors included Levensohn Venture Partners, St. Paul Venture Capital, and Selby Venture Partners. In 2002, these venture capitalists provided $8 million in finance. Additional investors included Meritech Capital Partners, a VC firm located in Palo Alto, California, that has backed some of today's leading technology companies, such as Facebook, Acclarent, Fortinet, and Tele Atlas; Split Rock Partners; Thomas Weisel Venture Partners; and W Capital, a private equity firm that participates in late-stage venture activities. Between 2002 and 2008, BigFix received a total of $36.4 million in funding from its venture partners, and CEO Dave Robbins had his sights set on making the company go public. He wasn't in a rush, saying that "Great businesses survive, no matter what the external environment."[19]

For two years in a row, BigFix received the Deloitte Silicon Valley Technology Fast 50 award, a prestigious award that ranks the fastest-growing companies in the San Francisco Bay Area. BigFix's 3,863 percent increase in revenues for the years 2002 to 2006 ranked third in the Software & Information Technology category in 2007, a remarkable feat: The average revenue increase of 1,455 percent is the norm. Numerous industry citations were awarded to the company, including the 2009 Visionary Quadrant, 2008 Perfect 5 Star Rating, and Best Buy *SC Magazine*, SC Industry Innovator Award, and 2007 eWEEK Excellence Award, among others.[20]

Despite the worsening economic climate in the United States, BigFix and its venture partners weathered the financial crisis and held on to their investments. BigFix's business strategy, which focused on the clear value proposition of technology that was able to simplify complex network security issues, eventually paid off in a big way. In July 2010, BigFix was acquired by computer giant IBM. *Bloomberg Businessweek* claimed the transaction was worth about $400 million.[21] The acquisition was spurred by IBM's need to fill a critical area for its clients, "since it allows many thousands of PCs to be updated simultaneously and within minutes of each other," a client issue that "needs a lot client support, which is where offerings from BigFix are so useful," said Al Zollar, general manager with IBM's Tivoli software operation.[22]

On the celebration eve of the exit, Dave Robbins raised the bubbly, toasting "And we cannot forget Keith Benjamin, a board member extraordinaire." The board member who stood by him for five years was now with them in spirit. Based on Keith's behavior as a role model, Dave offers these lessons for any venture capitalist who wishes to serve the CEO:

- *On value creation*: The most valuable inputs from the board member are (a) market analysis and research, (b) funding sources and relationships, (c) pattern recognition, and (d) recruiting of talent.
- *Venture capitalists should set expectations on their own roles as investors*: not what they aspire to do, but what they can truly do for the CEO.
- *Understand that the game of guiding a company is not perfect*. The first reaction is to fire the CEO when things go wrong. That may cause the situation to deteriorate further.
- *Each company's evolution and growth is unique, and cannot be artificially accelerated*. "Try not to compare every company's growth to Google."
- *On social capital*: It is in the venture capitalist's DNA to make introductions. But at times, these would neither be timely nor relevant. I would shield the business from some venture capitalists and duck when they tried to dump their network on me.
- *In the boardroom*: Know the big picture and ask the hard questions. Venture capitalists have an evolving thought process—they should challenge the CEO, be critical, and inspect every detail. But on the flip side, try not to lead every discussion or argue every minute detail. And some unsolicited advice for those board members who behave like proxy operators: Get the hell out of the fund if you want to run a company!

While the BigFix case study offers a CEO's views on VC value creation, here are a few related examples of how VCs can create value for portfolio companies.

Industry Expertise as a Value Driver

Industry knowledge, sector/domain expertise—the terms mean more or less the same in the venture business. Some practitioners have built their expertise by doing—starting companies—while others have gained awareness by observing—reading about trends and discussing opportunities with sector experts. The CEO of a portfolio company does not care as long as a practitioner is able to deliver tangible elements.

Consider David Cowan of Bessemer Venture Partners, who was an expert on Web security but has successfully morphed his expertise into other domains. "Over the years, Bessemer has made a number of investments in the Software as a Service (SaaS) arena. Our investments and knowledge within this arena has led to creation of unique metrics that are significant value drivers. We offer these to all our SaaS portfolio companies and it helps them to assess their own performance vis-à-vis the rest of the SaaS universe," says David.

Sales and Vendor Relationships as a Value Driver

Any venture-backed company needs rapid access to potential customers and vendors. A practitioner with a strong Rolodex can reduce some of this friction. "With one of our portfolio companies, I arranged and participated in at least 15 customer meetings in the first 12 months of our Series A investment. To get access to decision makers quickly is important for start-ups—essentially, you are accelerating the time to market." Lip-Bu emphasizes that a practitioner ought to be able to play a role in every stage of evolution—product planning, customer acquisition, manufacturing, and organizational development. However, a rookie practitioner can make a classic mistake of digging too deep. A mistake I have made too often is to assess the pipeline and challenge the CEO on the probabilities and timing of the sales. This becomes an exhausting affair for both parties and yields little positive outcome. Rather, a practitioner should understand the sales dynamics, as Ravi Mohan of Shasta Ventures suggests. "I recall my first board meeting where I wanted to conduct a review of the sales pipeline—it is a very common mistake and a low-level tactical move. I am now better in serving my CEOs by focusing on the high-level quarterly goals and by understanding the sell cycle, customers' buying motivations, and any friction therein. It is important to use the board meetings wisely so that the CEO can get the benefit of the board's time and intellect."

Business Strategy as a Value Driver

"One of the companies I invested in originally planned to develop a product—I convinced its leaders to build a services company. It was pretty clear that a services model would function efficiently and solve the problem the company was attempting to tackle," says Todd Dagres,

Founder of Spark Capital.[23] Todd got involved with Akamai's founders at a very early stage, during the Massachusetts Institute of Technology's $50K business plan competition, and helped shape the key elements of the company's business model. Akamai, which is a Hawaiian word meaning "smart," is now a publicly traded company with over $800 million in revenues.

As Brad Feld correctly points out, "Every CEO and company's needs are different, and there is no formulaic approach to value add. It is highly customized."

WORK PRODUCT AS A VALUE DRIVER: BRENT AHRENS, CANAAN PARTNERS

"During my early years, one of the CEOs of our portfolio company was in my face saying 'Hey, look, when have you done this before?' and my response was honest—I have not run a company before, but let me share a specific example. I described how I had developed a marketing campaign for a certain product line and its strong impact on sales."

By demonstrating his thoughtful approach, providing a tangible example, and supporting it with numbers, Brent was able to add value to the company while building a strong relationship with the CEO. This is by far the best way for a new board member to earn the CEO's trust and respect.

SETTING THE TONE THROUGH BOARD CULTURE

An effective board is active, one in which members know their boundaries. Boards can be categorized as:

- Active
- Moderate
- Passive

While early-stage venture boards are predictably active, individuals can be engaged or passive. In a small family of five to seven board members, each member wields significant power, which if misused leads to distraction and the destruction of value.

Healthy boards espouse key cultural aspects such as:

- Deep attention to details combined with macro views: the ability to step back and look at the forest through the trees.
- Promote inquiry and dissent: the ability to challenge management assumptions and to act in a nonthreatening and nonaccusatory manner.
- Minimize the minutiae: the ability to organize the quality of information and discuss key issues, not irrelevant ones such as leases and janitorial services.
- Control the flow: the ability to focus less on packaged information, leaving more room for open discussions.
- Establish a collegial atmosphere: the personalities promote open and honest discussions in a respectful atmosphere; the CEO feels challenged but never threatened and is viewed as an extension of this team.[24]

Board members also fall into certain categories—these create the fabric of the boardroom dynamics. These categories include the following:

- An authoritative pit bull, perpetually demanding higher sales revenues and lower burn rates, can create a culture of fear.
- The other end of the spectrum includes an utterly disengaged, passive board member. A practitioner describes this specimen as one who "starts every meeting by asking what the company does."[25] Such an overstretched director can never add value and does harm by distraction. Not reading the board package or being prepared for the meeting is one thing—not knowing what the company does is unpardonable and is similar to the inability to recall the names of your own children.
- Somewhere between the overstretched director and the micro-meddler sits the passive-aggressive, who can do much harm by manipulative behavior.

Experience and luminary status of other board members, interpersonal relationships between board members, and board-CEO dynamics define the underlying ethos. Like all relationships, this fragile web has a finite life span. However, the interpersonal dynamics of mutual respect and trust, preparedness, the energy, and the work ethic of each board member determine the duration of the relationships beyond the life of the investment opportunity.

Honest self-assessment of individual members as well as the entire board is crucial—eager beavers and passive padres can never build a company, but in all likelihood they will promptly take credit for all successes.

Practitioners agree that irrespective of the outcomes of the investment, the interpersonal dynamics of different members, especially in critical times, allow the building of strong relationships between practitioners as well as their venture firms.

Board Challenges

Venture capitalist board members face many pitfalls in helping govern their companies. As Andy Rappaport of August Capital noted, "A great board cannot make a great company but a bad board can kill a good company."[26] A badly functioning board can be characterized in many ways, but the fundamental shortcoming is not performing the self-checks necessary to ensure it stays cognizant of the real-time needs of company. A savvy venture capitalist board addresses surmounting crises head-on.

In the beginning, a venture company gets by on the momentum of an exciting idea or concept. It is not unlike a heady romance, where the founder, who is consumed by passion for an idea, meets a venture capitalist interested in investing and taking the company forward. Their courtship is mostly driven by the CEO's charisma, technical expertise, and deep and narrow ambition. The venture capitalist offers a steadying foundation, the financial stability through investment rounds, and a varied, helicopter perspective.

Andy Rappaport observes that "a CEO has to be a person who... focuses on one issue, a single set of objectives," while a venture capitalist board member is someone "who likes to take a broad view," which "provides a check and balance" to the CEO's intensity.[27]

Very few CEOs survive the travails of a venture-backed company from seed stage to an exit. Like any relationship, the visions and plans for a company's future can become misaligned between investors and the CEO. Harvard Business School's Noam Wasserman has labeled this situation the "paradox of success," where during the course of trying to raise money, the founder-CEOs "put themselves at the mercy of capital providers, increasing the hazard of succession."[28] As the company grows, any skill gaps between the abilities of the founder-CEOs and the organization's needs widen precariously. Venture capitalists should be quick to dispense with the unrealistic and romantic notion of the CEO who "goes all the way" in favor of a proactive approach that involves a candid evaluation of the CEO's strengths and weaknesses. Cracks in the relationship between the CEO and venture capitalist can easily lead to turmoil if not managed well. A common mistake on boards in the VC business, according to Promod Haque at Norwest Venture Partners, is "not taking timely action to change a nonperforming CEO for fear that it will rock the boat."[29]

Board members can also become vulnerable to management spin on information, relying too heavily on their CEOs for the details of the business. Venture capitalists who appointed CEOs may be unable to offer dispassionate or unbiased criticism of management actions or decisions. This type of dependency quickly becomes dysfunctional and can lead to opacity and misunderstanding.

Management Spin on Information: A $50 Million Lesson

From: Paul Johnston

Sent: Tuesday, September 30, 2008 11:08 Pacific Standard Time

To: Pete Solvik; Jonathan D. Roberts

Subject: Resignation

Jonathan and Pete:

This is a very difficult e-mail to write, but effective immediately both Parrish and I are tendering our resignation. We have both made a grave mistake by misrepresenting our revenue reporting to the board. Looking back at the time, we thought we would be able to right the wrong and correct our representation, but we have not been able to do this. Revenues have been overstated with a delta of approximately $400K a month . . .

So begins the sordid nightmare for a group of venture capitalists that has invested $50 million in this company. In 2008, Entellium, the Seattle-based company that was driving the next revolution of customer relationship management tools, came under intense fire. Entellium's four-year rise that garnered it numerous product design awards, accolades from *Business Week* magazine and Forrester Research, and a CRM Market Leader designation, ended with the arrest of CEO Paul Johnston and CFO Parrish Jones. In 2009, they were convicted of hatching a scheme that inflated revenue numbers to attract venture capital. The two colluded and kept separate books. Entellium's board was told that it had earned $5.2 million in 2007, when its actual revenues were around $1.7 million.[30] Like an elite athlete bafflingly tempted to take steroids, Entellium's CEO and CFO pumped up the company's success until it was almost hyperbole.

Johnston and Jones put up a show that dazzled investors, who forked over about $50 million in good faith. One of the biggest venture funds lost around $19 million.[31]

How did these industry stalwarts get defrauded? Pascal Levensohn, founder, Levensohn Venture Partners, and board member of National Venture Capital Association (NVCA) says, "When there is an opportunity for collusion, such challenges are likely to occur."[32] Levensohn recruited over 25 VC industry leaders to develop a series of white papers on how venture capitalists can improve their game as board members of VC-backed companies. Venture capitalists, most of whom are trying to be supportive and nurturing without being overbearing, can be vulnerable to such planned attacks.

GCA Savvian's Steve Fletcher is realistic about the challenges of a venture capitalist's role on the board. "If a company's executives really set out to defraud people, if they make up invoices or clients, it's difficult to detect as an auditor or a board member or an investment banker. The CEO and CFO are the most important executives of a company. In reality, most of your information comes from them."[33] In a small company of 15 to 20 employees, the primary board interactions are with the CEO and the CFO.

What are the lessons learned?

- *Cover the blind spots:* Blind spots in business often occur both when things are going badly and when the business is going well. Assistant U.S. Attorney Carl Blackstone, who prosecuted the case against Johnston and Jones, called Entellium a "legitimate company with a real product and real employees" with the only discordance being the inflated revenues from which Johnston pocketed about $1.4 million.[34] In other words, there weren't explicit red flags to board members about something fishy in the books. The numbers—even the exaggerated versions hammered up by Johnston and Jones—made sense and fit the story of a robust company like Entellium and its vibrant industry.
- *Put healthy skepticism to work by putting periodic reviews in place.* A study found that among 1,770 VCs who have taken at least one of their portfolio firms public, 196 (11.07 percent) of them have funded a fraudulent IPO firm, and 154 (8.7 percent) of them have backed an IPO firm that committed fraud after their exit.[35] Obviously, the VCs who backed Entellium are not alone.

  As a venture capitalist, it may be hard to question your charismatic and driven founder and CEO, especially when the numbers look great! Venture capitalists can avoid being hoodwinked by learning to intelligently question all the facts. For example, put in place safeguards like periodic in-depth reviews of sales or audits to dig deeper into financial records. Ask for customer lists with purchase order amounts and corroborate details in formal audits. Unfortunately, venture capitalists are also often put off by the extra costs of audits, which can be significant. Depending on the audit firm and the scope of work, this could be anywhere from $50,000 a year upward, and the cost rises quickly as the company grows. Still, as insurance, it is well worth the investment and peace of mind. Remember, the company is a partnership between the CEO and the board and its members. While the CEO is essential to the company's success, his or her leadership should be subject to checks and balances, which the venture capitalist provides by sitting on the board. This doesn't mean subjecting your CEO to interrogations for every decision or step taken or resorting to micromanagement techniques, which are tantamount to using a short leash that instills rancor and further alienates your CEO. A better strategy is developing a mentoring relationship with management that cultivates trust and openness.

■ *Enlist key players and enhance information flow.* In the case of Entellium, a stronger relationship with the business development team might have exposed deception sooner since collusion was largely confined to the CEO and CFO. "You always want the perspective of people who aren't on the management team and don't have a direct interest in sticking to the management team's story," advises Justin Hibbard of the research group Quidnunc Group, which conducts due diligence for venture investors.[36]

CEO Warning Signs

In the white paper, "Rites of Passage," Pascal Levensohn points to several CEO behavioral characteristics that may act as warning signs. The CEO:

■ Repudiates board input and stays the wrong course.
■ Is often missing in action.
■ Is defensive and combative with the board, stonewalling board inquiries.
■ Is not proactive in keeping the board informed.
■ Shirks responsibilities or passes the blame.

According to Pascal, if ignored, these warning signs can deteriorate into more serious mismanagement problems such as revenue shortfalls, gaps, and delays in meeting purchase targets or in completing contracts, and an exodus of employees.

Managing CEO Transition

Almost two-thirds of all venture-backed start-up companies replace their founding CEOs or top executives. Initiating and managing transitions during the changing of the guard is one of the most important decisions venture capitalists will make as board directors or members. Friction between the venture capitalist board members and CEO generally arises during these times. As CEOs build management teams by recruiting trusted team members, the risk of implosion during such times can be high. With their broader perspectives, venture capitalist board members can lobby to add talent outside the CEO's circle. This kind of strategic recruiting may call for the difficult task of moving founding members out of management seats and into more supportive, advisory roles.

Such transitions can be challenging for both sides—in the formative stages the VCs mentor the CEO, act as sounding boards, and even joke that they act as corporate shrinks. This build-up leads to deepening personal ties, but a practitioner needs to realize the consequences of any friendship. "One of the mistakes I made early on was trying to become friends with the entrepreneurs. You eventually learn that you can like them and admire them, but you don't want...you get too close to it and you get too close to them, and it sort of inhibits you in some ways," James Swartz of Accel Partners once stated.[37]

The best way to manage these changes is to anticipate them, monitoring for early signs of leadership problems, and acting quickly and decisively before any shortfalls lead to irreparable damage. One way to do this is for both parties to establish specific performance expectations. Annual reviews of CEO performance, including management team feedback, board member feedback, and input from other key stakeholders, are critical.

Besides value creation, the role of the board member is critical in assessing the performance of the CEO and helping identify and recruit other suitable members of the management team. Studies have shown that in venture-backed companies, management turmoil and change is constant, and roughly half of the CEOs lasted from business plan to IPO. Founders are unable to retain their roles as CEOs during the rapid evolution stages of the company—managing people, budgets, and technology in a rapidly evolving marketplace is rare. Thus, a practitioner needs to be prepared to identify and recruit key management talent. John Doerr of Kleiner Perkins identifies himself as the "glorious recruiter." Benchmark Capital went on to bring a top recruiter as a full partner in the firm. Leonard Bosack, along with his wife Sandy Lerner, formed Cisco Systems. Their tenure with Cisco lasted for four years after they raised their first $2.5 million Series A round from Sequoia Capital.[38]

In venture jargon, change management does not mean managing change, but quite literally, changing a member of the management team. "It's a tough decision and very disruptive," says Deepak Kamra of Canaan Partners. He adds, "It's much easier to assume that the CEO will eventually work out, so let's keep him." Thomas H. Bredt of Menlo Ventures points out that one of his portfolio companies had a very effective CEO who was able to build a world-class product. "The product risk was overcome and the team surpassed our expectations—the CEO was a great engineer who could get a product to market. After the IPO, we agreed that the founder would be better suited in the capacity of the chairman. Solidifying the company's position post-IPO required a different skill set." Organizational development and management, sustained growth, defending competitive jabs—all under the public glare of analysts—calls for a different timbre. Thomas points out that he had raised the CEO transition issues up front prior to making the investment.

> *By far, this is the biggest service any venture practitioner can do for the CEO—educate and alert the CEO, preferably prior to making the investment, that transition is normal.*[39]

As John Kenneth Galbraith once remarked, "The great entrepreneur must, in fact, be compared in life with the male 'epis mellifera.' He accomplishes his act of conception at the price of his own extinction."[40] People seldom grow from managing product development, to managing people, to eventually managing expectations in post-IPO public glare. As human beings, we rarely recognize our own shortcomings and inabilities when it comes to managing people, products, and capital. Practitioners need to keep watch for warning signs and be the catalyst.

Management of communication around this subject is critical. When the decision to replace the CEO is finalized, the board and the CEO would also agree on a clear message to be communicated to employees, customers, investors, and other stakeholders to assure everyone of the continuity and integrity of the company during the transition period.

Best Practices in Managing a CEO Transition

- Prioritize skills and experience needed.
- Enlist support: Ensure that the founder and the new CEO are aligned.
- Establish a new role for the founder ahead of time.
- Make the search priority one. One board member should lead the process.
- Choose the closer: Prime candidates usually need persuasion. One board member—the best closer—works with the dream candidate to close.
- Stay close to the new CEO: To ensure a smooth transition, maintain a high touch relationship in the first few months. Avoid complacency after the CEO arrives.

Causes of Stress within the Board: Performance and Emotions

In venture-backed companies, fragile egos and intensely competitive dynamic markets make for a highly charged board situation, writes Pascal

Levensohn. Venture-backed boards undergo considerable stresses when a portfolio company faces:

- Resource challenges
  - Sales growth is slower and/or
  - Cash position is weak
- CEO performance challenges
  - Milestones have not been met
  - Significant value creation steps have not occurred within projected timelines or prescribed budgets
  - Loss of key accounts or major clientele
- Market-based/external challenges
  - Constrained market conditions affect sales or future financing
  - Competitive forces disrupt the company's progress
  - IP-related matters cause unforeseen issues

When Arthur Rock resigned from the board of Apple, he was irritated by the chutzpah displayed by Steve Jobs. "They took a two-page ad in every newspaper you could think of, announcing that they were ready to ship the PowerPC, which I did not know they were going to manufacture—but that's not important—but that they were going to kill Intel. Literally—that's what it said. At that point, I resigned," he would say.[41]

Patterns of emotional behavior manifest in wide-ranging forms, including ego games designed to impress friends, actions taken to save face, self-interested actions, and personal vendettas, says Pascal Levensohn. Left unchecked, the force of emotion may compromise directors' abilities to promote the shareholders' best interests. An independent outside director can play a crucial role in defining the success of the company.[42]

Who Really Controls the Board? The Independent Director as an Adjudicator

The most dysfunctional boards I have seen have five to seven VCs who are piling on the management with words like "work harder, deliver more, and spend less."
—Chris Rust, US Venture Partners[43]

The role of an independent director can alleviate any vested behavior. "Allocating a tie-breaking vote to an unbiased arbiter commits the entrepreneur and venture capitalists to more reasonable behavior and can reduce the opportunism that would result if either party were to control the board," writes Brian Broughman.[44] Experts studied 213 venture capitalists' investments in 119 companies and found that venture capitalists control board seats in 25 percent of the cases, the founders in 14 percent of the cases, and neither in 61 percent of the cases.[45] In those 61 percent of the cases, the independent director acted as an adjudicator and likely brought the two sides to a common ground.

Various studies and anecdotal assessments show that independent directors were known by both parties in as many as 70 percent of the investments. "From a value-add perspective, access to independent thought leaders and leading executives is important for us," says Kenneth Van Heel, director of alternative investments at Dow Chemical Company.[46] Independent directors are brought in because they have the mutual respect of both the company and the investors, their behavior is objective and balanced, and they have strong reputations.

IMPROVING THE BOARD GAME

Being a good board member is not a complex affair, however, bad board behavior abounds aplenty. Like dysfunctional families, each board has its own quirks and challenges. But where a culture of trust and open communication exists, the boardroom can be a welcome arena.

Build a Trusted Partnership

Does the CEO know each board member's strengths and draw on these resources? Does the CEO feel secure and safe and discuss issues honestly and promptly? Does the CEO assign tasks to the board members effectively? "I really struggled to reconcile my role as a board member," says Brad Feld. Brad had formed companies, sat on boards and served as chair, and taken a few of the companies public. "It took me a while to firmly get my head set in one place where I focused on being the investor rather than the guy trying to run the company. It wasn't my responsibility to fix everything in the company, but to help the company win—I would provide feedback to the CEO and work for her. Trying to direct the CEO or entrepreneur does no good for any venture capitalist."

Ensure Open Communication Channels

Communication between board members needs to be open and frequent. The biggest mistake made by board members is to presume that there is consensus at the board—not bothering to ask others if they agree." I sit on four boards and find this happens all the time," says Pascal Levensohn. If board members fail to communicate critical issues in between board meetings, these can lead to surprises as well as inefficiencies. A common tactic employed is to discuss such surprises "offline" or delay the decision until a consensus is reached. Such behavior hurts the progress of the company, and very soon the CEO realizes that the board is playing the proverbial fiddle while Rome may be burning.

According to *A Simple Guide to the Basic Responsibilities of VC-Backed Company Directors*,[47] an open door policy between management and the board is equally crucial. Venture capitalists can share their wide range of experiences in other portfolios to benefit a company, particularly during critical moments of transition (e.g., when a company is about to consider an initial public offering). Venture capitalists can also give advice on organizational planning and compensation structures. They should also serve as sounding boards for their CEOs and carve out opportunities to mentor them. This means making themselves available for broad-based consultations even outside normal board meeting schedules.

As Brad Feld puts it, "With some portfolio companies, the tempo of exchange is different, it could be daily—multiple times a day. Some want to meet—it is always useful to get face-to-face, but I let the entrepreneur decide the interaction."[48]

A good board member invites and welcomes input from CEOs, non-venture capitalist directors, and other board members, including observers. Peer reviews and self-evaluations ensure greater accountability and better governance. Effective board members also avoid the distractions of board-room intrigue and political maneuvering and focus on the operational goals of their roles: promoting the best interest of the company and maximizing value for shareholders.

Qualities to be nurtured among members for an effective, harmonious board include strong interpersonal skills to manage the team dynamics and the relationship with management; pattern recognition skills to anticipate events and make tough decisions, often with little information; partnering experience to work with other investors with different financial stakes and to manage board meetings without getting lost in the mundane details; strong networking skills to reach out to contacts in the industry; and strong mentoring and hands-on, consultative skills with the CEO and top executives to maintain open lines of communication. One tool to foster openness within the organization is to hold board retreats during critical junctures in the development of the company. Unlike other board meetings, the retreat can be used to address critical issues lingering on the table with the help of an outside facilitator.

Avoid Complacency

For any portfolio company, venture capitalists should have an understanding of the company's competitive position in the industry to help it stay nimble and to make inroads in the market. Venture capitalists are expected to keep abreast of specific industry developments, as well as the current regulatory environment, to maintain oversight of rules and regulations, and to understand the governance requirements throughout the development of the company.

Align Interests of All Shareholders and Management

I have a test I use. Can I explain my decision as reasonable and fair to any shareholder group, not just my own?
—Andy Rappaport, August Capital[49]

In any company, the cast of characters includes various classes of shareholders, the management team, and the board. The interests of this cast, as described in the following section, can vary across the axis of time, value creation, and capital needs.

A VC Reports to Limited Partners and the VC Firm Any practitioner primarily seeks to maximize returns, and thus timely exits are essential. Strong returns allow the practitioner to raise the next fund and ensure longevity, possibly higher fees, and improved brand stature. Conflicts can arise when (1) Career: A practitioner seeks attribution quickly in anticipation of moving on from the current fund to greener pastures, (2) Fund-raising: The next fund needs to be raised and there are no successes to show, (3) Exit timing: A practitioner cannot see the growth trajectory or strong exit value within a meaningful timeframe, or (4) Financial: This company is becoming a sinkhole and the practitioner has "checked out." "Alignment does not matter when a company grows fast or craters quickly—you need alignment with the portfolio companies that are stuck in the middle," says Brad Feld.

Challenges among Shareholders Multiple classes of shares with multiple preferences stacked on each other creates a labyrinth wherein keeping track of each entity's agenda and economic interests can be challenging. Further, while the terms may be static, each practitioner and his or her fund's status is dynamic.

Any VC fund owns preferred stock, while the management may own common stock. Thus, any exit discussions where the management or common shareholders do not benefit would lead to frustration. In a few cases, the common shareholders have successfully negotiated additional cash prior to consenting to the sale of the company. According to one entrepreneur, the carve-out was offered only because the VCs were concerned about a possible shareholder lawsuit challenging the terms of the sale. In another case where the VCs lacked board control, the VCs offered a carve-out to obtain the support of the other directors for the sale.[50]

Cash Flow-Related Matters   If the burn rate is too high, management is seen as the primary culprit. The board and the CEO may disagree on the spend rate and priorities. Tension can arise over the priority of cash distribution at exit when the numbers are mediocre—for example, should accrued dividends, which primarily benefit investors, have a priority over management performance bonuses?

Performance-Related Challenges   Are you writing checks to defend sunk capital? Or to fuel growth? Consider the example of NEON, a health-care IT company backed by ARCH Venture Partners. The company had developed tools for hospitals to organize data and increase transaction speed. The target market never developed because the hospitals' IT protocol had not reached the point at which they could maximize the potential of NEON's technology. And any IT company selling to hospitals is leery about the sales cycle, which can be as long as nine months or more. NEON was one of the larger investments for ARCH and thus, the partners were investing a fair amount of time in trying to resurrect the opportunity. This conundrum has been faced by many practitioners when the initial thesis of an opportunity does not pan out. "The technology had to have a market somewhere...we just hadn't found it yet," Steven Lazarus, founder of ARCH, would recall. From hospitals, where the adoption for new technologies was sluggish, the company shifted its target market to Wall Street. Its technology was ideally suited for speedier transactions and messaging, and in five years the company grew to $180 million in revenues before it was acquired.[51] ARCH continued to support the company despite market-related challenges and it paid off.

Compare NEON with the defunct online grocer Webvan—termed as one of the most epic failures in the dot-com bubble fiasco, this company sold groceries such as bread and vegetables. Within 18 months it had spent $1 billion on several futuristic warehouses, promising to offer groceries in 30 minutes or less. Webvan's investor list was the who's who of VC—Sequoia Capital, Benchmark Capital, and several others. The company also raised almost half a billion dollars by going public (its stock went from $30 to six cents in a few months). Senior executives or investors did not have any experience in the supermarket trade—Webvan went from being a $1.2 billion company with 4,500 employees to being liquidated in under two years. "The presumption that you needed to get big fast worked for Amazon.com and virtually no one else," commented Gartner analyst Whit Andrews at the time of Webvan's bankruptcy.[52] His prophetic words rang true when, in 2009, Amazon resurrected Webvan and unveiled AmazonFresh.

In each of these examples, the underlying challenges of performance exist. Neither NEON nor Webvan was able to penetrate the market. However, the market conditions—the dot-com boom and bust—and capital needs of each business (Webvan needed *mucho dinero*, NEON did not) also act as criteria for decisions. Whatever be the reasons, the Webvan boardroom may have been much more challenging as compared to NEON.

Alignment of Exit Method, Timing, and Exit Value Successful venture capitalist board members have alignment and clear understanding of exit strategies as well as a strong sense of when a company has matured or is languishing toward failure. If a company fails to accomplish milestones, encounters dwindling resources, or suffers from competitive pressures—the exit method and value may be severely compromised. On the other hand, selling to a corporate buyer or going public on the stock exchange at the right time is expected to yield a strong outcome. But timing matters on exits, as does alignment of the stakeholders. If one venture investor is under more pressure to achieve an exit quickly than are other investors, the misalignment can impair the exit value. Further, if the CEO or the management team does not want to exit, the investors can end up with another set of challenges. These challenges are discussed in Chapter 12.

As the company evolves into maturation, it is rare and even unlikely that one individual will encompass all the skills necessary to guide the CEO and enhance value at every stage. Board members' ability to add value may diminish, and they need to cede their positions to more suitable peers within the firm. This rarely happens in practice—board members embed themselves within the company, especially as the company ascends to rapid growth. It's only during a crisis that disemboweling occurs. At the heart of the challenge is a rock star culture—practitioners become stars when huge exits and payoffs occur. The board members at the time of the exit are heroes who cross the proverbial finish line and enhance their resumes. But rotation for the sake of rotation can be challenging as well—a company may lose much-needed talent. Education of new members and their ability to build the right chemistry is critical. In the larger context, the rotation challenge may be less of an issue, but it still is a pertinent one.

SUMMARY

Good governance is akin to parenting—too lax behavior or micro-management leads to dysfunctional kids. A board member represents *all* shareholders (not just their financial interests), focuses on finding the right CEO, and then offers relentless support to her. Approving key strategic directions becomes easier with the right CEO.

A good board member first orients, then engages. Experienced board members are adept at "pattern recognition"—where lessons learned from various start-ups can be amalgamated to ensure mistakes are avoided.

Most rookie venture capitalists are bad board members. Akin to a new parent who struggles to understand his or her first child, a rookie practitioner stumbles all over, eager to display his or her acumen (or lack thereof). It gets worse if the rookie has arrived with an MBA, ready to divide the world into four quadrants. The only training ground for the rookie practitioner is the battlefield, but a view of apprenticeship, staying humble and serving is critical. Find the right CEO and offer her all you can. Entrepreneurs candidly speak of rookie board members as "He learned how to be a director. We paid the tuition," or "My strategy is to minimize the value subtracted."[53] Many CEOs joked that some venture capitalist board members were exceedingly valuable while other micro-managers were downright pains in the posterior.

Any board member should, in conjunction with the CEO, identify the value creation milestones. If the CEO is on target and plan, the best way to serve is *stay out of her way*. Much damage has been done with the intention of doing good.

There are innumerable factors in determining whether or not a company succeeds—but none is as important as the role of the venture capitalist board member. By their very nature, start-ups are not meant to be structured in a top-down, hierarchical way. More team-oriented than command-control, they must be managed from the ground up. A more engaged and flexible board member, ready to embrace and see opportunities in the challenges of growing a business can be an asset to the firm. The key is to balance the interpersonal abilities with skills in order to stay focused on those three magic words: maximize shareholder value.

In the following chapter, the fruits of good board membership—exits—are presented.

CHAPTER 12

Exit Strategies

For I must tell you friendly in your ear,
Sell when you can, you are not for all markets.
—William Shakespeare, *As You Like It*, Act 3 Scene V

A n exit occurs when a portfolio company is acquired, or its stock trades on the public exchanges. At those rare (and hopefully happy) moments when the capital invested completes a full circle—an investor "exits the investment" made by selling the stock of the portfolio company. LPs collect 80 percent of the exit proceeds while the GPs keep 20 percent share of the profits.

The two primary exit options, acquisitions and initial public offerings (IPOs), are reviewed in this chapter, along with private exchanges—an emerging option with implications for some highly sought-after Facebook, Zynga, and Twitter-like companies.

- *Mergers and acquisitions (M&A or trade-sale):* Mergers and acquisitions is the most popular path of exit for a venture-backed company. Also called trade sale, a portfolio company is sold to a larger company. The transaction nets a return for investors, who, in turn, share the spoils with their limited partners.
- *Initial public offering:* A highly desired badge of honor; investors list a company on a publicly traded stock exchange and sell privately owned shares for the first time to the public. Of course, fewer companies can demonstrate the growth and value to be considered IPO ready. And after they are ready, the Securities and Exchange Commission (SEC), the federal regulatory body, prescribes rules and regulations on public

TABLE 12.1   Returns: Or Why an IPO Is Better

Exit Path	Observations	Median IRR (%)	Mean IRR (%)	Standard Deviation
IPO	108	58.39	123.42	207.97
Trade-sale	423	18.32	75.32	408.27

Source: CEPERS, Frankfurt. For exits between 1971 and 2003. Data from Center for Private Equity Research, Frankfurt. Period from 1971 to 2003. Carsten Bienz and Tore E. Leite, "A Pecking Order of Venture Capital Exits "(April 2008). Available at SSRN: http://ssrn.com/abstract=916742.

offerings to keep everyone honest and protect that little old lady. Some venture practitioners treat the public offering as a financing event and not an exit. Compared to acquisitions, IPOs typically deliver a higher return to investors, as seen in Table 12.1.

- *Wall Street 3.0: Private Exchanges:* SharesPost and SecondMarket have sprung up, offering shares of sought after start-ups to eager buyers. After all, who does not want a piece of Facebook!
- *Redemption of shares:* Remember that redemption clause you negotiated—the one where you can treat your equity much like a debt instrument and trigger the repayment after 5 years! That is technically an exit but no venture practitioner worth his IRR speaks of redemption in public.

And yes, a write-off is technically an exit, but it doesn't need much deliberation in this chapter. Be assured that in your portfolio, the lemons, as depicted in Figure 12.1, will always ripen much faster. Stated differently, the losses occur much faster.

A good practice for GPs is to track the losses in a systematic manner. LPs certainly seek to understand the conditions and lessons learned with write-offs. After all, the goal is to avoid making the same mistakes again, or make new mistakes each time! Each exit path has its own advantages and challenges, as seen in Table 12.2.

PRECONDITIONS FOR AN EXIT

Certain preconditions need to be established prior to any exit overtures. These are discussed in Table 12.3.

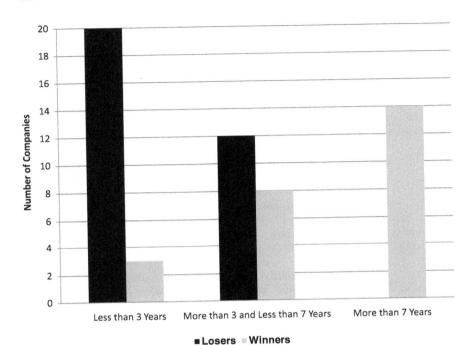

FIGURE 12.1 Lemons Ripen Faster than Pearls
Source: Jeffry Timmons, *New Venture Creation: Entrepreneurship for the 21st Century*, 5th ed. (New York: McGraw Hill, 1999).

Alignment of Interests of Stakeholders

Alignment of interests of various stakeholders can determine whether passage of an exit will be smooth or be a joyride to the suburbia of hell. The cast of characters includes:

- Board of directors, presumably with multiple investors, each with varying degrees of motivations and investor preferences
- Founders/chief executive officer motivations
- Common shareholders' interests

Naturally, the board exerts the maximum influence, but the role of other stakeholders is important as exits are being planned. Consider a Cisco executive who, while conducting due diligence, assesses the quality and character of the target company's management team. Cisco interacts with

TABLE 12.2 Pros and Cons of Exit Methods

Method of Exit	Pros	Cons
Acquisition (trade-sale)	Speed. Reduced regulatory challenges. (Assuming the FTC does not get involved!) Value can be lower in comparison to an IPO, but as many practitioners point out, it is efficient.	Takes two to tango. In some cases, earn-outs may be beyond the control of current management or existing investors. Founders or any other shareholders cannot retain partial ownership.
Listing on public exchange iInitial public offering)	Larger valuation in stronger market conditions. Can use stock for acquisitions. Improves stature and morale. Founders can retain partial ownership	Company needs to achieve growth rates that are higher than average. Expensive process. Regulatory and market challenges.
Private exchanges	Rapid liquidity. Higher valuations.	Awareness and demand for the companies needs to be high. No one is looking to invest in no-name companies. Value is determined by sheer frothiness and public market-like speculation.
Redemption	Ability to recover at least some capital, assuming company has some cash at hand at the time of redemption.	Dependent on company's ability to redeem, as well as other balance sheet obligations and board composition. Payouts could be spread out over time to minimize cash impact, further reducing any IRR.

the executives in an informal manner to explore short-term and long-term goals. "We look for culture, qualities, and leadership style. We don't care about the product that is on the manufacturing floor ... the second- and third-generation product is locked up in their heads," a Cisco executive points out.[1] John Chambers, the CEO of Cisco, laid out five guidelines for acquiring companies, including the "chemistry between companies has to be right" and "long-term win for all four constituencies—shareholders, employees, customers, and business partners."[2] If the founders and CEO of the target company do not see the exit as a win, it may show during

TABLE 12.3 Preconditions for an Exit

Preconditions for an Exit	Favorable Conditions	Unfavorable Conditions
Value drivers	Rapid sales and expansion, market leadership and proprietary position.	Flat growth, limited potential. Sagging morale. A dog. A distraction.
Board-investor alignment	Board members/investors are aligned with respect to timing and value of exit.	The largest investor wants that quick hit—a fund-raise cycle is coming up and we need that IRR! You want to stay! Or the largest investor (and the chairman of the board) is fatigued and wants to get rid of this dog. You, on the other hand, are a seed investor and control a fraction of the shares. And the common shareholders want to block the sale because those 3X liquidation preferences do not leave any crumbs for them.
Board-management alignment	Board and CEO/founders are in agreement with respect to timing and value of exit.	The investors want to sell. The CEO wants to grow. Investors sell—unhappy CEO ends up writing a book. What a wicked world! The CEO wants to sell—the investors want to hold and build value. A premature liquidity event for VCs!
Market demand	Buyers are kicking the doors down. A nice auction process is driving price and IRR to all-time highs. Sell this—and get that PPM ready for the next fund raise?	No market demand, but we want to sell. Hire an I-Banker, prepare a book, and start the selling process. With no bites and sinking cash position, attempt to raise a bridge note or a swallow a down round. Eighteen months later, shut the company down.
Macro conditions	Strong public markets and economic conditions.	Competition, erosion of margins, regulatory changes

buyer diligence. When Ted Dacko, CEO of HealthMedia, was getting ready to complete the sale of his company to Johnson & Johnson, he was not worried about the exit value as much as the team culture. "I wanted to ensure everyone understood the exit strategy and was aligned—we did not have any passive aggressive behavior," he says.

> We had a tough time convincing our board of directors who were also our investors to embrace many of our activities that would help build the Zappos brand and make the world a better place. The directors didn't fully understand or were convinced of things like brand or culture, dismissing many of these as "Tony's social experiments." Sequoia expected an exit in five years and hadn't signed up for these additional things. I was pretty close to being fired from the board. I was learning that alignment with shareholders and board of directors was just as important.[3]

Exit strategies, value, and timing evolve as the company matures. Practitioners have a strong sense of when a company has matured or is languishing toward failure. If a company fails to accomplish future-financing rounds, misses milestones and targets, exhausts ideas and resources, or sees its market shrink or shift, then it is critical to close down operations rather than to slowly wither into oblivion.[4] Conversely, selling to a corporate buyer or going public at the right time is certainly expected as a strong outcome. Timing matters. Premature efforts to drive exits can lead to depressed value or worse, no buyer interest. Sell too late and the dynamics may shift—potential buyers, market conditions, and the arrival of competition could impair the value. Mitch Lasky of Benchmark Capital points out that the window of exit opportunity can be narrow. "Look for that S Curve when growth and exit multiples are on your side," he says. See Figure 12.2.

Alignment of Exit Value: What's a Few Hundred Million Anyway?

At an appropriate time, specific exit values should also be discussed openly to ensure alignment with various stakeholders. For example, different investors may have conflicting valuations in mind. Examples abound where one venture capitalist was happy to part with the company for $100 million and another was expecting to turn at least $300 million.[5] If the liquidation preferences come into play and gravely impact the common shareholders, unpleasant situations, such as holdup of the voting process or worse, lawsuits, can ensue.

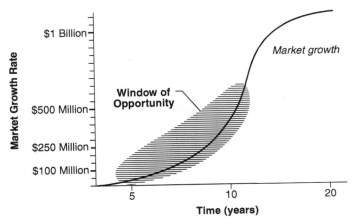

FIGURE 12.2 The S Curve of Exit Opportunities

ACQUISITIONS: THE PRIMARY PATH TO AN EXIT

In a study of 11,500 VC-backed companies that raised capital between 1995 and 2008, 65.21 percent, or approximately 7,500 portfolio firms, exited through either an IPO or M&A. Within this universe, the vast majority of investments exit via the M&A path and only 9.61 percent of them achieve exit via an IPO.[6]

As seen in Figure 12.3, acquisitions are significantly larger as compared to IPOs.

Acquisitions are the preferred path for most venture-backed companies due to speed and efficiency, as well as minimal regulatory challenges. Acquisitions offer larger companies much needed growth and expansion opportunities. And for venture investors, acquisitions offer an opportunity for a decent return. Consider Figure 12.4.

From 2002 to 2009, IBM acquired 70 companies, spending about $14 billion. By pushing these newly acquired products through an existing global sales force, IBM estimates it increased its revenue by almost 50 percent in the first two years after each acquisition and an average of more than 10 percent over the next three years.[7]

By rough estimates, Cisco acquired over 120 companies between 1993 and 2008—roughly an average of 8 to 12 companies each year. The first 71 companies acquired within an eight-year period (1993 to 2001) were at an average price of approximately $350 million. In that same period, Cisco's sales increased from $650 million to $22 billion, with nearly 40 percent of its 2001 revenue coming directly from these acquisitions.[8] By 2009, Cisco

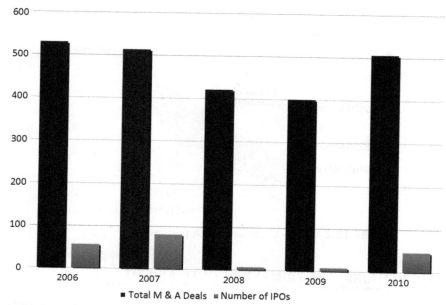

FIGURE 12.3   Liquidity Events of VC-Backed Companies
Source: Dow Jones VentureSource.

had more than $36 billion in revenues and a market cap of approximately $150 billion.

In 2010 alone, Google acquired 48 companies. For Google, the technology drivers have opened up new revenue sources. Its acquisition of Applied Semantics helped Google develop a text-advertising network called AdSense, now a multibillion-dollar revenue generator. Andy Rubin's start-up, Android Inc., was snapped up by Google and led to the development of what is now a leading operating system for smartphones.[9]

M&As are seen as the fastest way for larger companies like Google, IBM, and Cisco to expand, whether vertically or horizontally. Such diversification strategies can bolster companies' core strengths. VC-backed companies make strong M&A candidates as they "[offer] an established revenue/customer base [and] proprietary technology, [are] profitable and receptive to fair valuation metrics, [have] a unique and defensible market position, [and employ] strong management teams."[10] According to Larry Hrebiniak, professor of management at The Wharton School at University of Pennsylvania, this type of expansion leads to potential "synergies, cost reductions, or a combination of product line and structural change, because [the companies] look alike and are in some of the same markets."[11] As a

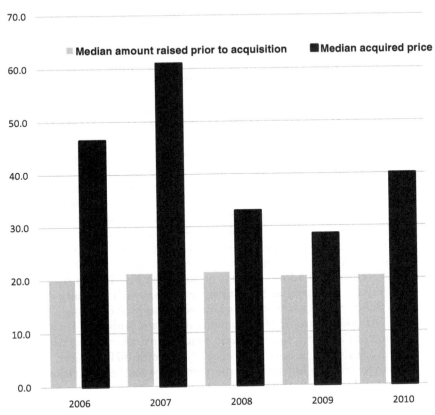

FIGURE 12.4 Acquisitions in Aggregate Yield Lower Returns
Source: Dow Jones VentureSource.

result, larger companies, especially the ones with significant cash, stagnant revenues, and limited growth potential, consider M&As as part of their growth strategy.

Key drivers for acquisitions are:

- *Improved revenues and profitability:* Cisco's sales increased from $650 million to $22 billion in the period from 1993 to 2001, with nearly 40 percent of its 2001 revenue coming directly from these acquisitions.
- *Operational synergies:* Larger companies seek to reduce costs and expand revenues and profitability by seeking synergistic companies that feed their value chain.

- *Vertical:* Vertical synergies occur when an acquirer moves vertically—up or down the value chain or supply chain. Also called forward integration or backward integration, examples include HP's acquisition of 3PAR to move into cloud computing, or Cisco's acquisition of Webex to expand its networking gear and voice-over-IP tools to Web presentation tools.
- *Horizontal:* Horizontal synergies occur when an acquirer moves to buy another company within a similar domain. Example: Oracle acquires Sun Microsystems.
- *Diversification of product lines to increase revenues:* Google, a search engine, acquires YouTube, an online video repository, to establish its ad revenues in the online video market. Amazon acquires Zappos to expand its offerings to shoes. Rich Levandov, an investor in several technology start-ups including Zynga, says, "Venture capital is about asymmetrical information and value—you know something that the buyer does not and you have something that a buyer wants—and wants now," he says. One of his portfolio companies, a start-up with an investment of $2 million, has no revenues. Five buyers are jostling to buy the company at $40 million or higher—it's not only Zynga's $3 billion valuation that keeps Levandov happy these days.

  Another example of asymmetrical value is StubHub. Rick Heitzmann of FirstMark Capital made a nice return when a portfolio company, StubHub, was sold to eBay. "Before StubHub, there was an opaque and muddy view of the secondary market for tickets. We were able to create value for both sides of the market, so revenues and growth followed. It was a good model." The company was profitable, with $15 million of total raise. "It is better to be bought rather than to sell, and we lived that cliché." When eBay came knocking, Heitzmann politely demurred, "We do not wish to sell, but if you are aggressive about buying, let's see your offer." Ultimately, StubHub was sold for $310 million—not too shabby for a company that took in just $15 million.
- *Geographic penetration:* Access to a new geographic territory, when conducted internationally, is also referred to as cross-border transactions.
- Quick, grab the technology before your competitor does: Google snapped up reMail, a popular iPhone application that provides "lightning fast" full-text search. reMail was yanked from the iTunes App Store as soon as it was gobbled up by Google. No predictions were made by either Google or reMail on the future of reMail. Will it be integrated with the Google Android mobile platform? Or worse, as TechCrunch's MG Siegler predicted, "they're [Google] just as happy

to kill off what is hands down one of the best e-mail applications on the iPhone—much better than the iPhone's native e-mail app."

■ *Quash any rising threats:* Apple bought Lala, a cloud-based Web streaming music service and within a few months shut it down. Lala users are angry; Apple is not—Apple bought Lala simply to take it offline because it didn't like the price erosion—10 cents per track charged by Lala as compared to 99 cents on the iTunes music store.[12] Better to get rid of it than to let it eat into your margins, or worse, let a competitor snag it and make the problem bigger.

OPERATIONAL SYNERGIES? IMPROVED REVENUES? REALLY!

Here are the real reasons why companies are acquired.
In his letter to shareholders in 1981, Warren Buffett writes about the three primary drivers of acquisitions—animal spirits (Don't just stand there, do something—buy a company), bigger is better (Ego—larger acquisitions are better), and undue optimism on post-merger integration (It will all work out—if not, all we lose is shareholder capital). Buffett writes "We suspect three motivations—usually unspoken—to be, singly or in combination, the important ones in most high-premium takeovers:

1. Leaders, business or otherwise, seldom are deficient in animal spirits and often relish increased activity and challenge.
2. Most organizations, business or otherwise, measure themselves, are measured by others, and compensate their managers far more by the yardstick of size than by any other yardstick. (Ask a *Fortune 500* manager where his corporation stands on that famous list and, invariably, the number responded will be from the list ranked by size of sales; he may well not even know where his corporation places on the list. *Fortune* just as faithfully compiles rankings of the same 500 corporations by profitability.)
3. Many managers apparently were overexposed in impressionable childhood years to the story in which the imprisoned handsome prince is released from a toad's body by a kiss from a beautiful princess. Consequently, they are certain their managerial kiss will do wonders for the profitability of Company T(arget). Such optimism is essential. Absent that rosy view, why else should the shareholders of Company A(cquisitor) want to own an interest in

T at the 2x takeover cost rather than at the x market price they would pay if they made direct purchases on their own? In other words, investors can always buy toads at the going price for toads. If investors instead bankroll princesses who wish to pay double for the right to kiss the toad, those kisses had better pack some real dynamite. We've observed many kisses but very few miracles. Nevertheless, many managerial princesses remain serenely confident about the future potency of their kisses—even after their corporate backyards are knee-deep in unresponsive toads."

All the other kids have one, what about me?
In another letter Warren writes:

"When a CEO is encouraged by his advisors to make deals, he responds much as would a teenage boy who is encouraged by his father to have a normal sex life. It's not a push he needs. Some years back, a CEO friend of mine—in jest, it must be said—unintentionally described the pathology of many big deals. This friend, who ran a property-casualty insurer, was explaining to his directors why he wanted to acquire a certain life insurance company. After droning rather unpersuasively through the economics and strategic rationale for the acquisition, he abruptly abandoned the script. With an impish look, he simply said: 'Aw, fellas, all the other kids have one.'"

Source: www.berkshirehathaway.com/letters/1994.html, accessed March 5, 2011.

If acquisitions offer an efficient mechanism for generating returns, who are GPs to judge these human fallacies of ego, mindless activity, and undue optimism? And as cash piles are hoarded by public companies, the animal spirits for acquisitions will continue. As of September 2010, U.S. companies had $1.9 trillion in cash sitting around, according to global asset manager AllianceBernstein.[13] European companies had the equivalent of $354 billion in cash. Here is to more acquisitions—after all, when was the last time you saw these public companies return money to the shareholders?

THE SELL PROCESS

Should the board decide to put the company on the block for sale, the process, as depicted in Figure 12.5, starts with dipping your toe in the water.

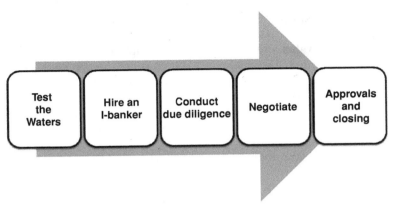

FIGURE 12.5 The Sell Process

Step 1: Test the Waters

Companies considering a sale generally hire a "sell side" investment bank to oversee the process of the company in a timely and efficient manner. Investment bankers charge a fee, typically, around 4 percent to 7 percent of the transaction amount, along with a retainership. At this stage, a company would invite investment bankers to propose terms and timelines and to demonstrate their industry awareness and connections. While these discussions ensue, the ineffective bankers will be eager to take the assignment and, after collecting substantial retainer fees, fail to deliver value. The low-level tactics include proposing significantly higher valuations to snag the assignment, and later, point to the buyer universe for poor outcomes. On the other hand, the best of the breed may not be willing to engage or sell something unless they believe the opportunity is meaningfully attractive to the universe of acquirers—and if they do, may propose a lower number to get the transaction completed fast. The company should seek the right balance between investment banker industry expertise, fee structures, target valuation range, and target time lines of transaction.

Company boards identify the investment bankers who have relevant knowledge of the challenges and opportunities of a particular sector and market conditions. Investment bankers are able to gauge the field, identify potential buyers, and know the potential hurdles and buyer objections. In determining the company's selling price, investment banks can provide fair assessments of value by analyzing the company's long-term prospects and current financials. Beyond providing these financial advisory services, investment banks identify potential buyers, solicit bids and review proposals, help companies select the most attractive candidates, and participate in the negotiations with interested parties.

At times, the value and visibility of the company may be such that an investment banker may be unnecessary. Or consider the approach of Heitzmann, who sold StubHub to eBay: "We deliberately built a board with tentacles in the potential buyer's market. You generally know someone—first-time entrepreneurs do not have much of a network—and that's where we come in. One of our board members knew people at eBay, and that's how it started," he says.

Bankers also bring about a degree of laziness in VCs, says Brad Feld of the Foundry Group. "On most occasions, with an investment banker, the price goes down," says Lindsay Aspegren. Lindsay, who was once with Goldman Sachs, has been an investor in technology start-ups for over a decade. Also, many buyers do not view the smaller investment bankers as credible and if the process is unsuccessful, the company is scarred—likely to be treated as damaged goods.

Step 2: Formalize the Process by Hiring an Investment Banker

At this stage, the board would hire an investment banker who will proceed within the following framework:

- *Process metrics and time lines:* Establish valuation guidelines, universe of potential acquirers, and steps/timelines for the process.
- *Presentation materials*: A teaser sheet, a set of slides, and relevant information memorandum.
- *First contact*: At this point, the I-banker blasts e-mails to the universe of acquirers, using teasers, which provide high-level information to acquirers. Teasers are typically a page or two long, with key highlights of the technology, revenues, and growth potential. Teasers do not disclose the name of the company and offer only some key points that get the buyers to the door to sign a nondisclosure agreement.
- *Screening the parties interested in the company*: Once the interested parties have been identified, and have signed nondisclosure agreements, these would be prescreened. This can be a nebulous step, as the goal of prescreening is to eliminate those who are merely seeking information without providing any insights into their process, motivations, or criteria. And beware of tire kickers. Brad Feld cautions that expressions of interest occur many times along the way. "It could well be corporate development guys from large companies just sucking info from entrepreneurs, or staying busy, doing their job. They may have no

money but are wasting an entrepreneur's time. We see many tire kickers and can help our entrepreneurs to cut through the noise—we know a lot of natural acquirers and we don't hesitate to call them when the time comes." Also, after the prescreening stage, companies choose to negotiate the terms themselves, without any substantial involvement from the I-bankers. Many intermediaries prefer to offer advice on the various potential outcomes based on negotiation parameters—mature I-bankers will seldom prescribe one path over another. The ultimate decision lies with the company.

- After a suitable buyer has been zeroed in on, the parties proceed to stage two of the process.
  - *Execute a letter of intent*: A letter of intent (LOI) establishes a level of commitment on both sides to proceed in a diligent and a timely fashion to finish what has been initiated. A LOI would include:
    - *Exclusivity*: The seller is engaging with only one party. This clause tilts the axis in favor of the buyer.
    - *Confidentiality*: This clause protects the seller's information. A must-have clause that does not impact the economic terms.
    - Broad parameters of transaction terms.
      - Due diligence
      - Conditions to closing
      - Employee matters
  - Suggested timelines
- Buyers may choose to offer a nonbinding LOI which is a two-edged sword. Further, a weak yet binding LOI does not accomplish much for the seller.
- Once the LOI has been executed, the buyer is aware of the negotiating advantage that starts therein. Other suitors usually step back at this point and the dance frenzy intensifies. A seller needs to ensure that the LOI has enough teeth in it to protect valuation and ensure that the diligence is completed with a sense of urgency.

Step 3: Conduct Due Diligence

Larger companies, and the buyer's counsel will engage in deep due diligence. Sellers establish a data room with relevant documents, which include:

- *Corporate records*: Certificate of incorporation, bylaws, board minutes, shareholders list.
- *Business records*: All material contracts of purchase, sale and supply agreements, research agreements, licensing and distribution agreements and government contracts, list of all assets and intellectual property.

- *Financial records*: All financial statements, receivables, loan and equity agreements, tax records. Copies of all placement memorandums, capitalization schedules, and equity amounts.
- *Employee records*: All employee agreements, consultant agreements, details of option plans and benefits (pension, health care) offered.
- *Legal*: Details of any litigations, pending or foreseen.

Step 4: Negotiate/Structure the Transaction

Typical elements of negotiation during the sell process include, besides valuation, the following:

- Asset purchase versus stock purchase:
  - Most acquisitions occur as asset purchases. This eliminates any unknown or contingent liabilities that a seller may assume as a result of stock purchase. Assets can be chosen ("You keep those desks and phone systems, we keep the IP and the customers") and allow for depreciation—a tax advantage.
  - In a stock purchase, the buyer can assume net operating losses (NOL) that the seller may have accrued, which may reduce the buyer's tax liabilities and augment the value. On the flip side, the buyer also assumes all liabilities, known or unknown. And yes, those old desks and archaic phone systems are a part of the deal.
- Cash offering, part cash and part stock, or all-stock transaction:
  - All-cash transaction is preferred by sellers and venture investors. Buyers can finance such transactions via external financings.
  - Stock transactions allow the seller to gain long-term economic advantages, and to be a shareholder to enjoy any advantages.
- Earn-outs and escrows: A buyer may believe that the value of the company lies in executing certain orders that generate revenues and cash flows or profits. Further, a buyer may establish certain targets and milestones for such an earn-out. Jack Ahrens of TGap Ventures tries to minimize any earn-outs: "The company is going to be controlled largely by the acquirer and so are the resources—people as well as cash. Things can get sticky pretty quickly when motivations change," he says. Depending on the sector, practitioners advise that approximately 15 percent of the value in earn-outs is acceptable. In the pharmaceutical sector, these percentages vary significantly and depend on the stage of drug development. Escrow percentages range from 5 percent to 15 percent and periods (12 to 24 months) are negotiated as buyer attempts to protect from any surprises and contingencies.

- Other terms:
  - ○ Representations and warranties made by the target company.
  - ○ Employees: Who stays, who goes.
  - ○ Employee options: Vesting schedule and acceleration.
  - ○ Indemnities offered by the target company.

Step 5: Approvals and Closing

The board and shareholders approve the transaction. The closing, a process during which the attorneys and key stakeholders execute final agreements, occurs on a set date. While these would historically happen in person, typically at an attorney's office, many of these are done virtually nowadays. After all, if signatures can be scanned and money can be wired, we do not need the general assembly.

WHEN AN ACQUIRER COMES KNOCKING

As they say, companies are always bought, never sold. Here are some points to consider when a potential acquirer comes calling.

- Technology companies seek to acquire innovative start-ups because larger companies are unable to innovate at a rapid pace.
- Acquisitions can be seen as a tactical way to recruit some very high-powered talent.
- Price, although important, is seldom a primary consideration in the acquisition. Several practitioners affirm that in many negotiations, the price effectively doubled by the time the transaction was consummated. This was not without due theatrics and emotional drama, but the sellers who held their ground and knew how to play the game were richer in the end.
- Eventually, acquisitions are a primary mechanism of growth for public companies.

THE BUY-SIDE ACQUISITION PROCESS

While larger companies seek certain features, product lines, or technologies, the first choice may be to build it internally. Any chief technology officer (CTO) of a company like Microsoft, Google, or Yahoo! will assert that his team can develop product internally, and do it faster and cheaper. However, in decisions where larger corporations look at make-versus-buy options, the CTO's ego and insecurities are not high up on the list. The potential for increased revenues, competitive dynamics, and financial growth and market timing comes into play. And this is where the CFO and the corporate development team display their acumen. CEOs love the process, too—at a very primal level, every CEO seeks to deploy excess cash to build a larger empire and demonstrate King Arthur-like prowess. And Warren Buffett's wisdom shows here: "Of one thing be certain: if a CEO is enthused about a particularly foolish acquisition, both his internal staff and his outside advisors will come up with whatever projections are needed to justify his stance. Only in fairy tales are emperors told that they are naked." Whatever the motivation is—technological, market driven, or ego driven—target companies and venture practitioners can benefit from such behavior.

The search process starts where the acquirer establishes certain criteria to narrow down the universe of potential targets.

Besides technological and market fit, examples of search criteria may include:

- *Size of transaction*: Consider the fact that Google has historically acquired a number of companies that are below the $30 million price tag. Examples include Adscape, now called Adsense ($23 million), and Blogger and WritePost, both rumored to be in the $10 million to $20 million range.
- *Geographic location*: Cisco is known to focus on the Silicon Valley area. John Chambers once stated in his acquisition strategy that "Geographic proximity is important. If the newly acquired firm is located close to Cisco, interaction will be easier."[14] The location also drives other intangibles—for example, Groupon's founders wondered whether this Midwest-based company would culturally integrate with Google!

But information flows both ways and the process of acquiring companies does not necessarily follow a prescribed, linear path. Many larger corporations rely on a network of relationships. For example, numerous Cisco executives serve on boards/advisory boards of start-ups. Such relationships provide key insights on technological developments. Investors too have found out that networks are an excellent mechanism to sell companies and generate returns in a consistent fashion. Larger companies also ask their sales team to keep an eye out for new entrants who may threaten their position. For example, Cisco heavily relies on its sales force to watch on new developments. And of course, venture capitalists are a great source of information. Of the various acquisitions made by Cisco, Sequoia—which originally invested in Cisco—had invested in at least 12 of them.[15] Sequoia was also an investor in YouTube, which was acquired by Google, one of its earlier portfolio companies. A study shows what most practitioners would intuitively know—that an acquisition is likely when there is a common venture capital investor linking the acquirer and the target.[16]

When any acquisition-related discussions occur, practitioners point to their duty toward shareholders of maximizing the outcome for all. Thus, in certain situations, bringing in an investment banker would be appropriate. For the investment banker, the goal of such an exercise is to drive the price up, or run an auction. If Google wants to buy a company, surely Microsoft would love to jump into the fray. Recall that when Google did a $900 million deal with MySpace, Microsoft followed soon thereafter and did a $300 million deal with Facebook. The investment banker would rush to gather additional interest from various parties and juggle with different buyers, all the time pushing the price as high as possible. The frenzy would culminate with a letter of intent with one of the suitors. At times, the buyer promptly locks up the game by proposing a "no shop" clause, where the target cannot indulge in the abovementioned exercise.

A buyer's due diligence process will occur in phases. The primary goal of the buyer is to ensure that the technology and teams are a suitable fit within its existing fabric. Thus, while the product lines, revenues, and markets are tangible, the softer challenges of postmerger integration are important as well. For example, Cisco sets short-term and long-term joint initiatives with the target's management team as a way to assess culture, management qualities, and leadership styles. They look for softer cues and watch if Does one person speak over everyone else? Do some people roll their eyes when the other is talking? Cisco negotiates directly with key individuals to identify their postacquisition intentions and also insists on employees waiving their accelerated vesting rights to ensure that they stay with the company postintegration. And valuation is not the most important negotiating point.[17] One Cisco executive remarked, "*Acquisitions are not financial—we do not do them because we can swing a good deal—they are strategic and help grow our company in the right direction* [italics added]."[18] "When a buyer seeks to make a strategic acquisition, the price is no longer a multiple, but could be significantly higher. As a practitioner, your goal is to understand that universe of strategic buyers," says Lindsay Aspegren of Northcoast Technology Investors. For larger companies, effective integration is key, or else the entire exercise is deemed a failure. Cisco has as many as 60 employees to manage the postintegration process. An integration leader is appointed, and within 30 days of announcement, HR lays out compensation plans for the team so that the talent pool can avoid uncertainty, stays, and focuses on creating value.

After the board approval and shareholder consents, the closing process begins. This process is as described earlier.

I'LL DO THE MACARENA FOR 17x IN 17 MONTHS

LinkExchange, an online banner exchange company, was acquired by Microsoft for its technology and customers. After Sequoia invested in LinkExchange, Tony Hsieh asked Michael Moritz of Sequoia to attend an initiation meeting with its six employees. After the introductions, the team decided they wanted to "move together in unison" and someone brought out a boom box. They started clapping, cheering...and as the song "Macarena" started, Moritz participated in the dance, as any good venture capitalist would. "I don't think words can truly describe what watching Moritz being forced to do the Macarena was like. It ranks up there as one of the strangest sights to behold," wrote Hsieh. "I had tears streaming down my face from laughing so hard."

Seventeen months after Sequoia invested $3 million, LinkExchange was acquired by Microsoft for $265 million. Moritz collected $50 million—a return of 17 times his initial investment in seventeen months. Time to do that Macarena again...and Moritz's turn to laugh.

Source: Adapted from Tony Hsieh, *Delivering Happiness: A Path to Profits, Passion, and Purpose* (New York: Hachette Book Group, 2010), 45–46.

DEAL KILLERS

According to Andrew Sherman and Milledge Hart, authors of *Mergers and Acquisitions* (AMACOM, 2nd ed., 2006), most transactions die due to:

- Price/valuation matters
- Terms and conditions
- Allocation of risk
- Third-party challenges such as federal and regulatory issues

ACQUISITION CASE STUDY: MINT.COM GENERATES 5x CASH-ON-CASH RETURN IN TWO YEARS

In 2009, Intuit, the maker of Quicken, decided it needed a makeover on its product line and offered Mint.com a buyout deal of $170 million.[19] In the day and age of Facebook, Zynga, and astronomical valuations, bloggers debated whether Mint sold out too soon.

The acquisition underscored a trend among software companies that wanted to extend their branding on the Web, where products are free and maintaining a suite of desktop programs brings in steady revenue. It also reflected a trend among consumers looking for easier ways to do their personal financial management. According to Brad Strothkamp of Forrester Research, Mint.com provided just the right amount of functionality without overwhelming consumers. "Quicken was a lot more than [many] people needed. Mint provides functions consumers want, but it isn't overkill."[20]

On many counts, the purchase garnered Mint CEO Aaron Patzer and his company a big win and rewarded early-stage investors. Still, with Mint.com increasing its user traffic and attracting rounds of investment and interest right before the buyout, could it have fetched a bigger selling price by playing the waiting game?

Mint.com was born out of founder Aaron Patzer's frustrations with the personal finance management software tool Quicken. Online banking Forrester Research analyst Emmett Higdon likened Quicken and other boxed financial management software to "something your dad uses."[21] Looking for something that was more user-friendly and that didn't feel like "a product from 1996," Patzer set out to create something different and targeted to the younger, iPhone-toting, Web-savvy users.

Launched in 2007, Mint.com grew to over 4 million registered users and now tracks about $175 billion in user transactions and $47 billion in assets.[22] A user-driven tool, it generates revenue by linking users to real financial institutions (such as commercial banks), brokerage accounts, credit cards, certificates of deposit, and other financial products, generating leads for these businesses from its wide user base. Mint.com also gathers details from where users shop and tracks how much they spend. This rich, merchant-level data is then aggregated to track the performance of industries and even individual stores. While Mint.com did not leverage this data in any directed way, only releasing certain charts and graphs that illustrate the occasional spending trend, its real value and service was still directed to users and financial institutions, not retailers.[23]

Mint.com's proprietary technology worked by centralizing all bank, credit card, mortgage, loan, and investment transactions from over 7,500 listed institutions on a summary page for users. Logging into Mint.com automatically synced all registered accounts, establishing a connection with the appropriate financial institution. An imprint of the account information offered users a way to monitor their financials without the need for accounting know-how. Users could view all their assets and liabilities without the need for tedious data entry or the cumbersome importing other financial software requires. What's more, all transactions in accounts added to Mint.com are itemized by category: for example, air travel, restaurants, or utilities. No transactions can be done through Mint.com—it serves only as a Web portal, summarizing and itemizing user spending, savings, and investment activities. Users can find out how much they are spending on interest on their credit cards, analyze their mutual fund performance, or check the value of their Apple stock.

Aside from displaying information, Mint.com also calculates budgets, shows cash flow each month, and offers users a range of financial products, listing the potential savings windfall each user could receive when signing up for a new account—for example, a certificate of deposit with a great introductory rate at Sallie Mae or a no-fee Roth IRA with Fidelity. By analyzing users' finances, spending habits, and demographic information, it automatically suggests products. If a user spends a lot on travel, he or she may receive a pitch for an airlines rewards credit card.

Mint.com has since expanded to other services, such as sending users e-mails, SMS alerts, and red flags on unusual spending, low balances, and upcoming bills. More proactive users can receive updates over their phones. iPhone users can even download a handy app at the Apple store. A public relations strategy based on a mix of word of mouth, use of the company's blog, Facebook, Twitter, and the iPhone app spawned Mint.com's rapid growth. In 2007, Mint.com received the TechCrunch40 top prize, bringing home $50,000.[24] It also received accolades from CNNMoney.com as a "top pick"[25] and from *Time* magazine as one of the top 50 web sites of 2008 and 2009.[26]

While investors were initially hesitant with Mint.com—with top VC firms Sequoia Capital, Greylock Partners, and Clearstone Ventures walking away—some started to take notice. First Round Capital's Josh Kopelman saw an impromptu demo of the product from Aaron Patzer at a networking event in 2006.[27] "Kopelman called me and I met with Patzer the next day. He was on to something—and it was clear to me that this young man was an execution machine. We handed him a term sheet in a matter of days," said Rob Hayes of First Round Capital. Hayes used his investment experience and product development skills honed at Palm to help Patzer build the right product, team, and business model.

By 2009, Mint.com had raised nearly $31 million in financing, including a first-round fund-raising windfall of $17 million from Benchmark Capital, Shasta Ventures, First Round Capital, and other angel investors, and an additional $14 million in a second round.[28] Mint.com received a valuation of $140 million at this round.[29]

The acquisition by Intuit, for the most part, delighted investors. Before Intuit's offer, Mint.com was valued at around $140 million, and

$170 million was seen as a reasonable offer, offering a five times return to total venture investment.[30] Still, many wonder whether Mint.com should have preserved its freshness a bit longer before joining hands with Intuit. "We could have sold for a lot more at a later date...the majority of the investors got a nice return. Everyone on the board was supportive of Patzer and his intention to sell the company," Hayes stated. Ravi Mohan of Shasta Ventures agrees: "Shasta was the largest equity holder in Mint and it was a great exit for us. Could it have been better—that is speculation, but we had to primarily support Aaron's goals."

> *Very large funds require massive wins...it is an assiduous problem of the venture industry—not the fault of founders. A $170 million exit is a life-changing event for the founder. As an investor, you cannot be misaligned with the founder and say that's a failure. If you do, you have the wrong product for the customer. A founder should not change the model to fit the investor's needs.*[31]

Both First Round Capital and Shasta Ventures are funds in the $200 million size range and thus could be satisfied with a $170 million exit. Postacquisition, Mint.com's Patzer became a VP and general manager of Intuit's personal finance group. He oversaw the integration of Mint.com technology into other Quicken products, including the ability to track spending, create custom budgets, and receive instant alerts on accounts from over 12,000 banks and credit unions.[32] Mint.com remains a separate entity. The two types of products—Web-driven Mint.com and desktop stalwarts like Quicken—will complement each other in the long run. And with 4.2 million users on Mint.com, Intuit may have snagged a winner.[33]

INITIAL PUBLIC OFFERING

Making the announcement to issue common stock on the public exchange, or "going public" for the first time, holds a special cachet in the world of VC-backed companies. Often marking the coming of age of companies, entrepreneurs see it as the epitome of success. But the regulatory and market complexities are significant and have impacted the IPO dynamics significantly. Across three decades, from 1980 to 2010, VC-backed IPOs as percentage of all IPOs is a mere 35 percent.[34]

In the 1990s, an IPO was within reach for companies with annual revenues between $30 million and $50 million that showed a profitable quarter and had a good board and management team. After the crash of 2000, larger, more mature companies with revenues of $150 million or more were seen as suitable candidates for IPOs. This had the effect of stretching out IPO timelines for companies.[35] In reviewing IPO trends of over 7,500 companies from 1980 to 2010, the median age of a company is 8 years. The lowest median age during these three decades was 5 years and the highest median age was 15 years.[36]

Tightening regulations in recent years have also increased the cost of going public. Companies face bigger regulatory burdens and liability and disclosure requirements, further eroding the preference for an IPO. In 2002, after the Enron and WorldCom debacles, the Public Company Accounting Reform and Investor Protection Act, or Sarbanes-Oxley Act (SOX), was enacted. The primary aim was to overhaul the financial reporting systems and push companies to develop internal control methods to ensure protection of investors. These regulatory demands required the companies follow a dreaded Section 404. Section 404 (a) of the act requires management to establish, maintain, assess, and report on the effectiveness of internal control systems over financial reporting. Section 404 (b) requires an independent auditor to assess these internal controls and the financial statements. A *Wall Street Journal* editorial stated: "That's as much bureaucracy as any human should be forced to endure under the Geneva Convention."[37] Compliance costs—internal labor costs and audit fees—for Section 404 range from $690,000 to $2.87 million depending on the size of the company. Of the 1,200 smaller companies that responded to the SEC survey, 69.7 percent bluntly said that they have considered going private. At least 44 percent of the larger companies, supposedly better equipped to manage the systems and costs, felt the same.[38]

Despite these challenges, 90 percent of firms surveyed separately indicate pursuing dual strategies in which they consider both an IPO filing and a trade sale for their portfolios.[39] While the pain is obvious, it is likely that dual tracks offer a better negotiation leverage. "Dual track for an exit? Now that is a problem we'd love to have," says Bryce Roberts of O'Relly AlphaTech Ventures, a San Francisco-based early-stage fund with investments in social media companies like Foursquare, bitly, and Tripit. If the company is ready and the markets are favorable, the IPO is certainly a better option because most M&A transactions don't generate the killer returns that IPO exits do. For example, in 2009, only a fraction of deals had a return of 10 times or higher.[40]

Because IPO-ready companies can be affected by market downturns and regulations, the volume of investment returns for VC investors may be driven more by M&A exits than IPOs. Consequently, venture-backed M&As are efficient and faster exit options. By 2013, the total consideration of venture-backed M&As is predicted to reach $60 billion per year.[41]

When a company decides to make an IPO, it registers its securities with the SEC for sale to the general public. From a business perspective, it is a culmination of a longer strategic plan for the company. For entrepreneurs, the priority is to expand capital resources by tapping into the public equity markets for additional investors. For more established businesses, it signifies an exit strategy or a way to solidify investments. The benefits and costs are manifold. The advantages are evident, including enabling access to capital, exposure, and prestige; facilitating future acquisitions of other companies (partial payments in shares); enjoying access to multiple financing opportunities such as equity, convertible debt, and cheaper bank loans; and developing increased liquidity and a ready exit strategy.[42] The costs are also not to be ignored: loss of privacy as to matters regarding business operations; competition; disclosure of executive officers' compensation, material contracts, and customers; pressure from shareholders to perform and meet market expectations; time-consuming diplomacy in undergoing periodic reporting to investors and shareholders and regulatory compliance.

Not an Endgame, but a Financing Event

According to Ernst & Young, around 70 percent of start-up companies fail before they reach their IPO potential, with the majority of successful IPOs mostly around for at least five years before the transition.[43] Once on the public market, these companies must compete with other IPOs. Only 8 percent of offerings are competitive in terms of value and fair market value offered by peers in the industry.[44]

The metamorphosis from a private company to a publicly listed company is a daunting process, requiring massive strategic planning and cost-benefit analysis of markets and products, value chain activities, infrastructure (e.g., business information systems, compensation, plans, and redundant assets), governance and management structures, and other business components—from both financial and legal perspectives.[45] The process itself, timed from the decision to go public to the day the IPO transactions are closed, varies significantly. Several factors will affect the time line, such as how well the process is planned, how well the company is positioned in the market, the abilities of the management team and advisors, as well as factors outside the control of companies, such as market conditions, and the current regulatory environment.[46]

Researchers point out that when public markets are favorable, the experienced venture capitalists are quick to take advantage. After assessing over 40,000 transactions spanning over two decades, authors Paul Gompers et al. conclude that not only are the investments of the specialized VC organizations more successful, but there is no appreciable degradation with changing conditions.[47] One more reason that a top quartile VC firm is so appealing!

The IPO Process: The Long and Winding Road

The IPO journey can be divided into many different phases in which the actual IPO is seen as a significant milestone in an otherwise complex structural transformation. According to *Ernst & Young's Guide to Going Public*, there are essentially three main stages:[48]

- A planning stage, where the company commits to diligent preparation that includes conducting feasibility studies and readiness checks on the business and financials itself, as well as the market.
- An execution or implementation stage takes place, where the right management and advisory teams are established; financial infrastructure and accounting, tax, operational, and IT processes and systems are assessed; corporate structure and governance are established; and investor relations and corporate communication strategies and plans are managed.
- Finally, the company reaches a realization phase, where shares are priced and the IPO transaction closes.

In this preparatory stage, which takes place about one to two years before the IPO is set to take place, a company does its homework to assess the readiness to go IPO.

- *Prepare a compelling business plan.* The business plan should be long-term, covering 24 to 36 months before and after the IPO to provide a clear road map that can be embedded early in the organization.
- *Benchmark the portfolio company's performance.* Before deciding to go public, companies monitor their performance, tracking growth rates, sales performance, profitability, and market share. Companies should also measure themselves on other benchmarks, such as ensuring that their products and services are well-defined and assessing their reputation among various market stakeholders (e.g., customers, analysts, and investment banks). Aside from financials, reputation and brand name are important intangibles for leveraging a company's strength in the public markets.
- *Is this a public-ready company?* A compelling business track record and a plan to demonstrate how IPO funds will fuel growth is key. Is there growth? Rising profits? In the management team, what expertise gaps need to be filled for operating a public company? Also, does the

company have adequate budgetary systems in place with financial information readily available on a monthly and quarterly basis? What are the state of investor relationships and the corporate structure for transparent reporting to shareholders? In a survey of global institutional investors, respondents ranked the top nonfinancial factors leading to IPO success.[49] In order of priority these are:

- Management credibility and experience
- Quality of corporate strategy and its execution
- Brand strength and market position
- Operational effectiveness
- Corporate governance practices

After this soul-searching of the first stage in the IPO process, the second stage is where the company begins the practical preparation toward going IPO. Once the decision is made to go public, the company starts shifting toward a public structure and begins behaving and acting like a public company.

Steps to an IPO

After an IPO readiness assessment is completed, the steps to an IPO, as presented in Figure 12.6, include selection of underwriters, conducting the road show, and demand assessment.

Consider the road map to IPO for Google. To comply with SEC rules, Google had to consider disclosing its financial information. It found itself in a position where it had more than 500 shareholders and had 120 days from the end of the year to file the financial statements. Google faced three

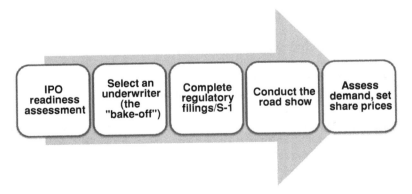

FIGURE 12.6 Steps to an IPO

choices: buy back shares from some shareholders, report financials publicly without selling any shares, or go public. Google had to present its financials by 2:00 P.M. on April 29, 2004. At 11:00 A.M., the company announced that it would be going public.

And prior to filing, Google realized neither NASDAQ or NYSE would list the offering, as they were short three board members. Companies preparing for IPO should take special care in building an independent and a strong company board that offers a broad mix of skills—from industry networks, technical knowledge, and expertise in business development to acquisition integration and financial analysis. Google was able to add three heavy hitters quickly—the president of Stanford University, the president of Intel, and the CEO of Genentech.

The "Bake-Off"   Investment banks compete for the issuing company's business during a process known as the "beauty contest" or "bake-off." The investment banks present their credentials to the company's board of directors, as well as their view of market conditions and challenges.

Company (or Issuer of Shares) Hires an Underwriter   The word *underwriter* is said to have come from the practice of having each risk-taker write his or her name under the total amount of risk that he or she was willing to accept at a specified premium. In a way, this is still true today. An underwriting syndicate brings new issues to market. Each firm takes the responsibility (and risk) of selling its specific allotment.

Underwriters or investment banks are hired to raise investment capital from investors on behalf of the company. This is a way of selling a newly issued security, such as common stock, to investors. Syndicates of banks (the lead managers) typically underwrite the transaction, which means they have taken on the risk of distributing the securities. Underwriters make their income from the price difference (the underwriting spread) between the price they pay the issuer and what they collect from investors or from broker-dealers who buy portions of the offering.

Google ended up with 31 underwriters—a long list, indicative of the eagerness of the middlemen. Several would drop off eventually. Credit Suisse and Morgan Stanley ended up with their names on the S1 filings.

File the S-1/Prospectus   Any company intending to go public is required to file a legal document known as the prospectus with the SEC. Registration is a two-part documentation process that involves Form S-1. Part 1 covers the prospectus, which serves as the primary documentation of disclosure to investors, detailing the operations and financial conditions of the company. Part 2 covers the supplemental information furnished to the SEC (copies of contracts, etc.). Once the SEC approves the company's registration statement, a final prospectus is released to investors.

The prospectus, which reads much like a business plan, includes the company's financial history and growth strategy, the details of its offering, and information on company management. It also outlines industry competition and other risk factors that investors would want to know in advance. In essence, the prospectus provides all the information investors need to know in order to decide whether to participate in the IPO. The preliminary prospectus is also known as a red herring because of the red ink used on the front page, which indicates that some information—including the price and size of the offering—is subject to change.

Quiet Period Begins   As soon as a company files a preliminary prospectus with the SEC, the quiet period begins. The company is prohibited from distributing any information not included in the prospectus. This period lasts for 25 days post IPO, after the shares start trading.

Sergey Brin and Larry Page did several things noteworthy at the time of the Google IPO, but the *Playboy* interview was the one that almost got them crossways with the SEC during the quiet period. A week before its celebrated IPO, the SEC caught wind of this interview, which had been conducted about five months prior. Eventually, this interview was included in its entirety in the S1 Prospectus as Appendix B. *Playboy* lost the exclusive interview to an inane SEC rule, and the media made some hay about it, as did the late-night comedians. As CEO Eric Schmidt quipped, it was a generic article, "without any pictures, I might add."[50] Phew!

The Road Show: Which City Are We In, Again?   Google did not have to struggle much with a road show as it decided to go down the Dutch auction path for selling its shares to the public. But the underwriter typically schedules dozens of meetings across the country. The CEO and his team, typically the CFO and other key executives, will join the tour during which the company pitches its business plan to institutional investors: mutual funds, endowments, or pension funds. At these meetings, the underwriter attempts to gauge the level of interest in the IPO, which helps lead to a decision on how to price the stock offering.

Book building is the process by which an underwriter attempts to determine at what price to offer an IPO based on demand from institutional investors. An underwriter builds a book by accepting orders from fund managers indicating the number of shares they desire and the price they are willing to pay. The book runner is the managing or lead underwriter who maintains, or runs, the books of securities sold for a new issue. Often the book runner is given credit for the total size of the deal.[51]

Following the road show, the company prints its final prospectus, distributes it to potential investors, and files it with the SEC.

Great Demand, or Put It on Ice?　And after all the road show presentations are complete, if the demand from the institutions is feeble, the underwriters will recommend that you put the offering on ice. Let it chill. And someday, hopefully, it will be springtime. Or if you are a Facebook or Zynga, skip this step and go to those secondary markets.

IPO Underpricing and Dutch Auctions

IPOs generate strong returns for investors, as seen earlier in Table 12.1 and here in Figure 12.7. But IPOs can be underpriced by as much as 15 percent, thanks to an incestuous relationship between underwriters and institutional investors.

The goal, when pricing an IPO, should be to establish an offering price that is low enough to stimulate interest in the stock but high enough to raise an adequate amount of capital for the company. The process of determining an optimal price usually involves the underwriters (syndicate) arranging share purchase commitments from leading institutional investors.

In order to balance the needs of the investor and the issuing company, the investment bank traditionally tries to price a deal so that the first-day

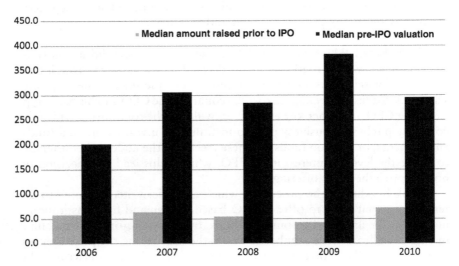

FIGURE 12.7　IPOs Can Generate Superior Returns
Source: Dow Jones VentureSource.

TABLE 12.4 Money Left on the Table: Instant Transfer of Wealth from Company to Those That Received IPO Allocations, Thanks to the Underwriters.

Company	IPO Offer Price	First Closing Market Price	Shares	Money Left on the Table ($M)
VMWare	$29	$51	33,000,000	$726
Akamai Technologies	$26	$145.1	9,000,000	$1,072
Goldman Sachs	$53	$70.3	55,200,000	$959
Blackstone Group	$31	$35.6	133,333,000	$622

Source: "Money Left on the Table in IPOs," Jay R. Ritter, University of Florida.

pop is about 15 percent.[52] This is a nice gift that benefits underwriters (the company pays the price) and their institutional investor friends—this incestuous cycle may seal the next investment opportunity that may be led by the underwriter.

Underwriters may claim that the effect of initial underpricing of an IPO generates additional interest in the stock when it first becomes publicly traded. But in reality, those institutional friends make an instant 15 percent. This results in money left on the table—lost capital that could have gone to the company had the stock been offered at a higher price. The company all along believes that the underwriters are representing its interests, but in reality the underwriters want to just get the deal done—the costs can be borne by the company, after all.

Table 12.4 outlines a few examples where either underpricing or frothy market conditions led to instant transfer of wealth from a company to those institutions that received IPO allocations.

The danger of overpricing is an important consideration for venture investors. If a stock is offered to the public at a higher price than the market will pay, the underwriters may have trouble meeting their commitments to sell shares. Even if they sell all the issued shares, if the stock falls in value on the first day of trading, it may lose its marketability and hence even more of its value. This can have emotional consequences and hence most companies would rather succumb to the 15 percent loss.

The Dutch Auction: Eliminate the Pop and Those Middlemen Google is an unconventional company in every way—even its IPO was a case study of sorts. Eric Schmidt, CEO of Google, did not like this pop—this 15 percent that should be in the hands of the company—and pushed for a Dutch auction. "I know this may sound like baloney, but we settled decisively on the Dutch auction after we got a letter from a little old lady who asked why she couldn't make money from the IPO the way the stockbrokers would. We thought she had a point about the basic fairness of the system," he wrote.[53]

A Dutch auction is an attempt to minimize the extreme underpricing that underwriters establish. In a Dutch auction, individuals could log on to their brokerage accounts and bid for a certain number of shares, say 500 shares. Or bid for shares for a certain amount, say $1,000. After the auction was completed, the company would establish a price and the individual bidders would receive a certain allocation of shares. "We liked this approach because it was consistent with the auction-based business model we used to sell our ads—it had a strong intuitive appeal for us," Google CEO Eric Schmidt would say.[54]

Such auctions threaten large fees otherwise payable to underwriter syndicates. Google had as many as 31 underwriters at the table when contemplating the IPO path, but ignored the conventional. Although not the first company to use Dutch auction, no company the size of Google had ever done such a thing. Google's share price rose 17 percent in its first day of trading despite the auction method. Wall Street was angry—it felt left out of one of the biggest IPOs of the time. "Don't bother to bid on this shot-in-the-dark IPO," said *BusinessWeek*. The *Wall Street Journal* ran a front page article—"How Miscalculation and Hubris Hobbled Celebrated Google IPO." Miffed underwriters actively discouraged institutional investors from buying, to punish Google, reduce demand, and send the initial price down. But for Google, a successful IPO was one where average investors, not necessarily big institutions, eventually gained from the underpricing.

IPO Deterrents: Regulatory Challenges Besides the dreaded Section 404 discussed earlier, there are plenty of deterrents to IPOs. The time, expenses, and scrutiny by regulators can be intense and demanding.

In a study conducted by Grant Thornton, authors David Weild and Edward Kim concluded that the deterrents to IPOs started when Wall Street ignored the small cap companies and thus killed the IPOs. The IPOs that raise $50 million or less declined sharply between 1996 and 2000. For example, in 1991, over 75 percent of all IPOs were in the sub-$50 million category and this number fell precipitously to below 20 percent by 2009. The losers in this trend were clearly those who profited from the IPO markets—VCs, investment bankers, and research analysts. The authors offer several recommendations, including an opt-in capital market and research requirements that provide the same structure that served the nation in good stead for so many years. This would revive the investment banks that supported IPO markets and possibly rejuvenate investment activity and innovation.[55]

In a survey of 116 private equity fund managers conducted by the Tuck School of Business at Dartmouth, 41 percent cited expenses of at least

$1 million in the first year of implementation alone for their companies due to the requirement to adhere to Sarbanes-Oxley regulations. More than one-third of PE firms reported that at least one of their portfolio companies was deterred from filing for an IPO as a result of these regulatory burdens.[56]

Post IPO: Should VCs Stay Engaged? After the rapture and thrill of the IPO settles, and the tombstones have been proudly distributed, a question comes up: Should a VC stay involved with a public company? A successful IPO outcome is a financing event and not a guarantee of long-term success of the company. With analysts and shareholders eagerly watching the ticker price run across the board at the stock exchange, the CEO is under pressure to deliver consistent earnings and growth. And this leads to an interesting conundrum for any practitioner: Should I stay and help the CEO become successful? Or should I keep my fiduciary responsibility to my LPs and move on to the next portfolio company? No easy answers here. Lip-Bu Tan of Walden International says, "I think it is a big mistake when a VC resigns from the board when a company is going public. That's when the CEO needs the most help. Being a public company is very unforgiving—the CEO is in the public eye and trying to live life by the quarterly earnings and with a VC's skills and expertise, you can help the CEO and the company to become a stable and a strong company."[57]

Seth Rudnick of Canaan Partners, who has led at least half a dozen companies to the IPO stage, differs in his views. "As a venture investor, you're looking at a number of metrics: What's best for the company, what's the IRR that you're getting for your investors? How do all the other investors in the company benefit? And those are all very complicated decisions. Frankly, at Canaan Partners we strongly urge all of our partners who are in companies that go public to get off the boards so that the decisions then become simply those that you would make as an investor rather than as a board member," he says. "I think you get too confounded, you know, you love the company, you want to stay on it, you want to stay involved but the dynamics are much different now."[58]

For Brad Feld of the Foundry Group, the choice is easy. "Forget your ego, do what your LPs want you to do," he says.[59] For a VC who is engaged with a public company, the responsibilities and liabilities become significant. Reporting, disclosures, insurance, insider trading issues—the game changes substantially. Factors such as the performance of the company, publicity, and liability risk are key parameters of consideration for any VC who wishes to stay on the board of a publicly traded company. In the proverbial limelight, public companies have a strong incentive to avoid any negative publicity that will adversely affect the stock price. Delivering financial statements in a transparent and timely way, whether annually or quarterly, gives investors and analysts continued assurance and confidence in the company. Companies that use IPO capital for growth purposes—to move into new markets, develop new products and services, as well as enhance marketing and branding continuously—keep investors happy. But in recent times, a third exit option—private exchanges—has evolved. Rich Levandov, an investor in Zynga, says, "Zynga could go public if it wanted to, but we choose not to. The secondary markets reduce some pressures on founders and investors."[60]

PRIVATE EXCHANGES: NECESSITY DRIVES LIQUIDITY SOLUTIONS

Till a few years ago, the prospect of selling shares of private companies may have been a challenge. But we have one more reason to be thankful to Facebook. A few big-name web companies have come on the scene in the past decade, prior to which it was inefficient for the investors on Sand Hill Road to enjoy a partial liquidity event. Wide-open exchanges for private company shares were pretty much nonexistent until now.

Now the trading of shares for private technology firms like Facebook, Groupon, and Twitter is becoming more and more the norm, with the revolution led by New York-based SecondMarket and Los Angeles-based SharesPost. In the first half of 2009, both of these firms started offering trading of private company stock.[61] Since then, there has been a groundswell of trading of shares of Silicon Valley giants such as Facebook, Twitter, and LinkedIn.

Venture capitalists have relied on two primary exit options—a trade sale via an acquisition or the IPO. Most firms that remain private offer some kind of ownership or stake to employees, venture capitalists, and other institutional investors. Some of these want to cash out, while others want to buy more. In the past, employees in private companies couldn't sell their shares for a reason—to incentivize increasing their value in anticipation of a future liquidation event. But in challenging times, "this incentive is now largely moot, since the IPO and M&A markets had effectively shut down," claims Greg Brogger, SharesPost's CEO.[62] To Brogger, the workaround of the private exchange makes sense and is a necessity. "People still need to buy houses and cars and send kids to college. [Having a private exchange] makes people's shares somewhat liquid."[63] What's more, most VC funds are 10-year funds. "They need to do something with their shares, and [private exchanges make] it possible to more easily close out at least some of their positions."[64] Finally, in an economic environment hostile to IPOs, a venue for entrepreneurs, venture capitalists, and employees to cash out makes sense. All these challenges present a ripe opportunity for innovative trading solutions—an if-you-build-it-they-will-come proposition.

Private exchanges generally function by having an intermediary take shares from sellers or companies and actively find buyers, a process that can drag into weeks—completely out of sync with the fast-paced world of trading. SecondMarket and SharesPost simplify the process by offering an auction-style system, formalizing the market-clearing process with more ease and transparency. So far, SecondMarket and SharesPost have been very popular. Brogger of SharesPost has cited angel investors and senior management of private companies as big users. "Those people are not necessarily looking to sell all of their position in a company, but want some amount of liquidity for their shares."[65]

Facebook, for example, has always been coy about its plans to go public.[66] But in a recent move that has set analysts and Wall Street buzzing, Facebook teamed up with Goldman Sachs, raising nearly half a billion dollars, as well as raising an additional $1.5 billion through a "special purpose vehicle" that enables the investment bank's clients special access to Facebook.[67] The move was riddled with legal complications (particularly, the SEC 500 shareholder limit). For Facebook to go IPO, the company has to release financial information.[68] In addition, with inflated valuation to over $50 billion, the pressure on pricing the shares appropriately will be a minor challenge, but the regulatory hurdles can be a deterrent. Early investors are especially keen on the legitimate transition/exit as a way to cash in some of their earnings. Heralding a new era of exits, Accel Partners sold about 15 percent of its stake ($517 million) in Facebook.[69] Activity on private exchanges, SecondMarket, and SharesPost intensified soon after the big sale. The following month, the average valuation of Facebook transactions on SharesPost increased almost 25 percent to more than $56 billion; SecondMarket reported similar swells with Facebook and other companies, transacting nearly $400 million in private company stocks in 2010.[70] While still a fraction of what is traded in public exchanges like the New York Stock Exchange and Nasdaq, private exchanges have brought a much needed third exit option to venture practitioners.

SharesPost versus SecondMarket

The two companies deliver their services in distinct ways. SharesPost works by connecting buyers and sellers through bulletin boards. Every private company on the site is represented on its own bulletin board, where requests are posted "with the highest price posting for shares at the top of the list for buyers, and the reverse for sellers."[71] Interested parties who want to buy or sell then visit the bulletin board and find the most attractive bid and ask prices—a process Brogger has dubbed "price discovery."[72] SharesPost handles the paperwork for transactions and clears all the money through an arrangement with U.S. Bank.

Not everyone can nab shares of offerings on SharesPost. While there are no limitations on sellers wanting to unload stock, buyers generally have to have substantial invested assets and experience under SEC Regulation D. Each transaction is a hefty, velvet-rope-worthy $2,500.[73] But SharesPost is also careful not to market itself as a brokerage firm that profits from the transactions by taking a cut. Instead, it charges a basic site user fee of $34 per month, and revenue is indifferent to whether transactions clear and whether the stock is sold. SharesPost has posted nearly 150 private company stock transactions a year since it started operations.[74]

SecondMarket employs a more traditional broker-dealer arrangement, overseeing trading and taking in commissions in the amount of 2 to 5 percent depending on the deal, equally split between buyer and seller.[75] While SharesPost uses a more hands-off, bulletin-listing system, SecondMarket can be likened to an electronic auction like eBay, with brokers waiting in the wings. Using the online bulletin board, sellers post their stocks. SecondMarket grades buyers based on the type and volume of deals they have done in the past or demonstrated an interest in. Buyers with the strongest grades get a call from a SecondMarket rep and begin the negotiation process. Like SharesPost, SecondMarket sorts out the paperwork, but it also pockets a commission.

SecondMarket seems to be outgrowing itself. It has started the networking process overseas with bankers and government officials and may be brokering deals with Asian shipping companies and palm oil plantations soon, as well as targeting companies in Israel, Brazil, and other emerging markets.

Trading in this way has raised concerns among investors and those involved in the companies about potential abuse, such as the flouting of regulations and laws, insider trading, or massive offloading or buying.[76] Still, people are hopeful about the future of private exchanges. Barry Silbert, SecondMarket's CEO, has boasted that this embodies "Wall Street 3.0"—defined as "using technology and doing things in a transparent way to bring trust back into the system."[77]

Private exchanges could also ultimately benefit an eventual IPO of a VC-backed company. Strong investor attention to companies on private exchanges acts as a barometer of success and could prompt bullish interest in firms before they debut on the public market. The frenzy of trading activity on private exchanges like SharesPost and SecondMarket for companies like Facebook and Zynga affirm their worth and can be the pilot run on their IPO-worthiness in the future. But as is evident, only those with mass recognition and demand can benefit from such exchanges. For the rest, the basics of value creation will be the order of the day.

SUMMARY

For any practitioner (and any LP), the exit of an investment is a much anticipated event. However, according to NVCA 2010 yearbook, as many as 30 percent of all VC-backed companies were either still hanging around in the portfolio or had quietly shut down.

Savvy practitioners do not necessarily aim for premature exits—rather they work toward building companies that generate value for customers, and are financially sound. For such companies, exit options are always plentiful and never at the mercy of markets. Alternate exit options, such as sale of the company to a private equity group, or redemption, are likely scenarios but not presented in this section.

This completes the major elements of the investment cycle. The final chapter touches on attributes and attitudes of successful practitioners.

CHAPTER 13

Summing Up

A Sherpa is someone who carries heavy payloads, up tall mountains, for low wages where the oxygen is scarce. There is no glow in this job ... it is a lot of work.

—K. Ram Shriram, angel investor in Google and Founder of
Sherpalo Ventures[1]

No other profession offers as great a combination of intellectual stimulation, financial gain, freedom/autonomy, and the thrill of building companies! The business of venture capital is an intellectually demanding, adrenalin-laden career path. A high-wire balancing act! Michael Moritz of Sequoia Capital says, "Every day is composed of a hundred soap operas—it's an exhilarating place to live and work."[2]

But how does one become a good player in the game of VC? The best advice I got was from Chris Rizik, a former VC who now manages a fund-of-funds. "A good VC has three qualities: First, have a good sense of the world around you and how it is changing. After all, we put money behind ideas that change the world—the demographic, technological—unfilled needs. You have to be open and curious to look out into the future.

"The second quality is Patience—nothing will be as fast as you want. A smart VC never panics or gives up when companies hit a bump. Those who are patient will not only profit but will ultimately succeed at the expense of those who panic. Patience should be married with intelligence—if you can no longer achieve the end game, it takes discipline to walk away and say, we are just not going to get there. Swallow hard and realize you just lost a few million.

"Finally, the third quality is to be fair with one and all. What goes around, comes around—in the end, the best VCs are people who were fair, were smart and treated everyone well. People seldom want to work with those who are out only for themselves."

And here are a few attitudes and aptitudes of successful practitioners—as you will see, there is no one quality, or a pattern, but these few stand out.

APTITUDES AND ATTITUDES OF SUCCESSFUL PRACTITIONERS

Successful practitioners demonstrate a strong drive, are unstoppable and tenacious, and are constantly evolving their own expertise and brand.

Drive: Entrepreneurial and Intellectual

"I don't think there is a good predictor that just because someone has an operating or entrepreneurial background that they are going to be a good venture capitalist. Conversely, if you don't, it doesn't mean you are not going to be a good venture capitalist," Mark Andreessen said once, while speaking at a Stanford Entrepreneurship forum.[3]

What is more important is that successful venture capitalists have an entrepreneurial mind-set—the ability to understand the basics of value creation. The background of some of the leading venture capitalists demonstrates no clear pattern. John Doerr of KPCB worked in engineering/sales roles at Monsanto and Intel. Vinod Khosla, who left KPCB to start Khosla Ventures, was the co-founder of Sun Microsystems. Tom Perkins had established his entrepreneurial credentials at Hewlett-Packard and University Labs, a company he led from launch to exit.[4] Consider these two diametrically opposite views on being a venture capitalist, the first from John Doerr of KPCB and the second from David Cowan of Bessemer Venture Partners:

I think you become a venture capitalist by being a great entrepreneur. As a successful entrepreneur, you can better figure out how to serve entrepreneurs in their mission. So those folks in the business school who figured they, like roll out of the womb born as a venture capitalist, I don't think they're going to be great venture capitalists. I think they should go get a job at a high technology company or a start-up. And then see if they want to step back from where the real action is into the world I work in, which is much more indirect and supporting entrepreneurs.[5]

As I was finishing up my MBA, I was told, "You don't have anything to bring to the table. The last thing a CEO wants is some snot-nosed MBA telling him how to run his business. So go get some real

experience." I had to reject the prescription and carve my own path.
Venture capital is what I really want to do. Operational experience
is a short-term advantage. It helps a venture professional to assess
and manage investment opportunities but only in their sectors of
expertise.[6]

David Cowan of Bessemer Venture Partners rejects the notion that even entrepreneurial experience is a prerequisite. "Entrepreneurs have expertise in certain domains. But in venture, domains shift all the time. And when exposed to any opportunity, those with operating expertise tend to try and fix things—that can, at times, be counterproductive," he says. Rightfully so, several practitioners who had very strong entrepreneurial background concurred that the hardest part for them was to transition from being a player to being a coach—to let go and let someone else run their own company. They get impatient, question the pace of execution, or the direction. Entrepreneurial success for VCs, if not modulated, can translate to being a royal pain in the rear for portfolio company CEOs.

Gibson Myers, emeritus partner, Mayfield Fund, once remarked, "Some people are just operating people. It's a whole different world to go to work, make things happen, be tangible, grow this, it's really yours. And those people don't transition to venture capital very well, because they want to operate. In venture capital, you're one or two steps removed from that, and you're advising. You have a relationship. You have a bunch of companies. You can't spend the time, so some just don't like it for that reason, or don't make it as a venture capitalist.[7]

While David Cowan does not feel that an entrepreneurial background is essential to be successful, his own entrepreneurial experiments started in high school when his father brought home an IBM PC. The heady days of DOS[8] and 5.25-inch floppy drives! David's father, an attorney of modest means but high ideals, constantly nudged David to take meaningful risks. The ingredients were right—mix some hardware, DOS, and a nurturing family with a Type A, and there you have it—an entrepreneur in the making!

David's first software product was market driven: It solved a real problem. At his father's law firm, young David saw that journals were circulated using distribution lists. Creating these lists was a laborious task—the variables were based on the reading preferences of each individual, the lawyer's seniority at the law firm, and the type of journal. David bought a manual, figured out the building blocks of a database management system, and developed his first software product. Built on dBase II, Dataroute could help design and manage the pecking order of distribution lists. The librarian at the law firm loved it: It reduced her workload of sorting and managing lists. And his father's firm became a reference account—a beta site, if you will.

David established his start-up, Cambridge Data Systems, and went on to sell Dataroute to several law firms on Wall Street, including major accounts like the Federal Reserve and even Microsoft's private library. "I could pay my way through college," he recalls. "You have to believe that the world can change ... be optimistic and at the same time be realistic and guarded, not romantic,"[9] says Terry McGuire, co-founder, Polaris Ventures, and chairman emeritus of the National Venture Capital Association.

Michael Moritz of Sequoia Capital does not have either entrepreneurial or operational expertise—he was a business journalist with *Time* magazine and crossed paths with Don Valentine of Sequoia while working on a book. Michael has gone on to invest in leading companies such as Google, Yahoo!, and YouTube and generate substantial returns for his investors.

Never Say Never: Be an Unstoppable Force

If you look at successful venture practitioners such as David Cowan, Jan Garfinkle, who started Arboretum Ventures, or Vinod Khosla, they all exhibit one special characteristic: Never take no for an answer!

Once Cowan was headed to enjoy a B-school break in Greece. When he reached the airport a few hours before his international flight, he discovered that his passport had expired ... just the day before.[10] Cowan decided to, against all odds, make an attempt to renew his passport and catch that very flight. Most international travelers would fret, fume, and head back home or to the bar. Cowan hopped into a cab, rushed to the passport office, filled out an application form, and realized he did not have the required photographs. He rushed out to take pictures, then headed back to the passport offices ... he waved his arms ... renewed his passport before you could gulp that cappuccino, and made a mad dash back to the airport. He found that his flight to Dallas, which would connect him to Athens, had just left Logan airport. S#$%%$##%$! But wait ... he discovered that he could hop on another flight to Dallas. En route to Dallas, he even asked the flight attendant whether they could "fly faster." A photo finisher as a marathon runner, he got on the Athens flight seconds—yes, seconds—before the gates were being closed. And when he did board the flight to Athens, he laughed out loud in triumph. At every step, every person David encountered—cab drivers, flight agents, passport officers, photographers, over 15 of them—said, "You will never make that flight." And David just kept on pursuing his goal with unwavering determination. That should give you an insight into how little he cared about public opinion or protocols. Or indulged in self-pity or remorse. Those who have read Cowan's blog[11] on this incident compare it to an episode of the famous Fox TV series *24*. Others say that this is a story for your grandchildren. "Amazing," "What a beautiful story," and "You had me cheering for you all the way" were some of the other responses. The entrepreneur in David is evident—get to the destination against all odds.

At Wharton, the admissions officer did not think Jan Garfinkle would be well suited for an MBA. Her background in engineering was not aligned with the mainstream approach of economics. And in the 1980s, Jan was the only female student in engineering and one of the few who wanted to pursue an MBA. Despite Jan's high scores on the GMAT, he suggested she should try her hand at something else. She ended up on the waitlist. A disappointed Jan headed out for a brisk jog and after 30 minutes returned to the admissions office to give it one more shot. Jan, who has mastered the gentle art of being assertive without being obnoxious, reaffirmed her desire to join Wharton and requested that the admissions officer reconsider. "He looked at me, bewildered, and then said, okay, well, come back tomorrow and we will get it done," recalls Jan, who completed her MBA at Wharton. She would go on to meet the future CEOs of Guidant and Medtronic through a summer internship at Eli Lilly and Company, and both would play an important role in the development of ArboretumVentures—her venture fund. Jan's career path would likely have headed in a different direction if she had given up.

And Vinod Khosla would have stayed in Pittsburgh if he was not persistent. While studying at Carnegie Mellon University, he was eager to reach the Valley. "The draw of the Valley for me is an entrepreneurial draw unlike anything else about United States," he says. He applied to the Stanford Graduate School of Business but was turned down. "They asked me to get some work experience. I did get a job in Pittsburgh and applied again, and of course, they turned me down again,"[12] Khosla would recount. "I yelled and screamed at the Director of Admissions. To get me off his back, he put me on the wait list." At his third attempt, Vinod was getting disheartened, but he did not give up. "Over the summer, I got to know everyone at the Admissions office; they became my friends. But even then, the Director did not let me in. The day before registration, I called him and said I am leaving Pittsburgh tomorrow morning. You like it or not, I am showing up at your door," he would recall. The Director finally caved in, and within a few hours, Vinod packed up and left Pittsburgh. "I had no place to go, so the Admissions Office staff put me up for a month," he remembers. And thus, he came to the Valley and founded a blazing start-up called Sun Microsystems and, after a successful stint at KPCB, Khosla Ventures.

Jack of All and Master of All

While there is no good predictor of what makes a good venture capitalist, some patterns are obvious. Those without substantial start-up or operating experience can gain an entry in the profession. At the entry level, passion combined with subject-matter or domain expertise matters. A PhD certainly helps. "Back in the seventies when I started, you could be a generalist and be successful in this business. As the business has evolved over the past 50 years, it has become a lot more focused around certain sectors and now, you need to be an expert in a few areas that matter," says Frank Caufield, the "C" in the legendary venture firm KPCB.[13]

While domain expertise may be a good starting point, it certainly is not of significant importance in the long run. David Cowan's example is striking. "In my 20-year career as a venture capitalist, I have invested in all kinds of domains and companies. For long-term success in this business, you have to think more generally and push yourself out of your comfort zone. You should be willing to reinvent yourself," he says. While a specialist in the technology sector, Cowan remains a generalist within the domain. He creates investment road maps and then, like the mythological Shiva, destroys them when the markets become heated.

When Seth Levine is not managing his investments at the Foundry Group, he blogs on how to teach your child to ride a bicycle. He says that a good practitioner needs to have some ADD—attention deficit disorder. In his "Attributes of a Good VC" blog, he jokes that ADD may be a necessary and a much-desirable condition to be a good venture capitalist. He writes:

> *The core of being a good VC is the ability to move from one thing to the next, often completely disconnected thing, quickly and without slowing down. Rare is the time when I sit down and spend a few hours doing something (anything) without interruption; so much so that I generally interrupt myself these days if I'm spending too much time on any one thing, but mostly because in any given day things just seem to come up constantly. With something like 8 companies that I actively work with these interruptions are all over the map—I may be helping one company sell its business, another raise capital, another plan for a strategic offsite and another with an executive search. Keeping all of this straight in my head is a bit of a task, as is shifting gears from talking about the tax considerations of a particular merger structure with one company to looking at moving into a new vertical market for another.[14]*

And how do the skills of a good practitioner evolve with the growth of the company? Promod Haque, managing partner at Norwest Venture Partners, says "Being a venture capitalist requires a varying degree of skills. At a seed stage, the skills required are different from say, investments at a mid or later stage." Norwest manages $3.7 billion in assets over multiple funds and Promod came to the world of venture capital with nearly two decades of operating experience. "At the seed stage, we have a founder and an opening—a white space in the market." A white space is defined as a place where a company might have room to maneuver in a crowded playing field. "The venture practitioner needs to have the ability to understand risk, validate ideas, and connect these to the market. Exploration and validation are key steps at this stage," Promod explains. "Now, as the company progresses, the skills to recruit people to a start-up become essential. A start-up is a no-name entity—the credibility and track record of the venture practitioner can be a tremendous asset in recruiting management talent. And you need talent that can grow the company—such talent is usually in high demand and otherwise would not be available to the start-up. In the early stage, the practitioner's ability to help the start-up to find customers is very important." And Fortune 100 companies—those marquee customers that all start-ups seek—unfortunately avoid start-ups. "They are trying to minimize the number of vendors and stick with the proven ones ... even if you get your foot in the door, these companies need time and ability to assess the new product. It's a significant commitment ... these are extremely busy executives and asking them to check a new product out requires strong suite of skills. As the company evolves further, the ability to syndicate the investment becomes critical. Other investors will look at how you are putting the investment rationale and leading the round," he says.[15]

A good practitioner has a mix of sales, technical, human resources, financial, and business strategy skills. And while entrepreneurial experience is important or even overhyped, several leading venture professionals do not have a string of start-ups to their name but demonstrate a healthy mix of these qualities.

Comfort in Ambiguity

Successful practitioners make rapid decisions in ambiguous, fast-changing environments. They are able to make good judgment calls even in trying circumstances. "Let me give you an example," says John Hummer, who is presently training for his pilot's license. "I was getting ready to land the aircraft when we noticed that clouds had descended below 800 feet. The tailwind was high at nine knots. Such a combination of cloud and winds is not conducive for a safe landing. We had a few minutes to process this information and make the call." John decided not to land the plane, and the instructor agreed, but now threw in the final emotional conundrum: "Now that you have decided not to land, add in a hypothetical situation that any pilot can face—your girlfriend is anxiously waiting at the airport for you." John promptly countered, "I can always explain the conditions to her and ask for forgiveness, but I cannot risk any lives ... no way! And this business is not quite different: you have to consider the key variables and make the judgment call or face the consequences."[16]

Relentless Focus on Value Creation

For most successful practitioners, value creation starts at home and extends to the entrepreneurs and LPs. Seth Levine of the Foundry Group advises that aspirants should know how the venture fund makes money.

> *Understand the math. As a non-partner you are fundamentally a cost center. The partners are quite literally taking money out of their own pockets and giving it to you. Rationally, they will only do this for one of two reasons—either you are significantly impacting their lives in a positive way that makes the trade-off worthwhile for them (you cost less than the marginal life benefit they get from having you around) and/or you will help create more carry (i.e., they can manage more deals with you around and therefore deploy more capital; you have a skill set that will positively affect the portfolio, etc.). If you fail to do these things you are just eating up management fees.*[17]

The successful practitioners started by creating value for the senior partners, the firm, their portfolio companies, and their investors. Those who are fixated on fame, fortune, and glory should head a little farther south of Sand Hill Road to Hollywood.

And while performance matters in the long run, in the short run it is more about the chemistry within the firm. Else adding value may be even a bigger challenge. Brant Moxley, managing director at Pinnacle Group International, an executive recruiting firm that focuses on private equity career opportunities, points out, "It's not as much about the quantitative skills as it is about chemistry and fit within a firm's culture. Your geek factor is not important, but the fact that you are fluid, smooth ... you can get inside the firm ... have a beer with the partners at 10 P.M. on Friday night. It is amazing how many times some very smart people were let go because they were lacking in interpersonal skills. At the end of the day, this is no different than a small business with about half a dozen people."[18]

Successful practitioners extend value creation into the community and beyond. Brad Feld reminds us that we should be a force for good in the world. When he is not looking at cool companies like Zynga or running marathons, he is testifying for creation of a start-up visa program and pushing for changes in immigration laws. Or helping entrepreneurs with the TechStars incubation program. When Jan Garfinkle started Arboretum Ventures, she launched Sprouts—a life sciences networking and educational event series in Ann Arbor. Todd Dagres, founder of Spark Capital and investor in Twitter, helped start a charity focused on vascular malformations and tumors that cause severe birthmarks and disfigurement in newborns.

A Balanced Yin and Yang

Most venture professionals agree that the required skill set includes a good mix of the yin and the yang—the head and the heart, or people skills and an analytical mind-set.

Rob Hayes, managing partner of First Round Capital, says, "The part that is really overlooked is that a VC needs to be a good therapist. Any CEO will tell you that it's the loneliest job in the world. You have to lead, be upbeat and confident . . . every CEO has doubts of hitting the next milestone, the next customer, or the next capital raise. A good VC is someone who can host an open, transparent discussion and even give them a pep talk. At times, the founders get at each other's throats. It's very easy for VCs to get prescriptive and that's not helpful—what is helpful is giving them the tools to manage the issues and become stronger."[19]

"VC doesn't necessarily take technical talent—it doesn't hurt—but it's more about people skills and the ability to assess whether there's a market for something," C. Richard Kramlich, founder of the leading venture firm New Enterprise Associates (NEA), once said.[20] The abilities to negotiate, to sell, and to build a strong network of relationships, along with a deeply analytical mind, are paramount in equal proportions. "Of course, there is this thing called judgment," Frank Caufield adds. And judgment is honed with experience. To sift through vast amounts of information, draw conclusions, and act in a somewhat ambiguous, fast-moving arena sums it all up.

Venture practitioners listed intellectual stimulation, financial gain, and freedom/autonomy as the top three reasons for seeking this career path.[21] Several practitioners I talked to also expressed the innate desire to "make an impact" and "to be a small part of something big." By investing in technologies and companies that change lives, practitioners believe that they will achieve their sense of purpose and life mission.

The profession is unique in that it provides the opportunity to interact with some of the best and brightest business, technology, and financial minds, all of whom are seeking new frontiers. There's no dearth of intellectual stimulation here!

If expectations of superior returns are tempered with reality, the road becomes easier—venture investing is a long-term play, not a get-rich-quick scheme. And generating returns for your investors comes first—you stand second in line. As Guy Kawasaki writes, who wouldn't want a job that pays $500,000 a year plus a piece of YouTube?

DRAWBACKS

There are a number of drawbacks to a career in venture capital. Steve Jobs of Apple fame does not seem to be impressed by this class as a whole—he once said VC "sounds like a bullshit job to me."[22] Entrepreneurs, particularly those who did not make it big due to paucity of capital, look at VCs as vultures, or worse, evil. And there are some 8,000 practitioners in the business in the United States, but few have consistently generated significant returns. You could very well end up in the also-rans.

Getting in is not easy, from a career perspective. And if you get in, the universe of top performers is very small. Mark Andreessen once said, "I don't believe there is such a thing as a VC industry. There are about forty firms that really do well as investors and over six hundred firms that will break your heart as an investor. A handful of firms generate all the returns and a lot of firms want to generate those returns."[23]

Playing this game with the "A" firms that matter is certainly not an easy task for wannabes. In a world of one-hit wonders, consistency matters. Andrew Metrick, a professor at the Yale School of Management and author of *Venture Capital and the Finance of Innovation*, has created a subjective top-tier list of venture capitalists, shown in Table 13.1. Top-tier venture capitalists get to charge higher profits—as much as 30 percent, as opposed to the standard 20 percent. Factors used in developing this list were consistency

TABLE 13.1   Top-Tier Venture Capitalists: A Subjective "A List"

Name	Founded	Capital under Management ($B)
Accel Partners	1983	$6.0
Benchmark Capital	1995	$2.9
Charles River Ventures	1970	$2.4
Kleiner Perkins Caufield & Byers	1972	$3.3
Matrix Partners	1982	$4.1
Sequoia Capital	1971	$4.0

Source: *Venture Capital and Finance of Innovation, Second Edition*, by Andrew Metrick & Ayako Yasuda (2010). Reprinted with permission of John Wiley & Sons, Inc.

of top-quartile performance, history of innovative strategy, and reputation in the industry.

Once you get in, staying in the business of venture capital is easy only as long as you can generate superior returns. Successful practitioners continuously need to adapt themselves over economic cycles and sectoral shifts. The one and only measure of the business: returns are a function of capital invested and time. So as the clock keeps ticking, your IRR keeps dropping. Worse, in bad markets and recessionary times, the ability to exit an investment slows down, not to mention the potential value of the return. But investors and LPs really don't care for any excuses. Be prepared to be voted off the island—your numbers will tell you when it is your turn to leave.

Finally, the business calls for the ability to handle multiple, complex, and pressing situations; to maintain your drive and discipline; to prioritize tasks; and to be comfortable with ambiguity. It calls for a mental tenacity—not becoming exhausted by the times you must say no, turn people down, or throw water on someone's great idea without being abrasive. Returns matter but how you play the game matters as much. And patience is a virtue as well as an asset when investments do not yield returns quickly enough.

WHAT ABOUT LUCK?

For a few chosen practitioners, the entry into VC was not an uphill crawl or a series of grueling interviews. It was a calling—a blaring siren. Bryce Roberts was planning to go to law school and in the interim decided to start a ski company in Jackson Hole, Wyoming. "One of my neighbors, a venture capitalist, invited me to sit in on pitch meetings and offer feedback," he says. Bryce went on to be the co-founder of O'Reilly Alphatec Ventures, which has invested in leading social media companies like Foursquare, Bit.ly, and Tripit.

Jack Ahrens, co-founder of TGap Ventures, has been in the venture business for over 30 years. Employed at a bank in Illinois, one afternoon he stumbled upon an internal memo that suggested his department was being shut down. "I was irritated and told my boss I would be leaving." His boss promptly jumped in: "We have a venture capital arm—what if we made you the president and gave you a raise?" "I took it—I barely knew what the heck venture capital was, but here I am some three decades later," says Jack. In these three decades, Jack has led over 35 successful exits, including twenty IPOs. Interestingly, neither Bryce nor Jack has the desire to grow his fund size beyond what is manageable. My own observation is that if they wished, they could easily raise a lot more capital and increase their fund size, but so far they have curbed any such inflated ambitions. For those who followed their calling, the ability to find strong investment opportunities, generate returns, and stay on the growth trajectory is not difficult.

There is no way of knowing whether you are a natural, as Sanford Bernstein puts it. Bernstein, founder of the investment banking firm Robertson Stephens and Company, had invested in venture funds for 20 years. "Some do it, some can't and like with athletes, there is no way of telling till they take the field," he once remarked.[24]

To prove they are good athletes, venture capitalists need to pick good investment opportunities. John Doerr used to say that training a new venture capitalist was not unlike preparing a fighter pilot for battle. It takes six to eight years, and you should be prepared for losses of about $20 million.[25] Not always! In its first fund, Hummer-Winblad invested in 17 companies, of which 16 yielded a positive return. Jan Garfinkle's Arboretum Ventures Fund I had two exits in quick succession that yielded strong returns—comfortably landing the fund in the top quartile. Recall that in interviews, both Jan and John were turned down by other venture capitalists several times!

It does help to have a reasonable measure of luck on your side. When Jan Garfinkle decided to raise her first fund, Arboretum Ventures, she met a leading LP over Chinese food to discuss her game plan. The meeting couldn't have gone better. Even the fortune cookie, now pasted in Jan's journal, said, "You will soon get something you've always wanted." David Cowan of Bessemer Venture Partners adds it all up nicely: "The one most important quality of a successful venture capitalist is LUCK."[26]

KEY TAKEAWAYS FOR PRACTITIONERS

It Starts with the Intention

A holistic approach to the business is essential; the best practitioners approach each situation with honorable intentions and aspire to be fair and balanced to one and all—at every stage of the game. No one can predict the outcomes but the ones who played the game well would pass the "front page test"—anything about them can be written on the front page of a newspaper and their mothers would be proud of their actions. As Eckhart Tolle, author and modern-day guru once wrote, "The outcome is inseparable from the actions that led to it and is already contaminated by those actions." It is better to be Gandhi than Gordon Gecko[27] in the game of VC or the game of life! The first and foremost takeaway is thus, integrity; the fiber of one's professional character. Where the financial stakes are high and one's growth in the business purely depends on IRR, integrity can be compromised quickly and Gecko-like behavior can be rampant. In the course of working on this book, I heard plenty of anecdotes where the spirit of Gecko was gaining ground over the spirit of Gandhi. Georges Doriot, rightfully called the father of venture capital, summarized it succinctly: "The chain of your activities keeps getting longer and it never goes away ... our lives form a tape over the years.... We carry it endlessly and we become a product of what we have done over time. Your accomplishments, your failures, the way in which you interact with people, they all become a part of your own personal tape"[28]

Besides greed, lack of ethical boundaries was evident—I heard sordid tales of practitioners who, under the guise of conducting due diligence, sought sensitive information from companies that compete with their own portfolio! When an eager entrepreneur thinks an investor is interested, they share all their sensitive information too soon. It takes inner discipline and the Admiral Stockdale mind (to do the right thing, even if it means dying like a dog when there is no one to see you) to stop the conversation and say, "We have a competing company in our portfolio—why don't you look it up first and decide if you want to discuss further, or share anything at all." I also heard other "stranger than fiction" tales of how practitioners treat portfolio CEOs, syndicate investment partners, and others in the ecosystem. The truth catches up sooner or later. One significant attitudinal flaw of this profession is arrogance—Brad Feld of the Foundry Group calls arrogance the biggest flaw a VC could have. When asked what he hopes of the VC industry, Fred Wilson of Union Square Ventures once said that there ought to be "a lesser number of a%%holes." In the game of VC, it does seem that ego may be indirectly proportional to IRR. Entrepreneurs see all and want to tell all—tired of being mistreated, now they freely share their opinions publicly on sites like thefunded.com. Some VCs cringe at the feedback—not Terry McGuire of Polaris Ventures, the former Chair of NVCA, who was voted as the best-loved VC.[29] A subjective and a populist vote with a small sample size, but nonetheless a title to be proud of. Entrepreneurs are generally not good at taking no for an answer, have strong opinions, and expect instant gratification—this creates a potential flashpoint in VC interactions. Opinions and egos abound on each side but those like Terry McGuire know how to strike the balance. Being responsive to entrepreneurs requires immense dedication—some entrepreneurs may have ideas that do not fit with your investment criteria, or could be less-than-promising. Yet others may be perpetually seeking attention, like wayward children. Yet others try to kick down your doors by sheer bull-headed force, rather than an intellectual play—a compelling business case. The best-in-class practitioners find an even-keeled way to respond to all without flinching. Some were of the opinion that they did not see the need to react to every little e-mail that came in—others were gracious and handled all entrepreneurs with amazing grace.

Winning Is Important, but How You Play the Game Matters

"Prejudice and opinion can preclude you from making an investment in a new area before it becomes hot," Michael Moritz of Sequoia Capital once remarked at a NVCA annual meeting. To see the big wave in a small crest requires a good mix of intellect, experience, and intuition. As it is often said, any fool can count the number of seeds in an apple; to predict the number of apples in a seed of a start-up is what matters.

When it comes to sourcing opportunities, proactive formation of companies via investment road maps can be an interesting cranial exercise. Opportunity and prepared minds often collide to generate returns. The mantra "Fail often, fail fast, and fail cheap!" is practiced by one and all. Can this be improved upon? Consider lessons from the parallel universe. In *Made to Stick*, Chip and Dan Heath describe how British Petroleum (BP) decided to reduce their "dry-holes"—the costs of unsuccessful drilling. It costs as much as $40 million to drill a large oil well. BP found that their estimates of hitting 1 in 10 were way off—they were actually hitting 1 in 100! Sounds like venture capital investments, correct? To avoid wasted expenditures, BP launched an ambitious "no dry holes" strategy. Explorers like to explore—it is education, they say! And they were irate. But the senior management stuck to their guns and, voilà, in 10 years, BP's hit rate moved from 1 in 100 to 2 out of every 3 wells! Put another way, from 1 percent to 66 percent! Agreed that starting and launching companies is quite different from drilling oil wells, and a number of beers can be consumed in this debate. But when was the last time a VC decided to improve their hit rate significantly, with a measured and a strategic approach BP style?

And the best practitioners resist the urge to negotiate every inch of the deal. Valuation debates are important but insignificant when it comes to good opportunities. A good practitioner knows the difference between value and price. Accel invested in Facebook at a $100 million valuation. Andreessen-Horowitz invested in Facebook at a $35 billion valuation. Kleiner Perkins invested $38 million in Facebook at a $52 billion valuation. At the time this book was going to press, Facebook was valued at $70 billion. And ask any LP, these investors are smart, the crème-de-la-crème of practitioners. The price per share was not important; the fact that Facebook still offered a potential for return was! The valuation conundrum is universal—in January 1801, Beethoven wrote to Herr Hoffmeister, a publisher, "I am offering to sell you a symphony. How much its worth is not really a concern to me because I am an incompetent businessman, bad at arithmetic. There ought to be in the world, a market for art. Artists would only bring their work and take as much money as needed." A streets-mart VC would have calculated Beethoven's hourly wage and concluded that the valuation ought to be the multiple of time invested and wages (all inclusive, worldwide rights, thank you very much!) A VC with an ivy league MBA would have inched a bit higher, with a Net Present Value / Discounted Cash Flow analysis. In either Beethoven's case or a Facebook investment, the valuation debate would be a travesty of justice to the potential therein.

The postinvestment phase—the part where the real work begins—does not draw much attention in the world. After all, as Peter Drucker rightfully said, "Deal making beats working. Deal making is exciting and fun, and working is grubby. Running anything is primarily an enormous amount of grubby detail work ... deal making is romantic, sexy. That is why you have deals that make no sense." Media loves to quote the premoney and exit values. In between those two events, what happens often makes or breaks the companies. If a practitioner can understand the risks and manage these effectively, she can improve the probability of strong returns. If the company fails to meet its milestones, the relationship between the VC and the entrepreneur can become tenuous—or celebrated, if all goes well. Christopher Columbus, the explorer who discovered America, is often celebrated as one of the first entrepreneurs, and Queen Isabella of Spain may well be one of the world's first venture capitalists. In a letter written in April 1502, Christopher Columbus wrote to his investors, the Governors of the Bank of St. George, Genoa: "Although my body is here my heart is always near you. The results of my undertaking are already being seen. ... The Holy Trinity may keep your noble persons in its guard, and increase the importance of your office." I have yet to experience such love from my portfolio company CEOs. When the relationship soured with his investors, Columbus was sued and landed in jail. Not much has changed in five hundred years!

And while practitioners plan their days and weeks in advance, the seasoned VCs know that you have little control over time. It is best to be flexible in managing priorities, as portfolio companies land into trouble.

Once an investment is made, a practitioner's eye ought to be on the exit. The longer it takes, the lower that IRR! But trying to push for a premature exit when the company is not ready is like Nikos Kazantzakis, author and philosopher, trying to rush a chrysalis to become a butterfly. He breathed his warm breath on the chrysalis, hoping to see this miracle occur quickly. What came of the effort was a dead butterfly, not to mention the guilt that goes with it. "In my hand I held a carcass. ... Years have passed but that butterfly's carcass has weighed heavily on my conscience ever since," he wrote in *Report to Greco*.

In a business where stakes are high and losses are aplenty, an even-keel mind makes the ride worthwhile—you cannot predict the endpoints. The Greek poet Constantine P. Cavafy wrote about the importance of the journey versus the destination in his all-time favorite poem, *Ithaca*. The road should be full of adventure, knowledge ... not expecting that Ithaca will offer you riches. While I wouldn't suggest that *Ithaca* be quoted in your fund memorandum or pitch documents (your LPs seek IRR; for poetry they may go elsewhere), to keep Ithaca fixed in your mind while making the voyage meaningful is what matters.

AS YOU GO FORWARD

At its core, VC is truly an apprenticeship business. If we look at this business, the first one-third of your career time is when you learn, the second is when you apply that learning with some degree of confidence, and the final third is when you start reaping the rewards. As it is often said, it does not take much to write a check and make investments—it is getting a return that matters! So as you go forth in the world of VC, keep the words of David Ogilvy, leading advertising executive, in mind: "Don't bunt. Aim out of the ballpark. Aim for the company of immortals."

About the Companion Web Site

The companion web site (www.wiley.com/go/businessofvc) offers various tools such as LP-GP Fund Due Diligence Checklist, Investment Due Diligence Checklist, Investment Summary format, and more. The companion site also includes external links to white papers and other industry guidelines.

If you have comments, updated links, or corrections, you can send them to the author at mr@thebusinessofvc.com.

Notes

Preface

1. "Microsoft Buys Skype for $8.5 Billion. Why, Exactly?" wired.com/epicenter/2011/05/microsoft-buys-skype-2/, accessed on May 30, 2011.
2. "Stumbling Venture Capital Industry Harms Start-ups and Innovation," by Peter Cohan, June 23, 2010. DailyFinance.
3. "Plenty of alternatives - But hedge funds and private equity have their limits," *The Economist*, Feb 28th 2008 economist.com/node/10716011.
4. Market Pulse: Alternative Assets Survey, 2010, J.P. Morgan Asset Management.
5. Steven N. Kaplan and Josh Lerner, "It Ain't Broke: The Past, Present, and Future of Venture Capital." *Journal of Applied Corporate Finance*, Vol. 22, No. 2, pp. 36–47, Spring 2010. Available at SSRN: http://ssrn.com/abstract=1649764 or doi:10.1111/j.1745-6622.2010.00272.x.
6. "Rightsizing the U.S. Venture Capital Industry," Paul Kedrosky, Ewing Marion Kauffman Foundation, June 10, 2009.
7. "Stumbling Venture Capital Industry Harms Start-ups and Innovation," by Peter Cohan, June 23, 2010. DailyFinance.
8. Gordon Hargraves (Rho Capital, a Fund of Funds) in discussions with the author, March 2011.
9. "Asian Private Equity—Will It Deliver on its Promise?" A Survey of Top LPs and GPs in Asian Private Equity, INSEAD Study on Asian Private Equity, 2010.
10. Angus Maddison, "Monitoring the world economy, 1820–1992." University of Groningen, Faculty of Economics.

Part One: Raising the Venture Fund

1. David Cassak, "John Simpson: Reluctant Entrepreneur," *In Vivo: The Business & Medicine Report* 21, no. 3 (April 2003), accessed January 13, 2011, www.denovovc.com/press/denovo-simpson.pdf.
2. Peter J. Tanous, *Investment Visionaries: Lessons in Creating Wealth from the World's Greatest Risk Takers* (Upper Saddle River, NJ: Prentice Hall, 2003), 69.
3. C. Richard Kramlich, "Venture Capital Greats: A Conversation with C. Richard Kramlich," interview by Mauree Jane Perry, 2006, accessed January 13, 2011, http://digitalassets.lib.berkeley.edu/roho/ucb/text/kramlich_dick_donated.pdf.

4. NEA was then a mere $125 million fund. Today, NEA's committed capital exceeds $11 billion.
5. News Release: "Boston Scientific Announces Offer to Acquire Guidant at $80 per Share," http://bostonscientific.mediaroom.com/index.php?s=43&item=376.

CHAPTER 1 The Universe of Limited Partners

1. John Maynard Keynes, *The General Theory of Employment, Interest, and Money* (New York: Harcourt Brace, 1964) 139.
2. David F. Swensen, *Pioneering Portfolio Management: An Unconventional Approach to Institutional Investment* (New York: Free Press, 2000), 92.
3. Keynes, *The General Theory of Employment, Interest, and Money*, 143.
4. "Global Alternative Investing Survey Results Report," Russell Investments, accessed January 23, 2011, www.russell.com/Institutional/research_commentary/alternative_investments_survey.asp.
5. "Asset Allocation, CalPERS, accessed on January 23, 2011, www.calpers.ca.gov/index.jsp?bc=/investments/assets/assetallocation.xml.
6. The ultimate value of the retirement benefit under a DC plan varies with the amount of contributions from the employer and worker as well as investment performance. DC plans differ on how much control the worker has over investment policy, but the worker usually bears most of the risks and rewards associated with variable investment performance.
7. Bank for International Settlements, "Institutional Investors, Global Savings and Asset Allocation," Report Submitted by a Working Group Established by the Committee on the Global Financial System, accessed January 23, 2011, www.bis.org/publ/cgfs27.pdf.
8. Canadian Pension Plan Investment Board, "CPP Fund $138.6 Billion," accessed January 23, 2011, www.cppib.ca/.
9. David F. Swensen, *Pioneering Portfolio Management: An Unconventional Approach to Institutional Investment* (New York: The Free Press, 2000), 18.
10. Yale University, *The Yale Endowment 2009*, accessed January 23, 2011, www.yale.edu/investments/Yale_Endowment_09.pdf.
11. National Association of College and University Business Officers, "Educational Endowments Returned 18.7% in FY2009," accessed January 23, 2011, www.nacubo.org/Documents/research/2009_NCSE_Press_Release.pdf.
12. http://foundationcenter.org/findfunders/topfunders/top100assets.html accessed March 13, 2011.
13. Joanne Fritz, "Corporate Foundation," accessed January 23, 2011, http://nonprofit.about.com/od/c/g/corpfound.htm.
14. Citi, *2009 Annual Report*, p. 235, accessed January 23, 2011, www.citigroup.com/citi/fin/data/ar09c_en.pdf.
15. GE Capital, Equity, "Info Center," accessed January 23, 2011, www.geequity.com/GEEquity/InfoCenter/infoCenter.html.

16. Kelly DePonte, "Funds of Funds: A Brief History," accessed January 23, 2011, www.probitaspartners.com/pdfs/FoF%20History%202005.pdf.

17. www.adamsstreetpartners.com/investment-programs/us-fund-of-funds.html accessed March 25, 2011.

18. Warren Buffett loves such business models and has a significant stake in Mutual of Omaha, an insurance company. From 1967 to 2010, Berkshire Hathaway's float increased from $20 million to $65.8 billion.

19. The Family Wealth Alliance, Seventh Annual Multifamily Office Study '10 Executive Summary, accessed January 23, 2011, www.fwalliance.com/store/exec-summary-7th-annual-mfo.pdf.

20. "SFOs in Action: How the Richest Families Manage Their Wealth," Knowledge@Wharton (blog), May 14, 2008, http://knowledge.wharton.upenn.edu/article.cfm?articleid=1964.

21. The level of involvement in the family business, however, varies widely by geography. Only 40 percent of American families in the sample are involved in the family business, compared to 70 percent of the Europeans and 89 percent of those from other parts of the world.

22. Capgemini, *World Wealth Report 2010*, accessed January 23, 2011, www.us.capgemini.com/services-and-solutions/by-industry/financial-services/publications/world-wealth-report-2010/.

23. NIST, Corporate Venture Capital (CVC), "Seeking Innovation and Strategic Growth: Recent Patterns in CVC Mission, Structure, and Investment," by Ian MacMillan, Edward Roberts, Val Livada, and Andrew Wang, June 2008.

24. Chris Douvos (TIFF) in discussion with the author, December 2010.

25. C. Richard Kramlich, "Venture Capital Greats: A Conversation with C. Richard Kramlich," interviewed by Mauree Jane Perry on August 31, 2006, in San Francisco, California, National Venture Capital Association, Arlington, Virginia (p. 69).

26. Timothy Recker (Chairman of the Institutional Limited Partners Association), in discussion with the author, December 2010.

27. Chris Douvos (TIFF) in discussion with author, December 2010.

CHAPTER 2   Fund Due Diligence

1. An excellent publication that addresses portfolio management: Thomas Meyer and Pierre-Yves Mathonet, *Beyond the J Curve—Managing a Portfolio of Venture Capital and Private Equity Funds* (Chichester, UK: John Wiley & Sons, 2005).

2. Lisa Edgar (Top Tier Capital Partners) in discussion with the author, March 2011.

3. Georganne Perkins (Fisher Lynch Capital) in discussion with the author, January 2011.

4. Kenneth Van Heel, (Dow Chemical Company) in discussions with the author, June 2010.

5. Lisa Edgar, "Are We Going to Make Money in This Fund?" PEHub (blog), September 7, 2010, www.pehub.com/81521/are-we-going-to-make-money-in -this-fund/.

6. Paul A. Gompers, and Josh Lerner, "What Drives Venture Capital Fundraising?" (January 1999). Available at SSRN: ssrn.com/abstract=57935 or doi:10.2139/ssrn.57935.

7. Private Equity International, *The Guide to Private Equity Fund Investment Due Diligence* (London: PEI Media, 2003), 91. The survey included responses from 313 institutions, 70 percent North America-based, with primary investing in PE and VC.

8. Sources of Capital for Michigan Venture Capital Firms and Entrepreneurial Companies. Professor Zsuzsanna Fluck, Director—Center for Venture Capital, Private Equity and Entrepreneurial Finance, Michigan State University, 2007.

9. AltAssets, "Institutional Investor Profile: Clint Harris, Managing Partner, Grove Street Advisors," September 4, 2002, accessed February 20, 2011, www .altassets.com/private-equity-features/by-author-name/article/nz1183.html.

10. Due Diligence Questionnaire. Available at www.pensionconsulting.com/ research_general_research.htm.

11. AltAssets, "Institutional Investor Profile: Clint Harris, Managing Partner, Grove Street Advisors," September 4, 2002.

12. Paul Bancroft III, "Early Bay Area Venture Capitalists: Shaping the Economic and Business Landscape," interview by Sally Smith Hughes, 2010, accessed January 13, 2011, http://digitalassets.lib.berkeley.edu/roho/ucb/text/bancroft_ pete.pdf.

13. Geoffrey H. Smart, Steven N. Payne, and Hidehiko Yuzaki, "What Makes a Successful Venture Capitalist?" *The Journal of Private Equity*, 3(4) (Fall 2000): 7–29.

14. "Specialization and Success: Evidence from Venture Capital," Paul Gompers (Harvard Business School), Anna Kovner (Federal Reserve Bank of New York), Josh Lerner (Entrepreneurship and Finance Units, Harvard Business School). 2009 Wiley Periodicals, Inc. *Journal of Economics & Management Strategy*, 18(3) (Fall 2009): 817–844.

15. Rebeca Zarutskie, "The Role of Top Management Team Human Capital in Venture Capital Markets: Evidence from First-Time Funds," *Journal of Business Venturing*, 25 (2010): 155–172.

16. Young Venture Capital Society Newsletter, Volume 1, Issue 2.

17. Yael V. Hochberg, Alexander Ljungqvist, and Yang Lu, "Networking as a Barrier to Entry and the Competitive Supply of Venture Capital," *Journal of Finance*, 65(3) (June 2010): 829–859. The authors conclude that there is less entry in VC markets in which incumbents are more tightly networked with each other. And the relationship factor seems to work both ways: A VC firm is significantly more likely to enter a market if it has previously established ties to incumbents by inviting them into syndicates in its own home market. In other words, venture capitalists will not cooperate with an outsider until they have quid pro quo access to the outsider's markets.

18. Ibid.
19. Alan Frazier, "Venture Capital Greats: A Conversation with Alan Frazier," interview by Carole Kolker, 2009, accessed January 13, 2011, http://digitalassets .lib.berkeley.edu/roho/ucb/text/frazier_alan_donated.pdf.
20. Steve Bird, "Private Equity . . . or Personal Equity? Why Who You Know Still Drives Venture Capital Returns," July 7, 2005, accessed February 20, 2011, www.go4venture.com/content/Case%20for%20Late%20Stage%20VC%20 (July%202005).pdf.
21. AltAssets.com Interview, 2008.
22. Robert Finkel and David Greising, *The Masters of Private Equity and Venture Capital* (New York: McGraw-Hill, 2009), 210.
23. *The VC View by Steven Lazarus*: Intellectual Asset Management magazine supplement, March 2005. "From IP to IPO, Key issues in commercializing university technology," accessed March 12, 2011, www.archventure.com/ archview.html.
24. Ann Grimes, "New Kids Arrive on the Venture-Capital Block," *Wall Street Journal,* February 25, 2005, accessed February 20, 2011, http://online.wsj.com/ article/0,,SB110928737299763683,00.html.
25. Kelly DePonte, "Emerging Managers: How to Analyze a First-Time Fund," accessed February 20, 2011, www.probitaspartners.com/pdfs/emerging_ manager_due_diligence_2005.pdf.
26. Kelvin Liu, "The Growing Importance of New and Emerging Managers in Private Equity," accessed February 20, 2011, www.institutional.invesco.com/ portal/.../II-IPCEM-IVP-1-E%5B1%5D.pdf.
27. Ann Grimes, "New Kids Arrive On the Venture-Capital Block," http://online .wsj.com/article/0,,SB110928737299763683,00.html.
28. Jean-Pierre Pipaud, "Emerging Managers: Elizabeth Flisser, Capital Z Asset Management," Emerging Managers Incubation (blog), September 22, 2008, http://emerging-managers.blogspot.com/2008/09/emerging-managers -elizabeth-flisser.html.
29. Kelly DePonte, "Emerging Managers: How to Analyze a First-Time Fund."
30. Ibid.
31. Grove Street Advisors, "Case Study 1," May 10, 2001, accessed February 20, 2011, www.grovestreetadvisors.com/news/gsa_case_study_01.pdf.
32. "CalSTRS AND CalPERS Unveil Emerging Managers and Financial Services Database," January 17, 2007, accessed February 20, 2011, www.calstrs.com/ newsroom/2007/news011707.aspx.
33. Ibid.
34. Women in Investments, Alternative Investment Management Program (CalPERS) presentation, February 10, 2009. www.calpers.ca.gov/eip-docs/.../ womens.../wiic-private-equity.pdf.
35. Ibid.
36. Sara Behunek and Mary Kathleen Flynn, "Closing the VC Gender Gap," *The Deal* magazine, July 2, 2010, accessed February 20, 2011, www.thedeal.com/ newsweekly/dealmakers/weekly-movers-and-shakers/closing-the-vc-gender-gap .php.

37. Women in Investments, Alternative Investment Management Program (CalPERS) presentation, February 10, 2009.
38. Oliver Gottschalg and Robert M. Ryan, "Advanced Private Equity Benchmarking," *Private Equity International*, February 2008, accessed February 20, 2011, www.peracs.de/report/PEI_61_Guest5.pdf.
39. Private Equity Growth Capital Council, "Private Equity FAQ," July 2008, accessed February 20, 2011, http://www.pegcc.org/just-the-facts/private-equity-frequently-asked-questions/.
40. David F. Swensen, *Pioneering Portfolio Management: An Unconventional Approach to Institutional Investment* (New York: Free Press, 2009), 75.
41. Kelly DePonte, "Lack of Access to Top Funds Is No. 1 LP Concern," *Venture Capital Journal*, May 1, 2007, accessed February 20, 2011, www.probitaspartners.com/pdfs/Lack_of_Access.pdf.
42. Ibid.
43. FLAG Capital Management, "Behind the Benchmarks: The Art of Private Capital Performance Assessment," November 2009, accessed February 20, 2011, www.flagcapital.com/pdf/Insights%202009%20November%20-%20Behind%20the%20Benchmarks.pdf.
44. Ibid.
45. Ibid.
46. Ibid.
47. Brian L. King, "Strategizing at Leading Venture Capital Firms: Of Planning, Opportunism and Deliberate Emergence," *Journal of Long Range Planning*, 41(3) (2008): 345–366.
48. Chris Douvos (TIFF) in discussion with the author, December 2010.
49. TIFF Advisory Services, "Marketable Investments," December 31, 2010, accessed February 20, 2011, https://wwws.tiff.org/TAS/reports/QRFinancial/MIQR/2010_4Q_MARK_INV.pdf.
50. www.adamsstreetpartners.com/investment-interests/fund-managers.html, accessed on March 25, 2011.
51. Christopher Rizik (Renaissance Venture Capital Fund) in discussion with the author, February 2011.
52. David J. Cowan, "Key Strategies to Successful Venture Capital," in *The Ways of the VC: Leading Venture Capitalists on Identifying Opportunities, Assessing Business Models & Establishing Valuations* (Boston: Aspatore Books, 2003), 60.
53. James R. Swartz, interview by Mauree Jane Perry, 2006, "National Venture Capital Association Venture Capital Oral History Project," accessed January 30, 2011, http://digitalassets.lib.berkeley.edu/roho/ucb/text/swartz_james_donated.pdf.
54. John Seely Brown, *Seeing Differently: Insights on Innovation* (Boston: Harvard Business Press, 1997), XXV.
55. Tom Perkins, *Valley Boy: The Education of Tom Perkins* (New York: Gotham Books, 2007), 120–121.
56. Tom Perkins, *Valley Boy: The Education of Tom Perkins*, 131.

57. David Cowan, "Road Map Investing," Who Has Time for This? (blog).
58. Vinod Khosla, Timothy D. Searchinger, and R. A. Houghton, "Biofuels: Clarifying Assumptions," *Science*, 322 (October 17, 2008): 371–374.
59. Brad Feld, "A Mental Model for VC Investments," FeldThoughts (blog), May 21, 2006, www.feld.com/wp/archives/2006/05/a-mental-model-for-vc -investments.html.
60. Brian L. King, "Strategizing at Leading Venture Capital Firms: of Planning, Opportunism and Deliberate Emergence," *Long Range Planning*, 41(3): "The Crafts of Strategy," June 2008, 345–366, ISSN 0024–6301, DOI: 10.1016/j .lrp.2008.03.006. www.sciencedirect.com/science/article/B6V6K-4SG558Y-3/ 2/e778b4d6d163c08c90470725da555b36).
61. Peter F. Drucker, *Innovation and Entrepreneurship* (Oxford: Butterworth-Heinemann, 1985), xiv.
62. Ibid.
63. AltAssets, "Investor Profile: Christophe Nicolas, Executive Director, Morgan Stanley Alternative Investment Partners," December 8, 2009, accessed February 20, 2011, www.altassets.com/private-equity-investor-profiles/article/ nz17499.html.
64. TIFF Advisory Services, Marketable Investments, December 31, 2010.
65. Lisa Edgar, "Are We Going to Make Money in This Fund?" PEHub (blog), www.pehub.com/81521/are-we-going-to-make-money-in-this-fund/.
66. Thomas Meyer and Pierre-Yves Mathonet, *Beyond the J Curve: Managing a Portfolio of Venture Capital and Private Equity Funds* (West Sussex: John Wiley & Sons, 2005).
67. AltAssets, "Institutional Investor Profile: Peter Keehn, Head of Alternative Investments, Allstate Investments, LLC," June 29, 2006, accessed February 20, 2011, www.altassets.com/private-equity-features/by-author-name/article/ nz8835.html.
68. Preqin Investor Outlook: Private Equity. "The Opinions of 100 Leading Private Equity LPs on the Market and Their Plans in 2011."

CHAPTER 3   Terms of Investment: The Limited Partnership Agreement

1. Howard Beber (Partner, Proskauer Rose), in discussion with the author, December 2010. Note: All quotes and information attributable to Beber throughout this chapter occurred during this discussion.
2. Alexander Peter Groh and Heinrich von Liechtenstein, "The First Step of the Capital Flow from Institutions to Entrepreneurs: The Criteria for Sorting Venture Capital Funds," working paper WP-795, IESE Business School, University of Navarra, Barcelona, Spain, 2009. www.iesep.com/Descargas/spdf/Gratuitos/ R160-E.pdf.
3. The Employee Retirement Income Security Act of 1974 (ERISA) is an American federal statute that establishes minimum standards for pension plans in

private industry and provides extensive rules on the federal income tax effects of transactions associated with employee benefit plans.

4. Kelly DePonte (Probitas Partners), in discussion with the author, August 2010.
5. Shelley M. Zoler, "Terms Limited Partners Are Looking for—An Update," VC Experts' Q4 2006 Roundtable video, 28:25. November 2006. http://video .google.com/videoplay?docid=4217714705619583874#.
6. Quoted in an article "Toward Transparency," by Alex Gove, Walden VC, *Venture Capital Journal,* October 2005, p. 48.
7. Timothy Recker, in discussion with the author, December 2010.
8. ILPA, "Private Equity Principles 2.0." Accessed January 17, 2011. http://ilpa .org/wp-content/uploads/2011/01/ILPA-Private-Equity-Principles-2.0.pdf.
9. Timothy Recker, in discussion with the author, December 2010.
10. Colin Blaydon and Fred Wainwright, Tuck School of Business at Dartmouth, "Limited Partnership Agreement Project: Results of GP and LP Survey," accessed January 17, 201, http://mba.tuck.dartmouth.edu/pecenter/research/pdfs/ LPA_survey_summary.pdf.
11. Kelly Williams (Credit Suisse), in discussions with the author, February 2011.
12. Anonymous institutional LP, managing $30 billion in assets in discussions with the author, October 2010.

CHAPTER 4 Fund Structure, Governance, and Operations

1. Union Square Ventures, "We're Hiring," accessed November 23, 2010, unionsquareventures.com/2008/02/were-hiring.php.
2. Gary Rivlin, "So You Want to Be a Venture Capitalist," *New York Times,* May 22, 2005, accessed January 13, 2011, www.nytimes.com/2005/05/22/business/ yourmoney/22venture.html.
3. www.adventurista.com/2008/04/vc-pre-mba-hiring.html accessed on July 3, 2010.
4. Rajeev Batra (Mayfield Fund) in discussions with the author, December 2010.
5. Robert Nelsen (ARCH Venture Partners) in discussions with the author, December 2010.
6. John Doerr, "Kleiner Perkins Caufield & Byers," in *Done Deals—Venture Capitalists Tell Their Stories,* ed. Udayan Gupta (Boston: Harvard Business School Press, 2000), 374.
7. David Cowan has ranked consistently on the Forbes Midas List—a subjective ranking of top VCs.
8. David Cowan (Bessemer Venture Partners) in discussions with the author, December 2010.
9. Geoffrey H. Smart, Steven N. Payne, and Hidehiko Yuzaki, "What Makes a Successful Venture Capitalist?" *The Journal of Private Equity* 3, no. 4 (Fall 2000): 7–29.
10. Punit Chiniwalla (Panorama Capital) in discussions with the author, September 2010.

11. Society of Kauffman Fellows, "Frequently Asked Questions," accessed January 13, 2011, www.kauffmanfellows.org/faq.aspx.
12. Ian MacMillan, Edward Roberts, Val Livada, and Andrew Wang, *Corporate Venture Capital—Seeking Innovation and Strategic Growth: Recent Patterns in CVC Mission, Structure, and Investment* (Washington, DC: U.S. Department of Commerce, June 2008).
13. A remora, also called a suckerfish, grows to about three feet in length. Using its suction cups, it attaches itself to a larger fish, typically a shark. The relationship, termed as commensalism, is a one-way benefit to the remora with no distinct advantage to the shark. The remora hitches a ride and feeds off the shark's scraps of leftovers. In fact, there is a controversy as to whether a remora's diet is primarily leftover fragments or its host's feces.
14. Brant Moxley (Pinnacle Group) in discussions with the author, July 2010.
15. Frank Caufield (Partner Emeritus, Kleiner Perkins Caufield and Byers) in discussions with the author, Aug 2010.
16. Lauren Fedor, "A History of Hedging," *Wall Street Journal*, June 12, 2010.
17. Harry Cendrowski, *Private Equity: History, Governance, and Operations* (Hoboken, NJ: John Wiley & Sons, 2008).

CHAPTER 5   Getting to the First Close

1. William H. Draper, III, "Early Bay Area Venture Capitalists: Shaping the Economic and Business Landscape," oral history conducted by Sally Smith Hughes in 2009, Regional Oral History Office, The Bancroft Library, University of California, Berkeley, 2008, p. 31.
2. I am grateful to Wilson Sonsini Goodrich and Rosati PC (WSGR), a leading Silicon Valley Law firm, for this information.
3. "Due Diligence in the Preparation of Private Placement" memorandum, WSGR Fund Services Group.
4. Robert Finkel and David Greising, *The Masters of Private Equity and Venture Capital*, McGraw-Hill; First edition (November 2009), 216.
5. "Working with Placement Agents," Morgan Lewis Deskbook Series, accessed January 18, 2011, www.morganlewis.com/vcpefdeskbook.
6. Ibid.
7. "What to expect from a placement agent: things you should know," Probitas Partners, accessed January 19, 2011, www.peimedia.com/Product.aspx?cID=5495_5538&pID=194135.
8. "Placement Agents Have Record Year as Private Equity Firms Fundraise," December 12, 2005, accessed January 18, 2011, www.sterlinglp.com/news/index.aspx?id=77.
9. Ibid.
10. Ibid.
11. "A Guide to Private Equity Fund Placement Specialists," Private Equity International (PEI) Media. http://www.peimedia.com/Product.aspx?cID=5495_5538&pID=201761.

12. "Placement Agents Have Record Year as Private Equity Firms Fundraise," December 12, 2005.

13. "How Pension Placement Agent Exploited Political Ties (Update1)," May 18, 2009, accessed January 19, 2011, www.bloomberg.com/apps/news?pid=newsarchive&sid=atwTqj6OjY7U.

14. Ibid.

15. "United States: California Restricts Use of Placement Agents," October 11, 2010, accessed January 19, 2011, www.mondaq.com/unitedstates/article.asp?articleid=112514.

16. "Carlyle moves away from placement agents," April 19, 2009, accessed January 19, 2011, www.ft.com/cms/s/0/7de19070–2d0b-11de-8710–00144feabdc0.html#ixzz1BWiGHIyT.

CHAPTER 6   The Art of Sourcing Investment Opportunities

1. David Kirkpatrick, *The Facebook Effect: The Inside Story of the Company That Is Connecting the World* (New York: Simon & Schuster, 2010), 116–121. In recreating this section, I have relied extensively on this book.

2. James R. Swartz, interview by Mauree Jane Perry, 2006, "National Venture Capital Association Venture Capital Oral History Project," accessed January 30, 2011, http://digitalassets.lib.berkeley.edu/roho/ucb/text/swartz_james_donated.pdf.

3. Randall E. Stross: *eBoys: The First Inside Account of Venture Capitalists at Work* (Crown Business, 2000) 216, 291.

4. William Elkus (Clearstone Partners) in discussions with the author, September 2008.

5. Chris Douvos (TIFF) in discussion with the author, December 2010.

6. Christopher Rizik (Renaissance Venture Capital Fund) in discussions with the author, February 2011.

7. "American Research University Data," The Center for Measuring University Performance," accessed February 1, 2011, http://mup.asu.edu/research_data.html.

8. AUTM 2009 Survey data of 300 research institutions, accessed February 6, 2011, www.autm.net/AM/Template.cfm?Section=Licensing_Surveys_AUTM&TEMPLATE=/CM/ContentDisplay.cfm&CONTENTID=5239.

9. Robert Finkel and David Greising, *The Masters of Private Equity and Venture Capital* (McGraw-Hill, New York).

10. Barry Jaruzelski and Kevin Dehoff, "The Global Innovation 1000: How the Top Innovators Keep Winning" (Booz & Company, Issue 61, Winter 2010).

11. Quoted in *Mac Week,* March 14, 1989.

12. David Scheer (Scheer and Company) in discussions with the author, August 2008. "Cholesterol Champions," accessed December 26, 2010, http://pharmexec.findpharma.com/pharmexec/article/articleDetail.jsp?id=109681.

13. Robin Wauters, "Venture Capitalists Get Grilled (And Pitched At Urinals) At #TCDisrupt," TechCrunch (blog) May 26, 2010, accessed on December 12, 2010, http://techcrunch.com/2010/05/26/venture-capitalists-get-grilled -and-pitched-at-urinals-at-tcdisrupt/.

14. William H. Draper, III, "Early Bay Area Venture Capitalists: Shaping the Economic and Business Landscape," oral history conducted by Sally Smith Hughes in 2009, Regional Oral History Office, The Bancroft Library, University of California, Berkeley, 2008. Accessed on July 3, 2010.

15. Arthur Rock, interview by Sally Smith Hughes, 2008–2009, "Early Bay Area Venture Capitalists: Shaping the Economic and Business Landscape," accessed January 30, 2011, http://digitalassets.lib.berkeley.edu/roho/ucb/text/rock_ arthur.pdf.

16. John Jarve (Menlo Ventures) in discussion with the author, September 2008.

17. Doc Searls, "A Talk with Tim O'Reilly," *Linux Journal*, February 1, 2001, accessed February 1, 2011, www.linuxjournal.com/article/4467.

18. "About O'Reilly," O'Reilly Media, accessed January 28, 2011, http://oreilly .com/about/.

19. Chris Douvos (TIFF) in discussion with the author, December 2010.

20. "It's about Results," TechStars, accessed February 1, 2011, www.techstars .org/results/.

21. http://ycombinator.com/atyc.html accessed on February 6, 2011.

22. http://ycombinator.com/atyc.html accessed on February 6, 2011.

23. Michael Arrington, "Start Fund: Yuri Milner, SV Angel, Offer EVERY Y Combinator Startup $150k," TechCrunch, January 28, 2011, accessed Feb 1, 2011, http://techcrunch.com/2011/01/28/yuri-milner-sv-angel-offer-every-new -y-combinator-startup-150k/.

24. Sarah Lacy, "How'd Sequoia Let Yuri Milner Grab this Sweetheart Y Combinator Deal," TechCrunch, January 28, 2011, accessed February 1, 2011, http://techcrunch.com/2011/01/28/howd-sequoia-let-yuri-milner-grab -this-sweetheart-y-combinator-deal/.

25. Data is from http://www.angelsoft.net, a leading software-as-a-service tool for managing angel networks.

26. Statistics from www.angelcapitalassociation.org.

27. Ibid.

28. Ibid. This is data from the year 2007: Substantial variations from these investment ranges have not been reported. Of course, we do not include super angels in these statistics.

29. Jeffrey Sohl, *The Angel Investor Market in Q1,2 2010: Where Have All the Seed Investors Gone?* Center for Venture Research: October 26, 2010, accessed January 13, 2011, http://wsbe.unh.edu/files/cvr-q1q2101_0.pdf.

30. Robert Wiltbank & Warren Boeker, *Returns to Angel Investors in Groups*. Lenexa, KS: Angel Capital Education Foundation, November 2007, www .angelcapitaleducation.org/data/Documents/Resources/AngelCapitalEducation/ RSCH_-_ACEF__Returns_to_Angel_Investor_in_Groups.pdf. "Exits from 539

angels [who] have experienced 1,137 'exits' (acquisitions or Initial Public Offerings that provided positive returns, or firm closures that led to negative returns) from their venture investments [between 1987–2007], with most exits occurring since 2004."

31. A well-managed network has a streamlined decision-making and negotiation process, typically managed by one angel representative. If each angel is to decide on her own, the terms, amounts, and so forth, the process can be fraught with challenges for both investors and entrepreneurs.

32. Tony Stanco & Uto Akah, *Survey: The Relationship between Angels and Venture Capitalists in the Venture Industry* (2005), https://www.equitynet.com/media/pdf/Survey%20-%20The%20Relationship%20Between%20Angels%20&%20Venture%20Capitalists%20in%20the%20Venture%20Industry%20(Tony%20Stanco,%20et%20al,%202005).pdf. The survey was sent to 2,156 venture capitalists and angels; 14 percent responded.

33. William R. Kerr, Josh Lerner, and Antoinette Schoar, "The Consequences of Entrepreneurial Finance: A Regression Discontinuity Analysis" (March 18, 2010). Harvard Business School Entrepreneurial Management working paper No. 10–086. Available at SSRN: http://ssrn.com/abstract=1574358.

34. Tony Stanco & Uto Akah, *Survey: The Relationship between Angels and Venture Capitalists in the Venture Industry* (2005).

35. Steven Mercil (RAIN Source Capital) in discussions with the author, December 2010.

36. OCA Ventures, "About OCA," accessed December 20, 2010, www.ocaventures.com/About/History+Page.aspx.

37. "Pledge Funds, Private Equity: Trends and Developments," Fish and Richardson, October 2007.

38. Arthur Rock, in an interview by Sally Smith Hughes, http://digitalassets.lib.berkeley.edu/roho/ucb/text/rock_arthur.pdf.

39. "Portfolio," Bessemer Venture Partners, accessed February 1, 2011, www.bvp.com/Portfolio/AntiPortfolio.aspx.

40. www.ovp.com/companies-we-backed/deals-missed.html accessed February 6, 2011.

41. Scott Duke Harris, "The Venture Deals That Got Away," *Mercury News*, August 10, 2008, accessed February 1, 2011, www.mercurynews.com/ci_10156479?nclick_check=1.

42. Alice Schroeder, *The Snowball: Warren Buffett and the Business of Life* (New York: Bantam Dell, 2008), 320.

43. Peter O. Crisp, interview by Carole Kolker, October 21, 20081, "Venture Capital Greats: A Conversation with Peter O. Crisp," accessed February 1, 2011, http://digitalassets.lib.berkeley.edu/roho/ucb/text/vcg-crisp.pdf.

44. Robert Finkel and David Greising, *The Masters of Private Equity and Venture Capital*, 215.

45. Deepak Kamra (Canaan Partners) in discussions with the author, July 2008.

46. A virtualization software company formed in 1998, now a publicly traded company with over $2 billion in revenues.

47. David Kirkpatrick, *The Facebook Effect: The Inside Story of the Company That Is Connecting the World* (New York: Simon & Schuster, 2010), 120–122.
48. http://blogs.wsj.com/venturecapital/2011/02/14/kleiner-perkins-invests-in-facebook-at-52-billion-valuation/ accessed April 2, 2011.
49. Keynote Speech, Michigan Growth Capital Symposium, University of Michigan, Ann Arbor, 2007. The full video can be found at iTunes: "Michigan Growth Capital Symposium 2007 Keynote Speaker—Ram Shriram, Founder Sherpalo Ventures."
50. Erik Lundberg (University of Michigan), in discussions with the author, December 2010.
51. Charles D. Ellis, *The Partnership: The Making of Goldman Sachs* (New York: Penguin, 2008), 188.

CHAPTER 7 The Art of Conducting Due Diligence

1. Vinod Khosla, "The Entrepreneurial Roller Coaster...High Highs & Low Lows," accessed February 6, 2011, www.khoslaventures.com/presentations/RCApr2003.ppt.
2. Peter Bevelin, *Seeking Wisdom: From Darwin to Munger* (San Marino, CA: PCA Publications, 2007), 220. Buffett mentioned these criteria at a press conference in 2001.
3. Warren Buffett, *The Essays of Warren Buffett: Lessons for Corporate America*, ed. Lawrence A. Cunningham, 2nd ed. (New York: L. Cunningham, 2008). Buffett defines "understanding a business" as "we have a reasonable probability of being able to assess where it will be in ten years."
4. Peter J. Tanous, *Investment Visionaries: Lessons in Creating Wealth from the World's Greatest Risk Takers* (Upper Saddle River, NJ: Prentice Hall, 2003), 79.
5. Ibid.
6. Warren Buffett, *The Essays of Warren Buffett: Lessons for Corporate America*, ed. Lawrence A. Cunningham, 2nd ed. (New York: L. Cunningham, 2008), 112.
7. http://egpeclub.home.comcast.net/~egpeclub/The_Warren_Buffett_Business_Factors.htm accessed on February 9, 2011.
8. *The Tao of Warren Buffett: Warren Buffett's Words of Wisdom: Quotations and Interpretations to Help Guide You to Billionaire Wealth and Enlightened Business Management* (Simon & Schuster, 2006), 14.
9. "First-Day Sales of Apple's iPad Fall Short of Sky-High Hopes," *Wall Street Journal*, April 6, 2010.
10. Steve Jobs; iPad2 keynote address, March 2, 2011.
11. Jim Rasmussen, "Billionaire Talks Strategy with Students," *Omaha World-Herald*, January 2, 1994, 178.
12. www.pbs.org/transistor/album1/shockley/shockley3.html, accessed April 12, 2011.

13. Joel N. Shurkin, *Broken Genius: The Rise and Fall of William Shockley, Creator of the Electronic Age* (New York: Macmillan, 2008), 181.

14. Ibid., 251.

15. Joel Shurkin, www.pbs.org/transistor/album1/addlbios/shurkin.html, accessed February 6, 2011.

16. Geoff Smart and Randy Street, *Who: The A Method for Hiring* (New York: Ballantine Books, 2008), 160.

17. Geoff Smart (ghSMART), in discussion with the author, December 2010.

18. Smart and Street, *Who: The A Method for Hiring*, 161–162.

19. Ibid., 162.

20. Kaplan, Kiebanov, and Sorensen, "Which CEO Characteristics and Abilities Matter?" http://www.nber.org/papers/w14195.pdf.

21. Peter F. Drucker, *The Effective Executive* (New York: HarperCollins, 2002), 1.

22. Paul A. Gompers, Anna Kovner, Josh Lerner, and David Scharfstein, "Skill vs. Luck in Entrepreneurship and Venture Capital: Evidence from Serial Entrepreneurs" (July 2006). Available at SSRN: http://ssrn.com/abstract= 933932.

23. Arthur Rock, interview by Sally Smith Hughes, 2008–2009, "Early Bay Area Venture Capitalists: Shaping the Economic and Business Landscape," accessed February 6, 2011, http://digitalassets.lib.berkeley.edu/roho/ucb/text/ rock_arthur.pdf.

24. Alex Pentland, "Defend Your Research: We Can Measure the Power of Charisma," *Harvard Business Review*, January-February 2010, accessed February 7, 2011, http://hbr.org/2010/01/defend-your-research-we-can-measure-the -power-of-charisma/ar/1.

25. Ibid.

26. Geoffrey H. Smart, "The Art and Science of Human Capital Valuation," 1998, accessed February 6, 2011, www.ghsmart.com/media/press/human_capital.pdf.

27. Ibid.

28. ESTJ, accessed April 12, 2011, www.myersbriggs.org/my-mbti-personality -type/mbti-basics/the-16-mbti-types.asp.

29. Steven N. Kaplan, Mark M. Kiebanov, and Morten Sorensen, "Which CEO Characteristics and Abilities Matter?" National Bureau of Economic Research working paper no. 14195, 2008, accessed February 7, 2011, www.nber.org/ papers/w14195.pdf.

30. Steven N. Kaplan, "Bet on the Horse: Determining Success Factors of New Businesses," Capital Ideas, accessed February 6, 2011, www.chicagobooth.edu/ capideas/dec05/1.aspx.

31. Patricia Sabatini, "Fibs on Resumes Commonplace," *Pittsburgh Post-Gazette*, February 24, 2006.

32. "Smith & Wesson Chief Quits Over Crime." *CNN Money.com*. February 27, 2004, http://money.cnn.com/2004/02/27/news/smith_wesson/.

33. Tom Perkins, *Valley Boy: The Education of Tom Perkins* (New York: Gotham Books, 2007), 137–138.

34. Interview with Theresa Mack, CPA, CFF, CAMS, CFCI, PI of Cendrowski Corporate Advisors in Chicago, IL and Bloomfield Hills, MI.
35. Avery Johnson, Jonathan D. Rockoff, and Anna Wilde Mathews, "Americans Cut Back on Visits to Doctor," July 29, 2010, accessed February 6, 2011, http://online.wsj.com/article/SB100014240527487039409045753956034327 26626.html?mod=googlenews_wsj.
36. Dan Bowman, "Healthcare on a Budget: A New Trend?" July 29, 2010, accessed February 6, 2011, www.fiercehealthcare.com/story/healthcare-budget -new-trend/2010-07-29?utm_medium=rss&utm_source=rss#ixzz1BiH0P8zl.
37. Deloitte Center for Health Solutions, "Retail Clinics: Update and Impli- cations," 2009, accessed February 6, 2011, www.deloitte.com/assets/Dcom UnitedStates/Local%20Assets/Documents/us_chs_RetailClinics_111209.pdf.
38. Ibid.
39. Anne Zieger, "Trend: Retail Clinics Expanding Range of Services," June 5, 2009, accessed February 6, 2011, www.fiercehealthcare.com/story/trend-retail -clinics-expanding-range-services/2009-06-05#ixzz1BiDk22Ak.
40. Deloitte Center for Health Solutions, "Retail Clinics: Update and Implications."
41. MinuteClinic, "Fact Sheet," accessed February 6, 2011, www.ibew110 .org/ASC/medical/PDF/Minute_Clinic_Fact_Sheet.pdf.
42. "MinuteClinic Closes $15 Million Tiered Financing Round Led by Bain Capital Ventures," September 13, 2004, accessed February 6, 2011, http://findarticles .com/p/articles/mi_m0EIN/is_2004_Sept_13/ai_n6190719/.
43. Anne Zieger, "Trend: Hospitals Mounting Attack on Retail Clinic Busi- ness," www.fiercehealthcare.com/story/trend-hospitals-mounting-attack-retail -clinic-business/2009-05-11#ixzz1BijdRZop.
44. Pamela Lewis Dolan, "Number of Retail Clinics Shrinking; Growth Slows as Partnerships Sought with Hospitals," July 27, 2009, accessed February 6, 2011, www.ama-assn.org/amednews/2009/07/27/bil20727.htm.
45. "Retail Clinics: Thousands on the Way?" July 19, 2006, accessed February 6, 2011, www.fiercehealthcare.com/story/retail-clinics-thousands-on-the-way/ 2006-07-20#ixzz1BiM82I7G.
46. Deloitte Center for Health Solutions, "Retail Clinics: Update and Implications."
47. Carol Wolf, "CVS to Double Number of In-Store Clinics after Health-Care Law, CFO Says," April 13, 2010, accessed February 6, 2011, www.bloomberg.com/ news/2010-04-13/cvs-to-double-number-of-in-store-clinics-after-health-care -law-cfo-says.html.
48. Deloitte Center for Health Solutions, "Retail Clinics: Update and Implications."
49. Antoinette Alexander, "Acute Visits Climb as MinuteClinic Preps for Rapid Growth Phase," January 11, 2011, accessed February 6, 2011, www .drugstorenews.com/article/acute-visits-climb-minuteclinic-preps-rapid-growth -phase.
50. Ibid. Also see Jacob Goldstein, "Retail Clinic Closures 'Not Unlike the Dot Com Bubble,'" Health Blog, May 7, 2008, accessed February 6, 2011, http:// blogs.wsj.com/health/2008/05/07/retail-clinic-closures-not-unlike-the-dot-com -bubble.

51. Amer Kaissi, "Retail Clinics: Did The Bubble Burst?" Healthcare Hacks (blog), January 22, 2010, accessed February 6, 2011, http://healthcarehacks.com/retail-clinics-did-the-bubble-burst.

52. Sandra Yin, "Surge in MinuteClinic Visits Could Signal Shift in Consumer Preferences," August 1, 2010, accessed February 6, 2011, www.fiercehealthcare.com/story/surge-minuteclinic-visits-could-signal-shift-consumer-preferences/2010-08-01#ixzz1BiEu2AbF.

53. Christine Blank, "Retail Clinic Growth Slows," January 15, 2010, accessed February 6, 2011, http://drugtopics.modernmedicine.com/drugtopics/Modern+Medicine+Now/Retail-clinic-growth-slows/ArticleStandard/Article/detail/651907.

54. Debra Wood, "Is the Retail Clinic Sector Slowing Down?" accessed February 6, 2011, www.nursezone.com/nursing-news-events/more-news/Is-the-Retail-Clinic-Sector-Slowing-Down_27582.aspx.

55. Terry McGuire (Polaris Ventures) in discussions with the author, January 2011.

56. Saras D. Sarasvathy, "What Makes Entrepreneurs Entrepreneurial?" accessed February 6, 2011, www.effectuation.org/sites/default/files/What%20makes%20entrs%20entl%20note.pdf.

57. Antoine de Saint Exupéry, *Flight to Arras*, trans. Lewis Galantiére (New York: Harcourt Brace, 1942), 129.

58. Jessica Livingston, *Founders at Work: Stories of Startups' Early Days* (Berkeley, CA: APress, 2007). This episode has been recreated based on PayPal founder Max Levchin's interview with Jessica Livingston.

59. Paradoxically, in Q4 2010, while Amazon posted its best quarter ever with $10 billion in sales, Borders was busy fighting bankruptcy. And it was no different for Blockbuster.

60. "Inside the Mind of Google," 2010, CNBC Interview with Maria Bartiromo.

61. Todd Dagres (Spark Capital) in discussions and e-mail communications with the author, 2008 and 2011.

62. Khosla Ventures, "What We Look For: Main Fund—What Matters," accessed February 6, 2011, www.khoslaventures.com/khosla/main_fund_wm.html.

63. Nichomachean Ethics, Book I, passage 3, accessed February 9, 2011, http://classics.mit.edu/Aristotle/nicomachaen.mb.txt.

64. Arthur Rock, interview by Sally Smith Hughes, http://digitalassets.lib.berkeley.edu/roho/ucb/text/rock_arthur.pdf.

65. William D. Bygrave, Julian Lange, Aleksandar Mollov, Michael Pearlmutter, and Sunil Singh, "Pre-Startup Formal Business Plans and Post-Startup Performance: A Study of 116 New Ventures," *Venture Capital Journal*, 9(4) (October 2007), accessed February 6, 2011, http://blog.guykawasaki.com/bygrave.doc.

66. Jeffry Timmons and Stephen Spinelli, *New Venture Creation: Entrepreneurship for the 21st Century*, 5th ed. (New York: McGraw Hill, 1999), 85.

67. James R. Swartz, "Venture Capital Greats: A Conversation with James R. Swartz," interview by Mauree Jane Perry, 2006, accessed January 13, 2011, http://digitalassets.lib.berkeley.edu/roho/ucb/text/swartz_james_donated.pdf.

68. As quoted by Vic Stretcher, founder of HealthMedia. Rick Snyder's fund, Avalon Investments, led an investment in HealthMedia, a healthcare IT

company that spun out of the University of Michigan and was acquired by Johnson & Johnson.

CHAPTER 8   The Basics of Corporations, Ownership, and Control

1. State of Delaware Division of Corporations, "How to Calculate Franchise Taxes," accessed on February 9, 2011, http://corp.delaware.gov/frtaxcalc.shtml.
2. The three corporate structures typically used to establish any company are C corporation, a limited liability company, and an S corporation. Most practitioners prefer to invest in a C corporation incorporated in Delaware for a number of tax, legal, and regulatory reasons.
3. David J. Brophy and Wassim Mourtada, "Structuring the Transaction: Term Sheet and Deal Structure," in *Taking Research to Market: How to Build and Invest in Successful University Spinouts*, eds. Kenny Tang, Ajay Vohora, and Roger Freeman (London: Euromoney Institutional Investment Plc, 2004), 169.
4. http://www.bothsidesofthetable.com/2010/07/22/want-to-know-how-vcs -calculate-valuation-differently-from-founders/ accessed on March 30, 2011.

CHAPTER 9   Valuation Methods and Other Voodoo Arts

1. David Kirkpatrick, *The Facebook Effect: The Inside Story of the Company That Is Connecting the World* (New York: Simon & Schuster, 2010).
2. Aswath Damodaran, "Valuing Young, Start-Up and Growth Companies: Estimation Issues and Valuation Challenges" (June 12, 2009). Available at SSRN: http://ssrn.com/abstract=1418687.
3. Rick Heitmann (First Mark Capital), in discussions with the author, Feb 2011.
4. Amy E. Knaup, "Survival and Longevity in the Business Employment Dynamics Data," *Monthly Labor Review* (May 2005), pp. 50–56; Amy E. Knaup and M.C. Piazza, "Business Employment Dynamics Data: Survival and Longevity," Monthly Labor Review (September 2007), pp. 3–10.
5. Aswath Damodaran, "Valuing Young, Start-Up and Growth Companies: Estimation Issues and Valuation Challenges." (June 12, 2009). Available at SSRN: http://ssrn.com/abstract=1418687.

CHAPTER 10   Structuring Investment Transactions

1. Mark Suster. Available at www.bothsidesofthetable.com/2010/07/22/want-to -know-how-vcs-calculate-valuation-differently-from-founders/.
2. Mark Suster, "Is Convertible Debt Preferable to Equity?" Both Sides of the Table (blog), August 30, 2010, http://www.bothsidesofthetable.com/2010/08/ 30/is-convertible-debt-preferable-to-equity/.

3. Mark Suster, "Want to Know How VC's Calculate Valuation Differently from Founders?" www.bothsidesofthetable.com/2010/07/22/want-to-know -how-vcs-calculate-valuation-differently-from-founders/.

4. Brad Feld, "Term Sheet: Liquidation Preference," FeldThoughts (blog), January 4, 2005, www.feld.com/wp/archives/2005/01/term-sheet-liquidation -preference.html.

5. Ibid.

6. Jonathan D. Gworek, "The Making of a Winning Term Sheet: Understanding What Founders Want," Morse Barnes-Brown Pendleton PC, June 2007, accessed February 9, 2011, www.mbbp.com/resources/business/founder_ termsheet.html.

7. Colin Blaydon and Fred Wainwright, "It's Time to Do Away with Participating Preferred," *Venture Capital Journal* (July 2006), accessed February 11, 2011, http://mba.tuck.dartmouth.edu/pecenter/research/VCJ_July_2006.pdf.

8. Rick Heitzmann (First Mark capital) in discussions with the author, Feb 2011.

9. Frank Demmler, "Practical Implications of Anti-Dilution Protection," accessed February 10, 2011, www.andrew.cmu.edu/user/fd0n/54%20Practical% 20Implications%20Anti-dilution%20excel.htm.

10. Based on a surveys conducted by law firms, Wilmer Hale and Fenwick and West.

11. Justin J. Camp, *Venture Capital Due Diligence: A Guide to Making Smart Investment Choices and Increasing Your Portfolio Returns* (Hoboken, NJ: John Wiley and Sons, 2002), 140.

12. While this may seem unimportant, I am aware of at least one situation where the founder of a venture-backed company died in a car accident. In another situation, the founder had an ugly divorce case that caused undue distraction to the board, shareholders, and the company while his ownership in the company was being divvied up.

13. Ted Wang, "Version 2.0 and Why Series Seed Documents Are Better Than Capped Convertible Notes," Series Seed (blog), September 2, 2010, www.seriesseed.com/.

14. Ted Wang, "Reinventing the Series A," VentureBeat (blog), September 17, 2007, http://venturebeat.com/2007/09/17/reinventing-the-series-a/.

15. Anthony Ha, "Ted Wang and Andreessen Horowitz Try to Reinvent the Seed Round," VentureBeat (blog), March 2, 2010, http://venturebeat.com/2010/03/ 02/series-seed-andreessen-horowitz/.

16. Kara Swisher, "Series Seed Documents—With an Assist from Andreessen Horowitz—To Help Entrepreneurs With Legal Hairballs," All Things Digital (blog), March 1, 2010, http://kara.allthingsd.com/20100301/series-seed -documents-with-a-big-assist-from-andreessen-horowitz-set-to-launch-to-help -entrepreneurs-with-legal-hairballs/. Mark Andreessen's venture firm, Andreessen Horowitz, was the first to agree to use Series Seed documents, followed by uber angel Ron Conway and VC firms including First Round Capital, SoftTech VC, True Ventures, Polaris Ventures, and Charles River Ventures.

17. Ibid.
18. Tom Perkins, *Valley Boy: The Education of Tom Perkins* (New York: Gotham Books, 2007), 112.
19. Jennifer M. Walske, Andrew Zacharakis, and Laurel Smith-Doerr, "Effects of Venture Capital Syndication Networks on Entrepreneurial Success." Babson College Entrepreneurship Research Conference (BCERC) 2007; Frontiers of Entrepreneurship Research 2007. Available at SSRN: http://ssrn.com/abstract=1060081.
20. Ibid.
21. Justin J. Camp, *Venture Capital Due Diligence: A Guide to Making Smart Investment Choices and Increasing Your Portfolio Returns* (Hoboken, NJ: John Wiley and Sons, 2002), 167–173.
22. Steven N. Kaplan and Per Strömberg, "Financial Contracting Theory Meets the Real World: An Empirical Analysis of Venture Capital Contracts," CRSP working paper 513, accessed February 11, 2011, http://ssrn.com/abstract=218175.
23. Ibid.

CHAPTER 11 Behind Every Successful CEO Stand a Few Good Board VCs

1. Brad Feld (Foundry Group) in discussions with the author, December 2010.
2. "The Basic Responsibilities of VC-backed Company Directors," a white paper by the Working Group on Director Accountability and Board Effectiveness. www.levp.com/news/whitepapers.shtml.
3. Seth Rudnick (Canaan Partners) in discussions with the author, September 2008.
4. William D. Bygrave and Jeffry A. Timmons, *Venture Capital at the Crossroads* (Harvard Business Press, 1992), 220.
5. Working Group on Director Accountability and Board Effectiveness, "A Simple Guide to the Basic Responsibilities of VC-Backed Company Directors," October 2007, www.nvca.org/index.php?option=com_docman&task=doc_download&gid=78&Itemid=93.
6. McKinsey Quarterly, February 2008 Survey on Governance. Of the 586 respondents, 378 were privately held companies, making it a relevant sample for the purposes of our discussion.
7. Adapted from "Introduction to Robert's Rules of Order," www.robertsrules.org/rulesintro.htm, accessed January 30, 2011.
8. Brad Feld (The Foundry Group) in discussions with the author.
9. Lip-Bu Tan (Walden International) in discussions with the author, December 2008.
10. PricewaterhouseCoopers, "Paths to Value," 2002. The Paths to Value study analyzed more than 350 R&D and services-intensive companies in the United States, Europe, and Israel that received seed or first-round private financing between 1999 and 2001.
11. "The State of the Corporate Board, 2007: A McKinsey Global Survey," McKinsey & Company, accessed January 30, 2011, www.mckinseyquarterly

.com / The_state_of_the_corporate_board_2007_A_McKinsey_Global_Survey_ 2011. A total of 2,268 respondents, including 825 directors and officers, contributed to this survey.

12. Fred Dotzler, "What Do Venture Capitalists Really Do, and Where Do They Learn to Do It?" De Novo Ventures, accessed January 30, 2011, www.denovovc.com/articles/2001_Dotzler.pdf.

13. Patrick Hoge, "BigFix Helps Companies Cut Their Juice Use," San Francisco Business Times, November 23, 2008, accessed January 30, 2011, http://www .bizjournals.com/sanfrancisco/stories/2008/11/24/story16.html.

14. Dave Robbins (IBM / BigFix) in discussions with the author, September 2010.

15. "BigFix, Inc. Secures $8 Million in Venture Funding; Leader in Patch Management Attracts New Funding From Levensohn Capital Management and Reinvestments from St. Paul Venture Capital and Selby Venture Partners," The Free Library, September 26, 2002, accessed January 30, 2011, http://www .thefreelibrary.com / BigFix,+Inc.+Secures+8+Million+in+Venture+Funding %3B+Leader+in+Patch. . .-a092811013.

16. Patrick Hoge, "BigFix Helps Companies Cut Their Juice Use," San Francisco Business Times, November 23, 2008, accessed January 30, 2011, http://www .bizjournals.com/sanfrancisco/stories/2008/11/24/story16.html.

17. "Miami Dade County Schools: BigFix Power Management Lowers Power Bills and Shrinks Carbon Footprint," October 2007, accessed January 30, 2011, http://www.energystar.gov/ia/products/power_mgt/MDCPS_Power_Mgt.pdf.

18. Patrick Hoge, "BigFix Helps Companies Cut Their Juice Use," San Francisco Business Times, November 23, 2008, accessed January 30, 2011, http://www .bizjournals.com/sanfrancisco/stories/2008/11/24/story16.html.

19. Ibid.

20. "BigFix Is One of the 50 Fastest Growing Technology Companies in the San Francisco Bay Area," October 2007, accessed January 30, 2011, http:// findarticles.com/p/articles/mi_pwwi/is_200710/ai_n21072006/.

21. Cody Barbierri, "IBM buys BigFix for Network Visibility and Compliance," Venture Beat, July 1, 2010, accessed January 30, 2011, http://venturebeat.com/ 2010/07/01/ibm-bigfix/.

22. IBM Acquires BigFix in Latest Corporate Acquisition," July 2, 2010, accessed January 30, 2011, http://www.infosecurity-us.com/view/10713/ibm-acquires -bigfix-in-latest-corporate-acquisition/).

23. Akamai went on to become a global giant providing services within the Internet/web domain and is a household name within the technology industry.

24. Allison Leopold Tilley, "Best Practices for the High Performance Board," podcast, accessed January 30, 2011, www.vc-io.com/governance.shtml.

25. Ibid.

26. Dennis T. Jaffe and Paul N. Levensohn, "After the Term Sheet: How Venture Boards Influence the Success or Failure of Technology Companies," November 2003, accessed January 30, 2011, www.equitynet.com/media/pdf/How% 20Venture%20Boards%20Influence%20The%20Success%20or%20Failure%

20of%20Technology%20Companies%20(Dennis%20Jaffe,%20et%20al,% 202003).pdf.

27. Ibid.

28. Pascal N. Levensohn, "Rites of Passage: Managing CEO Transition in Venture-Backed Technology Companies," January 2006, accessed January 30, 2011, www.levp.com/news/whitepapers.shtml.

29. Ibid.

30. Dan Richman, "Former CEO of Entellium Pleads Guilty to Wire Fraud," *Seattle Post-Intelligencer,* December 11, 2008, accessed January 30, 2011, www.seattlepi.com/business/391777_entellium12.html.

31. Kristie Heim, "Entellium CEO Pleads Guilty to Wire Fraud," *Seattle Times,* December 12, 2008, accessed January 30, 2011, http://seattletimes.nwsource .com/html/businesstechnology/2008499215_entellium120.html.

32. Pascal Levensohn (Levensohn Venture Partners) in discussions with the author, August 2010.

33. Constance Loizos, "Could It Happen to You?" *Venture Capital Journal,* November 1, 2008, accessed January 30, 2011, www.jphibbard.com/uploads/ VCJ%2011-01-08.pdf.

34. Christie Heim, "Entellium CEO Pleads Guilty to Wire Fraud."

35. Xuan Tian, Gregory F. Udell, and Xiaoyun Yu, "Disciplining Delegated Monitors: Evidence from Venture Capital," January 23, 2011. Available at SSRN: http://ssrn.com/abstract=1746461.

36. Constance Loizos, "Could It Happen to You?"

37. James R. Swartz, interview by Mauree Jane Perry, 2006, "National Venture Capital Association Venture Capital Oral History Project," accessed January 30, 2011, http://digitalassets.lib.berkeley.edu/roho/ucb/text/rock_arthur.pdf.

38. Carey, Pete, "A start-up's true tale: Often-told story of Cisco's launch leaves out the drama, intrigue," *Mercury News,* December 1, 2001.

39. Thomas Bredt (Menlo Ventures) in discussions with the author, July 2008.

40. John Kenneth Galbraith, *The New Industrial State* (Boston: Houghton Mifflin, 1971).

41. Arthur Rock, interview by Sally Smith Hughes, 2008–2009, "Early Bay Area Venture Capitalists: Shaping the Economic and Business Landscape," accessed January 30, 2011, http://digitalassets.lib.berkeley.edu/roho/ucb/text/ rock_arthur.pdf.

42. Pascal Levensohn, "The Problem of Emotion in Boardroom," *Directors and Boards,* Spring 1999.

43. Chris Rust, "Best Practices for the High Performance Board," http://www.vc -io.com/governance.shtml.

44. Broughman, Brian J., "The Role of Independent Directors in VC-Backed Firms," October 13, 2008. Available at SSRN: http://ssrn.com/abstract=1162372.

45. Steven N. Kaplan and Per Johan Strömberg, "Financial Contracting Theory Meets The Real World: An Empirical Analysis Of Venture Capital Contracts," March 2000. CRSP working paper No. 513. Available at SSRN: http://ssrn.com/abstract=218175 or doi:10.2139/ssrn.218175.

46. Kenneth Van Heel (Dow Chemical Company Pension Fund) in discussions with the author, December 2009.
47. Working Group on Director Accountability and Board Effectiveness, "A Simple Guide to the Basic Responsibilities of VC-Backed Company Directors," accessed January 31, 2011, www.nvca.org/index.php?option=com_docman&task= doc_download&gid=78&Itemid=93.
48. Brad Feld (Foundry Group) in discussions with the author, December 2010.
49. Andy Rappaport (August Capital) in discussions with the author, January 2011.
50. Brian J. Broughman and Jesse M. Fried, "Renegotiation of Cash Flow Rights in the Sale of VC-Backed Firms," *Journal of Financial Economics*, Vol. 95, pp. 384–399, 2010; UC Berkeley Public Law Research Paper No. 956243. Available at SSRN: http://ssrn.com/abstract=956243.
51. Robert Finkel and David Greising, *The Masters of Private Equity and Venture Capital* (McGraw-Hill; First edition November 2009), 216.
52. "The greatest defunct Web sites and dotcom disasters," CNET. 2008-06-05. Archived from the original on 2008-06-07. Accessed March 21, 2011, http://web.archive.org/web/20080607211840/http://crave.cnet.co.uk/0,39029477, 49296926-6,00.htm.
53. William D. Bygrave and Jeffry A. Timmons *Venture Capital at the Crossroads* (Harvard Business Press 1992), 220.

CHAPTER 12   Exit Strategies

1. David Mayer and Martin F. Kenney, professor, Department of Human and Community Development, University of California, Davis, "Economic Action does not take place in a Vacuum: Understanding Cisco's Acquisition and Development Strategy," BRIE working paper 148, September 2002.
2. Glenn Rifkin, "Growth by Acquisition" The Case of Cisco Systems," *Strategy and Business* (Booz Allen Hamilton, 1997) http://www.strategy-business .com/article/15617?gko=3ec0c accessed on December 13, 2010.
3. Tony Hsieh (CEO, Zappos), *Delivering Happiness: A Path to Profits, Passion, and Purpose* (New York: Hachette Book Group, 2010), 209–211. Tony tried to buy Sequoia's stock for $200 million, but eventually Zappos was sold to Amazon for $1.2 billion.
4. Paul Stavrand, "Best Practice Guide for Angel Groups—Post Investment Monitoring," accessed January 30, 2011, www.angelcapitalassociation.org/data/ Documents/Resources/AngelCapitalEducation/ACEF_BEST_PRACTICES_Post _Investment.pdf.
5. Working Group on Director Accountability and Board Effectiveness, "A Simple Guide to the Basic Responsibilities of VC-Backed Company Directors," www.nvca.org/index.php?option=com_docman&task=doc_download&gid=78 &Itemid=93.
6. Xuan Tian, Gregory F. Udell, and Xiaoyun Yu, "Disciplining Delegated Monitors: Evidence from Venture Capital," January 23, 2011, available at SSRN: http://ssrn.com/abstract=1746461.

7. Marc Goedhart, Tim Koller, and David Wessels, "The Five Types of Successful Acquisitions," *McKinsey Quarterly*, July 2010, accessed February 10, 2011, www.mckinseyquarterly.com/The_five_types_of_successful_acquisitions_2635.

8. David Mayer and Martin F. Kenney, "Economic Action does not take place in a Vacuum."

9. "Google Cranks Up M&A Machine," *Wall Street Journal*, March 5, 2011.

10. Montgomery & Co., "The Return of M&A: An Outlook for the Venture Industry," June 2009, accessed February 10, 2011, www.monty.com/pages/investmentBanking/TheReturnofMandA.pdf.

11. "M&A Is Back—But This Time, It's Different," Knowledge@Wharton, November 24, 2009, accessed February 10, 2011, http://knowledge.wharton.upenn.edu/article.cfm?articleid=2395.

12. www.wired.com/epicenter/2010/04/apple-kills-lala-music-service/ accessed February 21, 2011.

13. "Bankers, Investors Eye Companies' Growing Cash Pile," *Wall Street Journal*, January 4, 2011, accessed March 12, 2011, http://online.wsj.com/article/SB10001424052748704723104576061550087949700.html.

14. Glenn Rifkin, Glenn, "Growth by Acquisition."

15. David Mayer and Martin F. Kenney, "Economic Action does not take place in a Vacuum."

16. Paul A. Gompers and Yuhai Xuan, Bridge Building in Venture Capital-Backed Acquisitions (February 1, 2009). AFA 2009 San Francisco Meetings Paper. Available at SSRN: http://ssrn.com/abstract=1102504.

17. David Mayer and Martin F. Kenney, "Economic Action does not take place in a Vacuum," BRIE Working paper 148, September 2002.

18. Ibid., attributed to Michael Volpi, Chief Strategic Officer.

19. "Intuit's New Version of Quicken Gets Mintified with Financial Data Insights and More," accessed February 11, 2011, http://thegoodnetguide.com/tag/mint-.com/.

20. Aaron Ricadela, "In Buying Mint, Intuit Looks to Revitalize," *Bloomberg Businessweek* (blog), September 14, 2009, www.businessweek.com/print/technology/content/sep2009/tc20090914_208171.htm.

21. Jenna Wortham, "Intuit Buys Mint, a Web-Based Finance Competitor," *New York Times*, September 9, 2009, accessed February 11, 2011, www.nytimes.com/2009/09/15/technology/internet/15mint.html.

22. "Mint.com," CrunchBase, accessed February 11, 2011, www.crunchbase.com/company/mint.

23. Ibid.

24. Mark Hendrickson, "Mint Wins TechCrunch 40 Top Company Award; Takes $50,000 Prize," TechCrunch (blog), September 18, 2007, http://techcrunch.com/2007/09/18/mint-wins-techcrunch40-50000-award/.

25. "All Your Money at a Glance," CNNMoney, http://money.cnn.com/galleries/2008/pf/0811/gallery.web_sites.moneymag/2.html.

26. Adam Fisher, "50 Best Websites 2009," August 24, 2009, accessed February 11, 2011, www.time.com/time/specials/packages/article/0,28804,1918031_1918016_1917991,00.html.

27. Spencer E. Ante, "Mint.com: Nurtured by Super-Angel VCs," *Bloomberg Businessweek* (blog), September 15, 2009, www.businessweek.com/technology/content/sep2009/tc20090915_065038.htm.

28. Dan Frommer, "Personal Finance Startup Mint Raises $14 Million," *Silicon Alley Insider* (blog), August 12, 2009, www.businessinsider.com/personal-finance-startup-mint-raises-14-million-2009-8#ixzz1BKQgd0Fa.

29. Michael Arrington, "Mint Is Worth a Mint: $140 Million Valuation," *TechCrunch* (blog), September 2, 2009, http://techcrunch.com/2009/09/02/mint-is-worth-a-mint-140-million-valuation/.

30. Jim Bruene, "Is Mint Worth $170 Million?" *NetBanker* (blog), www.netbanker.com/2009/09/is_mint_worth_170_million.html.

31. Rob Hayes (First Round Capital) in discussions with the author (December 2010).

32. "Intuit's New Version of Quicken Gets Mintified with Financial Data Insights and More," http://thegoodnetguide.com/tag/mint-com/.

33. "Intuit's New Version of Quicken Gets Mintified with Financial Data Insights and More."

34. Initial Public Offerings: 1980-2010 Tables Updated Through 2010, as of January 2011. Jay R. Ritter, Cordell Professor of Finance, University of Florida.

35. Ibid.

36. Initial Public Offerings: 1980-2010 Tables Updated Through 2010, as of January 2011. Jay R. Ritter, Cordell Professor of Finance, University of Florida.

37. "Whatever Happened to IPOs? You don't have to be Sherlock Holmes to figure this one out," *Wall Street Journal,* Review and Outlook, March 21, 2011.

38. Securities and Exchange Commission, Office of Economic Analysis, Study of the Sarbanes-Oxley Act of 2002 Section 404 Internal Control over Financial Reporting Requirements, September 2009.

39. Center for Private Equity and Entrepreneurship, Tuck School of Business at Dartmouth, "Results of Survey of Private Equity Funds," April 2005, accessed February 11, 2011, http://mba.tuck.dartmouth.edu/pecenter/research/pdfs/exits_survey.pdf.

40. "Saying Goodbye," http://knowledge.wharton.upenn.edu/article.cfm?articleid=2440.

41. Montgomery & Co., "The Return of M&A: An Outlook for the Venture Industry," www.monty.com/pages/investmentBanking/TheReturnofMandA.pdf.

42. KPMG, LLP, *Going Public,* accessed February 11, 2011, www.kpmg.com/Ca/en/IssuesAndInsights/ArticlesPublications/Documents/Going%20Public.pdf; Ernst & Young, *Ernst & Young's Guide to Going Public: Lessons from the Leaders,* accessed February 11, 2011, www.ey.com/Publication/vwLUAssets/Lessons_from_the_leaders/$FILE/BE0067.pdf.

43. Ernst & Young, *Ernst & Young's Guide to Going Public,* www.ey.com/Publication/vwLUAssets/Lessons_from_the_leaders/$FILE/BE0067.pdf.

44. Roman Binder, Patrick Steiner, and Jonathan Woetzel, "A New Way to Measure IPO Success," *McKinsey Quarterly,* January 2002, accessed February 11, 2011, http://mkqpreview1.qdweb.net/A_new_way_to_measure_IPO_success_1538.

45. KPMG, LLP, *Going Public.*
46. Ibid., Ernst & Young, *Ernst & Young's Guide to Going Public.*
47. Paul A. Gompers, Anna Kovner, Josh Lerner, and David Scharfstein, "Venture Capital Investment Cycles: The Impact of Public Markets (May 2005). NBER Working Paper Series, Vol. w11385, pp. -, 2005. Available at SSRN: http://ssrn.com/abstract=731040.
48. Ernst & Young, *Ernst & Young's Guide to Going Public.*
49. Ibid.
50. Eric Schmidt, "Google's CEO on the Enduring Lessons Of A Quirky IPO," *Harvard Business Review,* May 2010.
51. www.investopedia.com/terms/b/bookrunner.asp, accessed February 21, 2011.
52. www.pbs.org/wgbh/pages/frontline/shows/dotcon/thinking/primer.html, accessed February 22, 2011.
53. Eric Schmidt, "Google's CEO on the Enduring Lessons of a Quirky IPO."
54. Ibid.
55. David Weild and Edrward Kim (Grant Thornton) June 2010. "Market Structure is causing IPO crisis – and more."
56. Center for Private Equity and Entrepreneurship, Tuck School of Business at Dartmouth, "Results of Survey of Private Equity Funds," accessed on December 25, 2010 http://mba.tuck.dartmouth.edu/pecenter/research/pdfs/exits_survey.pdf.
57. Lip-Bu Tan (Walden International) in discussion with the author, August 2008.
58. Seth Rudnick (The Foundry Group) in discussion with the author, August 2008.
59. Brad Feld (The Foundry Group) in discussion with the author, December 2010.
60. Rich Levandov (Avalon) in discussion with the author, January 2010.
61. Pui-Wing Tam and Geoffrey A. Fowler, "Hot Trade in Private Shares of Facebook," *Wall Street Journal,* December 28, 2010, accessed February 11, 2011, http://online.wsj.com/article/SB10001424052970204685004576045943100180026.html.
62. Rafe Needleman, "Sharespost Lets You Buy the Un-buyable," June 30, 2009, accessed February 11, 2011, http://news.cnet.com/8301-17939_109-10275505-2.html.
63. Ibid.
64. Ibid.
65. Benjamin F. Kuo, "Interview with Greg Brogger, SharesPost," June 17, 2009, accessed February 11, 2011, http://www.socaltech.com/interview_with_greg_brogger_sharespost/s-0022276.html.
66. Alexia Tsotsis, "Mark Zuckerberg: Facebook Will Not Go Public Anytime Soon," *TechCrunch* (blog), September 10, 2010, http://techcrunch.com/2010/09/10/zuckerberg-ipo/.
67. Ben Parr, "Facebook IPO Now Likely in 2012," *Mashable* (blog), http://mashable.com/2011/01/03/facebook-ipo-may-2012/.
68. Steven M. Davidoff, "Facebook and the 500-Person Threshold," *DealBook* (blog), *New York Times,* January 3, 2011, http://dealbook.nytimes.com/2011/01/03/facebook-and-the-500-person-threshold/.

69. Pui-Wing Tam and Geoffrey Fowler, "Hot Trade in Private Shares of Face-book."

70. Ibid. Also see Kathryn Glass, "Building a SecondMarket to Make Way for Wall Street 3.0," July 16, 2010, accessed February 11, 2011, www.foxbusiness.com/personal-finance/2010/07/16/building-secondmarket-make-way-wall-street/.

71. Benjamin F. Kuo, "Interview with Greg Brogger, SharesPost."

72. Rafe Needleman, "Sharespost Lets You Buy the Un-buyable."

73. Ibid.

74. Kathryn Glass, "Building a SecondMarket to Make Way for Wall Street 3.0," www.foxbusiness.com/personal-finance/2010/07/16/building-secondmarket-make-way-wall-street/.

75. Ibid.

76. Pui-Wing Tam and Geoffrey Fowler, "Hot Trade in Private Shares of Face-book."

77. Kathryn Glass, "Building a SecondMarket to Make Way for Wall Street 3.0."

CHAPTER 13   Summing Up

1. K. Ram Shriram, Sherpalo Ventures, founding member and angel investor, Google, keynote speech, Michigan Growth Capital Symposium 2007, University of Michigan, Ann Arbor.

2. Michael Moritz, "Future Opportunities," in *Venture Capitalists: Inside the High Stakes and Fast Moving World of Venture Capital* (Boston: Aspatore Books, 2000), 31.

3. Stanford University's Entrepreneurship Corner, Marc Andreessen, "A Panorama of Venture Capital and Beyond," accessed January 13, 2011, http://ecorner.stanford.edu/authorMaterialInfo.html?mid=2457.

4. Tom Perkins, *Valley Boy: The Education of Tom Perkins* (New York: Penguin, 2007).

5. Stanford University's Entrepreneurship Corner, John Doerr, "How to Be a Venture Capitalist," accessed November 26, 2010, http://ecorner.stanford.edu/authorMaterialInfo.html?mid=1281.

6. David Cowan (Bessemer Venture Partners), in discussion with the author, December 2010.

7. Gibson S. Myers, "Early Bay Area Venture Capitalists: Shaping the Economic and Business Landscape," interview by Sally Smith Hughes, 2008, accessed January 13, 2011, http://digitalassets.lib.berkeley.edu/roho/ucb/text/myers_gib.pdf.

8. DOS stands for Disk Operating System, one of the first operating systems, that was popular in the 1980s and the early 1990s. Windows eclipsed it around 1995.

9. Terry McGuire (Polaris Ventures), in discussion with the author, November 2010.

10. David Cowan, "Heracles' Marathon to Olympus, Athena Awaits," *Who Has Time for This?* (blog), November 3, 2005, http://whohastimeforthis .blogspot.com/2005/11/heracles-marathon-to-olympus-athena.html.

11. http://whohastimeforthis.blogspot.com/2005/11/heracles-marathon-to-olympus -athena.html accessed December 12, 2010.

12. Vinod Khosla, "Career: Learning from Failure Early On," Stanford University's Entrepreneurship Corner, accessed January 2, 2011, http://ecorner.stanford .edu/authorMaterialInfo.html?mid=19.

13. Frank Caufield (Partner Emeritus, KPCB), in discussions with the author, August 2010.

14. Seth Levine, "How to Become a Venture Capitalist," *VC Adventure* (blog), May 20, 2005, www.sethlevine.com/wp/2005/09/attributes-of-a-good-venture -capitalist.

15. Promod Haque, in discussions with the author, November 2010.

16. John Hummer (Hummer Winblad Venture Partners), in discussions with the author, August 2010.

17. www.sethlevine.com/wp/2005/05/how-to-become-a-venture-capitalist accessed December 12, 2010.

18. Brant Moxley (Pinnacle Group), in discussions with the author, October 2010.

19. Rob Hayes (First Round Capital), in discussions with the author, October 2010.

20. Gary Rivlin, "So You Want to Be a Venture Capitalist," *New York Times*, May 22, 2005, accessed January 13, 2011, www.nytimes.com/2005/ 05/22/business/yourmoney/22venture.html.

21. Geoffrey H. Smart, Steven N. Payne, and Hidehiko Yuzaki, "What Makes a Successful Venture Capitalist?" The Journal of Private Equity, Fall 2000, Vol. 3, No. 4: pp. 7–29.

22. Michael Moritz, *Return to the Little Kingdom: How Apple and Steve Jobs Changed the World* (New York: Overlook Press, 2009), 89.

23. Marc Andreessen, "A Panorama of Venture Capital and Beyond." Stanford University's Entrepreneurship Corner, May 13, 2010, (http://ecorner.stanford .edu/authorMaterialInfo.html?mid=2457).

24. Gary Rivlin, "So You Want to Be a Venture Capitalist," *New York Times*, May 22, 2005.

25. Ibid.

26. Seth Levine's blog, "How to Become a Venture Capitalist." http://www .sethlevine.com/wp/2005/05/how-to-become-a-venture-capitalist accessed on November 23, 2010.

27. Gordon Gecko, a fictitious character epitomized in the movie Wall Street with the mantra: "Greed is good."

28. *The Masters of Private Equity and Venture Capital*, page 203.

29. 2009 rankings, thefunded.org.

Suggested Reading

BOOKS

On Venture Capital

Venture Capital and Private Equity: A Casebook by Josh Lerner, Felda Hardymon, and Ann Leamon (John Wiley & Sons, 4th ed., 2008).

Venture Capital and the Finance of Innovation by Andrew Metrick (John Wiley & Sons, 2nd ed., 2009).

eBoys: The First Inside Account of Venture Capitalists at Work by Randall E. Stross (Ballantine Books, 2001).

Done Deals—Venture Capitalists Tell Their Stories by Udayan Gupta (Harvard Business Press, 2000).

On Private Equity

Private Equity: History, Governance, and Operations by Harry Cendrowski and others (John Wiley & Sons, 2008).

The Masters of Private Equity and Venture Capital by Robert A. Finkel, Prism Capital (McGraw-Hill, 2009).

On LP-GP Relationships

Beyond the J Curve—Managing a Portfolio of Venture Capital and Private Equity Funds by Thomas Meyer and Pierre-Yves Mathonet (John Wiley & Sons, 2005).

The Definitive Guide to Private Equity Fund Investment Due Diligence by Kelly DePonte, lead editor, Probitas Partners (PEI Media, October 2010).

On Term Sheets

How to Be Smarter Than Your Lawyer and Your Venture Capitalist by Brad Feld and Jason Mendelson, Foundry Group (John Wiley & Sons, 2011).

Term Sheets & Valuations: An Inside Look at the Intricacies of Term Sheets & Valuations by Alex Wilmerding (Aspatore Books, 2003).

On Due Diligence

Venture Capital Due Diligence: A Guide to Making Smart Investment Choices and Increasing Your Portfolio Returns by Justin J. Camp (John Wiley & Sons, 2002).

On Management Talent

Who—A Method for Hiring by Geoff Smart and Randy Street (Ballantine Books, 2008).

Whitepapers on Being a Good Board Member

A Simple Guide to the Basic Responsibilities of VC-Backed Company Directors by the Working Group on Director Accountability and Board Effectiveness, www.nvca.org/index.php?option=com_docman&task= doc_download&gid=78&Itemid=93.

After the Term Sheet: How Venture Boards Influence the Success or Failure of Technology Companies by Dennis T. Jaffe and Paul N. Levensohn, www.levp.com/news/whitepapers.shtml.

Rites of Passage: Managing CEO Transition in Venture-Backed Technology Companies by Pascal N. Levensohn, www.levp.com/news/whitepapers .shtml.

BLOGS

Thought-Provoking Blogs from Leading Practitioners

Fred Wilson, Union Square Ventures, *A VC*

David Hornik, August Capital, *VentureBlog*

Brad Feld, Foundry Group, *Feld Thoughts*

Ben Horowitz, Andreessen-Horowitz Ventures, *Ben's Blog*

Josh Kopelman, First Round Capital, *Redeye VC*

WEB SITES

VC and PE Career Opportunities

Pinnacle Group: www.pinnaclegroup.com

Glocap: www.glocap.com

eFinancialCareers: www.efinancialcareers.com

VIDEOS

Venture capital videos at Stanford University's Entrepreneurship Corner, http://ecorner.stanford.edu/index.html.

ONLINE PUBLICATIONS AND DATA SOURCES

For Daily Data Bytes, These Publications Are Helpful
- *Dow Jones VentureWire*
- *peHub*
- *TechCrunch*
- *The Deal*
- *VentureBeat*

Data Sources
- Cambridge Associates
- Dow Jones VentureSource
- Preqin
- VentureXpert

JOURNALS

- *Journal of Business Venturing*
- *Journal of Portfolio Management*
- *Journal of Private Equity*
- *Journal of Entrepreneurial and Small Business Finance*

These academic thought leaders frequently publish well-researched findings on VC—some of their papers have curvy Greek formulas that I don't profess to understand. Ignore these at your own risk:

- Colin Blaydon, director, Center for Private Equity and Entrepreneurship, Tuck School of Business at Dartmouth
- Steven N. Kaplan, Chicago Booth School of Business
- Andrew Metrick, Yale School of Management
- Josh Lerner and Paul Gompers, Harvard Business School

About the Author

Mahendra Ramsinghani has over a decade of experience with start-ups and venture capital investments. At Invest Detroit, Mahendra manages First Step Fund, a fund focused on micro-investments in preseed and seed stage companies. He has been involved in financing over 25 start-ups. Formerly, as director of Venture Capital Initiatives for Michigan Economic Development Corporation (MEDC), he led the legislation for two fund-of-funds programs that deployed over $200 million in LP investments in venture funds. Mahendra serves on the investment committees of three early-stage investment funds.

His background includes a bachelor's degree in electronic engineering and an MBA with a major in marketing and finance from the University of Pune, India. He lives with his wife Deepa and daughter Aria in Ann Arbor, Michigan.

Index

#

401(k) plans, 14

A

Acquisitions
buy-side, process, 297–302,
307–310
key drivers, 299–301
Advisory board, and PPM, 104
Ahrens, Jack, xxvii, 238, 339
Ahrens, Brent, 159, 160, 275
Allocations, and PPM, 94–95
Alternative assets, an overview, 6–9
Asset classes, 6
Risk, how to measure, 7
Alternative assets, future trends, 9
Andreessen, Marc, xvii, 173, 338
Angels. *See* Pledge funds
Anti-dilution protections, 242–244
Approval, sell process, 307
Acquirer, when comes knocking,
307–310
Armstrong, Jim, 165
Articles of Incorporation, 210
Asia and venture capital
investments, xxiv
Aspegren, Lindsay, 256, 309
Asset allocation strategy, 5

B

Background investigations,
importance, 192–194
Batra, Rajeev, 117, 163–164

Beber, Howard J., 89
Bernstein, Sanford, 340
Best-in class access, xix–xx
Bhatia, Sabeer, 225
Bird, Steve, 52
Board of directors
approval items, 246
causing of stress within board,
282–283
CEO, managing transition,
280–282
CEO warning signs, 280
challenges, 277–278
composition and orientation,
261–263
independent director as
adjudicator, 283–284
information, management spin,
278–280
practices, 263–265
roles and responsibilities,
257–261
self-evaluation, 262–263
Bono (U2 rock group), 52–53
Brandt, Kristine, 59
Bridge loan, 233
Brogger, Greg, 324
Bryer, Jim, 219, 228
Buffett, Warren, xxiv, 172,
174–175, 178, 179, 301,
307–308
Business model, reviewing, due
diligence, 201–203

Business plans
  competitions, 171–172
  weighing importance of, 203
Business strategy, as value driver,
    275–275

C
Camp, Justin, 248
Campus recruitment, of GP team,
    118–119
Capital
  contributions, 99
  sources of, 9–11
  supply and demand, xx–xxi
Caufield, Frank, 126, 334
Caveat Emptor, 151–152
Certificate of Incorporation, 210
Chief executive officers (CEO)
  board culture, setting the tone,
    275–284
  business strategy as value driver,
    274–275
  customer acquisition, 271–272
  director education, need for,
    256–257
  duties of successful, 256
  external environment, survival,
    272–273
  improving the game, 284
  industry expertise as value driver,
    273–274
  managing transition, 280–282
  perspective on VC value add,
    269–275
  Robert's Rules of Order,
    overview, 265–268
  sales and vendor relationships,
    274
  setting the direction, 270–271
  warning signs, 280
Certificate of Good Standing, 136
Chambers, John, 294

Charisma, as characteristic of due
    diligence, 184–185
Chiniwalla, Punit, 122
Clone, Bob, 43, 85
Closing, first. *See* First close
Closing process, 252–253
  conditions, 249
  initial, and PPM, 97
  preconditions, 136
  sell process, 307
Cold calling, source investment
    opportunities, 172
Communications, open, ensuring,
    284–286
Comparable valuations, 224–226
Comparison benchmarks, caveats,
    46–47
Coneybeer, Robert, 160
Conflicts of interest, and PPM, 105
Conversion of stocks at IPO, 248
Convertible loans, 232–233
Corporate Operating Funds, 27–28
Corporate research, source
    investment, 161–162
Corporate venture capital, 124–125
Corporation, formation, basics,
    209–218
Correra, Marc, 151
Corrigan, Wilfred, 164
Co-sale agreements, 247–248
Cowan, David, 68, 72, 74–75, 82,
    120, 331, 332, 334, 340
Crisp, Peter O., 172
Crockett, Catherine, 55–56
Customer acquisition, CEO
    perspective, 271–272

D
Dacko, Ted, 296
Dagres, Todd, 179, 202, 274–275
Damodaran, Aswath, 219, 227
Davidow, Bill, 256

Deal killers, 310–313
Decision guidelines, governance of
    GP LLC, 127–128
Defaults, and PPM, 102
Defined benefit (DB) funds, 12–14
Defined contribution (DC) funds,
    13–14
DePonte, Kelly, 39, 63, 69, 77–79
DFJ model, xxiv
Director education, need for,
    256–257
Discounted cash flow method,
    226–228
Discretionary distributions, and
    PPM, 95–96
Dividends, 244
Doerr, John, 120, 173, 178–179,
    252
Dolan, Peter, xviii
Donohue, Liam, 147, 161
Doriot, Georges, 341
Douvos, Chris, xviii, 29, 68, 84, 86,
    165
Drag-along rights, 247
Draper, Tim, 173, 191, 225
Draper, William III, 135, 164
Drawdowns, and PPM, 92–93
Drivers of valuation, 220
Drucker, Peter, 183, 343
Due diligence, checklist, 203–205
Due diligence
    airline captain approach,
        185–192
    art of conducting, 177–207
    assessing the market, 194–199
    background investigations,
        importance, 192–194
    business model, reviewing,
        201–203
    business plans, weight
        importance of, 203
    case studies, 195–199
    charisma, as characteristic,
        184–185
    checklist, due diligence, 186–187
    conducting, sell process, 305–306
    criteria, 178
    idea or product, evaluating,
        199–201
    interview categories, 187–188
    management, attributes,
        179–183
    management team due diligence,
        185–192
    market characteristics, 194–195
    qualities, 177
    serial vs. first time entrepreneurs,
        183–184
    what is important?, 178–179
Dugan, Jim, 170
Dunlieve, Bruce, 157, 256
Dutch auction, 321–322
Dylan, Bob, 77

E
Edgar, Lisa, 34, 36, 37, 84
Effectively connected income, and
    PPM, 105
Efrusy, Kevin, 155–156
Eligibility, and PPM, 93
Elkus, William, 157
Emerging fund managers, 53–60
    characteristics of good, 55
    criteria, 54
    how made, 55–57
    institutional allocations for, 58
    pension programs, and, 59–60
    why LPs seek, 54–55
Emerging markets, xxiv–xxv
Emerson, Ralph W., 72
Employee benefit plan regulations,
    and PPM, 96
Employment-related terms,
    248–249

Endowments, 14–17
  expenditures, statistics, 17
  pension funds, comparison, 17
Entrepreneurs, serial vs. first time,
    183–184
Exculpation and indemnification,
    and PPM, 103
Exit, preconditions, 292–297
  alignment of interest,
      stakeholders, 293–296
  alignment of exit value, 296–297
Exit-related provisions, 247–248
  redemption, 247
  drag-along rights, 247
  tag-along rights, 247–248
  co-sale agreements, 247–248
  conversion at IPO, 248
Exit strategies, 291–327
  acquisitions, 297–302
  acquirer, when comes knocking,
      307
  buy-side acquisition process,
      307–310
  deal killers, 310–313
  initial public offering (IPO),
      313–324
  preconditions, 292–297
  primary exit options, listed, 291
  private exchanges, 324–327
  sell process, 302–307
Exit value, alignment, 296–297
Expenses, and PPM, 100
External environment, survival of
    CEO, 272–273

F
Family offices, 25–27
  classes, 26
  objectives, 26
  statistics, 27
Farner, Pete, 180

Feld, Brad, xxiv, 76, 157, 203, 230,
    241, 258, 268, 275, 284, 336,
    341
Finance companies, 19
Firstbrook, Peter, 271
First close, getting to the, 135–152
  fund market materials, 141–142
  investors, target list, building,
      137–141
  lead investor, attracting,
      144–146
  momentum, communicate,
      146–147
  pitch, presentation, 144
  placement agents, role in
      fundraising, 147–151
  presentation slides, 142–143
  sweeteners, offering to attract
      LPs, 147
First close, statistics, 135–136
Foundations, 17–19
  asset allocation strategies, 18–19
  statistics, 17
  types of, 18
Fountainheads of academia and
    research, 160–161
Framework of entities, for funds,
    113–114
Frazier, Alan, 52
Fund investment strategy, 67–77
  dissatisfaction with some, 67
  evolution, continuing, 76–77
  health care, early based, 69–71
  inclusions, 68
  "me-too" category, 67–68
  sector-based strategy, 69
  "Shifts and drifts," 75
  venture capitalist, as founder, 72
  Web 2.0, and, 69
  well established, what is, 67–68
  white-space investing, 72

Fund managers, evaluating, 39–40
criteria for evaluating, 40
performance, 40
Fund market materials, 141–142
Fund performance measurement,
xxi–xxii
Fund size and portfolio
construction. *See* Portfolio
construction and fund size
Fund structure, 113–134
finding suitable partners,
125–126
fund governance and economics,
126–127
governance of GP LLC, 127–134
venture capitalist profile,
115–125
Funds of Funds (f-of-f), 19–24
features, 21–22
trends, 22

G
Garfinkle, Jan, 1, 125–126, 332,
337, 340
Garratt, Matthew, 118, 125
Gates, Bill, 162
General partners
administration and operations,
131–134
admission, membership, 127–128
carried interests, 129–131
clawback, and, 99–100
decision guidelines for, 127
definition, 33
governance, 127–134
PPM, 90
salaries and expenses, 128–129
termination, membership,
127–128
withdrawal, membership,
127–128

General Partner team, key
constituents, 114–116
Hiring, 116–118
Campus recruitment, 118–119
Proactive searchers, 120–121
Kauffman Fellows Program,
121–123
Corporate venture capital,
124–125
Gottschalg, Oliver, 65
GP-LP relationship, best practices,
107
Graham, Paul, 166

H
Hanson, Scott, 171
Haque, Promod, xxiii, 252, 256,
334–335
Hargraves, Gordon, xxiii
Harris, Clint, 48
Harvard Management Company,
xviii
Hayes, Rob, 337
Health care
bioinformatics, 70–71
diagnostics, 71
early based, strategy, 69–71
healthcare services and IT, 71
medical imaging, 70
Heath, Chip, 342
Heath, Dan, 342
Heitzmann, Rick, 163, 223
High-Net-Worth Individuals,
25–27
Hiring, of GP team, 116–118
Horowitz, Ben, xvii, 190–191
Hrebiniak, Larry, 298
Hsieh, Tony, 310
Hughes, Sally S., 184
Hummer, John, 2, 335
Hunckler, William III, 185

I

Idea or product, evaluation, 199–201

Improving the game, 284–288
aligning interests, 286–288
avoiding complacency, 286
building trusted partnership, 284
ensuring open communication, 284–286

Independent director, as adjudicator, 283–284

Information, management spin, 278

Initial public offering (IPO), 313–324
company hires underwriter, 318
Dutch auction, 321–322
filing of S-1/Prospectus, 318–319
financing event, as, 315–316
great demand?, 320
IPO underpricing and Dutch auctions, 320–321
post-IPO, 323–324
process, 316–317
quiet period, 319
regulatory challenges, 322–323
road show, 319–320
steps to an IPO, 317–318

Individual performance, 40–43
attribution, 42
investments, preconditions, 42
measurement, 42

Industry expertise as a value driver, 273–274

Institutional limitations, and PPM, 92

Insurance companies, advantages, 24–25

Interests, aligning
alignment of exit method, 288
cash flow-related matters, 287
challenges among shareholders, 286–287
performance-related challenges, 287–288
shareholders & mgmt, 286–288

Investment banker, hiring, sell process, 304–305

Investment
objective, and PPM, 90
period, and PPM, 97
process, 5
restrictions, and PPM, 101–102

Investment transactions, structuring, 229–254
closing process, 252–253
exit-related provisions, 247–248
milestone-based financing, 238–239
negotiation stress points, 230–238
other terms, 248–249
protecting your securities, 246–247
simpler term sheet, 250–251
structuring terms for target returns, 239
syndicating investments, 251–252
term sheet, spirit of, 229–230

Investors, target list, building, 137–141
screening LPs, 137, 138, 141

J

J-Curve, xxii
Jarve, John, 72
Jobs, Steve, 162, 184
Johnston, Paul, 278
Jones, Christopher, 124
Journalists and VCs, xxii

K

Kamra, Deepak, 173
Kaplan, Steven, 192, 254

Kauffman Fellows Program, 121–123
Kawasaki, Guy, 338
Keehn, Peter, 85
Key person events, and PPM, 101
Keynes, John M., 8
Khosla, Vinod, 75–76, 332
Kirkpatrick, David, 233
Kopelman, Josh, 80
Kramer, Oren, 151
Kramlich, C. R., 337
Kulkarni, Jayant, 171

L
Langeler, Gerry, 172–173
Lasky, Mitch, 177
Lazarus, Steven, 53, 145
Lead investor, attracting, 144–146
Lemmer, Mary, 117–118
Levensohn, Pascal, 255, 280
Leverage, and PPM, 98
Levine, Seth, 334, 336
Lewis, Sinclair, 177
Lilly, Eli, 2
Limited Partnerships Agreements, 89–111
Limited Partners
  comparison, 29
  investment process, 34
  stacking of, 240–242
  strategy, 5
  subpar, xx
  types, 5–31
Liu, Kelvin, 54
Livingston, Jessica, 166
Long, Augustine, 36, 54, 86, 149

M
Management
  aligning interests, 286–288
  attributes, 179–183
  execution, 182–183

fees, and PPM, 93–94
  integrity, 180
  team building, 180–181
Manager, top quartile, 61–67
  above average performers, 64
  measures of performance, 63–64
  priorities, 63
  statistics, 61
Market timing, 77–80
  strong market, and, 77
  rebalance by investors, 80
Mathonet, Pierre-Yves, 85
Mayleben, Timothy, 162
McGuire, Terry, 119, 341
Mercil, Steven, 169–170
Membership guidelines, of GP LLC, 128
Metrick, Andrew, 338
Meyer, Thomas, 85
Milestone-based financing, 238–239
Minder, James J., 193
Minimum investment, and PPM, 92
Mohan, Ravi, 48, 55, 141, 274
Moritz, Michael, 310, 329
Morris, Hank, 151
Morris, Paul, xxv
Moxley, Brant, 116, 336
Myers, Gibson, 331

N
Nabokov, Vladimir, 113
Nada, Hany, 57
Negotiation stress points
  bridge loan, 233
  convertible loan, 232–233
  preferred stock, as equity, 233, 236
  warrants, 236
Neis, John, 236
Nelson, Robert, 120, 161
Newhouse, Doug, 149

Network, as source of investment, 157–160

Networking, and proactive searchers, 121

Newton, Roger, 162

Nicolas, Christophe, 79

Noyce, Bob, 172, 220

O

Offering, and PPM, 91–92

Ogilvy, David, 135, 344

Olguin, Daniel, 184

Omidyar, Pierre, 157

One-off event, 46

Operations, of GP LLC, 113–134

Options, as type of warrant, 237–238

O'Reilly, Tim, 164–165

Organizational expenses, and PPM, 100–101

Orientation meeting materials, agenda, 261–262

Ownership and control, basics, 209–218

   authorized and issued shares, 211–217

   role of the board, 217–218

   shareholder rights, 217

P

Parallel funds, and PPM, 103

Partnerships, building trusted, 284

Performance and success, relationship, xix–xx

Pension funds, 11–14

   health care, and, 14

   investments, government mandated, 11, 14

   political interference, and, 14

   primary goals, 11

   sources, 11

   types, 12

Pension programs, emerging funds, 59–60

Pentland, Sandy, 184

Performance, fund, 40–52

   analyzing the data, 43

   comparison benchmarks, 46

   fund level performance, 43

   generalists vs. specialists, 51

   individual performance, 40

   metrics, evaluation, 43

   red flags, 48

   skill sets, identifying, 49

   soft skills, importance of, 49

   source capital, 51–52

   stability and alignment, 48

   team cohesion, dynamics, 48

   team dynamics, 47

Perkins, Tom, 72, 126, 251

Peterson, Tim, 126

Piggyback rights, 248

Pincus, Mark, 157

Pitch events, 163–164. *See also* Venture events

Pitch, presentation, 144

Placement agent, 35–36

   role in fundraising, 147–151

Pledge funds, source investment opportunities, 167–171

   angel groups, 167–169

   network of angel networks, 169–170

Plonka, James, 124, 206, 225

Portfolio

   aspects to ensure, 81–88

   building a portfolio, 86

   challenges to new entrants, 86

   construction and fund size, 80–85

   design, 80–81

   expected risks and returns, 11

   fitting in with current, 85–86

   matrix of relationships, 85, 86

rule of thumb, 81
summary, 84
Practitioners
  attitudes and aptitudes, 330–338
  balanced yin and yang, 337–338
  comfort in ambiguity, 335–336
  drive, 330–332
  jack of all and master of all,
    333–335
  never say never, 332–333
  relentless focus on value creation,
    336–337
Preemptive rights, 245
Preferred stock, as equity, 233, 236
Presentation slides, first close,
    142–143
Private exchanges, 324–327
  SharesPost vs. SecondMarket,
    325–327
Private placement memorandum
    (PPM), 89, 90
  advisory board, 104
  allocations, and, 94–95
  capital contributions, and, 99
  closings, additional, and, 97
  closings, initial, and, 97
  conflicts of interest, and, 105
  defaults, and, 102
  discretionary distributions, and,
    95–96
  drawdowns, and, 92–93
  effectively connected income,
    and, 105
  eligibility, and, 93
  employee benefit plan
    regulations, and, 96
  exculpation and indemnification,
    and, 103
  expenses, and, 100
  general partner, and, 90
  general partner clawback, and,
    99–100

institutional limitations, and, 92
  investment objective, and, 90
  investment period, and, 97
  investment restrictions, and,
    101–102
  key person events, and, 101
  leverage, and, 98
  management fees, and, 93–94
  minimum investment, and, 92
  offering, and, 91–92
  organizational expenses, and,
    100–101
  parallel funds, and, 103
  reinvestment of capital, and,
    98
  reports, 104
  risk factors, and, 105
  securities law matters, 105
  successor funds, and, 103–104
  tax distributions, and, 95
  tax exempt investors, and, 96
  tax matters, and, 104–105
  term of the fund, and, 97–98
  time and attention requirements,
    102
  transferability of interests, and,
    102
  withdrawal, and, 102–103
Proactive searching for GP team,
    120–121
Proactive searchers, and
    networking, 121

R
Rappaport, Andy, 286
Recker, Timothy, 29, 107
Redemption, as exit-related
    provision, 247–248
Reed, Ron, 201
Reed, Russell, 58
Regelman, Adam, 171
Registration rights, 248

Regulations, as challenges to IPO, 322–323

Reinvestment of capital, and PPM, 98

Reports, and PPM, 104

Risk factors, and PPM, 105

Rizik, Christopher, 42, 68, 144, 329

Roberts, Bryan, 121

Roberts, Bryce, 164–165, 314, 339

Robert's Rules of Order, overview, 265–268
   board action items, 266–267
   types of motions, 266
   voting on a motion, 267–268

Robbins, Dave, 270, 271

Rock, Arthur, 161, 164, 172, 184, 203, 220

Rozenblit, Igor, 35–36, 150

Rubin, Andy, 298

Rudnick, Seth, 83

S

S-1/Prospectus, filing, 318–319

Sahlman, William, xxiii, 221

Salaries and expenses, governance of GP LLC, 128–129

Sales, CEO perspective, 274

Scalability, xxiv

Scheer, David, 162

Schmidt, Eric, 201

Schwartz, James R., 206

SecondMarket, 325–327

Sector based strategy, 69

Securities, protecting, 246

Securities law, matters, 105

Sell process, 302–307
   approval and closing, 307
   conduct due diligence, 305–306
   hiring investment banker, 304–305

   negotiate/structure the transaction, 306–307
   test the waters, 303–304

Shareholder
   aligning interests, 286–288
   rights, 217

Shares, authorized and issued, 211–217
   capitalization table, 212, 214–217
   ownership dynamics, 212, 214–217
   preferred versus common shares, 212

SharesPost, 325–327

Sheshuryak, Sergey, 53

Shockley, William, 181

Shriram, K. R., 161, 173–174, 195

Shurkin, Joel, 181

Silbert, Barry, 326

Simpson, John, 1

Smart, Geoff, 182, 187–188

Snyder, Rick, 207

Source investment opportunities
   angels and pledge funds, 167–171
   art of, 155–175
   business plan competitions, 171–172
   cold calling, 172
   corporate research, 161–162
   fountainheads of academia/ research, 160–161
   network, the, 157–160
   venture events and trade conferences, 163–165
   venture farming, 165–167
   you win some, you miss some, 172–173

Springing warrants, 236–237

Stakeholders, alignment of interest, 293–296

Sturiale, Nick, 264

Success and performance, xix–xx
Succession, as axis of scalability,
    xxiv
Successor funds, and PPM, 103–104
Suster, Mark, 229
Swartz, James, 69
Sweeteners, offerings to attract LPs,
    147
Swensen, David, 8
Syndicating investments, 251–252

T
Tag-along rights, 247–248
Tan, Lip-Bu, 179, 181, 251, 268
Target returns
    anti-dilution protections,
        242–244
    dividends, 244
    higher liquidation preferences,
        241–242
    liquidation preferences, 239–240
    pay-to-play, 244–245
    preemptive rights, 245
    stacking of liquidation
        preferences, 240
Tavel, Sarah, 117
Tax distributions, and PPM, 95
Tax exempt investors, and PPM, 96
Tax matters, and PPM, 104–105
Team cohesion, criteria, 48
Term of the fund, and PPM, 97–98
Term sheet
    simple investment, for, 250–251
    spirit of, 229–230
Terms, other LP/GP, 105–106
Testing the waters, sell process,
    303–304
Thiel, Peter, 233, 238
Thompson, Rick, 160
Time and attention requirements,
    and PPM, 102
Timmons, Jeffry, 194

Top manager access, advantage, xix
Trade conferences, 163–165
Transaction, negotiate/structure,
    sell process, 306–307
Transferability of interests, and
    PPM, 102

V
Valentine, Don, 159
Valuation methods, 219–228
    comparable valuations, 224–226
    discounted cash flow method,
        226–228
    drivers of Valuation, 220
    VC method, simple form,
        221–224
Value creation, 267–269
Van Heel, Kenneth, 76, 80, 85,
    124
Valentine, Don, 186
VC method of valuation, simple
    form, 221–224
Venture capitalists
    becoming good, 329–330
    drawbacks, 338–339
    functions, 2
    going forward, as you, 344
    how you play the game matters,
        342–344
    investment in 1980s, xxi
    journalists, and, xxii
    luck, what about, 339–341
    number, xxii
    practitioners, attitudes &
        aptitudes, 330–338
    profile, 115–116
    takeaways for practitioners, get,
        341–342
Vendor relationships, CEO
    perspective, 274
Venture events, 163–164. *See also*
    Pitch events

Venture firms, evaluation by LPs, 36–38
Venture fund, 3
Venture farming, 165–167
Village Ventures model, xxiv

W
Walker, John, 189
Warrants, 236–238

options, 237–238
springing warrants, 236–237
types of, 236
Weiser, Marc, 117–118
West, Mae, 75
Williams, Jeff, 183–184
Williams, Kelly, 42, 57, 110
Wilson, Fred, 341
Withdrawal, and PPM, 102–103
Wozniak, Steve, 184